Theory of Strangers

Theory of Strangers

Science of People, Democracy, Non-Psychoanalysis

François Laruelle
Translated by Jeremy R. Smith

EDINBURGH
University Press

Edinburgh University Press is one of the leading university presses in the UK. Publishing new research in the arts and humanities, EUP connects people and ideas to inspire creative thinking, open new perspectives and shape the world we live in. For more information, visit www.edinburghuniversitypress.com.

Edinburgh University Press Ltd
13 Infirmary Street, Edinburgh EH1 1LT

Typeset in 11/13 Foundry Sans and Foundry Old Style by
IDSUK (DataConnection) Ltd, and
Printed and bound in the UK using 100% renewable electricity by
CPI Group (UK) Ltd

A CIP record for this book is available from the British Library

ISBN 978 1 3995 4923 3 (hardback)
ISBN 978 1 3995 4925 7 (webready PDF)
ISBN 978 1 3995 4924 0 (epub)

EU Authorised Representative:
Easy Access System Europe
Mustamäe tee 50, 10621 Tallinn, Estonia
gpsr.requests@easproject.com

MIX
Paper | Supporting responsible forestry
FSC® C013604
FSC www.fsc.org

This book is printed using paper from well-managed forests, recycling and other controlled sources

Contents

Welcoming the Stranger that One is: Translator's Introduction

I'm looking for
a man I don't know,
who's never been more myself
than since I started to look for him.
Does he have my eyes, my hands
and all those thoughts like flotsam of time?
Season of a thousand wrecks,
the sea no longer a sea,
but an icy watery grave.
Yet farther on, who knows how it goes on?
A little girl sings backward
and nightly reigns over trees
a shepherdess among her sheep.
Let us wrench thirst from the grain
of salt no drink can quench.
Along with the stones, a whole world eats
its heart out, being
from nowhere, like me.

Edmond Jabès. 'Song of the Stranger', translated by Rosmarie Waldrop. In *From the Book to the Book: An Edmond Jabès Reader* (Hanover: Wesleyan University Press, 1991), 10.

This is not a book that is solely meant to be read. It is to be lived. It is a book that is written in search of the Stranger, to welcome them – for they are who we are. We will learn to accept and say without fear: the Stranger and I are identical, in-the-last-instance alone.

Over the past decade and a half, the work of François Laruelle has amassed recognition from anglophone audiences for the inventive practice he introduces and rectifies in each work: non-philosophy. According to Laruelle, non-philosophy is the enacted pragmatic, critique and theory of philosophy when determined by the human-in-person, whose dictum or slogan is: 'man is not made for philosophy, but philosophy is made for man'.

The present translation of Laruelle's 1995 text, *Theory of Strangers: Science of People, Democracy, Non-Psychoanalysis*, comes after a long line of translations that span from some of his earliest reflections to his ultimate period of writing. In addition, the present work occupies a central thematic component for non-philosophy's development: the introduction of democracy into thought. And, lastly, as it is the translator's hope that the reader will recognise and agree before, during and after reading, *Theory of Strangers* is – alongside *Éthique de l'Étranger: du crime contre l'humanité* (Paris: Éditions Kimé, 2000) and *A Biography of Ordinary Man: On Authorities and Minorities*, translated by Alex Dubilet and Jessie Hock (Cambridge: Polity, 2018/Paris: Aubier, 1985) – a keystone text. It is the goal of this introduction to provide a brief overview of the text as well as reflecting on the following three facets of *Theory of Strangers*: its chronological placement, its shared thematic across this chronology, and its significance towards solidifying the basis for Laruelle's long-standing critique of humanity's judgement.

Theory of Strangers has three chapters that correspond to the subtitle of the work: 'Science of People, Democracy, Non-Psychoanalysis'. Prior to these chapters, each of which introduces and develops a unified theory between philosophy and a regional thought (such as the human sciences, democracy and psychoanalysis), Laruelle presents both a programme and a problematic. It is important for the reader not to gloss over these portions, as they provide the underlying framework: vision-in-man, and its distinction from humanisms and philosophical anthropologies. Without a critical read into vision-in-man, the reader may fall prey to misunderstandings to which the chapters all abide.

The first chapter introduces the principles of a science of people as the unified theory of philosophy and the human sciences. This chapter strives to criticise an invariant that is also present in *A Biography of Ordinary Man*: anthropo-logical difference, an invariant which assumes that humanism and philosophical anthropologies suffice to be able to determine or co-determine the real, man as Ego. By contrast, Laruelle's vision-in-man proposes through its unified theory a non-humanism, where it is man who determines philosophy, and not the reciprocal and reversible relation instituted by anthropological difference.

As a continuation of the first chapter, the second chapter introduces the principles of democracy as the unified theory of philosophy and the Stranger. While the previous chapter dealt with the real Ego, that is, man as the real of-the-last-instance, this chapter seeks out a way of representing the real as a unilateral subject: the Stranger. Likewise, where the previous chapter deals with a criticism of the invariant anthropo-logical difference, so too this chapter continues with the critique of ego-xeno-logical difference, the relationship between oneself and another. Such a critique, Laruelle argues, would be able to unmask the underlying or, rather, superior racism present in all philosophy. It also allows for a universal humanity to arise, ultimately providing the basis for a founding theorem of democracy. Without this science of people, a genuine non-philosophical definition of democracy is, if not impossible, at least rendered inconsequential.

Lastly, split into two sections, the third chapter introduces non-psychoanalysis (abbreviated to non-analysis) as the unified theory of philosophy and psychoanalysis. Whilst Laruelle utilises and draws from Lacanian psychoanalysis and its varying terminology, as well as various critics of and successors to Lacanian psychoanalysis – such as Gilles Deleuze and Félix Guattari, Jacques Derrida, Michel Foucault, Michel Henry, Alain Badiou and Daniel Sibony – the non-analysis introduced in this chapter provides a radical criticism of a complex that is far deeper rooted in the human unconscious than, as Laruelle argues, the Œdipus complex: the philosophico-analytic complex. Combining the previous chapters' stakes with the stakes outlined in this chapter, Laruelle's goal is to provide a radical reflection of the Real, what he calls the *Joui*, freed from the philosophical triangulation of psychoanalysis.

Readers of Laruelle may be familiar with how prolific a writer he is, so much so that he has compiled his work into various periods which reflect the movements or 'waves' of how he approaches his thinking. Each of the five waves is titled 'Philosophy', with *Theory of Strangers* inaugurating the period known as Philosophy III, consisting of writings that start from 1995 until the early 2000s. The only work still to be translated into English from this period is *Éthique de l'Étranger*. Philosophy III is most notable for rectifying a theoretical method called unified theory first introduced in *Theory of Identities*, which pairs yet without blending the theoretical and conceptual content of philosophy and another discipline (for example, as the reader will see below, philosophy and the human sciences, philosophy and politics, and philosophy and psychoanalysis). Instead of serving as a meta-conceptual commentary or criticism upon these two practices – for example, in terms of a unitary mono-disciplinary use of interdisciplinarity (such as a philosophy of psychoanalysis) – the unified theory couples each in such a way that their shared real object does not fall prey to theoretical capture or, to use Laruelle's parlance, where the theories become sufficient for this real object. With the addition of this translation (and with the hopes to have a translation of the book on ethics), the reader may finally have the opportunity to appreciate the development of Philosophy III with its vocabulary, methodology and framework for a score of different disciplines to be envisioned in a new light: non-Marxism as the unified theory of Marxism and philosophy, non-ethics as the unified theory of ethics and philosophy, non-theology as the unified theory of theology and philosophy, and so on.

In the case of the human sciences and philosophy in the sense of philosophical anthropology, their shared real object is the human, a consistent source of discussion and even debate in the work of Laruelle and secondary scholarship. Indeed, with the recent publication of *The Last Humanity: The New Ecological Science*, translated by Anthony Paul Smith (London: Bloomsbury, 2020/Paris: Éditions du Cérf, 2015), certain secondary scholars may still be confused by Laruelle's 'non-humanism' and defence of generic humanity even in the face of ecological devastation by human beings. Despite this, Laruelle's argument is akin to a variety of thinkers concerned with human emancipation, including Marx and Rousseau; the constant of non-humanism serves as an important guiding thread throughout *Theory of Strangers*, and it is up to readers to see the uniqueness of Laruelle's insights.

Lastly, as mentioned above, it is worth considering the significance of this work alongside *A Biography of Ordinary Man* and *Éthique de l'Étranger*. These works offer an intimate glimpse into Laruelle's stances as to why the 'human philosophy' of non-philosophy can and must be taken seriously. Furthermore, they provide a thorough critique of the philosophical invariants that dominate and structure the lived experiences of people: anthropo-logical difference and onto-theo-politics, for example. Indeed, with regards to the criticised invariants in this work and others, such as anthropo-logical difference and ego-xeno-logical difference, the overarching framework of non-humanism is offered as an alternative paradigm in contrast to philosophical anthropology and politics broadly construed. One can even go so far as to argue that without these invariants in the back of one's mind, the source of the reader's downfall and confusion may occur as a result. Any such scholarship striving to be 'faithful' to non-philosophy as a discipline would need to consider the careful attention present in this work and the overarching stakes of non-philosophy as a 'human philosophy'. It is a work that requires the reader to take on all the parts in their totality with a linear reading: one cannot, for example, jump to the chapter on non-psychoanalysis without understanding the prior chapters on the science of people and democracy.

Before moving into Laruelle's opening remarks, there are still reflections to be made regarding translation decisions. One of the most obvious translation decisions is to maintain *l'homme* as 'man' and the masculine gendered pronoun of 'he', but what will be clear from later parts of the reading is that I have chosen to make *l'Étranger*, the Stranger, without any gendered pronoun, opting for 'they' and 'them'. Likewise, when *les hommes* is present, I have opted for 'people' as opposed to 'men' to reflect the inclusive language of democracy. In addition, to retain the playfulness of the concepts, I have kept *Joui-sans-jouissance* and *en-Joui* in the original French. Following other translations of Laruelle's work, I have been careful to attend to the various conceptual genealogies of several frameworks, including the Heideggerian, Freudian, Lacanian, Deleuzean, Levinasian, Husserlian and Derridean frameworks (among a slew of others) interrogated here. I consulted a variety of sources from translators of these thinkers to provide not only a unique blend of each into one, but to also offer what may be considered as Laruelle's non-philosophical grafting from these frameworks into the new, more universal terrain.

One of the challenges of the translation was to come up with a way of reflecting the distinction that Laruelle makes between *rapport* and *apport*. Lacanian scholarship and some general understanding of French points to having the former translated as 'relation' in English, as in Lacan's statement *il n'y a pas de rapport sexuel*. However, this is not the case with the latter, with a variety of translations being, for example, 'input', 'contribution', 'participant', 'allocation', and so on. At first, I attempted to make the two terms rhyme in both English and French, with 'relation' and 'allocation', but I figured that this did not work with the intended connotations that Laruelle most likely wants to highlight. Instead, I opted for the distinction between relation and ration: the former implies reciprocity and exchange, whereas the latter an organised distribution of a fixed share from one side alone. Of course, rationing implies a scarcity of one or more resources, yet when put in the context of the One determining an order for thought, rationing is the minimal sense of giving a resource, wherein the One does not become divided into a portion. So to speak, the One is lent a hand simultaneously as it determines its side. It also helps that much later in the text, Laruelle distinguishes between *uni-lation* and *uni-apport*. In this way, uni-lation and uni-ration simplifies this distinction significantly more than how I previously envisaged. I have also translated *privation* as 'depriveness' as a contrast to *donation* as 'givenness', retaining 'privational' solely as its adjectival form.

In contrast to existing translations, I have sought to render any instance of *force (de/du)* X as 'X(-)power' rather than as 'force (of) X'. As mentioned in various instances of his own writings, Laruelle utilises the term *force (de/du)* X as an allusion to Marx's *Arbeitskraft* or labour-power, which is translated into French as *force de travail*. In a way, the bracketing of *du* in *force (du) Joui*, for example, implies a unilateral relation wherein the *Joui* is indifferent to the causality it determines or enacts. Therefore, one may bracket the hyphenation and still retain its allusion to Marxian terminology. Moreover, whenever a phrase included, for example, *non-positionnel (de) soi*, I have opted for a simpler reading that does not take on more words such as existing translations when describing, for example, a 'thought that is non-positional (of) self'. Similar to the above bracketing of (*de/du*), I have opted to translate these instances as, in the same example, 'non(-)self-positional'. This choice would make 'non(-)self-positional thought' easier to read with a flow and as an active description than the passive and clunky 'thought that is non-positional (of) self'. The only times that '(of)' or '(to)' are maintained are in phrases, for example, 'man (of) science', 'Essence (of) science' or 'given (to) man'. Regardless, the '(of)' and'(to)' imply bracketed intentionality and indifferent identity at the same time in order to limit distancing or difference. Retaining these instances of bracketing in English does not contradict the above changes distinct from existing translations. To put it simply, when there are ways to make reading easier for the reader without fundamentally altering the tone or intention of what is written, especially when the work seeks to introduce and welcome readers into a new framework, it is arguably better and more fruitful to make descriptions as active as possible to make these arguments compelling and worthwhile to engage in.

Wherever I needed to make interventions, such as translating and revising the term *unidentification* into 'uni-dentification' in the first chapter onwards, I do so with the intent to reduce possible misunderstandings associated with the reading. As an aside, in an attempt to utilise non-ableist terminology, I have sought to mitigate what may be inherently ableist French words (such as *muette*, *sourde* or *aveugle*) usually associated with philosophical and epistemological accounts of the sciences, and have attempted to render them to slight synonyms in non-ableist English. Finally, as one of the conventions of translating, at times I place the original French in square brackets for readers to compare. Doing this brings a sense of honesty and humility to the labour of translation, of which the original has the advantage not only of the thinker's voice, but it is also the source from which that intimacy is grounded.

I wish to express my gratitude to a number of individuals who took time to review the present translation, to share expertise and insight to the process. Thank you to Sylvia Nambiar, Brynn McNab, Taylor Adkins, Artem Morozov, Jacob Vangeest and Zach Walter. I also wish to thank Carol Macdonald of Edinburgh University Press for the opportunity to provide Laruelle's book for a wider audience of academics and non-academics. Lastly, I owe my deepest gratitude to both Anne-Françoise Schmid and, of course, François Laruelle: their inventive practices continue to inspire and guide me. It was my hope to have completed and published this translation while Laruelle was still with us. This translation, thirty years after its original publication, is dedicated to his memory.

Programme: Which One is the Stranger? A New Idea

Four problems make up the object of this essay, bringing about an identical solution for them.

1. Is the traditional antinomy between philosophy and the Human Sciences (in particular philosophy and psychoanalysis) an eternal and inevitable evil, or can it find a real solution? What is proposed here begins by renouncing any attempt of synthesis or philosophical 'resolution' just as much as any contrary exacerbation of scientific positivity – a solution that is in both cases *unitary* and would seek a third and superior unity, thus leading once more back to the old conflict without really dissolving it. We oppose the unitary solution with the idea of a *unified theory* – unified, not unitary. The idea consists in determining a radical or undivided identity of theory itself (the identity of philosophy and the Human Sciences) by the Real, rather than an identity of the Real determined by theory, which would divide it once more. This identity is posited *as a simple hypothesis* under these new conditions in terms of a conception of the essence of man as being the Real, 'Radical Immanence', 'Given-without-Givenness', or 'vision-in-man'. This conception is no longer entirely philosophical or has been repressed by the idealism of every philosophy. It suffices to make this hypothesis about man as the immanent infrastructure – a hypothesis scientific in kind but which is real, not logico-epistemological, one that is adequate consequently to the nature of its object – and substitute it for these transcendent and metaphysical entities such as the 'individual', the 'subject', 'consciousness' or the 'unconscious', to open up a new field of investigations that we call (inverting the plural and the singular) the 'science of people' [*science des hommes*] and no longer the 'sciences of man'. This discipline does not study the objects or properties that belong to philosophy and the Human Sciences, not competing with them on this point, but takes the knowledges [*connaissances*] that were first and

already elaborated by these conjoined disciplines as an object. This discipline is therefore no longer confounded with them, and their conflict stops being valid as the norm or authority for thought.

2. Is the antinomy between philosophy and democracy condemned to remain concealed and effective to the extent of this dissimulation, or can it find a solution? This antinomy is less apparent but softer than the first, though it is effective. Through its original and invariant – though very varied – structure of ontological objectivation, philosophy excepts itself – no doubt partially or provisionally, but this exception is constitutive – from its objects to the benefit of its discourse or excepts itself from its discourse to the benefit of its act. Philosophy is thus both anti-democratic and super-democratic and oscillates around a concept of democracy that it fails to establish in rigour and reality – that is, in its identity. The philosophical subject of the democratic enunciation just very provisionally and partially falls under the conditions that define the stated democracy. Man is divided between the philosopher, who states the democratic ideal of 'equality', and the man who is the object of this ideal and the one who can only claim to be the author of this discourse or appropriate it through the delegation to the philosopher. When it originates from the philosophico-political or when equality is not ordered by identity but dissolved in difference, democracy assumes that man is unequal to himself even in the affirmation of his equality or that one part of man remains 'minor'. This is a 'sought' and problematic concept, aporetic at worst, resolved at best in an unlimited becoming-democracy that continues to impose upon man the bar of anti-democracy and non-identity and to refuse man that he can fully access democracy or access it in identity. To put an end to the philosophical exception that extends into a super-human exception to man, it is necessary and sufficient here again to determine a radical, undivided identity (in no way, consequently, a 'totality') of the philosophical thus transformed and human multitudes, an identity of man, as we will see, in the state of Strangers. This is an identity that finds its real cause in this radical immanence that makes up the essence of people that we call elsewhere 'ordinary'. The ones whom the philosopher distinguished and hierarchised participate within 'ordinary man' equally without distinction or difference, without hierarchy: the everyman [*quelconque*] or vulgar man and the philosopher himself, thus restored in this use to their identity and its multiplicity.
3. Can the antinomy between philosophy and the Other Question or the Stranger Question, which does not stop being reactivated in contemporary thought, receive a solution? This antinomy is traditional within the Greek horizon of philosophy, but it has been exacerbated, radicalised and partially

resolved by Judaic thought and its affect of the Other person, from Freud and Wittgenstein to Husserl and Levinas. We take this kind of solution into account by transforming it under the general conditions of reality and thought that we postulate, with the goal of *resolving the inseparable problems of democracy and the Stranger together*. Hence, the following argument: if man finds his real essence in absolutely undivided immanence and experiences himself as a given-without-givenness, if man is neither the 'individual' nor the 'subject', neither 'conscious' nor 'unconscious', but what (to be quick) we will call vision-in-man or vision-in-Ego, an I that is neither 'subjective' nor 'objective' but self(-)immanent, then man is no longer *distributed* [*partagé*] between an I and an Other, the latter is no longer exterior or interior *and* exterior to the I, *but the immanent I also exists in a new structure that is the structure of the Stranger without 'leaving' itself – the I Stranger-exists* [*il existe-Étranger*]. If this I-in-I is real and defines every man, even 'the-foreigners', if the I-in-I is the guarantee that each man enjoys an undivided radical identity that can no longer be refused to them, then this same I can also be called under certain conditions, or in 'addition', a Stranger. In philosophy's traditional terms (albeit transformed under the conditions whose hypothesis we are positing), the I is 'real', and the Stranger is a 'transcendental' property of this I, which does not mean without consistency or 'unreal' in the vulgar or even ontological sense of the term. This is to no longer divide identity and the state of the stranger between two individuals or two people wherein one is subject and the other is not, or again wherein one affects the other and inhibits it as an Interdict: each man fully enjoys a radical identity and, for this very reason, is 'equipped' with Stranger-Existing. The Stranger is no longer 'the others'. In a sense, the Stranger is 'me' but on condition of understanding this I-in-I as a quasi-infrastructure and the Stranger as the quasi-superstructure in which the I-in-I exists. The formula, 'we are all strangers', ceases being an unthought slogan. It receives a theoretical pertinence but on the condition of ridding it of this little philosophical catchphrase, 'all', and substitute it with the identity of 'each-and-every-one' [*tout-un-chacun*] or seamless immanence which henceforth defines 'real' or 'ordinary man'. We condense this entire part of our investigations within the following formula that records the genuine causality of the I and the Stranger: *I and the Stranger, we are identical in-the-last-instance alone*. Or again: the Stranger is fully an I (I-in-I) but in-the-last-instance alone. We will explain these formulae which adjoin the causality called 'determination-in-the-last-instance' to radical identity. These formulae define what we call for reasons that are evident enough the *Theorem of Democracy*. We oppose this theorem to the vague and transcendent concepts of 'political philosophy' and to the philosophical exception to democracy. The theorem of democracy orients a theory of *the identity of Strangers.* It is in this last concept that the different directions of this essay converge: *the Stranger is the definition of man, the unity of philosophy and the Human Sciences, and the key to democracy.*

4. Can the antinomy between philosophical thought and theory of a scientific kind, beyond the particular case of the Human Sciences, receive a solution? We return to all of the previous problems, the first but also the second, and connect them within the third, which brings about the solution from the perspective of the object and, within the fourth, the perspective of theory. The theorem 'of democracy' is obviously not a mathematical nor regional theorem, it is a theorem with a real origin, where the real is neither regional nor fundamental, neither ontic nor ontological: Immanence-of-the-last-instance. Consequently, it is a *Transcendental Theorem.* It is no less scientific in kind or origin as it is philosophical, without which these rations give rise to 'synthesis' or 'resolution'. What we call the Immanence-of-the-last-instance, or the essence of man, indeed determines a 'science-thought' or a 'unified theory' that draws its materials (but only its materials) as its objects and operations, equally from the sciences and philosophy. Here again – despite the fact that it is neither the place nor the objective of this book to explain it – what we call 'vision-in-One' is the real cause of thought, the cause of a transcendental identity (to be determined) of science and philosophy, of theory and pragmatics. The 'science' that we reclaim is expressively in this sense a transcendental science, and the theorem of democracy, which bears on man as Stranger (and no longer on man's real essence alone), is its centrepiece. Then what can this mean for the set of our problems other than that the agent or the cause of the democratic enunciation is no longer the philosopher and that its object is no longer the philosophical 'subject' and its avatars, and specifically not the unconscious? This is the identity-of-the-last-instance of man as Stranger, the Stranger *qua* determined in-the-last-instance by the identity of the One-I. In this sense, the Stranger alone can 'stand' [*tenir 'sur'*] democracy upon a rigorous discourse and say what they do as much as do what they say. The discourse of democracy is marked by the immanence of a new performativity that no longer falls under the critiques that, for example, the thought of a Judaic origin could deservedly address the philosophico-linguistic concept of the performative.

If the unified theory of man culminates within the democratic theory of the Stranger, the latter can be specified a bit more by the recourse to the material provided by psychoanalysis. This is the 'unified theory' of philosophy and psychoanalysis, the generalised theory of the unconscious, which is also called non-psychoanalysis or less perfectly non-Freudian and non-Lacanian analysis. Non-analysis lifts one of today's most crucial antinomies with very extended variants (the antinomy between philosophy and psychoanalysis) thanks to a fundamental theorem parallel to the theorem of democracy of Strangers. If one formulates it summarily in psychoanalytic terms, which are undoubtedly still too undifferentiated, this theorem stipulates the following: *jouissance* determines-in-the-last-instance the unconscious as the dualysis of the philosophico-analytic imaginary. This formulation abbreviates a more complete and even 'heavier' (albeit typical) formulation of a theorem. Indeed, if we oppose to the unitary and amphibological concept of '*jouissance*' the unperceived distinction of analysis (but a founding one for non-analysis) of the '*Joui*' and '*Jouissance*', we will say: *the Real or the* Joui-sans-Jouissance *determines-in-the-last-instance (through the organon of* Jouissance*) the Unconscious as dualysis of the transcendental appearance that the philosophico-psychoanalytic symptom is.* Of course, this is a provisionally unintelligible and complex formula since it puts in relation new uses of the concept of the 'real', 'symbolic' and 'imaginary' that non-analysis transforms from analysis, but we suspect that it displaces outside of their constitutive claim and emplaces as simple (that is, 'imaginary') material (and therefore without negating them strictly speaking) the guiding and pertinent formulae of Lacanianism: 'the unconscious is structured like a language', 'there is no sexual relationship', 'the One is not' (but) 'there is some One', and so on. This treatise's third chapter will be the term-by-term presentation and commentary on this theorem.

Undoubtedly, you might be wondering about the meaning and interest of this elaboration, and you might be tempted to see in it what nevertheless it is not: a meta-philosophy, a meta-politics, a meta-psychoanalysis. Like non-analysis in particular, this 'Theory of Strangers' in general has no empirically descriptive or prescriptive claim. It neither describes foreigners [*étrangers*] from the perspective of their assumed political or cultural reality nor symptoms from a new psycho-pathological perspective. By this very fact, this theory has no ontological and philosophical claim, whether questioning or normative: it is not a philosophical 'solution' to the 'Other Question' or an ideologico-political 'partisanship' regarding the 'problem of foreigners'. As for non-analysis, it is also not a new 'theory' or 'version' of the unconscious, its philosophical reappropriation. Their signification and pertinence are 'transcendental' in the rigorous sense in which this term designates predicates or properties that do not add anything to the given, do not add anything real to the Real (here, the One or the Ego) and do not add anything effective to effectivity (here, the socio-politico-cultural context or even the symptom, and so on), but that pertain to the already constituted knowledge and 'manifestation' of which they make a *theoretical use*, knowledges about man produced by philosophy and the Human Sciences (and, in this case, psychoanalysis). The meaning of this type of theory is to reveal, with the ration of these primary knowledges, the Stranger as such in each man, or the Universal Unconscious, to constitute a genuine intelligible and democratic order not of 'Other People' [*Autrui*] alone but of Selves-as-Strangers [*des Moi-comme-Étrangers*]. If the theory does not claim to therapeutically intervene in so-called everyday reality as much as a politics, a philosophy or a psychoanalysis would claim to do, it nevertheless does transform empirical givens (cultural, linguistic, analytic, political, and so on) which are also philosophical or philosophisable givens, but in view of including them within a relatively autonomous order or realm of the democracy-of-Strangers. The theory does not claim to transform them in view of themselves or to change them empirically. Therefore, it is not the theory's problem to intervene in the assumed situation of foreigners in the historico-cultural sense, not even to reformulate a 'philosophy of the Stranger' or respectively a 'philosophy of the Unconscious'. By radicalising it, we extend to philosophy itself (and to analysis and politics) the clause of relative philosophical indifference to the empirical. Philosophy already needs empirical givens but does not really modify them insofar as they belong to the order of the primary or empirical given – the share of contingency. We extend this contingency of the given to philosophy and the Human Sciences themselves; henceforth, it is a simple material of which a ('transcendental' but precisely more 'metaphysical') thought makes use, a theoretical use. Its ultimate meaning is to bring man (that is, the Stranger) the possibility of an immanent *jouissance* of what otherwise he is affected by [*ressent*] in pain and worry of the war and the violence which drives culture, language, society – philosophy, too, which adds to this discontent. This is why it can manifest and contribute to constituting non-political democracy as the 'transcendental order' of the Stranger and, within the Stranger's specific order, the non-analytic destiny of the 'subjects of the unconscious' that we are.

The treatise is arranged in the following way:

The *Problematic* draws up a table of the set of themes, objectives and objects of a science of man as Strangers and presents the fundamental concepts of what we call a 'unified theory'.

The chapters that form the body of the text develop the unified theory in its domains [*ressorts*], objectives, its theoretical context and strive to undoubtedly very schematically put this new discipline in place, each time in accordance with the material.

The first chapter posits the prolegomena to any future science that would present itself as human; simultaneously, the human cause of-the-last-instance of this science (the Ego as vision-in-man); the necessity of a material constituted by philosophy and the Human Sciences; and finally, the great traits of the specific essence of man-as-Stranger which is the object of the new science of people.

The second chapter specifies this science of humans (or gives it its entire object) as a theory of Strangers and implements the previously posed principles. It passes from the Ego to people, from the cause to the object of this science. It is in all respects the central part of this treatise and what is the most innovative of it within the present investigations. The second chapter strives to knot within one, same transcendental theorem defining man as Stranger(s) the reality of its object: the rigorous knowledge of man as Stranger(s) and the conditions of a real democracy. This theorem opens a new field of objects and investigations and opposes itself, through this identity in the mode of the last-instance, to philosophy (political or not), which proposes of man or democracy only a 'unitary' theory or which begins by separating, dividing and hierarchising them.

The third chapter implements the previous two chapters regarding the case of psychoanalysis. It is an introduction to non-analysis or non-Freudian and non-Lacanian analysis: how could this discipline proceed, what concepts elaborate on the case of psychoanalytic discourses treated as meta-human? Obviously, the point is only that some indications are destined to show the reality of this new field of research and to 'force' (if it is possible) the inevitable resistance of psychoanalysts. This chapter presents two difficulties for which we must excuse ourselves to the reader, precisely, about the reading: the chapter assumes assimilated, on the one hand, the problematic of the previous chapters and the author's way of thinking and, on the other hand, the author's material (Lacanian theory) truly reduced to its elementary framework, a 'standard' and nearly scholastic Lacanianism, but which is quite sufficient for a first elaboration of non-analysis. Finally, its allusive, abrupt, compact character, stripped of any textual location, is explained by this (not discounting any available time for the future towards a research into the non-analytic field): we have chosen to throw into battle all of our available weapons, or, in the game, we have chosen to fold all of our cards, abandoning this construction site to the interest (or disinterest) of young researchers – to their spirit of invention as much as their courage. Considering ourselves in a state of emergency, we have thought that it was better to wildly reclaim a new terrain than to magnify the pedagogical precautions and transitions, in order to furnish a kind of memento (even an indigestible one) of possible problems and solutions. A difficulty of interpretation ensues: it can pass for a supplementary attempt at philosophical meta-psychoanalysis, an interpretation absolutely contrary to its meaning, since it is rather non-analysis which rightly makes the meta-human character of psychoanalysis appear and its supersession illusory (the transcendental illusion) from the essence of immanence of man [*de l'essence d'immanence de l'homme*]. The most general project of non-analysis would be to institute a use of analysis that liberates it from its amphibological blend with philosophy, but not from any relation to philosophy.

The entirety can also be read as a critique of the judgement of humanity such that it is formulated and comprised within philosophy in general. Then, the point is to 'sensitise' the reader, this spontaneous philosopher, to the antinomies that render contradictory the judgement of humanity and towards the necessary passage from the judgement to the scientific problem of man. The science of the essence of people as Strangers posits the conditions that suppress these antinomies, and which give to man the thought that he merits and the science the cause that inscribes it in the heart of the human real. Here and there, some very brief indications regarding a pragmatics of philosophical humanism and in general the pragmatics of Human Sciences, a pragmatics included within a first theory of man, specify the meaning of this treatise.

Problematic: On Man as a Scientific Continent

Homo Sive Scientia

We are attempting to think the beautiful formula, man of science, attempting to make it into a hypothesis, and attempting to experiment upon it in view of a new scientific continent: *Homo sive scientia.* Let us translate it as: 'man, ergo science (of man)' – our new *cogito.*

Philosophy and science maintain dissymmetrical relations with man. Philosophy claims to bring man his fulfilled essence; science is silent concerning man or only knows man as a seemingly rather absent object of the Human Sciences; he seems quite absent from the conditions and foundations of any science. The first seems to defend man, while the second forgets or reduces him. Here, we would like to change the general hypothesis and suggest that what we have just described above is a double appearance, undoubtedly an objective appearance but one that is quite possible to rectify by thinking man and, consequently, the relation of these two types of thought otherwise; that their opposition stems from the fact that philosophy, no more than science, does not know man and that introducing man 'between' them is sufficient to cease hostilities that were based solely on ignorance and resistance. Then, it is philosophy that would globally devalue man precisely because it would like to change and overvalue man in its own way through sufficiency; and it is science, on condition of enriching its concept and no longer reducing it to merely a science of objects, that now (accompanied by philosophy deprived of its sufficiency) would protect man and science would be protected by him in the real. Man's essence is perhaps not in these shifting and changing figures of sand and water that philosophy gives to it. Perhaps the essence of man could be kept within itself just as much as in the apparent positive forgetting and scientific silence concerning man. We are not saying that, unlike philosophy, science does not think – for it is possible to make a thinking use of it while conserving its nature as science, a hypothesis that we are experimenting with – but only that it does not speak like philosophy. The silence of science perhaps suits man if he is, as we believe, the most silent being and if beings of silence alone can make language speak rather than letting themselves be spoken by language – which is all of philosophy.

Homo sive scientia, the formula which serves as our new hypothesis concerning the relations between science, philosophy and man, means that a god is made (of) [*pour faire (de)*] philosophy, but man alone is made (of) science, which does not mean that science exhausts man. For us, this formula has always appeared in an absolutely certain yet absolutely opaque feeling, without clarity or distinction: it speaks in some way without speaking, like science itself. And it is not a saying originating from the Western tradition nor a philosophical thesis. Perhaps it is an axiom, freely posited no doubt, but one that participates in the kind of neutral internal power of axioms without a philosophical effect. Even if they are not intuitive, even if they are silent, these are axioms that are deprived of any transcendent ontological reference, instead having a weight, an intrinsic ontology which makes the axiom-form imposed as it is without further justification through a sort of strictly internal consistency. The hypothesis of a possible affinity of man's essence and the axiomatic form, however, makes no sense in the strictly logical comprehension of axiomatics, and even less sense in its ontology, whether it be Aristotelian or something else. It could be that if the axiom does not have or no longer has a transcendent ontological foothold, it nevertheless finds a reality that suits it and to which it is adequate to in this silent and full presence of the real. In short, the good use of science and undoubtedly philosophy would be the work neither of the Being of onto-theo-logy nor of the logico-formal Void, but of a human reality that is quite capable of being formulated or given in the form of the axiom or hypothesis. With this cause of science that science does not exhaust, we are finally closer to an experience of man that is neither Greek nor Jewish.

Philosophy's 'man', the one who is so weak and so effaced by Being and its avatars, could have only entered the scene of thought masked and falsified: *daimon*-man, creature-man, individual-man, subject-man, overman-man, *Dasein*-man, and so on. Repressed and 'forgotten' by so many adventures that did not really concern man, he had to make way for philosophical anthropoids. Just as we had to return to the old 'madness' beneath 'mental illnesses', perhaps we will have to return to this idea of 'man', abandon the subject and the individual, the agent and the actor, the analysand and the man of words, and make humans once again a new idea in thought.

Therefore, rather than adding a supplementary touch to the uncertain figure that the Greco-humanist tradition has bequeathed to us, we are proposing as feasible the institution of the most general science of man *qua* man and of man existing in the multiple state. Man is neither confounded with the 'subject' of the philosophers nor with its twin and opposite concept the 'individual': man is the being-human (of) man as he is postulated immanently, no longer by the Human Sciences, but by a science that is specific to its object and method (even more rigorously still, as we will come to establish it) by a unified theory of philosophy and the Human Sciences. We had to suspend most of the doctrines that philosophy holds concerning man, as well as the facts under which the Human Sciences has concealed man's being-human; we had to forge other hypotheses that could explain the object of the new science and distinguish it from its philosophical images.

There are four hypotheses that form a system and that correspond to the theoretical discoveries gradually conditioned:

1. The Ego has for its constancy what we call the 'One', the Real when it is understood as immanence, but as the radical form of immanence: as self(-) immanence rather than immanent to something else (to Being, Substance, Subject-Ego, and so on). Thus, we are radicalising the original philosophical ideas of 'transcendental immanence', 'internal transcendental experience', and so on, but by dissolving the amphibology of the immanent real and the transcendental. We are definitively excluding any nothingness, any reflexive or perceptive distance from the One; we are suspending any transcendence of it, any decision and ontological position (that is, any auto-position) of it. We state that the One is non(-)self-decisional and non(-)self-positional, that it is absolute inherence without self(-)distance; or, again, because it is not reflected, we say that the One is self(-)affect or better yet: Affected-without-affection, that the Real is nothing other than this ordeal of the affect of self(-)immanence. Finally, we say that the real-One is absolutely distinguished in this way from the World and in general from Being, that the One is not the One-All but the One-without-All.
2. The being-human (of) man, due to its 'epistemological status', is only thinkable as an object of a unified theory, an object no longer of philosophical theses or the positive sciences but of a system of hypotheses or axioms whose nature is no longer solely scientific but identically transcendental or of 'real' origin. The science of man thus only exists as a 'unified theory' of philosophy and the Human Sciences, as a *mathesis transcendentalis* of lived experience, in a non-rationalist sense (to be specified) of these words.
3. The being-human (of) man, beyond the I or the Ego but always from the point of view of its reality, only exists in the state of 'Other', that is, identically in the state of Multiple and Stranger. Through his scientific concept,

man only exists as a multitude of Strangers, a way of giving meaning back to the old concept, *multitudo transcendentalis*, and of positing democracy in the very heart of the science of people.
4. The being-human (of) man, from the perspective of its knowledge, allows us to define a good use of these meta-human discourses (philosophy and the Human Sciences) henceforth as simple material for this new science. Because this new science presents itself as a unified theory, it is distinct from unitary theories (philosophical anthropology and the Human Sciences) but capable of procuring their intrinsic identity from them. At the same time, this new science is a pragmatics of these disciplines and conducts a real critique of the anthropological antinomies of philosophy or the antinomies of the judgement of humanity.

Unitary Theory and Unified Theory of Philosophy and the Human Sciences

The construction of a new discipline is a poorly elucidated theoretical problem: by way of spontaneous philosophy, we give ourselves two or several already constituted disciplines in general that one treats as pertinent and 'real' or given presuppositions, and one strives more or less empirically or in an aprioristic way – through overlaps and transferences, in general through a more or less differentiated synthesis of problems, procedures and concepts – to constitute and define a new 'domain' or quite simply a body of objects and articulations that have all the *ad hoc* traits of bricolages and artefacts. This empirico-philosophical fashion cannot be our own, for it obeys an implicit logic that emerges from that which we call the Philosophical Decision, and which defines the unitary mode of the constitution of a discipline through division, the inequality of hierarchy and a supplementary synthesis. We exposit this in priority under the name of the 'idealist triad' before posing the entirely different problem of a 'unified theory' of the Human Sciences and philosophy: no longer an apparent creation of science under the authority and in the spirit of philosophy, but rather a unification of the sciences and philosophy equally in a more potent discipline. A unitary theory of their relations would renew somewhat differently their conflict of hierarchy and their war since time immemorial by assigning the unification of the Real to the theory itself; a unified theory seeks within a new experience of man and of the Real to 'simplify' and render immanent the identity of theories themselves. The 'means' that it uses for this end, opposed to the idealist triad, is what we call the Real as One or the Ego-of-the-last-instance, or, again, as 'vision-in-man'. It allows us to only posit their necessary equality in the form of their identification-in-the-last-instance, which really destroys their inequality or their difference without thereby resulting in their confusion. This brings about a peace and democracy among them that they have never known. This is a new 'logic' of the relations of philosophy and the Human Sciences rather than a philosophical logic of them. The point is to give our formula its positive and radical meaning: *Homo sive scientia*, a formula which is not immediately or spontaneously given by science and even less by philosophy in any case but elsewhere than in them, even if it must be constructed through them and with their ration.

How can philosophy believe to be able to constitute a new science and, in particular, a science of man? Philosophy does not always explicitly undertake one such constitution or reconstitution – it cannot always do so, even though it has endlessly attempted to proceed with it – but there is a certain way of imagining new sciences 'in the spirit' of philosophy or wanting to 'ground' them afterwards, rather than in the spirit of science itself. The formation of new knowledges [*savoirs*] is an enterprise that responds to certain invariants of two types: one set of invariants can be scientific, the other set can instead be philosophical and precisely give rise to a 'knowledge' rather than a science or a 'scientific continent'. Even if philosophy is not always required and is also sometimes displaced on this continent, what is essential to these invariants that make up the Philosophical Decision is found and is symptomatic here. More profoundly than 'analytic' transference, there is a procedure of transference proper to the philosophical style and responsible for promoting the constitution of a new formation of knowledge.

Schematically, this procedure consists in: (1) isolating, in one determined 'positive' science, a precise and assumed complete empirical theory (analytic geometry, mathematical physics, thermo-dynamics, and, to take some recent examples from Lacanians, a mixture of the signifier and logic and, from the post-Lacanians, axiomatic set theory); (2) then transposing it into the essence of a particular science (psychoanalysis for example, and, in the foreseeable future, a science of the human real); (3) implicitly postulating, given the assumed philosophical unity of 'essences' or the ultimate unity of the Real, that this particular science contributes in determining – both in its own mode and in a universal form or with a philosophical ambition – the essence of science and in explaining the possibility of other sciences. Therefore, this procedure brings three dimensions into play: (1) a particular theory, a sequence of knowledges [*connaissances*] or an already elaborated and validated knowledge [*savoir*]; (2) a particular science erected on this knowledge elevated to the dignity of a science with a specific object; (3) the essence of science, anticipated and postulated by the previous terms and responsible for assuring their unity or their communication in return.

This triad is neither arbitrary nor contingent. The trinity of invariants of any philosophical decision (that is, the ultimately specular circle of a Dyad and a Unity) will be recognised here. The Dyad is the Dyad of the object-theory and the new science erected upon it; and their Unity is represented by the science of sciences, philosophy or a scientific heir of philosophy, which is both particular and universal and which functions as a 'middle-term'.

This procedure combines abstraction (a knowledge locally produced, abstracted from its process of formation and elevated to the state of the essence of science) and unitary transference (to another object, here man, at least through the unconscious). Obviously, in the case concerned, one can carefully distinguish between the massive transference of mathematics to so-called man (the Human Sciences), their ontological investment (a new experience of Being as inconsistent Multiple), and finally a simple vague resonance between the unconscious and mathematics (at the level of the 'letter'). The latter two specific cases represent a critique of the Human Sciences, but it is no longer sufficient here because the transference involved originates elsewhere and is more powerful. It is now of the nature of a philosophical decision and affects analysis itself as one of its objects. However, to be fair to the subtlest attempts, we will say that if they still resort to this triad as the mode of constitution of a discipline, to abstraction and unitary transference of the essence, they then limit its scope due to their sense of alterity and simple 'resonance'. However, the problem is of knowing if the constitution of a science can completely eliminate, as we believe, this recourse to the weak identity of 'resonance' itself and to all mathematico-philosophical exchanges or reciprocities. The ultimate relevance of these types of apparently scientific procedures seems to us, moreover, to stem from philosophical logic rather than from science.

This procedure of the philosophical 'triangulation' of science is here called 'idealist'. Why? Because another conception of the relations of science and philosophy equally rather than a new philosophical combination is possible, one that denounces within this combination an absolute idealism. Another conception – that is, otherwise than epistemological, or otherwise than re-appropriable by a philosophical decision. It is a conception that excludes the congenital idealism of philosophy or where the known Real (the One-in-One or the One-without-Being) is no longer given and constituted through its knowledge, where the known Real is no longer confounded with objectivity through which it alone is known. We call 'idealist' a conception of science that reduces the known real to the knowledge of the Real: this is the very foundation of the procedure of idealist abstraction. Idealism indeed proceeds towards the abstraction of knowledge outside its reference to the known Real in-the-last-instance and distinct from the object of knowledge, and then supposes that the theory is near the Real itself with some nuances, that set theory can, for example – by right and all nuances bracketed – function as a new ontology (Being-*qua*-Being as pure multiple) or rather as the Other of classical ontology, that it can exhaust the essence of the human and science in which it would not be a simple local and contingent knowledge. The (ontological) objectivation or any other form of transcendence – which is, however, nothing but a particular, 'occasional' moment ordered to the Real itself – then contributes towards constituting the order of essences. This procedure can only introduce into the sciences once more all the aporias that make up the Philosophical Decision and its innate idealism. Philosophy is made to 'resolve' these aporias, that is, to simply displace them after having posed them. Even in psychoanalysis and not only the most specular of the Human Sciences, it is always this supplement, this horizon, this guardian . . . dedicated to the exploitation of man.

Now, how do we conceive a unified theory of philosophy and the Human Sciences, that is, a unified theory of man? It is under this title that we understand a 'human science of man' or again a 'science of man's essence (of) man', that is, the inclusion of the essence as human (neither anonymous nor ontological) essence within a theory of the scientific type and as its object. This is a paradoxical project: the sciences that are called 'human' are sciences of the object 'man', object sciences, but they are not sciences of the essence; as for philosophy, it bears on essence without genuinely being a science. Therefore, by what condition can we conceive a genuine science – in the same way as 'the sciences' – but one that would bear on the essence of man rather than on an indefinite spectrum of predicates and properties that are supposed to belong to man? In one such theory that is called 'unified', it is philosophy that brings about the dimension of the essence, even if the concept would be 'modified' in the operation, and it is the Human Sciences which brings about the dimension of science, even if as well its concept would be 'modified'. Science obviously knows the universal, but the universal is oriented about the object and not thematised as such, as is the case in philosophy under the name 'essence'; and philosophy also has an 'object' of a special kind, the object that corresponds to philosophical interest. How we constitute the human, non-objective essence into an object that is nevertheless of the rigorous scientific type is another way of formulating our problem. Its solution requires that it would be very precisely elucidated by what we can understand, on the one hand, by 'modification' and, on the other hand, 'unification' or the identity that, beyond the real-One itself, will speak about science and philosophy.

A radical identity of science and the (human) essence implies a modification of their relation of unitary synthesis such that it is traditionally posited under the final authority of philosophy. What identity and what distinction matters if the unitary unification – what we call the Philosophical Decision – also acts through identity and distinction? What is their mode of identity and distinction in a simply 'unified' theory? This type of distribution is equivalent, beyond the simple real-One, to what we call 'the One-of-the-last-instance' or again, as it happens, the Ego-of-the-last-instance, an entirely new way of identifying and distinguishing. Unlike the mode of the most general philosophical synthesis, called the *Same*, that contains the triad that we have spoken about, that is, an invertible or reversible hierarchy, and therefore a circularity and a simultaneity, the One (of-the-last-instance) on the one hand does not participate, unlike the Same, in the identity that it realises or determines, but keeps itself in-One and remains inalienable; on the other hand, the One determines outside of it and after it *a radical identity, absolutely without difference, and a unilateral duality or a duality without reciprocity*, for example a duality of science and essence; and, finally, this is obvious so that this identity cannot be contradictory, the One involves considerable modifications of the concept of essence, and therefore a modification of philosophy (and the Human Sciences insofar as they bear constitutive philosophical presuppositions). These three moments – this is the fourth trait of a unified theory in this mode – do not form any circle of the 'Same', not forming a reversible, that is, philosophical or unitary process, but are 'unilaterally' arranged according to an irreversible order.

Thus, we seem to construct *a priori*, through its cause, the concept of a unified theory of the Human Sciences and philosophy. Indeed, this is because, in its principle at least, it cannot be drawn from either of them, which are nothing but its materials or rations, but must precede them, be independent of them, being neither a science nor a philosophy subject to proceeding once more empirically through them and falling back into the unitary rut. However, the idea of an *a priori* construction is very insufficient and represents a falsification of a philosophical origin. The One called 'of-the-last-instance', the One that is a cause and not only in-One, is a 'pure' transcendental of a new philosophically unprecedented type rather than a simple *a priori* philosophically posited in a circle with experience. In philosophy in general, as one may recall, transcendentals designate 'categories' of a superior degree, more universal still than categories, or that transcend them and that are called (such as the One, Being (and being [*Étant*]), the Contingent, the Multiple, the Good, the True, and so on) real in the sense of *res*, but without contributing nothing 'real' to it nor equivalent to its properties as *res*. Conserving the idea of a transcendental sphere, we conceive it entirely otherwise than philosophy as soon as we say that it concerns the Real-as-last-instance. The One such that we understand it, when it is cause and not solely the simple Real, indeed possesses the following decisive characteristics to explain what we have previously posited as radical identity or the unification of science and philosophy:

1. The One is no longer a 'conceptual', abstract or ideal transcendental, it is a sphere of transcendental experience or real-experience-in-the-last-instance. The One is no longer related to the Real as a predicate but as determined-in-the-last-instance by it; and the Real is no longer on its side identical to the *res* as being, the Real is a phenomenon through and through or Given-without-Givenness, an absolute given without an operation of givenness, and an identity through and through; the transcendental participates in the Real without itself being the Real or a part of the Real.
2. This identity determined by the One is the only transcendental that is now not convertible with Being to which it is related or in which it is said. Being is, on its side, a transcendental of the second rank or a derived rank; in philosophy, Being is a mixture of the transcendental and transcendence; here, Being is Transcendence whose essence is this transcendental identity that is said from it but without still forming a mixture with it.
3. The One is said in an absolutely universal way, more than supracategorial, of Being and being, that is, the empirico-ideal and transcendent sphere that we call 'effectivity'; the Real but also the transcendental therefore absolutely distinguish themselves from effectivity even if the Real is related to the transcendental.
4. The One is said universally (this is the universality of the unified theory) of effectivity but in no way in the manner of a predicate that is said of . . . or attributed to . . .; the One does not have the causality of the predicate or the form (and otherwise furthermore does not have the causality of one of the three other causes: agent, matter, end), but possesses the causality called 'Determination-in-the-last-instance', a universal causality that only can be valid *for* Being and being, for the sphere of effectivity, because this cause is neither alienated in its material nor in its effect.
5. The One is the causality of the Real, but precisely of a real that is neither empirical nor ideal; neither ontic nor ontological, but phenomenal throughout: as such, the One is the real cause of produced knowledge or the unified theory. It is in no way a cause whose reality would be exhausted in knowledge or science (as in idealism) but whose reality defines a real order of knowledge, the identity precisely of the essence and science as being of-the-last-instance.
6. Finally, and this is perhaps its most important trait here, this sphere of transcendental experience that is immanent in-the-last-instance is the specific essence of man beyond his real essence (vision-in-man). It is this sphere that will be deployed as the Universal Humanity of Strangers.

These few schematic indications allow us to construct the concept of a unified theory of philosophy and the human sciences as soon as we introduce 'among' them, or rather, in each of them, the hypothesis of this experience of man. However, if the One-of-the-last-instance defines a new experience of the transcendental, it conserves from it an essential trait to radicalise it: it adds nothing effective to effectivity, but modifies or acts upon it by contrast in a precisely and solely transcendental way. This original causality passes through two operations that define the determination in-the-last-instance or explain what we must understand by the unification or identity of theories: (1) a radical identification without difference or synthesis, what we call, given its origin within the One and its non-return upon it, a *uni-dentification*, what we will therefore distinguish from any philosophical synthesis where the synthesised terms modify in turn the essence of the synthesis and circularly penetrate within it (uni-dentification is non-circular, without auto-position, and is a 'simple' transcendental identity); (2) an equally transcendental suspension of the philosophy-form or the mixed-form or the claims of the Philosophical Decision, a suspension that does not either let itself be co-determined by what it suspends but by the One, and what, for the same reasons as previously, we call *uni-lateralisation.* It is this double acting in which the One is capable under the conditions of Transcendence all by remaining in-One that is very different from a 'transcendental reduction' that is always more or less circular; or again under the conditions of the causality of Being and its four metaphysical modes that suffer from the same defect. However, it modifies rather the experience that we have of science and philosophy, but it only modifies them transcendentally, not effectively; and it acts upon what of them is given from our transcendental point of view, namely their relations and them alone. Let us explain these two points.

First point: the science of the human essence that we lay the foundations of here does not in any way propose to philosophically intervene within philosophy (a new anthropological decision, for example) or in the Human Sciences; not more than does it propose to project one of them (linguistics or psychoanalysis) upon philosophy as is done now. Inversely, the recourse to the Human Sciences in the elaboration of this theory does not imply that they would be constitutive of it. We will say that the transcendental causality of the One upon the Human Sciences and philosophy, as a Determination-in-the-last-instance, which does not modify them in their effectivity or does not even claim to propose to do so in a new concept, has as a correlate (itself included in the concept 'unified theory') their use not as a cause or a constitutive element of this new science, but solely as material, as an occasional cause and ration. If the transcendental such that we understand it is not an effective (ontic or ontological) predicate of the Human Sciences and philosophy, if it transforms them but without modifying them in their own mode, it is equally as non-effective that it requires them, outside of any ontic or ontological causality (such as form, agent, matter and end), simply as a cause that is called 'occasional'. Having no effective efficacy, no model either in the Human Sciences and in a philosophy, the causality of the One (of the essence of man) gives rise to a specific science, the identity of science and the essence (here the human essence). It forms a new and autonomous discipline, irreducible to these objects such that they are unitarily disjointed and synthesised in distinct disciplines. Its goal above all is not – despite the prevailing theme of the 'unitary theory' – of carrying out a new synthesis. It has no goal nor objective, no finality, but enjoys its own identity and the use that it makes out of the rations of existing disciplines. If otherwise it can be interpreted as a transcendent 'unity' of philosophy and the Human Sciences, then this is an effect of its transcendental power of identification, a transcendental that resides elsewhere and anteriorly within the One; an appearance that arrives upon it in addition and that can always give rise once more, in the mind of philosophers, to the confused dreams of the encyclopaedia or the system of culture, the negotiation and hybridisation of knowledges, and so on.

Second point: a unified theory means a certain type of equality of science and philosophy, invited to stop their combat and renounce their authoritarian and hierarchical style. This is not an equality abstracted from a hierarchy, interiorising or repressing it in the way of the philosophies of equality, as if one would put science and philosophy back in a 'face-to-face' towards a new conflict. Realistically, the transcendental 'apparatus' of radical unification without difference brings within a unilateral or irreversible relation (therefore, without confusion or amphibology) on the one side the identity of science and man – precisely to rethink from top to bottom as the object of the new knowledges to produce – and on the other side their predominant unitary mixture, sometimes philosophical, sometimes belonging to the 'Human Sciences'. On both sides, it always concerns their relation, either a new relation determined-in-the-last-instance, or a traditional and unitary relation. Even in the unitary situation, the relation of their exclusive or inclusive disjunction, they are inseparable, one because it aims for the essence of others, and the others because, as sciences or so-called as such – but we do not judge this – they constitute an alterity or a stumbling block for the philosophy that is determined in accordance with them.

Thus, we do not give ourselves 'science in-itself' in the way of a philosophical hypothesis, or the 'fact' of science in the epistemological manner and through a typical abstraction of philosophy, but rather we give ourselves the indivisible and complex bloc of the philosophy-of-science. The transcendental causality of the Determination-in-the-last-instance is then responsible with extracting from this mixture not the One itself – the One is already manifest – nor even the identity of science and the human essence, but the content of this identity: the 'Essence (of) science', and what can specify and make it known with the ration of the mixture and through the suspension of the claims of the mixture. We no longer believe that the 'mixture' – the philosophical form *par excellence* – only concerns philosophy and not science; we no longer believe that we know science *a priori* and in its essence through its surreptitious confusion with the One; we no longer believe that the Philosophical Decision would be a void form, a formal outfit thrown onto science, the One then manifesting science outside of any residual relation to philosophy, in the way of the essence of science 'in-itself'. This is why the object of the unified theory – far from any surreptitious scientism – is the uni-dentity of science and essence. In a more general context, we call this the Essence (of) science; and in the most restrained context of this treatise, we call it the Human Essence (of) science or again the man (of) science, a formula to comprehend according to strict uni-dentification, as an identity absolutely indivisible but without confusion. Under the name that is still to-come 'Stranger', this identity will be the cause and the object of the science of people as the democratic science of Human Multitudes.

For all these reasons, the science of the human essence cannot be a positivist and scientistic overthrow of philosophy like the philosophy-of-the-Human-Sciences, neither can it be this revenge of a new form of the hermeneutic and cultural appropriation of them. Philosophy is not unilateralised, reduced to the state of occasional material, without radically being identified equally – subject to this transcendental causality that modifies it profoundly, it and its experience of the essence – to science. Correlatively, science is not unilateralised, suspended in its effectivity and its claims to philosophy without the Human Sciences being on their side. Rather, the problem is to change the form of their relation, to substitute their unitary relation which remains under philosophical domination with a relation of 'unification' that would rather be drawn from the transcendental dimension such that, at least, we have defined it.

Without a doubt, within their unitary mixture, philosophy aims for science in its essence, proposes to access it and ground it. One is also tempted with subtracting this essence 'in-itself' of science from philosophical authority, to globally 'abstract' science from it, but this is an ultimate philosophical illusion: what would be subtracted from philosophy will not be science but its essence, for the essence has been posed and brought into science by philosophy itself. Rather, it is therefore necessarily a new experience of the Essence (of) science, the inclusion of the problematic of essence within the heart of science, that the One can manifest, obviously withdrawing it from its philosophical interpretation.

Perhaps, one will then ask why we 'call' this 'unified theory' 'science' rather than 'philosophy'? Of course, with the unified theory indeed being a matter, from our point of view, of an absolutely new or emergent theoretical genre that is neither philosophy nor science in the sense of separate effective sciences, there are constraining reasons to call this 'science' rather than 'philosophy', at risk, it is true, of a scientistic misunderstanding concerning the exact nature of this project that is not a simple positivist reversal of philosophy but of the identification-in-the-last-instance by the One. Here, the One becomes the real cause of the 'unified theory' itself having fallen outside of any science and/or philosophy (but, under certain conditions, in no way outside of this theory itself) and its efficacy cannot be exercised under the banner of one or the other. The One saves the unified theory from science and philosophy, even if it saves it, it is true, from itself. Therefore, if the One itself does not allow us to name the project, it must be so in accordance with the material, precisely through its aspect as a 'unified theory' or again, as we call it, a 'science-thought', which gives what is essential to the argument. However, even from this point of view, it seems that no privilege of science is possible and it seems rather inadequate to still speak of a 'science', even if it were a science (of) the Human Essence (of) science. We no longer think the project through its terms, but we think the terms through the project, for in a 'unified theory', the material is not 'philosophy-as-such' or 'the Human Sciences-as-such', but their indivisible mixture such that philosophy (or epistemology) in a dominant way projects it through its affection by science. Therefore, no one will find here a new thesis about what we call 'science' or 'philosophy' in-itself, about the relation to the Real that they claim to maintain – an epistemology or a philosophy of philosophy. Among the Human Sciences and philosophy, there are some relations to the Real, and there are some in a blended state – this is all that we are allowed to say: for us, this is a contingent given, if at least it is presented, on the basis of which we do not construct the concept of a unified theory in an empirico-aprioristic or circular way, but what we utilise contrarily as a ration, for transcendental or non-effective reasons, in view of their unified theory. Therefore, we will make note of this: the expressions 'the science of the Essence (of) man', 'the human science of people' and the 'science of humans' that we inevitably use in this essay have no other necessity than empirical paleonymy (the overthrow of a predominantly philosophical hierarchy) transmitted by the material, and always risks being read exclusively as a 'science', in the general habitual sense, and is therefore susceptible to receiving a scientistic meaning, even when the point is to simply save science from philosophical authority without giving it a 'positivistic' importance. For us, these are simple indications of rectification that must themselves be rectified. Precisely, the expression 'science' is allowed if it is no longer assumed, as philosophy wants it to be, exclusive of the essence. A unified theory is in any case a science, but more than a science: it is the use of the essence. Its concept must be therefore necessarily 'completed', 'unified' more exactly, without this being in the least distorted. Neither complement nor supplement, when it is enrooted in the real of the One as vision-in-man, the transcendental is a grace that leaves everything intact by absolutely changing the experience that we have of things.

What are the practical consequences of this new theoretical genre here presented and, again, in what way are we a scientist or a philosopher? The theme of the essence, as we know, makes no declarative sense for the effectively existing sciences, but for philosophy and, hence, for the problem of a unified theory. Then, it is essential to not imagine this identity of science and philosophy (of essence), of the science and man (the human essence) in an exterior or epistemological way, as if one is given the existing sciences as relevant (beyond their simple state as material) to then pose the thus naively philosophical problem of their essence, *eidos* or Idea, and so on. The Essence (of) science, the man (of) science is said of a radical identity such that it is one with the suspension of the philosophical economy of terms. By eliminating the traditional relations of science and philosophy, we evidently eliminate their epistemological version: a unified theory is the real phenomenal content of this artefact that is called epistemology. It furthermore does not unify in exteriority heterogeneous domains ('theory' and 'thought') in the way of a master-key and distorted 'hybridisation' of disciplines, but is immediately installed within a unified practice of science (and) philosophy and 'grounded' in a transcendental immanence that, being of-the-last-instance, respects the autonomy and the specificity of the disciplines in which it does not claim to intervene inopportunely. However, it appeals to scientific and identically philosophical operations, but only within this context and under this reservation; consequently, without proposing their reciprocal dismemberment or systematic interference. We substitute the old philosophical thesis of the convertibility of philosophy and science (with some nuances) that nourishes many contemporary enterprises with their identification-of-the-last-instance and its critical effects.

A unified theory is a new theoretical genre, distinct from the sciences and philosophy as much as the One-in-One is distinct from Being. The solely transcendental introduction of the problem of the essence (Being) within theory itself leaves scientific work open, allowing us to conserve it in its integrity but no longer in its naivety because it is ordered to the Determination-in-the-last-instance which does not inter-vene but which uses it within its own sphere. Here, therefore, in this theory and thanks to it, the point is to be or remain a scientist without becoming a philosopher who requisitions the Human Sciences for their benefit; and the point is to be or remain a philosopher without dismembering or negating philosophy in a positivist way, but without either exercising it in the naivety and spontaneity of its claims. This science of the essence is also or still a science of objects: simply, this science is integrated now within the only ensemble capable of not distorting it. If their 'object' is no longer the same, there is only between them a transcendental 'conversion', there is only a transcendental difference, ontico-ontologically void, of a strict identification. Even if this is not a science in the sense where science is opposed to philosophy, it is as much and at least a science (moreover: 'unified'). By 'adding' the One-of-the-last-instance to the sciences and philosophy, thus contributing a transcendental modification upon them, we change nothing of them, of their concept, but we install by contrast an autonomous discipline that integrates them without distorting them by one another. It is a discipline that manifests their essence of unification by revealing it not as a still hidden or implicit essence, but as an essence that they ignored or repressed. Therefore, it is even allowed to speak of science for it is a science, but an insufficient one. We must transcendentally specify or enrich its concept: a . . . first science, for example, or one science, a 'unified' . . . theory, or a . . . transcendental science.

As a transcendental concept, a unified theory therefore has no relevance for the sciences and philosophy in their spontaneous exercise and cannot either be judged in the name of them. A unified theory is another emergent dimension, another theoretical problem not convertible with the ontico-ontological sphere, which is here discovered with man or the One and what they cannot pose: the problem of their real constancy of knowledge, the transcendental ingredient which inhabits knowledges. This new object defines a new discipline that uses the occasion or the affect of constituted knowledges to know it. Let us add that it is in this sense alone that one such theory, whose object is rather the identity of science and the essence, can also be called 'science of the One' and provide it with conditions, and therefore can claim in turn for object – under certain conditions – the real of the One or the Ego. It then prohibits the hasty conjunction of the empirical and philosophical concept of 'science', or the twin idea of a pure and in-itself science, with the concept of the 'One' even when it is already defined by its radical immanence.

Having described the unified theory of man from its first ingredients or its cause, we can perhaps re-describe this theory if not more empirically at least more concretely by speaking of philosophy itself and the Human Sciences.

On Philosophy as the Superior Form of Bio-Technology

The previous position of the problem allows us to 'reread' the philosophical presuppositions concerning man otherwise. What is the most general problem that a science of humans has to pose and resolve if we try to imagine it through philosophy? All the ethical, legal and technological, scientific as well, all these problems, bio-technology as a whole for example, revolve around an immense and miniscule question that almost all present, in which some admit its importance, but before which all renounce returning to the human kaleidoscope and occupy themselves with constructing what they call 'man' with heteroclite morsels, this tired caryatid of Greek being and what the Human Sciences are responsible for bearing. This directing question that has not yet become a true solvable problem as such is that of the indivisibility of man. Insofar that the being-human of man is given in the mode of a *de jure* indivision is, for some, an ideological or religious fantasy but not a scientific 'given'; for others, this should undoubtedly be an obligated point of departure for any reflection, but of a solely 'philosophical' reflection upon man. Among the first, who are imperceptive enough to not see that the refusal of indivisibility is a very specifically philosophical obsession (at once Greek and Judaic) rather than a scientific rule as to the object 'man', and among the second, who make this indivisibility a moral and fantastic idea, honestly a transcendent and exterior idea, it is impossible and it is not necessary to choose either.

Concerning man precisely, we still keep on deciding on man. Sometimes man is a god, sometimes man is a wolf for man; sometimes man is an image of the creator or even an echo of Being; sometimes man is an autonomous I or rather the Other-man; sometimes man is an accident or even a substance; sometimes man is a slave or rather a superman and a sovereign. We do not hesitate in dividing and dismembering man through a philosophical surgery that preceded modest bio-technologies for a long time. We do not see that these decisions that make us sometimes creators equal to God, sometimes the simple doctors of the essence of man, also make us non-humans equal to the wolf. This is called philosophy, an activity that does not stop dissolving the existing figures of man to recreate new ones, to proclaim the end of man, or the end of some of man's images, to then reproduce other ones, to revolutionise without discontinuing the seat of the human being to better assure oneself of man. As for a science, man is but a question to deliver to disciplines – the Human Sciences – that have not wanted to assume the human meaning as it is of their object nor of which did they know how to give a scientific rigour. Philosophy as much as these disciplines, both fascinated by their conflict, refuse to admit that they are the Other of the human, rather than the human as the Other of these 'sciences', a distant Other like a horizon that is utterly unthinkable.

Philosophy is a thought whose form and consistency are very special. It possesses an invariant structure that is found within all philosophers under multiple variations and that we will call the 'Philosophical Decision': it is a structure with 2/3 terms, a triad of simultaneous terms essentially, and therefore arranged according to relations of hierarchy, domination and subordination which, contrarily, do not exclude different types of distance or difference in which philosophy regularly attempts to prevail against metaphysics.

In Platonic terms but generalisable to any philosophy, to philosophise: (1) is to first posit a dyad of terms, a pair of opposites or contrasted terms, eventually an empirical multiplicity, that already have the form of a hierarchy themselves. This hierarchy can be grasped empirically, from below on one the side of its terms; or it can be grasped universally from above and by the dominant term - no matter: under these two forms, one traces a line of demarcation, a border, making the decision among types of reality with unequal ontological value but remain simultaneous within the hierarchy. To philosophise: (2) is to then posit an instance of a superior unity, the One after the Two, but prolonging the Two of the hierarchy; the One is both interior to the Two, identical to one of its terms, but also exterior to it: the One and the Two form a new hierarchy. Therefore, it is after decision or demarcation that Unity as synthesis and as system arises.

Two important remarks: (1) duality is always raised and interiorised within the One; but it is rather the duality that is the motor or determination of philosophy; it never leaves the coupling and its hierarchy, and this up to the heart of synthesis; the decision is determinant of philosophy, even if Unity is dominant: Unity, a divided as much as indivisible Unity, reigns but does not govern; (2) the contradiction of the Two and the One is resolved under the form of a circle; the circularity, of course more or less open or broken - and it can be considerably broken, dispersed, disseminated, and so on - defines the essence of philosophy: this is its order form to it, its generalised hermeneutics. It can be worked upon, deconstructed, subsisting as repressed as what is specific to the philosophical argumentation.

We can deduce the great invariant traits of this structure of the Philosophical Decision of its concept of man:

1. The essence of man is first the being-divided, taking the form of a doublet or a hierarchy: the division between a subject and an attribute (man as an animal . . . a religious animal, a political animal, a speaking animal, a metaphysical animal); between a subject close to the empirical or animality and an attribute open onto the universal (the rational, the collective, and so on); between a subject and itself as identical to the signifier or the unconscious, and so on. Man is the system of this devaluing and this overvaluing:

between the philosopher and the everyman, between the philosopher and the private man or the 'idiot', between the analyst and the analysand, it is always the same more or less 'isolated' and disidentifying hierarchy.

2. Philosophy submits the essence of man to its teleology, claiming to intervene and change it in accordance with the essence of Being or the ends of thought. Philosophy is the superior form of bio-technology, presenting itself as the superior, 'transcendental' technical object of the government and transformation of the living. Like bio-technologies, philosophy cuts into the human identity, deciding that man is a wolf or god; eagle or lamb; master or slave; sovereign or subject; soul or body; understanding or intuition. Philosophy does not stop revolutionising man's seat, concerning man, and rendering man problematic, and so on.
3. The essence of man is then in man's becoming: the animal-man as a 'bridge', as a continuous becoming, the becoming-animal of man and the becoming-human of the animal. As a consequence: man begins in the pre- or inhuman and results in the superhuman. It is not only Nietzsche but the whole of philosophy in reality that only knows the inhuman, the all-too-human, the superhuman, all of its declinations, but ignores the radical 'human'.
4. Therefore, man is not for philosophy a first given, outside of the question and givenness; rather, man is first a confused and blended matter, to breed or educate (philosophy as pedagogy, discipline, even breeding), so that man is rather a terminal question (Kant), an object who is only realised at the end of philosophical time or through becoming, through labour, through history, and so on. Consequences: (1) human identity is barred, repressed and 'constituted' through the identity in becoming of philosophy; (2) the man of philosophy is a moving body of unstable figures or masks; hence, the obliged theme of the 'death of man'; man being confounded with philosophy and its movement can only be born and pass away, dissolve with philosophy, and can be born from philosophical limitlessness and enter back into it; (3) man is an empirico-philosophical doublet; the essence of man is a difference. Let us sum all of this up as 'Anthropo-logical Difference': this is the invariant of the relations of philosophy with man.
5. The subsets of philosophy called anthropology and humanism are just apparently contrary to ontology and metaphysics; rather, they are commanded by them through the general hierarchy that submits man to Being, *Cosmos*, *Physis*, God, Spirit, the Subject, *Dasein*, and so on; but within this hierarchy, these all represent a local exacerbation of man, an attempt to save man, but on a still philosophical mode.
6. Philosophy speaks of man but thinks to another thing, to a transcendental anthropoid, to the image of a divided and doubled being; a folded and

specular being, the 'doublet' has all the characters of a demon – not the Christian demon but the Greek *daimon*; of the being who reunites contraries, the sky and the earth; the being of the between, the border and the leap beyond the border. The demon is not quite god, and even less the unique God, but the demon is closer to a multiple god. The philosopher is this amphibological being as the excellent or superior form of man. However, does man have to be and become a 'superior' being? Can man open himself up to the super-human or extra-human? This is what philosophy believes. However, do we need, as man precisely, to share this philosophical belief?

On the Indivisibility of Man as a Theoretical Object

Rather than carve out the human object at the discretion of this idealism and this will, we make the hypothesis that a really human science that stops being a conglomerate of disciplines will take man as real or the lived experience (of) indivision for an object rather than this nebula of fantastic and changing images. A rigorous discipline that does not have man for stake but first as a cause, and which will distinguish the cause and the 'affair', will begin indeed with the position of the human indivisibility as a theoretical problem. Hence, the double refusal of its philosophical position as a question that ends by negating or dividing it; and its position as a transcendent, religious indivision utterly foreign to man. A science of man-*qua*-man, not man *qua* desire, power, language, society – this precision thus distinguishes this science from the Human Sciences – is given in a system of axioms whose principal axiom is the following: man is man because man is man rather than because man is; man is 'man-in-man' or 'vision-in-man'. The 'being of man' is a dangerous formula that abbreviates it, so more completely and more rigorously: the being-human (of) man. The first philosophically divides man and abolishes his essence-(of)-human-identity, putting a blank or a void within it that it does not see itself; the second begins by restoring man's essence, that is, man's identity-*qua*-man, and by subtracting it from the anonymous and universal powers that have captured it, reduced and dispersed it at the discretion of the great attributes or the multiple ways in which it is said and determines the economy of the Human Sciences.

Thus grounded in its object science has the unique goal of rendering explanatory and critical the identity of man, immanent rather than fantastic and exterior. Science does not constrain us necessarily to abandon this definition of man, as the Human Sciences thought it had to do and which has been led by philosophy into this rut; but it makes us an obligation, by contrast, to displace it from the mystical and transcendent terrain – the philosophical terrain still once and through another turn – onto the terrain of the most immanent practice of thought.

The solution to the most general problem of a science of humans consists therefore in positing indivisibility in the mode whose science as a unified theory 'postulates' its new objects or posits its 'discoveries'; and to proceed towards recasting it, which ensues from the theoretical field currently occupied by the Human Sciences and philosophical anthropology. The principle of this mutation lets itself be summed up as thus: stop considering man in his identity as the regional 'object' and philosophically 'objectivated' object of a knowledge and treat man rather as a first given, a Given-without-givenness, a given that is not objectifiable or transcendent, both as an emergent theoretical discovery and as the object of a system of axioms. It is a change that takes on the form of a substitution whose meaning is perhaps other than revolutionary: it is not a new anthropology that is substituted for an older anthropology or a new figure of man that is substituted for what history has effaced, but what is substituted is the scientific conception of man (in the transcendental sense defined previously) for the philosophical or anthropological conception that is still the nourishing soil of the Human Sciences. First of all – before any further precise analysis – 'scientific' means that instead of considering the human identity as a problematic and attempting a supplementary combination of their indivisibility with the procedures of technological division that philosophy exercises upon man as being-in-the-World and being-in-the-City, being in History and Life, we will assume the already stated response: man is already given and his indivisibility is already granted – to then draw the theoretical consequences and describe in some way this science from within itself instead of cobbling it once and for all from an *ad hoc* concept.

This solution may surprise the philosophers who object to a vicious circle to better give the change concerning theirs that is rather real. In science, and above all in its axiomatic dispute, there is no circle between the object and its theory as there is one in philosophy, for this is precisely on the condition of giving ourselves or rather letting-ourselves-be-given man in his indivisibility, treating man as an absolutely first given or a given immanent to themselves, as the cause (of) science rather than as the philosopher's object – their 'Fact' or their 'Idea' – that we are given the means to procure the theoretical field that is the most adequate for this object. Let us stop manipulating the fantastic philosophical images of man, and treat man both as an innovative discovery and as the object of a system of axioms, at least 'real' axioms for the point, indeed, cannot be that of a logical and symbolic axiomatisation of the Human Sciences, but rather of what little by little will prove a genuine 'human' axiomatisation of the Human Sciences.

The novelty of the argumentation is first to bear on the object of a science as much as a philosophy rather than on a philosophy alone. Under the word 'man', we can no longer understand the anthropoid entity of 'Anthropo-logical Difference', as if the point was to continuously transform with additives and complements and in a scientific 'direction' the philosophy of man; in some way: an anthropology-as-rigorous-science. This discipline as well is an aborted dream. By 'man' we mean who or what is postulated immanently without the determinant supplement of a philosophical decision, and as its 'real object' by the science of man so man must be real or more than simply 'possible'.

Another novelty is that not only the experience of man but the status or function of man in argumentation completely changes in relation to philosophy. Here, let us take science in its axiomatic dimension and compare it to philosophy's way of doing. In philosophy, man fulfils a mixed function: man is both a given and a demonstrated. Given as a postulate who serves to demonstrate or ground judgements that are related to man or the World; and demonstrated or, through its properties, the object of demonstration and argumentation (analysis, synthesis, dialectic, and so on). Man's status is mixed and shared: semi-given, semi-deduced. Hence, the circle of any anthropo-logy or again the convertibility of man and man's 'science', philosophy assumes some nuances, indeed to a near differe(a)nce, the reciprocation of the object and its discourse. The unified-theoretical position of the problem brings about a radical clarification within the relations of man and science. On the one hand, it imposes us to choose, and on the other to order. To choose between the given or rather the deduced-from-the-given: man and the science of man are either one or the other, but not, each of them in a chiasmus, both at once. To then order: first man, who is but a pure and simple Given-without-givenness, and not a deduction; then the science of man or the theoretical representation of man that is deduced from its object rather than simply given as it is or, more rigorously, making up the object of a transcendental inference. More concretely: there is no scientific position of the problem of man except if one makes man the object of axioms but 'real' axioms, and exactly: transcendental axioms or axioms themselves determined in-the-last-instance by their object. A being is simply posited or given without being in any way demonstrated: it is no longer a question of deducing the existence or at least the reality of man from *Cosmos*, *Physis*, God, Being, Philosophy, and so on. We must resolutely abandon these coteries that envelop man: the created-being, the thinking-being, the being-there or *Dasein*, the superman, the savage, the flesh, the being-in-the-World, the subject of the unconscious, and so on, which are definitions and postulates of the philosophical type and therefore circularly blend the given and the demonstrated; which ground themselves empirically and intuitively on empirical givens without solidity; and utterly prohibit any science of man because they divide the proof, making it vicious or interminable. Such that man is postulated by science, man is a philosophically non-defined and philosophically non-demonstrated first term. If man is 'posited' as given or real, it will no longer be through a philosophical operation of position and decision, therefore the auto-position of the I, for example in the way of Descartes, Fichte and even Husserl. We must think of man as simply 'postulated': this does not mean unreal or problematic, to the contrary, but simply posited and no longer philosophically auto-posited, and even as what, in man's real essence, excludes any position.

By postulating the reality of man no longer as the ob-ject but as the object of axioms for this science, by thus unsettling the theoretical status of human disciplines, we obviously prohibit the old conversions, the old exchanges of man with science, thought, philosophy, and so on, all of which the philosophical tradition attempted to inscribe man within the World, the City, History, the Unconscious, Language, and so on, in the goal to become the master of man. Man is the only being deprived of contraries and neighbours - this is the requisite of a science that strives to do right to the status of man that we call the 'individual' [*individual*] rather than individuel [*individuel*], given the means to think the radical undivided without contradiction which does not stop slipping out of the very fat or clumsy hands of philosophers who only produce man as an already divided or general, not really universal, concept. Philosophy is made for *Kosmos*, *Physis*, *Polis*, *Ousia*, for Desire, Language, and Power; it has never been made for the individual but only for the concept-of-the-individual as the undivided inscribed within transcendence, in Leibniz's fashion for example.

As for the theory of man, it also undergoes this radical clarification with the help of the axiomatic instrument. The theory of man stops being of the nature of an auto-position that anticipates its object or impinges upon it, positing it as a presupposition. The theory - as a simple theory - is strictly inferred from its inalienable object within it, deriving from it rather without determining the object in turn: we call cause-of-the-last-instance what is opposed in this way to the presupposition. What can science do? Philosophy prevents us from knowing. We do not know what science could do under certain conditions, what it could think also and precisely think about the most individual. However, we can know on the obvious condition of delivering science from its logical and formal use, from its technological interpretation as 'techno-science', and finally from its philosophical ontologies; to extricate the immanent transcendental exercise of scientific thought by giving it precisely a real cause - man. Then, we discover that the 'unified theory' is the most adequate order-form for man and man's identity; we discover that a science through Identity, and perhaps of Identity, is quite possible. This order-form is the order-form of a thought rather than a knowing and it rejects the order-forms of philosophy or the Human Sciences either to the state as simple experimental material, or simple models of interpretation. The science of humans does not suggest man – this is the customary idealism of philosophy that, from its operation, bars reality – but to think man as given-before-thought; to think as priority, rather than primacy, of man over man's concept or over 'humanity' . . .

On Man as a Cause for Science

Touching on the relations of science and man, perhaps we have gone a bit quick, burning stages that we will have to cross once more. These relations are harder to clarify than the relations of philosophy because man is not manifest there. For this problem, we must invent a method and precisely a method of the scientific type, rather than a philosophical strategy. Therefore, concerning science, we will give ourselves a corpus of objects or particular phenomena and a general hypothesis of explanation. These new objects will be the meta-scientific or philosophical discourses that describe the essence of science; not any such particular science, but what invariants of scientific thought because they postulate that science-as-such exists without being thereby an abstract generality. Indeed, through what phenomena can science be given or announced because it is not through the knowledges produced by such and such particular science? Through meta-scientific descriptions provided by the philosophies of the sciences and epistemologies – this is inevitable. Our corpus is therefore constituted by mixed phenomena at the intersection of the sciences and philosophies, there, and only there, it is a question of the essence of sciences. What are these phenomena? Let us classify them under three rubrics that therefore concern science, invariant rubrics that cross through philosophies and epistemologies:

1. The relation of science to the Real would be a divided relation: on the one hand, it would be a science of the phenomena *qua* objects in the philosophical sense of the word 'object' (produced through an objectivation) and, on the other hand, it would assume, even beyond this always intelligible objectivity, a relation to a more remote reality, to a real-in-itself of Nature and its properties; science would contain a primary realist, naive, philosophically or rationally unintelligible postulation; a relation to being [*Étant*], but a relation deprived of Being, for example, or one that would not explicitly pass through the thought of Being, rather forgetting it.

2. Science would not think: this would be an experience of the Real that is ignorant [*aveugle*], opaque, unresponsive [*sourde*] and silent [*muette*], deprived of meaning, a symbolic manipulation and sometimes even a calculation; its operativity would exclude thought and speech - science would not speak, it would be technicist and naive, and so on. This is also an invariant of the philosophies of the sciences; it is more or less honoured or recognised, sometimes refused by good will; but we believe that it is very profoundly inscribed in the same philosophical way of thinking. From Plato to Heidegger, science does not think (the Real), it dreams, and the very existence of epistemology is installed within this philosophical repression of science and only wants to save it on the basis of the transcendent image that philosophy has transmitted upon it - an image identical to its repression.
3. Science would not have an essence or specific identity. On the one hand, it would not itself pose its authentic relation to the Real; to do so, it needs the services of philosophy. On the other hand, it could not think itself, and rigorously, there would be the positivist and absurd project of a 'science of science', a philosophical project in its intention, but there wouldn't be a science of the essence of science. It is philosophy that takes on this role of a science of the essences. This refusal to grant science a specific essence is identically the refusal to grant it an intrinsic identity. It is submitted to the philosophical order that appropriated it, that divides it and rejects its realism as transcendent and unintelligible. This submission has a philosophical history, the history of nihilism where the theoretical dimension of science is mitigated and reduced little by little: it is reabsorbed in a Nietzschean way within the formations of power-knowledge (Foucault), or in the refusal of the true real (Deleuze); pragmatically, within the acts of communication or consensus; epistemologically, within argumentation and controversies; sociologically, within the politics of science and the relations internal to the laboratory as a micro-society, and so on. This nihilism signals the refusal to grant science a proper essence and the dissolution of its identity in 'the' sciences - in knowledges.

Therefore, these are our phenomena: not the sciences but this philosophical description of science, organised according to the fundamental invariants that cross nearly all philosophies. The problem is now the following: can we formulate a general hypothesis that responds to two conditions: (1) allowing us to explain all these phenomena in a sufficient and coherent way, that is utterly not 'repressing' without a vicious circle; to find them a unique cause and consequently provide its theory; and (2) to explain them by critiquing their immediate appearance (here, philosophical or epistemological) under which they first present themselves; and therefore to find an explanation more universal than their philosophical explanation. The philosophical explanation is indeed our object, our 'phenomenon', the meta-scientific reality that we must explain and that cannot thus be worth its own explanation. The theory to produce must function as a rectification of epistemological representations, modifying the theoretical field which has science as an object by introducing into this field new theoretical objects that philosophy can no longer master but that exceed it through their power to open, concerning science itself, a 'space' of new knowledges. It is evident that we renounce carrying out a philosophical and epistemological surveying of the sciences to catch sight of man there, for we will only find the man of philosophy: for example, the transcendental subject as the subject of science according to the neo-Kantians, or the transcendental ego according to Husserl. Rather, we try to practise something that possesses in any case a 'science' side upon philosophical or meta-scientific materials. Concerning this method of the resolution of philosophical problems, we will give some details to finish, but, in any case, it cannot be a matter of 'philosophy as rigorous science'.

We will formulate this theory that must explain the described phenomena very schematically from its main piece that will have the advantage of leading us to the problem of man. Do not forget the posited conditions: explain the three mentioned phenomena sufficiently, give them a positive meaning and full intelligibility, but by separating them from their philosophical auto-presentation. This general hypothesis is evidently the following, that (1) of the Real understood as One-in-One, vision-in-One, rather than as Being; (2) of the One as the cause of an identically philosophical and scientific thought – of a theoretical use; and finally (3) of the real of the One-cause as hypothesis, as we have already said, of the scientific type rather than solely as a philosophical category or object, rather than as one of the transcendental categories of ontology.

What can explain this hypothesis of phenomena that we have posited, and, in turn, what do they require of this hypothesis within the formulation of the One?

1. The One as immanent real, on condition that it will be posited as a cause of science, explains that the science, such at least that it is included within a unified theory which it makes use of, would be fundamentally 'realist'; that it postulates an indestructible or unexchangeable reality to which it is submitted and which is its genuine object below phenomena. If, as must be so given its essence, it is more posited as the cause-of-the-last-instance or inalienable within the phenomena, this explains that this use of science

would not be immediately realist, that it destroys the realism postulated by philosophy through or in terms of the phenomena alone. The One gives a full and positive meaning to an immanent or postural realism.

2. The One as immanent vision-in-One, without reflection, if it is the ultimate cause not of science but of the use of science as a unified theory, explains that science can be rendered as thinking, that it is related both to the Real and to itself within an immanent relation, outside of any reflection or consciousness; that it is transformed into a calculation invested by a thought experiment, but an absolutely opaque or unreflected thought. Here again, the One gives a positive and implicit meaning, a right to the opacity of science and prohibits the transcendent division or the opposition between calculation and thought, between reflection and manipulation. It is from calculation that the One institutes an immanent use.
3. Finally, the One gives to science an inalienable identity, integrating it to an order of thought autonomous in relation to philosophy, and equally in relation to knowledges to which it is not reduced; and relatively autonomous in relation to the One. This type of identity is specific: it is at once without consistency, without any philosophical form, syntax or closures; and is consistent or 'finite' in a strictly intrinsic way. This use generalises the properties of scientific knowledge that enter into this order as absolutely multiple (more than fragmented or catastrophic); absolutely finite or consistent each time (more than 'reified' into 'states of affairs', 'bodies' or 'objects'); absolutely universal (more than 'general' and 'total'); and absolutely rectifiable (more than 'open').

If now it is inevitable that this One of immanence would be the very essence of man rather than a metaphysical entity, the Ego in the radical sense of the term, then this transcendental pragmatics of science, respectively the Human Sciences, is the human work *par excellence.*

From Man as the Cause for Science to the Science of People

The One-of-the-last-instance explains sufficiently and positively all the phenomena that philosophy solely 'explains' by partially negating or denying them, barring, devaluing them for its benefit. Now, this One, what is it? What or which one is the One? As we will implement them, neither through its internal essence nor through its function the One is not this transcendent ontological or metaphysical entity arranged within the neighbourhood of 'Being', which is rather the critic of the One. On the contrary, through the characteristics that we have assumed of the One, it has all the characteristics of man. No longer by definition the man of philosophy and the Human Sciences, a man who is always divided and unrealised, but of the essence of man insofar as this essence is man-in-man or vision-in-man.

Here again, the approach should have a scientific side: let the One be such that we have posited it with its properties (the self(-)immanence, self(-)affect and cause-from-immanence of science-thought); it is suffice to formulate the hypothesis that it concerns man, that it is a matter of explaining all these phenomena and to destroy or critique - for it never is a matter of a simple tautology - the immediately philosophical and negative, representative and metaphysical interpretations that we have necessarily given once more, firstly, of this One that we will pose. Here, we will not do this demonstration, but we will conclude upon it that our science, if it destroys the metaphysical images of man, can produce knowledges about man that postulate and protect man in his integrity or identity.

Perhaps it is fruitful, after so many systems about the 'individual', the 'subject', '*Dasein*', the 'flesh', and so on, to return to the old name 'man'. It is to be given the constraint of having to respect human identity against the techno-philosophical obsessions of its distribution and the horizon of anthropo-logical difference that the Human Sciences still harbour. Recognised as the cause of the unified-theoretical use of the sciences, man is hardly an immanent requisite of this practice: rather, it is man's very existence, at least man's immanent reality if not man's effectivity. It is to cut short and definitively the anthropologisation of the sciences (for example, the sociology of scientific research) as to a social and technical objectivation of man. Against the circle of these two normalisations, we are given the means to enroot science in an instance that is more real and more 'objective' than simple self-consciousness and its correlate objective ideality - this is a transcendent foundation of science and what ruins it rather.

For we who attempt to reconcile man and science in this resolutely non-philosophical and non-Greek axiom: *Homo sive scientia*, we seek out their identity rather than their difference or dispersion, the Identity of each of them, insofar as the identity, in priority, of man alone as the cause-of-the-last-instance for science, rather than an encompassing synthesis of the philosophical type, for example humanism and the Human Sciences. Therefore, we must reprise this problem of indivisibility in a fresh way, to make it change terrain, and render it scientifically treatable and accessible. It is on this condition that the problem of 'bio-technologies', for example, which is unsolvable or contradictory in philosophical terms, can rest upon a less aporetic basis.

Therefore, we will state some propositions concerning this man in man's relation to the sciences and their theoretical use, which will distinguish this man from the man of philosophy. These distinctions are solely valid for man's real essence and in no way exhaust the science of people in which these distinctions are just the hypotheses and what we have not yet described.

1. Man is absolutely real through his essence: neither effective nor worldly like a being, neither unreal nor imaginary nor mental like Being. Radical immanence is not immanence to the Ego, but the Ego itself.
2. 'Real' man (which is a pleonasm) unilaterally precedes anthropo-logical difference, its 'humanist' avatars and images.
3. There is a human identity inalienable within philosophy or elsewhere, inalienable within the 'subject' and even 'the individual', in 'consciousness' or 'the unconscious'.
4. Man is the cause not of science but of a unified-theoretical use of science, or again: man is the cause for science and the cause of its theoretical use.
5. Man is the cause and not the 'subject' of science; a cause-of-the-last-instance and not the cause of an ontological type (form, matter, end, agent).
6. Man allows us to distinguish science as theory and the theoretical use of existing science, which is entirely different.

It is with these distinctions that we pass from the problem of man as the cause of the theoretical use of the sciences or the cause 'for' the sciences to the new problem of a human science of people: To what conditions can man posited previously as the cause of this new scientific-type discipline, become in turn the object of the science? This is the science's originality: it cannot begin by reducing man, as the Human Sciences do, to the state of the transcendent object of the philosophical type to then mathematicise or treat man through an entirely other procedure. This science treats man as its real object under the new condition of having first posited man as the cause-of-the-last-instance and thus protected from a transcendent objectivation woven within the transcendental illusion of philosophy. In his essence, man is the cause of a new use of science, but science can bear in turn upon the essence of man and make this man-cause in turn a theoretical object.

However, this science cannot proceed unless it is based this time upon the data that anthropology and the Human Sciences represent. Indeed, these give us 'man' but by partially leaving man's essence undetermined (as equally undetermined as the essence of science), only determining man's essence empirically through the supposed 'human' properties but which are meta-human and drawn from transcendent man or man inscribed within the World. Anthropology and the Human Sciences only know man from mixed traits or properties of the philosophical kind even when he is produced by scientific procedures, and are globally inhuman or only concern the attributes of man (sexuality, power, language, economy, and so on). Now, these primary knowledges produced by these sciences and these primary concepts produced by these philosophies are what serve as object-phenomena for a new discipline that must completely determine the essence of man this time in a rigorous mode. Therefore, we will distinguish the real object of this science, the Human Essence (of) man; the cause of this essence, its identity of One-in-One or Ego-in-Ego; and finally its object-phenomena, philosophical anthropologies and the Sciences of man – 'meta-human' discourses.

It is evident that the way in which we will sum up the enterprise could give rise to the appearance of a new circle and therefore a new theoretical failure for the philosophers: a science of man-as-cause of science. Do we not therefore create a new aporia, the aporia of the programmes of philosophical foundation?

1. Touching on the new science itself, it cannot be a matter of a vicious philosophical project of a science of science, comprised as the science of knowledges or a science of empirical theories (this is precisely a philosophical ambition); but of a science (or unified theory) of the Essence (of) science, an essence that is in no way reversible or convertible with already produced knowledges from elsewhere (and utilised as a simple ration or material), this essence being determined in-the-last-instance by a real cause which is inconvertible with any such thing.
2. Touching on man, we will likewise say that it cannot be a matter of a vicious philosophical project of a science of the human sciences (of empirical knowledges produced by them); but of a theoretical use of the Essence (of) man and which uses – yet as simple data or material – already produced knowledges that are not convertible with this essence, it also being determined-in-the-last-instance by the human identity that is absolutely inconvertible.
3. And, finally, touching on the combination of these two moments, as we have said it is not a question of immediately and nothing further from man as the immanent cause for science to man as the real object of one science. However, this human identity, which is undoubtedly the very reality of science, can necessarily become in turn an object of a theoretical type, thus susceptible to be determined by science. The human identity can become this real object only by passing – but in a mode that does not alienate it – through the general conditions that belong to the scientific objectivity proper to the unified theory; that therefore there is beforehand a specifically human objectivity distinct from the real essence (the One) or

the vision-in-man as the cause for science. Then what is this specifically human essence beyond the One or the Ego? Man – because we cannot yet demonstrate it here – can only be in turn the object of one science under the objective form where man is the multiplicity or multitude of people, not 'in general' or a multitude of Egos, but of the Ego-as-Stranger(s). It will be necessary to specify the relations between 'man' and 'people' or – which is certainly the same thing – between the human identity and the Stranger who is said in the multiple. The science of man is first the science of Strangers and it is under this latter condition that a science of the human identity can be envisaged.

Science and Meta-Science

Without a doubt, philosophy is superhuman and inhuman, but globally and from the perspective of science, philosophy is meta-human. Our interest in treating it so is to take it as a discourse that aims for the essence of man, but in the mode of an illusion which the unified theory utilises to determine this essence more rigorously, even if it means undoing it. The meaning of the engaged operation is the following: it is, if you will, to invert the meta-human discourse concerning the essence of man and to make it pass from the point of view to the simple object of a new discipline; to treat, for example, the way in which philosophy anticipates the essence of man and man's properties in view of containing his knowledge within the enclosure of anthropo-logical difference, as the corpus or the object of a new radically human science through its cause and its main object. The method utilised refuses the philosophical surveying of man and science, the epistemological and anthropological universals; it treats these representations as meta-scientific and meta-human discourses which it converts into simple data for a new discipline. Thus, we substitute in general philosophy not with a science of philosophy but a unified theory of philosophy, that is, a science of meta-scientific discourses. This new paradigm of intelligibility, which is nothing other than a human science of meta-human discourses, is what for philosophy and the Human Sciences that accompany it can only appear as a gauntlet that must mobilise their resistance. Without speaking of this paradox that a science of humans, being precisely the 'simplicity' of their essence, must accept giving the appearance of a hyper-speculation outside of any reasonable limit, yet what it solely attempts to do is to bring speculation to the service of man. However, if this enterprise appears abstract and meta-anthropological, like a supplement to the current sciences of man, this is an appearance from a philosophical origin. The point is to be the most real and the most concrete enterprise, too close to be seen otherwise than within itself.

This is the principle of the mutation introduced within the thought of man, the necessary condition to make man the object of a solvable problem without rejecting or abandoning man once more – as philosophy could not avoid doing so – to the Human Sciences. The repeated assaults carried out by philosophy to extract a science of man from the facts have all failed for fundamental reasons, philosophy being not more a science of man than it is a genuine science of Being and above all a science of the One. Even though this would only be one moment among others of its operation, our project passes through the suspension of these attempts and through the 'inversion' of the guiding hypothesis: instead of giving ourselves the man-of-philosophy in view of correcting man and making man the object of a science which is assumed to be more rigorous, we give ourselves this discourse as meta-human rather; but we first give ourselves man as man is postulated and treated by a science as a unified theory and we explain how this unified theory represents and explains this man with the help of this meta-human discourse thus 'internalised'. This is probably but an apparent inversion, if, at least, the reality is that philosophy 'revolves' around science rather than science 'revolving' around philosophy and, moreover, if reality excludes that everything turns and revolves in permanence, if it rather distances philosophy from it and consequently the philosophy of science as well. This destruction of the Copernican Revolution within the horizon of the majority among us still thinks of the being-human as the fact of a science that will recognise the identity of man and science as being of-the-last-instance.

Even though we do not develop it in this treatise as much as it would be desirable, one of the most important consequences of these investigations and the global change of hypothesis that motivates them is the new status of the Human Sciences and philosophical anthropologies. It is no longer a question of refusing the first or critiquing them in the philosophers' fashion – we have become indifferent to the Human Sciences/philosophy combat and we do not take any part in it. Therefore, the point is no longer to ground them within an irenic and syncretic philosophy: we do not give ourselves the fact of these sciences or these anthropologies to ground it. We abandon this old, impossible philosophical programme of a foundation of the Human Sciences and directly seek within man and man's being-given-without-givenness what can no longer 'ground' but 'determine-in-the-last-instance' (as we say) a human theory or human science of man.

However, what does it mean 'to think the Human Sciences' if the point is to think them in a mode that would be equally scientific and no longer ground them? A discipline that is more universal than them, however, as is a unified theory of man, will reduce them to the state of ration or material on the one hand, simple models on the other hand, that are destined to interpret under restrictive conditions - the very conditions of anthropology and its transcendence - this discipline and its axiomatic side. It is with this double relation that the last hand will be put towards the constitution of man into a scientific continent, capable of unifying and allying from within - without a unitary philosophical will - the varying human disciplines. The two problems of a general science of humans and a theory of the Human Sciences are therefore more than correlative: they are identical. The science of humans can only be realised by one such use - with its inductive side and its axiomatic side - of the sciences that have been called 'human' in a way that appears now partial and restrictive. A unified theory of man is then capable of reorganising the general economy of knowledges, to redistribute Intelligence, Cognition, Knowledge, Thought, Philosophy itself, and Human Sciences outside of philosophical authority. While philosophy lets itself be besieged by the innumerous knowledges produced by the Human Sciences - Artificial Intelligence included - and can only attempt to interiorise and dominate them, instituting a combat which it has lost in advance because it only wants the combat for itself, a universal science of man, because it is a science rather than an 'ideology', and universal rather than regional or fundamental, can unify these knowledges without claiming to once and for all give them a foundation or the rule of operation. If philosophy is an activity of foundation and operation together, a theory unified 'in-man' is identically a theory and a use, that is, the full and positive concept of thought.

One last precaution without which this project would risk being badly understood: through its side called 'axiomatic', the point cannot be that of an axiomatic artificially transferred from exact sciences. It must be adapted to this new object that is neither logical nor mathematical but 'human', constituted by real lived experiences in the radical sense; and integrated within a unified theory in the mode of identity which tolerates it. The science of people is necessarily a *mathesis transcendentalis* that has radical lived experiences or immanent phenomena that form the essence of man as an object, but insofar as he is posited and acquires a transcendental and objective status that renders human immanence finally accessible to a science. The point is to identically experiment on and axiomatise in-the-last-instance and to do so upon data constituted by the Human Sciences themselves.

Let us call this mutation a non-Rousseauism, which does not above all mean that it would be contrary to Rousseau. It is through many psychological traits and theoretical formulae that we will not otherwise deepen that this essay is akin indeed to the Rousseau-thought that it attempts to 'generalise' in a 'non-philosophical' mode. However, the quasi-scientific generalisation of

Rousseau can only give rise to a non-Rousseauism. To suppose that Rousseau was indeed the Newton who brought order into the moral and human world is still an order that is a bit exterior and philosophical, and honestly anthropological, that he left an imprint upon man, not having known how to universalise this order as much as possible in the theoretical mode. Others have tried after him, whose traces we walk along once more to attempt to mark out a practicable pathway. Rousseauism is now a model that restrictively interprets the most general science of man.

Chapter I
Principles of a Science of People as the Unified Theory of Philosophy and the Human Sciences

The Principle of a Future Science that would Present itself as Human

To whoever strives to lay the foundation of a science of man, there are two already explored paths immediately proposed by the tradition: a new version of the metaphysics and politics of man, dogmatic humanisms (Hobbes, Locke) or critical humanisms (Rousseau, Kant, Fichte); and a synthetic and empiricist doctrine tainted by philosophy, leading the existing Human Sciences once again to a new deal with a near supplement of 'reflection', 'culture', 'dialectics', 'hermeneutics' and now 'communicational theory', and so on. We discard these two paths together – sometimes alternating, sometimes complementary and blended – in view of founding a human science of man: they are neither sufficiently human nor sufficiently rigorous, as they ignore the essence of man as much as the essence of science.

Within the elaboration of one such science, we can no longer help ourselves with these old guiding threads. Contrarily to philosophy but especially outside of philosophy, this is because we treat the essence of man, his identity of Ego-in-Ego or vision-in-man, as a new idea, as the equivalent of a scientific-type of discovery which does not yet have the adequate theory of its reality. Such that we remain within philosophy or within the Human Sciences, man is proven [*éprouvé*] as a being without an identity or his own essence, constituted by exterior predicates that divide him and whose being [*l'être*] is uncertain and unreal. A science cannot be content with an object as aporetic and motley as the one that these twin disciplines provide it. When it is a unified theory, the specificity of a science is for its object to let-itself-be-given – here, not 'man' in general, but what we will call man's 'Essence (of) man'; to thus itself define what it understands by 'object' or the 'being-given' and to not let them be defined from outside by philosophy or the Human Sciences alone. One such science thus manifests two requirements. Firstly, to renounce subsuming man under one philosophical decision that is too general and too particular; to submit man to ready-made disciplines for a unitary and abstract concept of man, a concept that is both too broad and too narrow for man. Rather than several sciences for one unique, ideal and transcendent man, who is but one of the philosophical universals, it is a well-founded science for people in their multiplicity; and rather than the 'sciences of man', it is the 'science of people': only one science determined by the being-given-in-the-last-instance of its object can here resolve the paradox of the being-human of man as identically solitary and multiple, and avoid his unitary confinement. Secondly, indeed, it is to go from the essence of man, of the being-human such that it is given, to science, rather than from existing sciences to an already alienated man which they complete by fragmenting and rendering hypothetical. What does this radical yet special priority ('in-the-last-instance') of the object that conditions without circularity – in a non-philosophical or non-fantastic way – the science of itself mean? The question is no longer *What is man?* and whether he can be the object of a science, even if he can be its 'subject', because this philosophical question divides its object to better subjugate him. Rather: being given the being-human of man, his identity that is fully human, what then results for his science? How is man, rather than the 'subject', the cause of science, a science that is truly speaking inferred from man?

Indeed, it is in man himself, in his radical being-given alone, pushing away the positive or explicitly philosophical disciplines which immediately offer their services, that we seek that which may render not only possible and necessary, but simply real, a 'human' science in all senses of the word. Instead of going from the sciences or philosophies that already exist concerning other objects towards man and defining man in an operatory and idealist way as an overlapping point or locus of convergence of techniques and procedures made for these other objects, we start from man in his radical identity and ground upon him a scientific discipline that is *a priori* adapted to him, a 'human' science from the outset, albeit rigorous. In the so-called 'Human Sciences', human designates a synthetic object, as a synthesis of already-produced scientific knowledges; or a general and composite predicate which serves as the universal predicate for these knowledges – Language, Power, Unconscious, and so on – that function as the genuine subject-object or 'empiricities' of these sciences. This inversion of the 'normal', that is, 'human' relationship immediately alienates man within knowledges that were not produced concerning him. In the formula 'human science of man' by contrast, human no longer designates a residual predicate obtained through convergence, but first, in priority, the real phenomenal content, that is, inalienable within knowledge, of man as the cause (of) the science of man; then, the object of this science, or what we call man's Essence (of) man. The wild [*sauvage*] transference of scientific technologies, to which most of the human sciences boil down, *de jure* alienates the cause (of) science and even its object from science itself such that it already exists. By taking the object of science from the cause (of) science, from the human first radically given in its essence, we contrarily find a science that *a priori* excludes this alienation. Taking the human identity as a guiding thread, being given it as already 'real' and, with the help of the existing theoretical field (philosophy and the Human Sciences), content with drawing the consequences for a recasting of the theoretical field, is not to commit a vicious circle; less so, in any case, than to take philosophy and its presuppositions as a guiding thread, and perhaps even less so if one wants to wonder – as one must – what 'being given' [*se donner*] and 'being-given' [*être-donné*] mean when it is a matter of a science of real essences rather than a philosophy of possible essences or an empirical science of facts.

Therefore, we renounce the formula 'science of man', which viciously blends within philosophical generalities of already-elaborated knowledges and transcendent philosophical decisions, for this more rigorous formula: 'human science (by man) of man's Essence (of) man'. Man is no longer for us a philosophical question; he is a problem that must be resolved within the immanent limits of the practice of a unified theory. A unified theory presents philosophical and scientific aspects without being precisely a unitary (philosophical) synthesis of philosophy and the positive sciences; they are aspects which come from what it uses of both as simple rations or materials that it validates under the condition of the real identity of man. These rations are combined within the formula that designates no longer the cause but the object of this theory, namely the Essence (of) man, which we must determine little by little. This object displaces dogmatic or critical philosophies (of the 'individual' and the 'subject') as much as the Human Sciences, but it cannot thus displace the problem of the knowledge of man onto a terrain other the field of idealism and positivism unless because it is the object of one 'theory' that admits the human identity is no longer reducible to it nor even to this object, but, rather, the human identity is their cause or determination-in-the-last-instance. These are the first fundamental distinctions: (1) the radical human identity, the I-in-I as the cause of the new science of man; (2) the Essence (of) man as the object of this science; and (3) anthropological philosophy and the Human Sciences are reduced to simple materials from which this theory deduces a double, philosophical and scientific, ration.

The alternative to the specular couple of the Human Sciences and philosophy thus presupposes a simultaneous re-elaboration of the essence of man and the essence of science as unified theory. Apparently, this new path could pass for an exterior or post-*factum* synthesis of the Human Sciences and philosophy; in reality, it is a matter of their identity before their disjunction into opposite and complementary decisions; nevertheless, it is a matter of their identity that we will call 'of-the-last-instance'. Here again, we assume this posture within the elucidation of the principles of this science of people, instead of projecting a transcendent metaphysical image of people or an image already objectivated without a prior elucidation of the phenomenon of the being-given of man. Philosophy and the human sciences alienate their object, separating man from himself and from what he can do. Sometimes they make him an empirical fact, sometimes a fact of rational nature (a *factum*), sometimes an Idea, instead of being placed back into the very posture of science-thought such that the radical human identity determines it, and being content with describing and knowing him (as 'people' or as 'Strangers'). Science – and above all the science of people – cannot not utilise the data of ideologies and, in general, philosophical positions; it is constrained to do so anyway, already occupying the space which it itself wants to conquer. However, it knows that its object is solely overdetermined by these formations, rather than determined by them, and that it is assured with finding within the real of its 'object' more than its object strictly speaking: the cause of itself. Science is spontaneously limited to the immanence of its practice and knows that it does so in good rights; it knows that its identity as a science is there and that it has no need to be founded by philosophy or assured by the Human Sciences, which it only uses as rations that are not determinant of the essence of its object. We do nothing but practise here, without going beyond it towards philosophical positions, a science that is not an avatar of philosophy; a science that knows that it is itself real without being existent in the factual way of the Human Sciences or the way in which philosophy exists as an Idea. What can one science therefore mean when it is not reducible to the philosophical meaning of these words when it is said that it is 'being given' man as its object? The givenness of the being-human is perhaps that which escapes from all ontology and all phenomenology of givenness as much as that of position.

The Duality of the Givennesses of Man: The Human-Given-without-Givenness and Meta-Human Givenness

To demonstrate it, we must return to this triviality: man is the given or object of this science. It is a vague and confused generality with which epistemology is often satisfied, but which we must now begin to clarify here. What does 'being-given' mean here when it is a matter of man on the one hand, a unified theory on the other hand, and no longer a philosophy or a science assumed 'in-itself' and separated? Touching on man as an object of one such science, we argue that there is a duality of heterogeneous givennesses, two radical concepts – not without a relation – of the being-given and not only one – even divided – as philosophy and the Human Sciences presuppose it: on the one hand 'man' such that they present him, as 'human phenomena' or 'objective givens'; and on the other hand man as the immanent phenomenal essence such that these disciplines by definition do not present him. The ambiguity of the word 'object' is thus dissolved: there are the 'objective givens' and there is the real or the 'cause' of the science – two immanent postulations. We begin with the latter as it is *de jure* first.

1. It treats Human Identity – we will use the term 'Ego' – as given rather than as assumed given: therefore, as a Given-without-Givenness, *de jure* anterior to any givenness, even if it were reduced and immanent, that would once more initiate and divide it. Touching on the idea of a given-without-givenness, we will distinguish (1) the non-donative, valid only for the Ego and meaning that Human Identity is neither auto- nor even hetero-donative; that, consequently, it is not donative of anything nor given through a givenness regardless of its origin; and the non-auto-donative or the non(-)self-donative, not valid for the Ego but valid for the concrete man inferred in priority from the Ego – we will call the Stranger – meaning that the Stranger is, to the contrary, given by a givenness although it is itself non(-)self-donative. Therefore, it is to treat Human Identity as real by itself, in its identity, rather than through the transference from the reality of other objects (desire, language, politics, economy, and so on) with the fragments of which philosophy attempts to reconstitute this identity that it does nothing but divide and render transcendent once more. What this science postulates is something other than a convertibility – like the way of the convertibility of the One and Being – it is the already self(-)given radical identity of the One-without-Being. We will treat this real identity (of) man as its cause-of-the-last-instance, consequently excluding the simultaneous rational and empiricist procedures and ontology of the Human Sciences, which are not given man himself but exterior, fragmented and specular images, too general in any case and too narrow – the images of an anthropoid being.

A science that is human by the reality of its cause rather than by hallucinatory desire possesses the equivalent (nevertheless understood in an entirely different mode than the philosophical and which we must elucidate soon) of the transcendental power that classically belongs to philosophy. 'Transcendental' means that this science (1) is related in priority to the Real itself, or, here, consequently, to the radical identity of its 'object' rather than to the (philosophical or other) representations of it; (2) that it is directly related in itself, in its essence as unified theory, without passing through the mediation of any such philosophical decision; yet (3) unilaterally or without which it determines this object in turn, so inalienable in it, a cause that we will say that it is then only 'in-the-last-instance' the cause of science. In any case, regardless of the style of this transcendental dimension, this is to exclude that it be constituted by a simple extension or prolonging of the existing sciences of man. These sciences are hidden philosophical decisions that refuse for themselves this transcendental dimension radically understood; they are mixtures of the philosophical decision and a mathematisation that ignore themselves in their nature as a mixture and are content with operating wildly, exercising their pretension as a science in a positivist fashion, not elucidated elsewhere; and deciding *a priori* on their object, carving it up as a result of empiricist decisions, instead of receiving it and letting itself be affected by it without claiming – in all senses of the word – to distribute it.

This essence of man – like the cause of 'his' science – means that he is treated as a new 'discovery-' or 'hypothesis'-type of theoretical object, one which does not yet have the knowledge that it requires, but which is destined to transform the former theoretical problematic in the face of which it emerges as unprecedented. A specific science of man cannot receive its object from philosophy, a somewhat worn-out object without unity, if not the exterior unity of philosophy, in the way in which the Human Sciences borrow theirs from it here and there and in particular from history. Its philosophically paradoxical force is to immanently let-itself-be-given an 'object' that it cannot distribute and which is *de jure* anterior to it, therefore, no longer an object in reality; it is also to be situated not in the afterwards of man but in that which, in some way, is deduced from him; and, lastly, it is nevertheless to not break the immanence of this being-given by the precession of that which is given. If this discipline is really a unified theory rather than a separated science or philosophy for which, to the contrary, the object and thought mutually anticipate and encroach one another, and wherein a unique identity is distributed, then it must posit the identity of man, inalienable or of-the-last-instance, with an absolute inequality, the dissymmetry without reversibility of thought which follows from this object without distributing its reality, without claiming to determine it in turn. Man and the science of man are no longer reversible or convertible as philosophy would postulate it – the 'last-instance' prohibits it. It combines the immanence of thought, an immanence received from its cause, with this inequality of thought with its cause that is never resorbed. This absolutely novel or emergent theoretical order-form, in relation to the philosophical circle, is equivalent to the great anti-idealist but also, as we now see, anti-positivist rule that prescribes going from the being of man to science rather than the inverse. To determine a science by its 'object' of-the-last-instance makes no sense here unless the object is no longer empirically pre-understood in the element of philosophico-anthropological exteriority or transcendence, and unless its givenness is annulled in its essence of the Given or the phenomenon of radical immanence.

Indeed, the point is to dismiss the spontaneous idealism of the philosophers and epistemologists – the idealism also of the phenomenological givenness and its diverse variants – that believes that it is science that constitutes its object and not only its knowledges. The 'opposite' alone grounds in-reality the autonomy of science, without otherwise regressing to a dogmatism which would be nothing but a new version of metaphysical dogmatism such that it is found in the classical philosophies of man as an 'individual' or to a new version of critical humanism. This transcendental and ergo non-dogmatic, real and ergo, non-idealist or non-criticist, non-transcendent cause-of-the-last-instance, demonstrates that the reality of this human science cannot be acquired from the outside with the coalition of the Human Sciences, nor even tinkered from within as a result of reflexive, hermeneutic or deconstructive decisions; it also demonstrates that it must be acquired in an originary way and first given in its 'object' or its cause before any decision, rather than conquered by a philosophical or epistemological will of science. Not more than as philosophy dissolves the reality of its object in representations that do not describe its essence but do not belong to the human phenomenon as simple objective givens, this science's own reality is not dissolved within the possibles of the philosophical decisions or technologies of the Human Sciences. There is not only the autonomy – as contemporary thinkers believe – but there is also the reality of man and science: they must be reckoned with together.

2. On the other hand, if one such theory must be human in its effectivity rather than through hallucinatory desire, it truly possesses an 'empirical', not 'empiricist', side. It is given a field of phenomenal properties under the form of discourses of philosophies and the Human Sciences considered as meta-human. We therefore understand empirical in an *a priori* way, without decision or selection, open to all phenomena called 'human', including philosophical decisions which give these phenomena their meta-human dimension. It is therefore no longer a proven or disguised metaphysics that would submit man to the prior authority of a decision that anticipates and breaks the phenomenal unity of the object; rather, it is a science capable of elaborating and presenting the conditions of a constitution of 'man/people' [*homme(s)*] – philosophical decisions included – into a new scientific continent

alongside others. The material of this unified theory is therefore, first, the undecidable 'set' of meta-human discourses (anthropological or otherwise) that are situated beyond the Essence (of) man but that, in any case – we will not discuss them here – 'make claim' [*prétendent*] to man. Nevertheless, this science strives to reduce them in-the-last-instance to the immanence of man. Therefore, they must be recognised or required, not simply as ambiguous 'regional givens' but as objective givens for this science and for it alone. They are, therefore, givens that are contingent first in their order, simple objects or 'phenomena' which can no longer exceed this state except, as we will say, as an 'occasional cause'. This is because through its science-aspect, the theory of people necessarily requires that the givens, on the side of its immanent cause, present themselves as what it has not created, a contingent 'empirical object' that it must receive. However, this object required in its occasional contingency is posited from the outset, not as an ambiguous 'ensemble' or 'totality', but as the identity (itself without a philosophical choice or decision of exclusion and/or inclusion) of virtual philosophical dimensions and the facts whose blend makes up the complexity of 'human phenomena'. The rule of absolute emergence is also valid for the empirical object and implies that it is not simply a mixture of phenomena called 'human' and philosophical decisions, but their aprioristic identity, the identity of the fundamental (the philosophical) and the regional (the Human Sciences): it is an identity that is not only the identity of the 'theoretical' and the undecidedly 'factual', but an identity of the *a priori* (of the philosophical and the scientific). It is not a question of 'complex' or 'total' facts in an originary way, but the constitution of philosophy and the Human Sciences into a genuine *a priori* donor of human phenomena.

With this exigency, the vicious circle or *petitio principii* that grounds the Human Sciences as much as philosophy is challenged a second time. These disciplines now 'globally' yet *de jure* belong to man as simple objective givens or material of science. They can no longer contribute in founding, determining or constituting this science itself, which rests on another principle, a principle unknown to these sciences and philosophy. The science of man will no longer be circularly an ingredient or a part, either abstract or concrete, of its corpus of 'facts' and knowledges. Even if it becomes acceptable (as a 'real' hypothesis 'in-the-last-instance', not as a hypothesis in the unilaterally scientific sense) that man and man alone is the cause of this science, there is no longer a circle, a philosophical circle in general or regardless of its mode, between man as the 'cause-of-the-last-instance' and as 'objective givens' of this science. There will be two absolutely heterogeneous givennesses of man, two givennesses which will no longer be the result of a division and unification: they will form a dual or static structure required by the real conditions of science and such that it does not reconstitute any *petitio principii*.

Only one sort of radically immanent non-phenomenology - of description and phenomena outside of phenomenological codes or codes of the *logos* - can retrieve under the morass of philosophical decisions this identity of a science of man capable of letting-itself-be-given or rather receive them twice and not only once (even if 'divided'). The science of man obliges us to take the word 'object' in two meanings without common measure: as given by philosophical givenness or transcendence and especially as given-without-givenness or cause (of) science. Within this non-decisional identity (of) man, this One of immanence, resides the primitive, philosophically unviolated unity of man and the science (of) man, rather than the divided and derived unity of man and the philosophical decision.

Glanced from outside, outside of itself, for example by a philosophy, oe such science will be received naturally as a still philosophical albeit self-contradictory attempt. The dissolution of the amphibology of man and the decision, the real and the possible, immanence and transcendence, will be experienced as the attempt of a monstrous synthesis; in all cases, it will be experienced as an Other-of-philosophy. Of course, this is to describe their exact relation, which is more than inverse, that the unified theory of man is occupied with: it is philosophy that is the Other of the cause (of) science, the meta-human dimension; it is not man who is the Other of philosophy. Man is the measure of all things - of the Whole itself, of Transcendence, Nothingness, Reason, the Other, and so on; on condition - obviously - that he stops being measured by a decision-of-totality or that the measure stops being reciprocal or reversible. This science is neither identifiable by an existing empirical human science for it possesses a transcendental root so radical and so inalienable that it breaks the philosophical circle; nor is it identifiable to a philosophy for it is genuinely one empirical science beside others. We must distinguish the genuine empirico-transcendental duality from the empiricist-transcendental doublet.

This solution is therefore not an exterior (empiricist) synthesis nor interior and exterior (philosophical) synthesis of the Human Sciences and philosophy. Rather, it is the identity of which both are perhaps born - but this is a hypothesis which we forbid ourselves - on the mirror of philosophy through the disjunction of one philosophical decision. One such synthesis does not procure any genuine change of terrain, any real mutation, but simply a supplementary 'revolution' on the spot. The key of a science that would be human through its essence even before its data would be - human, albeit without anthropological idealism - cannot be found except in its object understood in priority consequently to its meaning of its cause, not in the sense of 'objective givens'.

We will now examine each of these two givennesses.

The Non-Donative Ego or Vision-in-Man

What must the being-human (of) man be if his science requires that it be necessarily accompanied, without contradiction, with another 'empirical' givenness of itself that is both contingent and necessary? What must the essence of man be that explains that he can be given in two heterogeneous ways and not in the philosophical way, only once 'divided'? We have already posited this essence from a hypothesis, precisely a 'unified theory'-type of hypothesis, not logico-epistemological or philosophical, but real-in-the-last-instance. This hypothesis stipulates that the essence of man must be a given-identity-without-givenness or in a mode that, for positive reasons, excludes the mixed phenomena in the midst of which the Human Sciences and the phenomenology of varying types of givenness proliferate. Because man is self(-)given in a mode that belongs to immanence alone, outside of any relation-to . . . intentionality and transcendence, outside of any nothingness, scission or self-alienation, without the mediation of the *logos* or the decision, the givenness itself, man's essence is this non-relation(-to-)the-Real in its lived indivision, below any 'internal relation' (Husserl, Wittgenstein), which is always decisional: a non-decisional, non-donative and non-positional identity. The immanent 'phenomenon' of man is below any phenomenality described by phenomenology, as man is below any criticist decision because man is constituted by the lived experience (of) an internal identity which is never given within the form of a philosophical decision or its innumerable avatars (soul, substance, individual, subject, consciousness, *Dasein*, and so on). Rather than a *factum* in the analytico-critical faction, a mixture of the *a priori* and the empirical which is auto-developed like philosophy itself, rather than as well an absolute withdrawal, man is non(-)self-decisionally and, therefore, non(-)self-donatively given in a real rather than transcendental or aprioristic experience destined to inform an empirical experience. As an experience that remains in-the-Ego, man is a real who here loses the status of the 'given-givenness' mixture, definitively emptied of his worldly and transcendent contents in general – including reason as decision. Man is non-intentionally self(-)full [*empli (de) soi*]. We call 'vision-in-man' this filling, this being-full-without-fulfilment [*être-empli-sans-remplissement*], indiscernible from man himself. The human is no longer and has never been (if not from philosophical illusion) a simple predicate, a mode, or a difference . . . a duty or a bridge . . . towards another thing, a givenness of his being, and so on. The guiding thread constituted by the first and nothing-but-Given, the Given that precedes any scientific, legal, ethical practice, and so on, related to man, is neither the problematic Idea of humanity, nor the socio-historico-anthropological Fact of the human species; it is what we must call the being-in-man, man-in-man, or again, vision-in-man . . .

With this self(-)inherent Ego, it is the human itself that is as such given (to) man. Man is his own 'object' without passing through the Other man or intersubjectivity (another form of submitting to the universal). Man is the only being who brings about with himself a real or ante-logical Identity. Far from being a wolf or a god for himself, what he is only outside of his essence, man is human 'for' and above all 'in' himself, fully-human. In opposition to the anthropoid images that people the sky and earth of philosophy, which are all interiorly divided, problematic and proliferating, is man whose indivisible self(-)given reality holds him not on the margins of the World, but well before the World in the simplicity of his immanence. From anthropological or anthropoid images of man to the immanent lived experiences as lived experiences (of) a non-donative immanence, such is the reduction that the unified theory of man imposes.

The most human 'phenomenology' is the non-phenomenology that discovers it is possible to renounce the point of view of the *logos* as determinant, and it is one that strives to know immanent, non-donative phenomena without claiming moreover to constitute or deconstruct them. An absolute science of phenomena describes them as deprived of 'logical', 'ontological' or ultra-ontological phenomenality. Thus, a description of the phenomenal reality of man utilises the philosophico-scientific *logos* as a simple 'material', but it is not reduced to it. This inverse reduction of the *logos* (or phenomenality) by the phenomenon itself in its absolute autonomy is not possible unless the phenomenon is definitively saved from its empirico-positivist status and described as the absolutely, not relatively, immanent lived experience (of) givens, as the specific *Erlebnis* (of) the non-donative One. Such phenomenal givens are deprived of all forms of transcendence, as much 'critical' or 'decisional' transcendence as – 'withdrawn' or deconstructive transcendence.

Everything in thought begins with science as a science 'of' the Real that finds within it its cause-of-the-last-instance, and everything begins in science with the undivided identity of man. The 'transcendental theorem' that grounds this general discipline shall be a reformulation of the *cogito*, which we will examine later on. It will deduce some axioms including the following one that 'completes' for the moment philosophical forgetting or repression: man is the being-man (of) man and no longer solely the being-of-man (*Dasein* . . .); or, man is the one who still specifies the question '*What does it mean to be for man?*' Philosophy and the Human Sciences are inscribed within the elision of human identity, of which they do not see that they have sacrificed it for their own transcendent finalities that it is worth taking the pain to say that they are 'all-too-human' [*trop-humaines*]. It is useless to change philosophy, to substitute an existentiel [*existentiale*] thought of *Dasein* with anthropologies of the subject, if it is to continue to not see that this repression of human identity is that which allows the tautologies and vicious circles of philosophy and the Human Sciences. Science begins by re-establishing the complete formulation of a hypothesis whose truncated and lacunary character would justify anthropological fantasies. It helps us to detect this blank and to 'fill' it with a special, nothing-but-full-immanence identity that contains no parcel of social, political, psychological nor even phenomenological transcendence.

Therefore, if a resolutely 'empirical' science of man (and perhaps even every science) can be despite everything 'transcendental' in its origins, it is certainly not so in the way of philosophy, Kantian for example (the distinction of the fact and the law), which is now in any case cast out on the side of meta-human material. Rather, it is transcendental through the Real, through the non-decisional and non-donative Identity that makes up the absolute being-given of man. Both traits together make up one authentic 'thought'. However, this identity is no longer mediated by the philosophical decision, its 'difference' and 'circularity', and through the very varying modes of them. Thus is definitively broken – not in philosophy where it remains what it is, but for this science – the empirico-transcendental doublet. Nothing, not the least politico-anthropological, philosophico-worldly, phenomenologico-donative parcel, is retained nor included within the essence (of) the immanence of man (but not within his existence as Stranger). Man is not only, as philosophy believes, the relation of a function or a transcendental dimension for . . . experience. Man is this lived ante-philosophical paradox, a lived experience (of) immanence which is enjoyed before any sensible or intellectual 'intuition' whose minimal conditions are otherwise not here reunited. The being of man is already real before being realised; self(-)given in an immanence which escapes from any intuition, which is always objectivating or simply donative. Man is the reality and therefore the immanent legitimacy of this so-called 'philosophical misunderstanding' that Husserl spoke of concerning transcendental realism, the one which he otherwise confused, like any consequent idealist, with a mixed realism, as much transcendent as immanent. Man is therefore more than a simple philosophical misunderstanding and an incomprehension of critical or phenomenological idealism: man is the philosophically, phenomenologically unreceivable, the first non-philosophisable. In truth and in irony, man is worthy of the name Transcendental Idiot when his essence will be completed.

This man, the man-without-Being and man-without-World, regarding whom it is worth the pain to remark once again that he does not have the 'illuminated' and dogmatic form of intuition, signals the end or more exactly the loss of validity and the displacement – the actual or achieved transcendental reduction – of classical and critical humanism, his always partially exterior and transcendent philosophical 'figures'. To simplify, somewhat in the way in which Fichte, for example, characterised idealism and materialism to oppose them, we could say that there are only two possible interpretations of the being-human (of) man: either through transcendence and decision (or one of its forms), and this is idealist humanism (always somewhat 'revolutionary' or 'negative', and so on) or even phenomenological humanism (the givenness of man's being); or through immanence alone, the only lived, non-decisional and non-donative 'instasis' [*instase*], and this is the theory of man as absolutely anterior to the disjunction, itself philosophical, of the Human Sciences and philosophy, positivism or criticism, and so on. Escape is not possible: it suffices to conceive any such form of transcendence as belonging to the essence of man even if it were then reduced to the proper immanence of givenness, to make the latter a simple mode of the former or universal entities which his whole being, such that he is postulated by an immanent science, otherwise refuses. Philosophy has no 'ontological' means to realise what it would like to make man: an absolute (by proxy), it cannot do anything here except contradict itself, making man a mode of another thing and who does not have his ultimate reason within himself. For example, Humanist Idealism is first idealist before being humanist and ends up doing its part to man: by dividing man into mixtures of transcendence and immanence, givenness and the given, of which man is nothing more than a mode, a mode of a transcendence too old for him, the foam of a nothingness more original than him, the effect of a decision or an undecidable more singular than him, and the offspring of an unconscious more universal than him. It is to this dissolution of man by all forms of transcendence – even liberty, even nothingness beyond natural particularities (for man in his being is a radical 'undivided' absolutely anterior to any natural or social particularity) – to his dissemination (as if the deconstruction of teleological humanism could be also the deconstruction of man himself), and to his constitution by the different types of appeal, that the science of people is opposed, the destruction of the amphibology of philosophy and man which would dissolve the being-human.

The Givenness of Meta-Human Knowledges and its Relative Autonomy

The duality of givennesses is static in the sense that no blend or becoming will communicate with its terms; however, it is not transcendental, being the place of strictly scientific labour where man's Essence (of) man – the Ego and the Stranger – is determined by and within a production of knowledges which require the help of a meta-human given.

Let us return for a moment to these 'givens' of a science of people. Because such givens, contingent *qua* 'materials' or 'objects', would be necessary, because they have a 'relative autonomy', this is an internal or transcendental exigency that draws its cause within the radical (yet not exclusive) autonomy of the Real Ego, but its reason is in science itself.

This relative autonomy takes on a very particular form that distinguishes it immediately from the form of the object in the philosophical sense of the word, which is apparent because the object and its objectivity make a circle with the essence and, in particular, with the essence of science. On the contrary, a science that breaks the specular doublet of the empirical and the transcendental (the idea of the *a priori factum*) can function only as an actual and achieved reduction of the most general philosophical form and its most constant mode, objectivation, and to liberate the relative autonomy of the empirical givenness.

On the one hand, by requiring the indifference and equivalency of all humanist or anthropological decisions, this science rejects them to the state of simple empirical phenomena. Philosophy makes up an integral part of the objects of a science of man and can no longer pass for a superior science of man or for the genuine remedy to the Human Sciences: philosophy is only the 'meta-human' form of these discourses, the universal materiality that a science requires as its material. Even philosophical humanism, legal and critical rationalism for example, belongs to the empirical object of science rather than to the essence of science.

On the other hand, if science is given a material that now contains these decisions as an *a priori* identical in-the-last-instance to factualisation and no longer as the *factum*-form of the object or the philosophical-type of *a priori*, a givenness which is no longer a philosophical decision of empiricism that contains the very undecidability of man and his associated philosophical representations, the function of philosophy is now the function of what we call an 'occasion' or 'material'. This form – there are other ones, in particular the form of the non-auto-positional objectivity typical of the unified theory, but we will examine them concretely in the next chapter about the 'Stranger' – is the first of the aprioristic structures of the scientific representation of man, so that the correlation of theoretical objectivity, non-auto-positionality itself, and this materiality forms a new duality, the aprioristic structure of the science of man. Here again, this is a duality-without-scission: it does not break effectivity 'into two', for example: it does not intend 'to break the history of humanity, of philosophy or anthropology, into two'. As a 'static' and phenomenal duality, it is the very instance of the universal that precedes the knowledge that will be given to it and the one that commands it as a simple non-constitutive yet solely specifying description. Generally, a unified theory does not claim to intervene within effectivity that is given to it, but simply to make use of it. A science of man, describing this duality, does not add a supplementary division or a new philosophical decision to the weight of divisions that humanity bears.

The Object of Science: Universal Humanity or Strangers

With the non-donative Ego in general, we only possess the real essence of man, in no way yet the concrete man or Universal Humanity. To obtain Universal Humanity, we need a double structure or, more rigorously, a duality of structures: on the one hand, the 'Ego' or its real essence, which is an identity; and, on the other hand, the 'Stranger' or 'Existence', which is an original (unilateral) type of duality. These terms no longer have their metaphysical meaning of origin here, as we will see the reason later on, but they are necessary and inevitable as a philosophical material or rationing. What we call (as a very general, unique term) 'man' is not only concrete or absolutely autonomous; man is also a complete being. We express this duality of structures (a radical identity, a unilateral duality) literally in the concept Indivi-duality. This fundamental notion of a theory of people as Strangers does not obviously designate the individual in the analytico-dogmatic sense and even less in the psycho-sociological sense.

The Identity of the Ego, though absolutely solitary, does not therefore remain 'solipsistic'. It is accompanied by a structure of universality that is non(-)self-decisional and non(-)self-positional, a new duality caused in-the-last-instance by the Ego and in an occasional way by the meta-human material, and what we call the 'Stranger', which is here, therefore, a structural and transcendental concept. The Stranger is a duality without analysis (the 'individual') or synthesis (the 'subject'), *de jure* anterior to the analysis which would determine them and to synthesis which would reunite them within an ultimate humanist purposiveness. Therefore, this duality has two poles: on the one hand, the pole of real, non-decisional and non-donative Identity and, on the other hand, the relation which this essence extracts from the contingent (identically theoretical and factual, politico-analytico-and-so-on . . . philosophical) data of human phenomena. We will remark that the Stranger is not the relation of the Ego with the World, a synthetic relation of reciprocity and convertibility, but it is the relatively autonomous relation extracted from the World (the meta-human mixture) and is received or lived in-Ego or in-Man without being a relation to the Ego. The Ego is so concrete that it does not enter into any relation but can receive or tolerate one in its own mode of the Ego. This is why the Stranger is a duality that presupposes the Ego but that is absolutely rejected outside of the Ego, a unilateral duality received in-Identity without constituting a real part of it. By contrast, this duality is rooted within the Ego and takes it as its reality while it does nothing but take up a support or occasion, effectivity, on the adverse term that is contingent as the 'givens' of a science are.

What is this region of Humanity, the region of complete or effective man, that is, as well, the region of the science of this man? If man is no longer defined by the transcendence of Being and by the figures that it supports (creature, individual, subject, consciousness, and so on), but rather the One alone, there is also transcendence in general where the Ego is not engaged but it engages as 'human', on condition, however, that it would be a transcendence that is irreversibly inferred from this being-given of the Ego. One could say of man that being real or solely given by his essence that he is not [*il n'est pas*] but that he can use Being, he can extract Being from its philosophical form, mixture or blend – Ontological Difference or again Anthropo-logical Difference – giving Being a purely human real essence or identity, depriving it consequently of its difference-form or mixture-form, its fold-form to the benefit of a non-auto-positional, non-auto-donative form. The experience by man of his humanity is an experience of a simple transcendence, an exteriority that does not transcend a second time through a (re-)folding upon itself, an exteriority that is given one-time-each-time without being re-given. It is a transcendence, if you will, but one that has the property of each time entirely and unilaterally being deployed not from or through the Ego, but in-Ego, being consequently simple and not folded again upon itself as philosophical transcendence is, the transcendence of the 'object' and its modes (consciousness, subject, individual). An opening-without-decision, open-without-horizon-nor-project, a transcendence-without-the-operation-of-transcendence – this is the only kind of static opening or one that would be really infinite, without an internal limitation, without transgression nor superseding, without progress nor perfectibility. It is the only opening that, because it is no longer blended with the real essence of man; it is the only transcendence that, because it is grounded within the real essence of man without being issued from it through an operation of nothingness or transcendence – like its redoubling or its fold –: this opening and transcendence can be the 'correlate', autonomous like the essence but relatively to it, of the absolutely autonomous being of man. This is 'Humanity' strictly speaking, of which we say that it is not the dwelling of the Ego – the Ego does not dwell – but uniquely the dwelling of Strangers. Without a fold, without an exterior content either, it is probably too universal to let itself be filled by the Time to-come, Duty, Labour, Communication, but it possesses a specific and original content to determine – these 'Strangers' that we are. Man, in his complete essence, thus possesses, without it being affected in his concrete essence, a radical opening that he is the only one to determine and that is grounded in his non-decisional and non-donative autonomy.

Such that it is exercised in the lone 'de-duction' of the Ego-given-at-first, taking it as a unique guiding thread, a science is assured to not return to Anthropo-logical Difference, to man divided unitarily by philosophy. Against the operation of which it is customary, we indeed have first simplified and un-folded the essence of the Ego; we have emptied it of its universal determinations grounded on transcendence (the World, Being, Reason, the Moral Law, Nothingness, the Call, Communication, and so on), thus reaching man as the radical which precedes any philosophical radicalisation, as the lived indivision which makes his phenomenal content alone absolutely real. Therefore, we could have symmetrically emptied the universal opening of its foldings, its particular contents (also the World, Reason, Being, Nothingness, Call, Communication, and so on), or rather the residue of the auto-positional form common to all its predicates, and which would close it in an ecstatic-horizontal way or fold it back upon itself. To render it even more universal, to give it its *de jure* universality (including the Stranger), we have simplified and unfolded Humanity, making it a hyper-philosophical generality. Let us call this in opposition to the cosmo-logical or cosmo-philosophical enclosure: Universal Humanity. Man is this Idiot who also exists as Universal Humanity or as Stranger.

The cross of philosophical humanism is obviously the problem of the identity of man understood as a simple unity of a duality, synthesis or correlation regardless of its mode (soul/body; form/matter; reason/sensibility; sovereign/subject; man/world; consciousness/unconscious; and so on). This unity is aporetic, both impossible and required, as soon as man becomes a mixture, a unitarily divided and therefore problematic being, and when this poverty of humanism is confused with a poverty of man, this philosophical division with the Indivi-duality that forms the Ego and the Stranger. The 'dual' man is the only non-mixed being of 'creation', the only 'being' deprived of contraries. Even philosophers sense his division as absurd or scandalous, that they cannot ignore because they are the ones who put him there, and that they nevertheless cannot sur-mount. Man is a unilateral duality rather than a dividing/divided being or an amphibology (from which *Dasein* does not escape). Man is the lived experience of Radical Identity and it is rather Being that he brings about to the World from his outside-of-the-World. Whether he is found also in the World, subject to all the crossings and all divisions, but they remain definitively contingent and do not reach his essence itself, is something other than a new avatar of the philosophical division: it is the duality of his givennesses that is not 'in the World' or 'effective' then metaphysically idealised under the form of identities; it is human alone, of a real origin, and therefore nothing-but-transcendental. The transcendental effectivity of man, his being-divided in multiple ways, is no longer his reality; it is only one of the two sides of the duality, its contingent side as a 'given' or 'material'. For the unified theory, there is no problem of soul and body, no philosophical hypothesis about their unity 'in-itself' or about the essence of man; the soul/body unity is a philosophical or effective question, not a real problem. The real is 'in-man' rather than 'in-itself' or 'for-itself'. It gives rise to the duality of the Ego and the Stranger, which does not pass once more over the unitary philosophical breaks because it globally rejects them as one of its poles, the most exterior one. The two givennesses of man do not therefore overlap the divisions of mind and matter, reason and sensibility, self and non-self, consciousness and the unconscious. These divisions are further teleological closures and aporias, while the duality – the Indivi-duality – is a radical opening, anterior to these divided anthropological images. The Ego-as-One is thus accompanied by an opening that is from the outset infinite rather than progressively opened or unfolded/re-folded. It prohibits meta-physical flight as much as the philosophical attempts of suture, normalisation and closure. It is a matter of a positive non-articulation of two givennesses, a duality that is non(-)self-donative and non(-)self-positional – a determination-in-the-last-instance. We do not above all say that man is the Other, the point of opening, resistance and flight from Nature, the City and all closed systems; nor do we say that he is the ultimate opening of a supplementary synthesis which would more or less refuse to close itself. Man is precisely the only being who would already be the Stranger and consequently without a contrary: because man is given twice, in a non-unitary or non-mixed way, and because he cannot therefore self-contradict himself more than be realised dialectically.

This duality breaks the circularity of the 'subject' and the 'object' and presupposes, obviously, a 'unilateral' experience of subject and object entirely different from the duality of philosophy and the Human Sciences. As for the redistributing of the empirical and the transcendental on a duality of this type that excludes outside of it the empirico-transcendental doublet, it in parallel implies the remodelling of these dimensions. This is the simultaneous end of transcendental idealism and empirical realism; the first is replaced by a real-transcendental duality, the second by a transcendental-*a priori* duality which testifies to an equally scientific and no longer solely philosophical empiricism. Together, they maintain the non-relation, the irreversible 'relation' of a static duality rather than the reciprocal or circular relation of the Philosophical Decision.

The Ego, The Stranger, Science

The problem of the relation of theoretical discourse with its cause, with its object, and finally with its givens (here, meta-human statements), is complex. A transcendental science is distinguished from a philosophy and distinguishes itself against its unitary will by its experience of the anteriority of its cause and by the experience of the necessary contingency or relative autonomy of its empirical object, which is no longer the result of an objectivation/decision, but the effect of a more profound asymmetrical or irreversible relation between the cause (Ego), representation (Humanity), and its materials. Whereas a philosophy places a reciprocal or reversible relationship between them, one such science will say that its discourse of knowledge uses meta-human knowledges in view of knowing Humanity.

The Ego is the Given that precedes Givenness-as-theory-of-the-Given, and Givenness is deduced from the Given rather than constituting the Given. By its very existence, Givenness indicates the fully-being-given of the Ego, but does not contribute towards determining it as if it would support still being the object of an intentionality or a being-in . . . being-in-man rather than in-the-World. In the 'science (of) man', the (of) indicates that science is inferred from the being-given of the human, not that it aims for it like an object. The problematic of the man-object and its correlative, the man-subject, must be reverted back to the state of the model and serve as a simple material for a recasting of the theory of man. Inversely, the Ego, because of its anteriority over it, cannot be said, subject to epistemological idealism, as 'immanent' to science, to the representation of man – or Humanity. The Ego is nothing but self(-)immanent and forms a cause through or from immanence and not only 'immanent' cause. Whereas philosophy places between them a reciprocal determination, immanence places between them a determination-in-the-last-instance: this is what we thus call the causality of the Ego which is exercised in unilateral dualities without being alienated in them. However, this form of causality also reigns, though less radically, in the duality of Humanity and meta-human givens. Hence, a certain number of consequences:

1. Because there would not be a reversibility or convertibility between man and his science, between the 'cause' and its 'effect', because the Ego destroys this convertibility, this thesis must be understood in priority in relation to it. However, this thesis is what makes the science (of) the Ego, precisely because it does not constitute its reality, a 'real' science although in-the-last-instance, a 'transcendental' science (in a non-Kantian and non-Husserlian sense). Human science thus avoids having to fall back under

philosophical legislation, sinking into the circle of the decision of givenness and seeing its reality dissolved in it. Therefore, if the Ego is not the thought or representation of the Ego, by contrast the Stranger is, in a still limited sense, the theory of the Stranger: if not through their real essence and through their essence of universal transcendence, then at least through the theoretico-empirical indication and specification of it – this point will be elucidated in the theory of Strangers strictly speaking. Subject to this reservation, the description of the transcendental and aprioristic structures belongs to man and his theory – as a real-science-in-the-last-instance would like. These structures define an indissolubly phenomenal and theoretical space of a new kind, distinct from the philosophical and the anthropological. On the theoretical plane, it is the space of the real hypothesis, the induction and deduction of 'human theorems' from axioms themselves formulated by utilising the objective givens provided by philosophy and the Human Sciences. On the phenomenal plane, it is the phenomenon of a transcendental structure of Humanity delivered from the auto-positional and auto-donative form. The science of people is first a posture of immanence as to its cause; but it is then and on this basis a play of operations of induction and deduction which have the goal of 'producing' the Stranger, that is, to assure of their phenomenal givenness.

2. A transcendental science does not co-belong to its object or is not a part of it, but irreversibly or non-specularly 'reflects' it. The Ego, the non-given-given [*donné-non-donné*], determines beyond itself a given object of a givenness, the identity of the Stranger and science. This region that is also both the region of Humanity and science indicates or makes known that it is a concrete thought or the real science (of) man without transcending towards its cause or reaching back to man as to its foundation. It is this unreflected self(-)reference of thought that we call, in the progress of these investigations, its uni-flection. In contrast to this foundation that Being has never been but only was, the non-donative Ego has stopped being the foundation of thought or competing against Being [*l'Ego non-donationnel a cessé d'être le fondement de la pensée ou de concourir à ce fondement qu'il n'a jamais été et l'Etre était*]. It is rather indicated from itself as the effect (of) man and his identity, and this directly in an immanent way without transcending. The Ego is a radically unreflected essence: if a god or a demon introduces reflection into the World, man introduces outside of the World, but for the World, nothing but the 'uni-flected' thought of science such that it is determined-in-the-last-instance by the vision-in-Ego. By contrast, philosophy and the Human Sciences that think according to the order of the regional or the fundamental isolate attributes or generalities that they

assume to be human, transcend towards a 'subject' which is more a thing than an identity; towards a generality and a totality which 'goes beyond' man because, from the outset, they lack the identity of man as the new object susceptible with unsettling the Greco-philosophical problematic of individuality. On the contrary, a theory of humans manifests them without having to aim for them or intention them - to represent them - by a supplement of transcendence (this can be a 'withdrawal' or 'step-back'). The Ego brings about alongside the theory the order or posteriority, the place for the second or science, but it is not itself submitted to this order as to an encompassing and superior hierarchy in philosophy's fashion. The Ego is not ordered by the World, but it brings about the order that emplaces the World from the Ego but after it. Far from being assigned to a place within the cosmo-logical ordering, the Ego emplaces the *cosmos* and invalidates the most profound Greek presuppositions as to 'the place of man in the World'. This is the end of the cosmo-political paradigm.

3. Humanity is a dimension of phenomenality and 'presentation' more universal still than the World and that thus accompanies the Ego. Science protects this space of universal presentation by emptying it of its anthropological and philosophical models, it 'creates the void' to yield to the knowledge and thought of man as Humanity, which thus accesses a dimension more universal than philosophical representation. Humanity is simple as identity itself, not distributed; philosophical representation is always divided, doubled, and choked up in the proliferation of its entities and doublets. The science of people is liberated as an absolutely unlimited, not teleologically closed space of transformation and production of new statements about the Stranger, not 'about' the human identity which it immanently indicates without claiming to transform it. We will not confuse the aporia of the philosophical decision that, in this sense, is never closed, or is only opened by closing itself and, in the best case, is only closed by opening itself - and this uni-versal opening of Transcendental Humanity which accompanies the Ego. It is an opening with an immediate non-ecstatic-horizontal structure; it is an abstract space in relation to the space filled by philosophy, it is void of any Structure, Difference, Dialectic, empty as well of any Project with its dimensions of Duty, Time, Faith - but, maybe, not empty of 'Strangers'.

Consequently, there is no synthesis to expect of this duality, no progress or meaning of history, no ultimate teleology of 'reconciliation' or 'conciliation' for this Universal Humanity of Strangers. At least such that he is included in science, torn from philosophical tradition and ends, man is an Ego-without-history because he only has himself to worry about; and man is an Ego-without-becoming because his autonomy is so radical and so sufficient that he experiences, by contrast, Humanity in the current or achieved state. Humanity is deprived of contraries or divisions (material/ideal; object/concept) as much as the Ego itself is. If the Ego has no contraries, Humanity nor its science cannot moreover have any: either in themselves or outside of themselves where philosophy fails to oppose itself to them. A science that respects the specificity and autonomy of its object can do nothing but imply the theoretical rejection of philosophical humanism, even with the Judaic conceptions (the emphasis on alterity, exteriority and resistance), the science of humans has already broken off in a founded and non-contradictory way.

On the Science of People as the 'Unified Theory' of Man

With the duality of the givennesses of man, it is the ensemble of the philosophical presuppositions of humanism and the positivist presuppositions of the Human Sciences that are found invalidated. For example, the system of the double Kantian question within which the question could be divided: *'What is man?'* (1) is there a fact from the Human Sciences and (2) by what right, upon what foundation are these sciences related to their object? This system is taken out of play. A science grounded in the reality of the being-given-without-givenness of its object, rather than in the transcendence of a philosophical givenness, begins to the contrary by placing man out-of-the-question. Man is no longer a problematic being by his essence; his thought or his theory alone are problematic. Because his being would be out-of-the-question explains that his theory would not be out-of-the-question or must be rectified, even refounded 'from him' and now with help of the simple meta-human material from the Human Sciences and philosophy. The theory does not start from these sciences and from their anthropological image as from a fact upon which it would reflect to seek its condition of possibility: rather, it 'declasses' them as a material or even as a restrained model of interpretation of this science of man which is so general it is the science of people. It starts from the duality of the Ego and the Stranger, which is neither a fact nor the possibility of a fact, but the givenness of a transcendental identity emerging 'dually' in the face of its own thought or rigorous representation; and what it must know is this Stranger, as an Ego that precedes them *de jure* and that it cannot therefore determine and transform, through which it is content with inducing and deducing its universal representation with the help of a material. Not only does it postulate the originality and primitivity of the being-given of man, but that which follows: the irreversible radical distinction, the unlimited duality of the Ego and the Stranger, the

Stranger and their knowledge. It is simultaneously the nature of the 'discovery' of the Stranger, the scientific 'new object' unintelligible in existing theories; and the necessity of unsettling existing theories to render them adequate to this object.

Thus, it stops problematising the being of man to reason in the following way: granted man as self(-)identity, what results through induction and deduction, what consequences result for the theoretical knowledge of this object? Instead of alienating its object in transcendence by a philosophical decision that would claim to co-constitute it and therefore transform the essence of it in the gesture of interpreting it, instead of dividing it by defining it through 'consciousness' or through the distinctions of the subject/attribute type, and so on, it is given it in a way which remains immanent, and it manifests it as being nevertheless anterior to it that it is rectified in accordance with it, rather than the opposite. If philosophy destroys through its idealism the undivided essence of man in the name of his transcendent representations that it sets out to protect – philosophy is the guardian of Being, of Difference, and so on – science destroys through its immanent 'realism' these representations, invalidating them and protecting the essence of man which it determines in a simple knowledge. If there is one problem that may be its own, it is the transcendental problem of the reality of its object; and if there is one way of thinking that would be proper to it and distinguish it from the Human Sciences as from philosophy, it is the way of thinking of an irreversible order or a priority of the object over the thought of the object, a priority which has this as an original that it does not forbid thinking the given, as philosophy would object to. We must describe this order more precisely, but it is essentially identical to the causality of man as determination-in-the-last-instance.

This means that man is precisely no longer an object in the philosophical sense of the word; it also means that science is not objectivating, in its essence at least, for otherwise it utilises the 'objective givens' and even philosophical objectivations, but as 'simple materials' that no longer have the object-form. It no longer thinks within the object-form, but in the discovery-form or given-form that is non(-)self-positional and non(-)self-donative. Regardless, without claiming to constitute an 'object' because it is already given fully and non-constitutively when it is set in motion, rather, despite its posteriority or secondarity, it is the thought (of) this object. Man, the manifest-in-man, is also manifested by and for science: as man is, not as science is; but manifested as man is through the global existence of that which science is and as science is.

Through the existence of these two heterogeneous modes of givenness nevertheless articulated without contradiction, man is a discovery without equivalent in the Greco-anthropological horizon that only knows a unitary or differenciated mode of givenness. Science invalidates all anthropology as it does all phenomenology of man: indeed, they can do nothing but begin by dividing his being, projecting upon him the operation and structures of decision, losing identity to the benefit of 'difference' and the 'same', substituting himself in reality with their object. Science knows him and thinks him without being substituted for him or being the equivalent of him: for science, man remains an absolute and inexhaustible given, precisely because through his essence he is reduced to his identity alone, freed from the transcendent attributes which would make him into a being [*être*] of the World, sometimes a being [*étant*] amongst beings, and sometimes the being-of-beings [*être-des-étants*]. Reduced to his sole identity-constancy, he is announced as a quasi-scientific type of object as unthinkable within the current theoretical horizon (humanism) as any such new 'particle', 'law' or 'theory'.

The solution of the theoretical problem of a science of the essence of man therefore consists in changing the terms and the order of the philosophical question; to think on the basis of a response that is not prior (preparatory . . .), but rather first, and to order theory to its object. It displaces 'first philosophy' as long as its object is thought as given before being 'first', without reversibility, as the real anteriority (to) thought and ordering it. It is outside of the question now to want to continuously pass, through additives and correctives, transferences and transformations, complements and supplements, from philosophical anthropology and the Human Sciences to this general science of people. This science begins with the immanence of its 'object' precisely because it has never first been a Human Fact or an Idea. This is why we begin by discarding all existing facts and theories like all philosophical questions. Finally, it is man who gives this discipline its meaning-as-science, which it cannot draw exteriorly from within a philosophy or within the 'scientific' facticity of history, linguistics, anthropology, and so on. However, it is also his anteriority as a 'new object' that explains that we do not yet have the adequate theory of man, the one which unilaterally follows him, rather than anticipating him.

A 'unified theory' kind of science therefore has no (philosophical) foundation but a cause: no foundation, and even less a determinant region. This science is neither regional-empirical, nor fundamental-ontological, but strictly immanent with a domain of the 'one-Continent' [*Continent-un*] type, the identity of a region and a horizon. Man has never been – except in restrained interpretations – this dispersed and contingent being of the Human Sciences; nor this ecstatic-horizontal being or projected being that philosophy describes to us and which is nothing but an image where it gazes complacently. Philosophy has populated its sky with anthropoids (*cogito*, the soul, thought, superman,

Dasein, and so on), the proper creatures of philosophy, its demons and its gods, and which it breathlessly renews, as they are threatened by metamorphoses and ruins which it brings about to them as a way of life. We understand that philosophy and the Human Sciences have repressed man in the name of humanity itself, understood then as a too general attribute and a transcendental abstraction. Both have abandoned the vision-in-man to be dedicated to attributes among which they have separated the vision from itself and dispersed: society, desire, power, language and the unconscious . . . These entities, whose whole 'reality' holds to a decision of auto-position, are transcendentals that speak of man as being and assume an ontological horizon as the multiple significations of which man is said, so that man and humanity - and humanism - are reciprocal . . . However, if the Human Sciences and philosophy, once again, have taken the problem empirically or the other way around, on the bias of significations of which the being-human is said, and have sought the unifying subject or foundation of these significations, the unity of Being and man, one science begins from an emergent and, consequently, strictly speaking non-'empirical' object. The significations or categories of which the being of man is said can 'decide' and ground new 'sciences', but they will never be sciences adequate to their essence and their cause, but simple inter-disciplinary connections, interferences or vicinities.

The *Cogito Sum* of Man as Stranger

We will describe the most fundamental requisites of a science of man: on the side of its cause, its object and its materials, rather than its operations. Philosophy can do nothing but repress or deny them through idealism. Nevertheless, it is rather what science postulates as 'given', and what it knows in an unreflected way, adapted to the theoretical type of a knowledge that cannot be reflected upon and within its object, and whose criteria are rather belonging to an immanent practice, a less objectivating one, but consequently the most philosophically 'ignorant' [*aveugle*] and 'naive'. Neither philosophy nor the Human Sciences can do right to human identity, which they confuse with the multiplicity of 'human facts' - social, political, psychological, and so on - or with the being-of-consciousness that is division, alienation and transcendence. A science of people cannot be constituted with pieces taken from these transcendent machines: politics, economy, psychoanalysis, and so on.

Therefore, there is only one solution: taking as a guiding thread the real hypotheses of the Ego, then Humanity or the Stranger, as qualitatively heterogeneous givens that are nevertheless undivided in-the-last-instance, and elucidate their theoretical form in accordance with this precession; to describe them from the interior of themselves without ever exceeding them from a philosophical position. Our problem – rather than asking ourselves if one such science can be given, if it is possible, and if it is the possibilisation of the fact of the Human Sciences, and so on – is to precisely start from the phenomena of its cause, the Ego, and its object, Humanity, and to render them theoretically intelligible because they are not yet or not at all intelligible in the horizon of philosophy.

Obviously, it is the entire philosophical argumentation that here undergoes a mutation of both a theoretical and pragmatic kind: the given, thought, their order, the hypotheses, axioms and principles, experiment [*expérience*], and so on, everything changes when man appears outside of the circle of the philosophical family. We are constrained to seek a theoretical 'syntax' or 'order-form' that would be adapted to the emergence of man before his theory, a precession that we know that does not belong to Being nor the Other. We need a syntax that requires science to abandon its Greek and Judaic presuppositions and render it adequate to its new object. All by being rigorous in fidelity to its object, one such science remains a thought rather than a calculation or a ratiocination; it remains an immanent theoretical use of meta-human knowledges that it does not produce but receives from elsewhere; to which it impresses finally a theoretical order unknown to them and which 'expresses' the Human Identity and its priority over thought; it is an order which does not institute it once more from a philosophical distributing, difference or mid-dle [*mi-lieu*].

Therefore, we will not believe that it aims or intends for the Ego and even Humanity as a philosophical kind of ob-ject in general, a phenomenological ob-ject in particular, or that it must finally think man 'directly': this is always to imagine it as an object. It does not propose experiencing the undivided identity (of) man in some way directly and through a sort of intellectual intuition or anthropological intuition. It has no intuition (which is always objectivating, despite everything) of the Ego and Humanity; but it manifests them through its mode to it, as they are manifested in their mode to them. The meaning of the hypothesis: man is the (irreversible) cause rather than the (reversible) object of his science, is to eliminate between man and representation any structure of transcendence (consciousness-of . . . or being-in . . . and even withdrawal . . .). Science as such cannot hope to transform man himself but only his representation. It is the dignity and rigour of science to protect him 'as he is' against the assaults of the Human Sciences; not to limit this phantasmatic project of transforming him, but to be foreign to him – unlike philosophy which hallucinates him.

To now describe the most general mechanism of the reasoning that is the theoretical order-form ensuing from man, let us return for a moment to two postulates of all possible anthropo-logy; let us return to the Anthropo-logical Difference that feeds the Human Sciences and, in any case, philosophical humanism. The first postulate is the postulate of a dyad or coupling (soul/body; myth/reason; subject/object; given/givenness; nature/society; subject/sovereign; individual/society; structural difference, and so on, and the one that condenses them all: *anthropos/logos*); and the second postulate is the postulate of a unity that balances this dyad by making it into a triad. Let one take the pain of examining the simplest and most invariant ultimate foundations of that which is given for the Human and Social Sciences, and one will not find anything other than an anthropo-logical duality and a 'strictly' speaking human or super-human unity. These dyads are functionally equivalent to a near hierarchy: in any case reversible or convertible, even if it is always with a lot of nuances, differences, slippages, shifts between primacy and hierarchy – for example, that of the 'unity-of-man' over the couplings that constitute it. Through this reciprocal determination that is their own, the two anthropological constituents become the 'differential' elements of this basic structure of the Human Sciences and philosophical humanism.

Let us suppose that we now treat this 'Difference' as a particular meta-human knowledge to which we will apply the order-form that we call Determination-in-the-last-instance or Transcendental Duality, the specific syntax of a unified theory. It stipulates that any such statement or postulate of anthropology must be transformed either into a given, hypothesis or axiom, or into a theorem which one deduces from this given, but which cannot be both at once. Anthropology and even the Human Sciences precisely treat their basic statements, theirs or other more specific ones, as principles or as philosophical-type 'postulates': they are both given and demonstrated to a simple near difference, therefore mixed and circular from the theoretical point of view; they are bi-lateral or convertible dualities. Therefore, it is a radical theoretical clarification that the axiomatising aspect of the Determination-in-the-last-instance introduces into anthropo-logical difference by suspending it as 'difference' or the reversibility of contraries. However, axiomatisation is but one aspect of this 'real logic'. It is a transcendental order irreducible to deduction as to induction, but one which allows for a use of them, so that the terms that fulfil the 'axiom' and 'theorem' functions are not exchangeable as they are, despite everything, from one formal system to another system. Not only is each ingredient of the Philosophical Dyad, each postulate liberated from its own identity, but it enters into the specifically transcendental order that the irreversible Unilateral Duality (the Stranger) be now inferred from the priority of Real Identity (the Ego). This order imposes treating each of them not only either as an axiom or as a theorem but, because it is real and not logical, the one (the Ego) as a given and the other (the Stranger) as givenness rather than given, but not as fulfilling both functions at once. This is to renounce this mixture by which the basic philosophical anthropo-logy of the Human Sciences wants to win on all counts and loses man.

In any case, we must also choose and order the terms instead of binding philosophical amphibologies. We must choose, but by phenomenally 'realising' the terms (the meaning of the given and givenness is no longer philosophical), and by ordering them according to their type of givenness which foresees the new theoretical order-form. The Ego is a given-without-givenness, a purely immanent identity which now precedes couplings, or, rather to which the anthropo-logical couplings give rise – the Stranger – within the theoretico-pragmatic space of the 'unilateral' structure. This axiomatisation is neither empirical – by definition – nor logical – it is not a logicised axiomatics, but 'human', finding its element in the being (of) man rather than in the being-formal or void of logic. Nevertheless – or because of this – it is strictly immanent or transcendental, including the experience of the being-given (of) the Ego which, of itself, without making an appeal to some philosopher *ex machina*, suspends their claim. Therefore, it stops being empirically and intuitively validated by the transcendence of man-in-the-World: it no longer describes social, historical, analytic human phenomena, and so on. It breaks the anthropological circle for a finally rigorous thought, in such a way that one no longer, even sporadically, recognises within the 'fragments' the objective appearance of a circle.

The Ego's restitution of its status as a Given, ergo as cause or the first – priority is not here an attribute, it is an internal exigency that science itself posits concerning its cause – therefore institutes a transcendental order distinct from the order of anthropological contents (the great attributes or empiricities that ground the Human Sciences and their exteriority); it is also distinct from a 'rational' order which is always mixed in philosophy: philosophical-and-regional (geometric, arithmetical, physical, and so on). This scientific and real order nevertheless contains no parcel of regional (ontic) or even fundamental (ontological) rationality for the reason that its emergent cause also contains – in its essence at least – no ontic nor even ontological determination. Man is 'in-man': this is why he is neither Being [*Être*] nor being [*Étant*], which are for him nothing but models that restrictively interpret him on the basis of initial non-human conditions. Man is the bachelor (of) Being, delivered from the linings, envelopments and folds of philosophy.

The following is the '*cogito*' of man, of man as Stranger rather than as the 'subject': if man and the science of man are, one or the other, either given-without-being-demonstrated or demonstrated-and-inferred-from-the-given, it is therefore (ergo) that man is given without being demonstrated (thought), and that his science as Stranger is deduced or induced from him without being given as him. This '*sum cogito*' of man as Stranger is transcendental, that is, as much an immanent 'deduction' as an 'immanent' induction: I am (in the sense where my 'being' is being-in-man), therefore I think myself as Stranger; or again: I think man as cause-of-the-last-instance of thought, therefore he Stranger-exists. Thus, we pass from the philosophical plane, which is always semi-real and semi-theoretical and blends its discourse and its object, to the theoretical plane, which precisely is nothing but the order of knowing without also and directly participating in the order of the Real, unless this is in-the-last-instance: the transcendental is 'real' without distributing the Real. The incestuous confusion of man and science by which the latter becomes an 'abstract' part of its object or its corpus would prohibit the very constitution of a science and would deliver the authentic form of their identity to the unlimited fantasies of the anthropo-logical circle. The bi-lateral anthropological duality stops being convertible in itself and with the Identity (of) the Ego. The Identity (of) the Ego is no longer an object of knowing but a 'real' hypothesis or an axiom for a science-thought; the anthropo-logical duality is a material of which the Ego or more precisely the Stranger already extracts and specifies themself within the order of knowledge.

In relation to the Human Sciences and philosophy, it is a matter of a 'non'-anthropological and 'non'-Copernican break in general and, in particular, as we will examine later on, a 'non'-analytic break. Indeed, man is an anthropologically and psychoanalytically invisible discovery, a blank within the philosophical and analytic horizon, but this non-seen in priority results from a decided foreclosure of the being-given of the Ego. We must nuance this: unlike the Stranger, the Ego itself precedes its denegation, it is not constituted by this always secondary repression, and it is indifferent to this philosophical resistance. Within the complex human posture, that is, in the Ego (of) the Stranger, the Ego therefore precedes the scientific break and is not reduced to it, while the givenness of the Stranger must reckon with it. Indeed, science contains an 'analysis' and a displacement of this resistance at the same time as the emplacement of philosophy – humanism, in particular – as the restrained interpretation or 'particular case', even if it is not exhausted in these effects. Man as both Ego and Stranger is already-there, that is, in-man, not as Being anticipating thought or even the Other inhibiting thought, breaking and differing/deferring it, but as a scientific discovery that solely, without strictly speaking anticipating it, precedes theory. In particular, it no longer is a question of a 'deconstruction' of anthropology or the 'ends of man' that would assume them as still essentially valid, nor is it an amendment to philosophy and its humanism; nor even a supplement of scientific rigour for philosophy and a supplement of philosophy for the Human Sciences; but rather, a qualitative mutation within the thought of man-*qua*-man.

'Already-there' is said absolutely of the first Given alone as Ego, and relatively said of the Givenness as Stranger. The science of people has not taken place; man even has not taken place in the way of a possibility to reiterate through thought.

Man is given with a philosophically unprecedented though entirely positive constancy, as an emergent 'object', a hypothesis through which the theoretical field is restructured. One such science does not have to reprise, comment or even deconstruct the philosophies of man and the Human Sciences to which it would have granted a prior pertinence. The object of this science, being real well before being first, is not a presupposition or a premise. It suffices that it is manifested in a mode to it and in its identity finally, so that these disciplines that prevent man from constituting himself into a scientific continent do not miraculously dissolve themselves into 'ideological clouds', but in one fell swoop lose their validity which is nothing but their pretension. It is with their now philosophically inert material that it becomes possible to construct the theoretical field adequate to man. The most real thing that science brings about – that is, the most genuinely revolutionary – is this postulation that the problem of man is if not resolved, at least *de jure* solvable if it is correctly posed, posed as a problem not as a question, if man stops being a philosophical concept or an entity transcendent to consciousness (the Other or the Unconscious) to become a 'given' through immanence, delivered from the ontological or even analytic transcendence that always invests the philosophical use of hypotheses or axioms.

The Stranger as the Subject of the Science of People and Democracy

The solution to the traditional problem of the relations of subjectivity and science rests here on the distinction made between man as the Ego, as the real cause of science, and the specific subject of the Ego, the subject of Universal Humanity, a function that is not held by the Ego. Among these aprioristic structures that constitute the space of the Stranger and that give rise to rules of use of philosophical material, which we will examine only in the next chapter, we indeed distinguish a certain 'non-auto-positional Unity', the moment of subjectivity constitutive not of the Real but of its representation alone. The Ego is not the subject of science, with the latter function being a proper structure of the Stranger and brings it together. Man as Ego and the subject of Humanity are not reciprocal; this is an end set to philosophy as the Copernican thought of 'Absolute Subjectivity', not only a change within the phenomenal experience of the subject itself. In general, this means that the Stranger alone is now the subject – not the cause – of the science of people and, for example, the theory of democracy. Through its essence, the Ego is not 'subject', that is, barred, 'decided' or objectivated, therefore subjugated; the Ego is too real to be only the 'subject' in the philosophical way, but it is not so furthermore in the 'non-philosophical' way. By contrast, there exists a subject-function, a theoretical *a priori* specific to the universal representation of Humanity that is not more divisible/barred than the Ego itself. This function can empirically be held by any such term drawn from philosophy but is required as a non-defined philosophical term; it will receive a constancy undoubtedly called 'subjective' but in the unreal or objective mode of the Stranger. The irreversibility that places the duality of the Ego and the subject 'in relation' protects man and science from their reciprocal invasion, from their mutual 'constitution'. This is to refuse all subjectivation, sociological then metaphysical, of science. It is also to recognise that man, in his real essence, is not alienated or subjugated, nor produced as the subject by the knowledge that he produces.

Therefore, we will say of the transcendental science of people that it is 'human' fully but not, for this very reason, 'subjective', even if it possesses one such subjectivity-function; that man is its cause, that the Stranger is its subject or its organon, while a god or a demon is the 'subject' – in all senses of the word – of philosophy. This is to liberate thought from the dreadful discourse of alienation, the discourse of 'objectivist' and 'positivist' objectivity with which philosophers overwhelm it. Its cause protects science from definitively falling under the law of the subjectivation/objectivation couple, the genuine alienation.

If one has understood the proper meaning of the unified theory, the way in which it destroys philosophical amphibologies, one will no longer be shocked that we argue that it is the identity, to the nearest last-instance, of Humanity and the most universal thought; and even, provisionally using an even more 'subjectivist' model certainly more subject to misunderstanding, the identity of the lived experience, of the 'affect' – the content of the Ego-in-Ego – and 'theory'. In the priority-based sense where it is cause-of-the-last-instance and then an eventual object of theory, the lived experience or 'affect' is no longer obviously aimed for or constituted by theory, it is no longer an ob-ject defined by a whole categorial system, by a 'saying' that would be furnished by the ontological horizon – it is not the self(-)affect, but rather, the Affected-before-any-affection. The language that our science uses now is nothing but meta-human, secondary, or occasional, it is the 'correlate' of the following: the most universal discourse presupposes the most indivi-dual Affected, but not reciprocally. The Affected is the determination-in-the-last-instance (of) the theoretical as such of which it needs, but the theoretical cannot be its correlate unless it does not co-determine it. This is not to confuse science and the subjective affect as philosophy can always do so, of which it is a *de jure* possibility. It is hardly necessary to specify that it neither grounds science upon a transcendental solipsism. On the one hand, man does not ground, he determines-in-the-last-instance; on the other hand, as real individual, man does not give rise to solipsism precisely because he is the Real outside-of-philosophy and because solipsism is an intra-philosophical object that only has pertinence for whoever already lacked the real-One; and finally, the Ego or One-in-One lets the Stranger exist in the state of multitudes. This identity-of-the-last-instance of the old 'contraries' lets-them-be in general without overlaying and dominating them with an encompassing unity, nor does it tolerate when philosophy, indiscreet, comes to break this entirely unilateral identity of the human real and rigorous representation, an identity which therefore excludes under all their forms the unitary and finalised syntheses, the interventions destined to divide or fold each of the terms in presence in order to 'yield' a philosophical surplus-value from them.

The science of humans is summarised in an *Ego cogito* that we must now understand in a non-Cartesian sense, as the unilateral duality of the Ego (*sum*) or cause of science, and the *cogito* as the subject-of-science or the specific subject of the *cogitatio*. This *Ego cogito* institutes a non-Copernican discipline or a discipline outside-the-'subject'. As we have said, the articulation of the Ego and the Stranger is the object of a genuine transcendental (or real, not logico-geometric . . .) theorem. The Cartesian *cogito* remains meta-human; it is nothing but a half-philosophical, half-scientific axiom, a mixed given conditioned by an ontology (a theology, a cosmology) and by particular or regional sciences (geometry); but whose purely transcendental validity has not been freed. Its real 'dualysis' reduces it to the state of simple material or a restrained model of interpretation of the universality and validity of the theorem of the Stranger. It roots the science of man in its cause: not in some anthropo-logical or transcendent philosophical entity, in any unconscious or Other, but within the vision-in-man that is the ultimate resource of this science and manifested by the very existence of it.

Science arrives [*advient*] where man is in-man and man is Stranger, not where man is the 'subject', the 'creature', 'reflection', 'consciousness' or 'being-there'; and it en-sues (from) man rather than it be-falling [*ad-vient*] upon him. We must oppose philosophical sufficiency, which is illusory, with the sufficiency through internal solitude, through intrinsic identity. Man is not the finished product [*fini*] of anything else – of an Other – man is the intrinsic finish [*fini intrinsèque*] or Solitary who precedes any finitisation. Therefore, it is rigorous and sufficient to say that the nature of man is man rather than the wolf, the animal, the super-man – rather than philosophy. Science is the set of the conditions of reality (the being-given (of) the Ego) and rigour (the scientific structures of Humanity) that henceforth prohibit one to confuse the significations of which man has been credited with his essence itself.

Against Dogmatism: A 'Non-Copernican' and 'Non-Rousseauist' Mutation

Man is real and therefore first or foremost, defining an order; he is not dominant and does not enjoy any primacy. This means that man is not the beginning or the foundation, the origin or the difference within the origin, and so on, but the cause that renders possible the knowledge (induction and deduction) of the aprioristic structures of the Stranger. This is to be done with him as a foundation (or aspiring for it in vain), as the last end (he does not have an end and even, as a cause, excludes all ends with philosophy), as a principle (man is not a divided beginning having power-over . . .). Yet more than an answer preceding the call of the ontological question, man is the 'Answered' who, with this title, precedes the act of the answer itself, the Given that precedes his givenness. The most human answer is the following: granted man *qua* man or in his identity, what then results for thought and how does it deduce man's representation, how does it carry out the recasting of his classical or philosophical concept?

This logic is the consequence of what we call 'vision-in-man'. The radical realisation of the Greco-Christian *topos, 'What is man?* presupposes more than amendments or correctives to philosophical anthropology: rather, it presupposes a change of terrain. It presupposes letting-itself-be-given as a basis no longer philosophy, which does not have a basis, but man as this real basis for philosophy.

That which has answered, the non-positional and non-donative Ego, is the object of a hypothesis, in no way the object of a thesis or a principle – the Ego is no longer a metaphysical 'entity'. Man-*qua*-man emerges less beyond the ontological horizon (which is still a transcendence), that he is announced as the cause of an order so universal that he can inscribe metaphysical transcendence itself within it as a 'particular' or restrained case. It stops being assumed given within the element of exteriority to be experienced as given-in-man. This is no longer an ontological presupposition: How would a simple hypothesis be dogmatic? Despite the inevitable appearances, one will avoid seeing anthropological dogmatism here. Even though rigour requires us to go from man to the thought of man, rather than the inverse as idealism and criticism want to, there is no pre-critical decision in the position of the problem, but an immanent or transcendental posture which is nevertheless scientific as much as philosophical.

Philosophy is too idealist, decisional and positional, to be able to elucidate the essence of man in a rigorous way otherwise than through the questioning reiteration and within a horizon too broad and too narrow for him: too broad for his essence-of-identity, and too narrow for the thought that ensues from him and which is an even more universal representation than philosophy. The philosophical approach is here more than inverted or 'revolved': it is in priority displaced and emplaced as a simple material and 'model' by human reality itself. Therefore, there can be no question of a supplement to the 'Copernican Revolution' of the subject. It is a scientific mutation, a genuine emergence of the given, a new 'fact', rather than a philosophical reiteration of possibilities pre-traced within the horizon of the tradition. And it is a non-Copernican mutation by which man as Stranger does something other than take the place of the divided philosophical 'subject' because he emplaces or reduces the Copernican subject to being a restrained interpretation or an axiomatic 'model' of this general science of man. The order imposed by man upon thought undoubtedly means that the object no longer revolves around the subject but, more profoundly, the revolutionary axis of the subject and object – the Copernican dyad – is abolished, and thought does not revolve around the object anymore. There would be dogmatism if thought revolved around man given as a transcendent fact, so that it is he who, ceasing to be the ob-ject to become a cause, emplaces thought by stopping its movement. In a universal space of man, for which it is nothing but an experimental material or a model, the Copernican Revolution stops reversing and revolving; it becomes 'non-'revolutionary.

Theoretical non-Rousseauism, that is, Rousseauism in a unified-theoretical mode, is not content with designating a 'welcome space' for the Human Sciences: it is an identically scientific and human dimension in-the-last-instance. The principle of the general science of people is that the identity of science and the identity of man are 'the same thing', that man is not a philosophical animal but, with some nuances, a man (of) science. The man who seeks his salvation does philosophy. The man who knows that he is already saved practices the vision-in-man as the most human thought, which does not mean the most existential or the most too-human thought. This science-thought is foreign to philosophy as much as to the constituted sciences – to their conflict, rather, because it maintains a relation with their identity and because it does nothing but refuse the lack of humanity in the Human Sciences and the lack of science in philosophy.

On the Good Use of the Human Sciences: Meta-Language, Material and Model

How do we generalise the Human Sciences without reverting once more to philosophy? We do so by treating them as meta-human, as the simple meta-language of the science of people. Therefore, through another science, necessarily, but a science grounded on more universal principles and on a greater adequation to man, capable of inscribing them within its own theoretical space as on the one hand experience and on the other hand a model of interpretation, rather than empirical givens to 'go beyond' and 'interiorise' within the 'concept'. It is forbidden to us to claim to continuously pass, through successive interpretations, from the Human Sciences to the new unified theory. They are still impregnated with philosophical presuppositions and the unelucidated recourse to mathematics to describe the human object. The science that we elaborate must be 'discovered' with an original theoretical syntax and adapted to the new object, even if it maintains, then and on this basis, the narrowest relations with the material of the Human Sciences.

Of the two competing postulates of philosophy, we have seen that a unified theory would differenciate the one as an axiom and the other as a theorem, prohibiting each term from having these two uses simultaneously. How is this a non-anthropological generalisation of the Human Sciences? The reason of this gain in universality by which the science of people is opened, and opens for the Human Sciences an unlimited theoretical space of rectification of its representations, is that thought no longer functions towards two *de jure* equivalent postulations from the point of view of the possibility of theory, but towards one alone – the being-human (of) man as given of the Ego – and the second – the anthropological duality – now appears with some nuance as 'useless' or rather contingent from the point of view of the cause and even the object of science, not more useful than a simple material and a model. One such generalisation belongs to the scientific and no longer solely philosophical type of generalisations; it belongs to the 'non-Euclidean' or 'non-Newtonian' type – we call it here: 'non-Rousseauist' or 'non-anthropological'. It reduces the current sciences of society and man to the state of simple knowing, the providers of meta-human statements regarding man-in-the-World or man-in-Society, then in the state of 'restrained' interpretations.

The axiomatic gain in universality is obvious: the theory of man stops being constituted and enclosed by Anthropo-logical Difference; closed up by the teleology bound by anthropology itself. Anthropology cannot give rise to any science, its argument being vicious and grounded on a finality of thought. It is an effect of meta-language and, rather, it is towards its exclusion as a so-called hypothesis and towards its reduction to the state of material for a theorem, the Stranger's theorem, that a really general science of man can be grounded. It is to acquire a universality in relation to which the universality of the Human Sciences would appear as restrained to the meta-linguistic 'conditions of existence' that precisely belong to Anthropo-logical Difference. Humanity gives rise to a 'scientific continent' when its identity is discovered and manifested within a knowledge that is from the outset outside of the restrictions of the 'fundamental'-type (philosophy) or 'regional'-type (the Human Sciences); when it is irreducible to the facts and 'objective' givens of the disciplines that bear on man-in-the-World or man-in-Society. By becoming contingent for the Ego and even partially contingent for Humanity, the anthropo-logical postulate becomes philosophically inert and liberates a diversity of meta-human knowledge, without special pertinence but of which the theory uses freely. Because the being-human (of) man excludes man from having a contrary, the science of people is grounded on free axioms (or the possibility of axioms) rather than correlations of philosophical 'postulates'.

We may draw some consequences regarding this non-philosophical generalisation as to the status of the Human Sciences, before applying the rules later on especially in the case of psychoanalysis (see Chapter III).

Now, it is absurd to negate or even philosophically 'criticise' the Human Sciences. A unified theory of man is in the state of suspending their sufficiency, that is, their secret claim (a genuine transcendental illusion) to reach the reality of man and even simply the reality of his attributes. Thus reduced, they are not effectively 'destroyed', but transformed into simple means of knowledge. To start, at the beginning of the process, they are transformed into material, inert from their own point of view, sterile and not re-employable by themselves, having lost the little reality that made them transcendent to man. This material, non-defined and non-elaborated from their own point of view, is by contrast re-employable by this general science in view of axiomatising the Human Sciences (we will give a short example with psychoanalytic material).

With this science, therefore, it is no longer a question of interiorising or sublating meta-human knowledges, appropriating them in the philosophical mode and thus depriving them of their effective scientific dimension. The vain combat that grapples them with philosophy is not regrettable in only one sense and on only one side, but, like any combat, two sides at once. The scientific generalisation of knowledges, even if they were of the human-in-the-World or the human-in-the-City, and so on . . . is not their philosophical generalisation. The philosophical generalisation captures and interiorises them to a machine that is foreign to them, that extracts from them for its own benefit a surplus-value of reality and authority; the scientific generalisation universalises them in a mode of thought which does not do violence to them. There is an abyss between treating them (psychoanalysis, for example) as empirical givens with the help of which one produces meaning, truth and value, but that one rejects in their materiality and empiricity far from 'thought', and treating them as authentic sciences in their order – the order of the production of knowings or knowledges that bear on man-in-the-World – but as restrained models. The axiomatic aspect of the new discipline and its generalisation neither diminishes nor falsifies the sciences.

On their side, the Human Sciences undoubtedly lose their will – philosophical will, more than simply 'metaphysical' – to substitute themselves for philosophy and constitute a new paradigm of science and thought. However, they do not lose this authority by being overthrown [*renversées*] by another discipline. The sciences that we call of the 'unified theory' kind – which are sciences that are thematically sciences of essence, rather than object sciences, grounded on the identity of science and the Real in-the-last-instance – do not overthrow existing sciences, as they are not hierarchising but function towards priority (and therefore a superior universality) rather than primacy. In addition, if their generalisation is with a human origin, if they displace and emplace the 'positive' sciences as models instead of philosophically overthrowing them, the sciences do not become their slaves but a material to distribute within a now unlimited space that man has not opened but accompanies him and that is no longer closed up by any philosophical teleology or so-called 'ends of man'. As cause (of) science, man has no purposiveness [*finalité*]. This is one effect of the human generalisation of the Sciences of man to finally come upon [*advenir*] where man is, and, rather, to be-come [*de-venir*] from their cause-of-the-last-instance.

This is a new meaning of the 'demarcation criterion'. The point is to no longer distinguish between philosophy and science in 'general', that is, still epistemologically or methodologically, but between the Human Sciences – insofar as they participate in the same transcendental illusion as philosophy – and the general science of humans that reaches its real cause, man, as much as possible without returning to philosophy. The line of demarcation no longer passes between science, reduced to theories which would be falsifiable, and philosophy, which would not be falsifiable; but it passes between the transcendental or non-human meaning of these sciences and the human or immanent meaning of their unified-theoretical pragmatics. Here, the demarcation has acquired a pure transcendental origin, no longer of a philosophical and partially transcendent still origin. Only science as unified theory, now identical with the thought of the Real, can posit its demarcation with philosophy.

Their use as 'material' or 'model' obviously presupposes the equalisation [*la mise à égalité*] of the Human Sciences: not some in relation to others where they are in conflict, but in their common relation to their generalisation by identity. This is the Equivalency Principle of the Human Sciences, a transcendental rather than empirical equivalency, but one that henceforth – from the strict point of view of their 'humanity – prohibits hierarchies, primacies and privileges. Introducing democracy into the human use of sciences, 'deducing' them from their unique human cause, is a scientific task rather than a political one, but it is the only real task that relates itself to the politics of science and, soon, the politics of research programmes.

Their axiomatisation introduces the transparency of rules, rules manifest to man and science, exhaustively enumerated and capable of hunting down what subsists of 'theoretical' mystery, enigma, fantasy or miracles, or even contrary to theory, for example the miracle of 'linguistic rationality', the miracle of 'communication', and other *ad hoc* disciplines. This is not at all to exclude from the science of people, on the contrary, these two limits that designate the 'empirical' and the 'mystical' in exteriority. Understood in all of its phenomenal or human reality, it is a 'thought experiment' [*expérience de la pensée*] insofar as it re-introduces within its cause this mystical exteriority and in its object this empirical exteriority that philosophy and, consequently, the Human Sciences rejected as non-rationalisable. Such that it is postulated and posited in the way of axioms that are nevertheless real, the Ego is no longer divided, semi-rational, semi-mystical and semi-philosophical. The Ego is fully its own identity that, for its own account, draws and validates from mysticism the meaning of radical self(-)immanence; from science the meaning of the axiomatic order of reasons; from philosophy the meaning of the transcendental; from empiricism the meaning of experience; from philosophical rationality the meaning of an *a priori*, universal and necessary space of thought; and from logic the meaning of a quasi-symbolic and quasi-formal use of natural and/or philosophical language, doing right to the automatic writing within even the most thinking thought from where the philosophers intended to hunt it out. Man, thus understood as the Ego (of) the Stranger, is the suspension of positivism, scientism, idealism, empiricism, and so on, the suspension of all philosophical positions which are nothing but deviations of the science of humans as much as they are normalisations of its object. Rather than it not making itself rejoin or coincide *ad infinitum* all the edges through which the Human Sciences, philosophy, mysticism, psychoanalysis, and so on, touch one another by repelling each other, this science thinks each of them in their identity, but insofar as it precedes their disjunction and insofar as it is the cause which allows their theoretical rectification, indeed their theoretical recasting, and their equal distribution upon the scientific continent.

From 'The Anthropological Demon' to the Stranger

We will call 'the demon's theorem' or the 'the superman's theorem' the founding theory of anthropology and the Human Sciences according to which between man and his theory there is necessarily a 'common form', structure or syntax of the type of a demonological being or a being of a mid-dle, in which they are convertible or exchangeable to some near nuances. This form is obviously the fold-space or doublet of philosophy specified to man. This 'theorem' grounds the Human Sciences, which have not invalidated it despite the background mythology and fantasy that inhabits it. Man and anthropological discourse thus form a dyad in which they unite and surmount their opposition under the form of a superior being: a superman, a man-*par-excellence*, a sovereign subject – or quite simply a philosopher . . .

Regarding this mimesis or specularity, neither the thinking tautologies of the 'Same' nor the deconstruction by the 'Other' can deliver man, condemned to mirror himself in philosophy as in his Other, or in his Other as in himself. Between man and man, there would be one common form that allows him to represent himself. This imagery, this speculative thing without spirituality, which is at the origin of the myths of 'intersubjectivity' and 'communication', dissolves in his reflection, itself double or divided, the phenomenal reality of the Ego and the phenomenal reality of Humanity. Anthropology and the Human Sciences emerge from an imaginary experience of man that philosophy encloses within the magic circle of its images as if it was itself interminably fascinated – the family circle, all these circles constituting the familial double of the being-human. The true familialism, its most extended concept, is here, and no deconstruction can suspend without remainder this anthropo-logical mimesis, this specularity according to which only the similar knows the similar, and man accesses man in a superior intersubjectivity. By contrast, what alone can reduce, explain and emplace this 'theoretical' imaginary is the unilateral order of the unified theory. This incestuous thought of anthropology and the Human Sciences, an incest as the very being of man, is dissolved by the induction and deduction that the non-figure of the Stranger opposes.

Such that he is postulated by science and its unilateral duality, man does not fall into any philosophical dualities, decisions or alternatives (soul/body; mind/extension; ontic/ontological; subject/object; lived experience/objective; individual/species; but also naive/reflexive; self/other man; solipsism/intersubjectivity; historical/social; political/mystical, and so on). As we have said, these decisions are at most materials or models that interpret the general science, and the unilateral duality between the Ego and Stranger is not one of these decisions. It does not even think within the afterwards of man – man is not an 'Other' – another subject or the absolute Other – but within that which is determined-in-the-last-instance, an order both posterior and belonging to posteriority. The partially transcendent structures taken from the World and philosophy, such as the creature, the subject or ego, self-consciousness and *Dasein*, intentionality and being-in-the-World, are nothing but imageries of speculation but in no way how man is presented through or from himself, within the de-duction of that which he is or as the Stranger that he is. Dialectics, reflection, phenomenology, hermeneutics, and so on . . . are suspended as soon as the nothing-but-human identity is re-established and suppressed the 'blank' that gives rise to anthropo-logies or the forgetting of the (being-) human to the benefit of his being *tout court*. The elucidation of the essence of man is particularly kept in check – by measure of its will – when the thinker describes man's meaning-of-being in accordance with the meaning of Being in general and introduces inside the internal identity a distance, a difference, indeed an 'absolute transcending' under the pretext of expelling the 'cogitative' form and all the even more transcendent modes of givenness.

In the space of the transcendental theory, the theory of the humanity of Strangers, the statements have a non-philosophical and apparently contradictory form. For example, if the word 'humanise' can be intransitive, we will say: the human [*l'homme*] does not humanise, or man determines humanisation. These are statements that suspend the validity of philosophical tautologies of this kind: the human humanises (the world worlds, the nothing nothings, and so on). More generally, a science of man can do nothing but deliver man from the anthropo-id [*anthropo-ïdes*] envelopments, linings and matrices within which philosophy encysted him: the being-created or creature; the individual; the subject; the demon; the thinking and reflexive being; consciousness-of; spirit; being-in-the-World and being-there; the sub-man and super-man; the unconscious; the barbarian and the savage; the political-/religious-/lingual-/metaphysical-animal, and so on. Philosophy is a vast sky of humanity-fiction where anthropoids, prosthetic people, surrounded and supported by prefixes (the in-human, the all-too-human, super-human, trans-human, and so on) occupy the folds or inter-worlds of systems. Let us begin by flattening or unfolding the philosophical *cosmo-logos* and make these demono-logical beings that are not man fade away, they are only the speculative images of man, and assign them rather to a place and a function, finally real, as simple models interpreting this science. Man is neither a being-of-the-project – a project that we must reopen – nor an event that has taken place, a simple possibility that we must repeat, comment on and interminably deconstruct to realise it. Proceeding within the de-duction of man and ordered by him, it does not think him as an omnipotent fantastic being floating in the future nor as a distant figure in the past and dissolving under the repeated assaults of history. Between man and his scientific representation, between the scientific representation rather and the data of the Human Sciences, there is, if you will, a 'common form', but it is the *a priori* common form of the unified theory, and it stops being a common instance to the two parts, a dominant and synthetic one, a sort of 'common sense' proper to philosophy. It is a uni-versal, that is, unilateral structure without reciprocity; it is an absolute or non-specular reflection.

'Non-Humanism' and the Critique of Humanist Imagery

'Humanism' is the ensemble of the philosophical images of man, rather than the rigorous knowledge of man. Humanism is one form of speculative imagery, the product of an undoubtedly transcendental imagination, understood in a very general sense as an operation of the synthesis of contraries or as One-of-the-Dyad. We call image in the philosophical sense the product of the reciprocal speculation of contraries, with the image always being the double or divided reflection; it is to this we will oppose a transcendental science as the simple, uni-lateral or non-specular reflection (of) the real. This is not to injure or decry philosophy, that is to say that it lacks the spirituality and meaning of the 'internal', that philosophy is an operation of projection of pure images, that, in particular, philosophy does not know man but only representations of man. Humanism claims to engross man with such images, and it fills him with transcendent and unsuitable models (transcendence in general is made for the *Cosmos*, *Physis*, *Ousia*, Duty, and so on . . . but not for man). Humanism associates man by force with speculative representations that he does not need. This Principle of Sufficient Humanism (sufficient for . . . man) orders by submitting man to a capital of philosophical decisions, a capital of meaning, truths and values destined to assure the transformation of the essence of man in accordance with Being, Reason, Spirit, Revolution, and so on. Rather, human science retrieves the power of man to transform philosophy, and the human transformation of philosophy is something other than the opposite of the humanist exploitation of man.

This is because 'ordinary man' or the Stranger is for the philosopher the object of a double operation: the ordinary man is divided by the one who is the excellent or universal man, and therefore sub-humanised; then he is the doubled by the latter, becoming both singular and universal, the common and philosophising man. This operation is the absolute condition of all humanism:

every man is associated or connected to a philosopher as the excellent and universal form of man. Humanism and what the philosopher thinks of man is not what man thinks (of) himself. The famous critical slogan, 'think for yourself by putting yourself in someone else's shoes' [*penser par soi-même en se mettant à la place de l'autre*] has a very precise real meaning: double the other by thinking in his shoes and for him, and, inversely, let me be doubled by the one who thinks in my shoes [*doubler l'autre en pensant à sa place et pour lui; et inversement: me laisser doubler par lui qui pense à ma place*]. This reciprocity is the real phenomenal content of 'communication', the recognition of the reciprocal mastery and slavery of people.

Without being opposed to it, that which strips this operative and technological humanism and sends it back to the Transcendental Illusion is what we call 'vision-in-man', the transcendental and non-aprioristic fact that man thinks, acts or prescribes from deep within himself, with his own thought rather than with the help of a(nother) Thing (Reason, the Law, and so on) or an Other (thing) (the Other, the Unconscious, and so on), which are nothing but an occasional cause for him. Vision-in-man is the affirmation that man does not need rescue from predicates to be what he is; such as the predicate of Reason or even this new predicate – after Language, Power, Writing, and so on – which is Communication. Man does not think outside of himself, with the prisms of Reason or the bolstering of an assumed universal Communication but which is not, in any case, when compared to the universal space of the unified theory, or that it is only general/total, once more divided. Man thinks from his own depths, which is his intrinsic finitude: a sufficient human reason which is no longer a pathological affection of Reason but an absolute immanent given, lived as such by man and what we will call again here the 'Ego'. It is from these intrinsic finite depths that he takes his power to use Reason and Communication rather as simple occasions, not as tools: this would be a misunderstanding concerning the essence of man, his technological normalisation. Finite – ergo uni-versal – pragmatics is scientific, and it does not belong to the technological and transcendent order. Through the sufficiency of his finitude, man defines one sphere of absolute ante-communicational reality, more radical than any 'ante-predicative'.

Rather than a god or a demon, man is the only being who brings to the World, from before the World, the reality or identity of philosophy and science. He is the only one who opposes the philosophical divisions with the transcendental immanence of a non-decisional and non-donative lived experience (of) indivision. Let us say this with precaution: what we call the 'unified theory' is the 'spontaneous philosophy' of real man, what he thinks (of) himself, that is, by himself, before his philosophical images or representations, though not independently of them. This reality certainly does not mean that one extracts from the transcendent man of philosophy and his humanoid images a trait that is judged as remarkable: Reason, Language, Communication or any other predicate, to then give it a function of the total unification of experience. This 'realism' is transcendent just as transcendental: it is one philosophical position among others and the fully designated adversary of Transcendental Idealism. Man himself indifferenciates [*indifférencie*] these philosophical positions by the duality of his essence – the Universal Humanity of Strangers – and his effective existence.

From this point of view, the being-given of man particularly invalidates several antithetical philosophical positions. On the one hand, a phenomenological humanism that would still associate the 'non(-)self-positional' to an ontology of transcendence and an intentionality dooming humanism to become what it is: a by-product of ontology. On the other hand, the deconstruction of this humanism and other ones: man is not the Other (of) man, the Real is not the impossible delimiting ontology and phenomenology, the Real is vision-in-man, that is, 'in-One'. More than an Undeconstructible, man is that which indifferenciates and renders contingent the undecidable decision of deconstruction: man is the first of the non-philosophisables. Finally, legal rationalism, Fichte's for example, a solution that is worth a few words. Still restrictive, it submits man to humanism and projects a particular – 'rational' – content into the Self and its opening, forcing one to confuse them in an amphibological way. Fichte does nothing but eliminate 'general logic' from the Ego, but in no way does he eliminate what essentially still remains of it under the form of the *logos*, transcendence or decision – the heart of all philosophical logic – and falls once more into the transcendental illusion that he nevertheless denounced, but of which he made a too narrow concept. The entirety of Fichte's philosophy is then developed as a logic of philosophy instead of being an inductive as much as axiomatic science of philosophy as meta-human alone. Once more, it completes itself in the identification of the being-of-man with an ecstatic-horizontal opening that is still – measured to Humanity or the Stranger which accompanies the radical being-immanent of the Ego and considered within its intimate structure – a particular and folded space, an enclosure. Every philosophy of man can do nothing but 'return' to Fichte; a science will only return to him as a symptom and a reserve of meta-human indications, rather than as to this science itself. Fichte represents the maximum of what a philosophy can critique of Being and programme the future in favour of man. Otherwise, Fichte does not sufficiently radicalise the non-decisional and precisely non-positional essence of the Ego, nor does he give the transcendental illusion all its breadth beyond 'dogmatic' metaphysics alone, so that Humanity as a second region accompanying the Ego still remains equipped with a philosophical decision contracted within a fold and restrained to the particularity of transcendent contents like the Moral Law, the Time of the project, and Rational Faith. Newly anonymous, made of projective structures on the way, Humanity is not yet recognised as identical to the Stranger.

Only a really uni-versal 'non-Fichtean' thought, where Fichteanism would be nothing more than a particular case or a material, a sort of necessary meta-language though without autonomy, can recognise the undivided real within man and save the immanent human phenomenon from transcendent philosophical apparatuses that it immediately transforms into the simple *a priori* of experience. Whereas Fichte brings the philosophical decision to the limits of what it can do without breaking the ultimate restrictions of humanist imagery, whereas he thinks man within the bounds of reason, the problem of a science of people is entirely different: conceiving science and humanity within the bounds of the Ego (of) the Stranger, for these bounds of the science of people are not at all the bounds of Reason. The unified theory is not rational in the philosophical sense of this word, which is perhaps the only sense. It is first real, which is perhaps the best way of saying that it is not irrational. 'Reason' is a mixture whose bounds are both internal and external, immanent and transcendent; however, the unified theory is the intrinsic finitude of knowledge which contains and maintains not only the Ego but the Stranger themself within their positive bounds; which stops making it into a being of the project; and which renders possible a Uni-versal Humanity, one that is undoubtedly contingent, in relation to the intimately finite being of the Ego, but which 'destroys' the divided/folded pro-ject, the closed opening doomed to infinite perfectibility to which philosophy reduced man.

Critical humanism and philosophy in general, even the deconstructions, postulate human reality and the lived experience of the infinite, and attribute to man the onto-theo-logical vicissitudes of God, whereas the Stranger as a unilateral duality completely de-finalises the project from any metaphysical or onto-theo-logical dimension. Humanism remains a transcendent or imposed theory where man is nothing but its subject [*l'assujetti*]. As always in the Copernican Revolution – which is not a science of the subject [*sujet*] but a 'theory' of objectivation by the subject and itself – man is not the authentic 'subject', that is, the cause (of) science or the Stranger.

One will object that this 'opposition' (it is not one, but a unilateral duality of man as Stranger and philosophy) is a half-Rousseauist, half-Stirnerian residue, in any case an impossible thesis provided that the analysis is carried out up to the ultimate conditions of the philosophical – up to the ultimate forms of 'transcendence'. Precisely, an analysis of the invariant structures of the

Philosophical Decision and that which cannot be stopped on its path, that is, towards transcendence, may only make one perceive that the immanent, non-decisional phenomenon of the Ego is regularly presupposed by transcendence but not elucidated by it; that it is required to make philosophy real rather than simply possible, but without ever being described in its intimate constitution. The non-Copernican Ego that transcendentally precedes the philosophical decision in-the-last-instance has nothing in common with its anarchist avatar, which is a mode issued from the decomposition of this decision. Only a misunderstanding of a metaphysical origin concerning the Ego and its science, concerning their identity-of-the-last-instance, can make one believe that the vision-in-man is the 'Transcendental Unity' of philosophies or its complement and its empirical double. The man to which all philosophy thinks, even humanist criticism, is ontologically a mixture; whereas the man of the vision-in-man is this Transcendental Idiot of an ante-decisional simplicity.

The ensemble of these new perspectives concerning man constitutes a sort of 'non-humanism' rather than an anti-humanism, a science of man more universal than any philosophy that is capable of integrating it as a simple meta-language without authority and then, pragmatically, as the *a priori* of all experience. Critical and legal humanism, to reprise this example, is henceforth one decision among others, to the nearest reserve of its particularly actual symptom-function, a representation which requires being 'rectified' and inserted into a knowledge destined to describe in-the-last-instance the vision-in-man itself. The non-humanism that results is the ensemble of rigorous knowledges relating themselves to the Ego and to the Stranger; it is not a negation of humanism – we will explain a few of them in the following chapters. Humanism is a restrictive thought of man, of which we know that it is subtended by a unitary postulate that only one science can suspend and is formulated thus: man is necessarily associated once and each time only one humanist thesis, once and each time only one decision. A science of people is grounded on the suspension of this postulate, which is not necessary for the being of man, and substitutes this postulate with another one: to the man who is nothing but man necessarily corresponds no particular humanist decision, or rather what corresponds to man, nevertheless as contingent, is an infinity of decisions including certain ones which may be called entirely particularly 'humanist'.

Transforming the Knowledge of Man, Rather Than Man Himself

As a philosophy, humanism identifies two activities that only a transcendental science can distinguish: elucidating the essence of man, but also claiming to come upon man in his essence through this operation of elucidation. Whereas the 'Philosophical Decision' is the amphibology of these two operations, one such science protects the first, renounces the illusions of the second, and replaces the aberrant and dangerous project of a transformation of the Real (of the essence of man) with the project of a real transformation (of the effectivity of man). In essence, this principle grounds more rigorously than any transcendent ethical postulation the bounds of possible action regarding the human being. The new rules that implement the induction and deduction of the Stranger through the Ego make use of the statements from the Human Sciences, but not from man himself. We must globally reduce the techniques of the human body, for example, bio-technologies, to the state of restrained models that 'interpret' the transformation of the science of man, his knowledges, rather than man himself. Not more than he himself uses transcendence to think transcendence, but thinks one-time-each-time in the immanent mode a unique or simplified, non-folded transcendence, man is not directly transformable by science, which, by contrast, uses under certain conditions and always in the name of his identity bio-technological transformations or other transformations as materials. Everything of man that is philosophisable belongs only to the objective givens that a non-philosophical science by itself requires. For example, the observer-observed relation, which is more or less undecidable, is rather 'real', but this word here means 'existent' or 'effective'. Only man through his essence is real, only human phenomena are effective. As such, this relation belongs to the objects of a science, but not to its Essence (of) science, and does not contribute to defining it subject to dissolving once more its reality in universal instances (Reason, Being, Consciousness, Language, Communication, Spirit, Matter, and so on). The cause (of) science is not reduced to the observer, and the observer belongs to the 'objective givens' rather than to the essence of science. The duality of the unified theory is non-positional (of) its objects and is never related to them in an objectivating way: it is philosophy which does this and the one that attributes this alienation to it.

The human unilateral duality (the Ego, the Stranger) means that man is the real base, in some way the ultimate phenomenal content of all possible 'infrastructure', and that it is on this basis and by the means of knowledge that it becomes possible to transform the social, political, philosophical aspects, and so on, of his existence as Stranger. The point is to go from the untransformable reality of man, incapable of progress, perfection and destruction, racist or otherwise, incapable of 'perfectibility', to what it allows in transforming effectivity by the means of knowledge, rather than starting from effective man, already interpreted and transformed by philosophy, to transform him again somewhat more. Nothing, if not good will – and yet . . . – distinguishes the perfecting and destruction of man; and nothing, unless it is the philosophical decision as the ultimate authority subjugating man, distinguishes good will from the pure will to power. We must finally choose: either the ultimate authority and violence of philosophy that decides on the essence of man and confuses science and decision, science and will; or a human science that will have over philosophies not only the advantage of theoretical rigour, but the advantage of ethical rigour. It is the advantage of considering man as un-transformable in his essence and thus possessing an absolute measuring standard nevertheless in-the-last-instance of the transformations of transcendent human phenomena that it is scientifically and ethically possible. Genuine humanism is not a supplement of decision to the being of man; it is the one that is grounded where man really is and alone the 'cause' and then 'subject', Ego then Stranger. This is why man must be protected not only from dogmatic metaphysics but, beyond it, from any form of transcendence – from philosophy as such. Ethical and legal rationalism appear to us as not strong enough for the goals that they fixed: perhaps precisely because they still reason in terms of finality. In its stead, only one human science liberates man from any philosophical purposiveness and, opposite of what is done ordinarily, submits philosophy to man by means of a human science and pragmatics of philosophy (under the name 'non-philosophy').

To summarise: philosophy attempts to alienate man, believing that it has succeeded, but has failed; by contrast, there are true alienations, including this philosophical belief itself; and, finally, a science of man is a science of these alienations, but it is a science which is itself non-alienating. The humanist decision must arrive [*advenir*] where man is and thus be rendered human.

Chapter II

Principles of Democracy as the Unified Theory of Philosophy and the Stranger

On the Science of the Essence of Man as the Science of Strangers: The Theorem of Democracy

The investigation into the conditions of democracy is an obliged exercise of philosophy and politics. Among these conditions, however, one has not been clearly identified as such, perhaps because it questioned the most general presuppositions of philosophy (political or not) and, consequently, the very possibility of a rigorous or adequate thought of man first, and then the status of the political.

This condition is itself a universal or exceptionless solution, a solution which is itself 'democratic'. It is a solution to the problem of the essence of man and, in an imperative way as well, to the problem of the Stranger with which democracy is inseparable. What does this mean? It means that the 'subject' of the democratic statement would in turn and would only be a Stranger, the only otherwise possible Stranger. This means that the subject of democratic theory consequently stops exempting themselves from this status of the Stranger and enjoys the privileges of the philosophising subject who claims to grant their status to man and therefore to the Stranger. Political or not, philosophy elaborates concepts of democracy that claim to be valid if not *de facto* at least *de jure* for all people – philosophy therefore assumes itself as being the 'superior form' of democracy. These concepts are obviously variable and are nevertheless recognisable by certain invariants that express this claim but very quickly avow their limits: these are the invariants of a discourse that is in reality solely meta-democratic. Such that it is defined in general, democracy is nothing but a transcendent ideal distributed between the two worlds the 'I' and the 'Stranger'. Cut off from its own power, divided or barred by philosophy and its onto-politics, democracy is and remains impossible, oscillating between the fact and the ideal and in many other cleavages.

We only succeed in resolving the problem of democracy – that is, in posing it first correctly on the theoretical plane – by renouncing the semi-democracy of the philosophers to pose the hypothesis that any man, absolutely every man, a philosopher or not, is no longer an element of the Whole or the City that is presumed to alone be real, but each man is a solitary I whose solitude is neither numbered nor unnumbered, and draws up a theorem from this solitude according to which they are, under certain conditions, also a *de jure* Stranger in a multiple state, a state which is no longer numbered – the Stranger is neither Robinson nor the philosophical critique of Robinson. The exceptionless universality of the Stranger that we include in the complete concept of man, subject to their relation to the World, is the radical condition of democracy. If, first, it is the I who can be Stranger rather than the one who I find confronting me (the alter ego), then the problems of intersubjectivity would be theoretically resolved and the thought of it pacified.

A theory of the essence of people as Strangers, existing as immediately as the democratic theory itself without being a 'political' theory, is offered so as to reunify these two worlds in a unique law as separated as the Earth and Sky. Perhaps 'reunifying' is not the best concept. Philosophy is already this permanent unitary and superior synthesis, an auto-position of the transcendent sphere of politics and onto-politics. Rather, what matters is a theorem, not a thesis, of democracy, and it is the central piece of a 'unified theory' that is only unified, not unitary or amphibologically confounding the I and the Other. This theorem renders democracy real, and not only possible, unifying from within its two separated parts, redistributing the economy of the I and the Stranger in accordance with their immanent relation called 'of-the-last-instance', refusing to distribute power over two neighbouring entities and to attribute power entirely to the existent-I-(as-a)-Stranger . . . We are not sure of it, but it is perhaps the fantasy that democracy would be grounded on reciprocity or reversibility that makes the philosophers and their good, all-too-good will cower, without speaking about 'intersubjectivity', and that democracy consists in sharing power on the basis of an alienating distribution of the I and the Other (and the modes of the Other: the rival, the competitor, the minoritarian, the excluded, the marginal, and so on, who or which are rather obviously practical realities but with no theoretical significance). Let us first reformulate our concepts of the I and the Stranger in accordance with their identity-of-the-last-instance; let us return to democratic immanence, to its radical phenomenon; let us suspend our beliefs and our political, onto-political decisions that are nothing but meta-democratic decisions; let us put ourselves back in the being-human (of) the Stranger – this is the only programme that would itself be practically democratic because it is theoretically democratic, defining a democratic opening distinct from any political plane, finally giving its radical meaning to the expression 'the actuality of democratic man'.

Finally, who is the stating 'subject' of the theory of democracy? It is not the I-in-I for whom the problem is not posed being given their ultimate structure. Rather, the stating subject is the Stranger insofar, at least, I and the Stranger are identical-in-the-last-instance. The Stranger alone has the correct or adequate, that is, democratic point of view concerning the theory of man and, hence, the theory of politics: the Stranger does what they say and says what they are.

The Ego-Xeno-Logical Constitution of Philosophy: On the Stranger as Difference or Identity

Our most general way of thinking – philosophy – is a practice of aporia and a culture of discontent, and the question of the Stranger is the henceforth dominant form of this old philosophical discontent, one that renders the discontent a bit more manifest and makes up the conjuncture, like a surplus symptom. Never as much as today has philosophy confessed that it also has 'societal problems'. On no question as much as the question of the Other has philosophy exposed its fragility and powerlessness, manifesting one such opportunist good will under the form of the ideology 'communication'.

We can give numerous versions of the invariant structure of philosophy (Dyad + One). In terms of Myself and the Stranger, in human terms in general, this invariant structure takes the form of a softened Ego-xeno-logical Antinomy or Difference that, in its own way, is not specifically political but emerges from the constitution of philosophy. Ego-xeno-logical Difference is the matrix, like the *a priori*, of the different types of relation that common sense, carried on by philosophy, could have imagined between the I and the Other. It does not concern one particular, historical position of the problem, but the transcendental horizon of questions and partisanships (political ones for example) on this problem. This horizon is political but as much 'fundamental' and, for example, phenomenological (Husserl, *Cartesian Meditations*) or even the deconstructive positions on phenomenology (Heidegger and Derrida) that are content with still, despite everything, repressing this invariant. The ego-xeno-logical logic indefinitely stokes these mixtures of the I and the Other that philosophy unceasingly redivides, redoubles, redistributes, magnifies and displaces. Thus does philosophy only extend its powerlessness or its repression of the problem of what we must call the identity of the Stranger. Philosophy has always undergone the most extreme difficulties in recognising a positive status to the Stranger and even to simply recognise the Stranger's *de jure* existence. When it wants to do so, when it does not say that the I exists without reference to other people (Descartes), philosophy presumes that the Other is produced by the I on the model of the I, that the Other is essentially 'constituted' by the I (Husserl); philosophy diminishes the autonomy of the Other-Person and makes them into a simple mode of the I. Then, it is undoubtedly progress to either reciprocate the I and Thou (Fichte), or to think 'difference', for example, concerning the Stranger. We even believe to have reached the *nec plus ultra* of the thought of the Other when we invoke 'our differences'. However, reciprocation, like difference, is the complete opposite of a 'solution'. Both are simple modes of an aporia, the aporia of philosophy itself. We are not sure that difference, as always anonymous and undetermined, would be a very rigorous concept on the theoretical plane and very effective on the practical plane. All these problems have undoubtedly been reactivated by the 'deconstructions', the great doctrines (Wittgenstein, Heidegger, Derrida) that have recorded the irruption of the question of the Other as such, occasionally under Levinas' 'radical' impulsion, on the margins of the oldest question of man. The question of man, posited under the Kantian form of the 'subject' – the first appearance of the Other – has not been resolved because philosophy does not bring about a solution. The question has been revived and reopened more crucially through this second discovery of the Other, a discovery that is more powerful than the discovery of the 'subject', even capable of deconstructing the subject. But the discovery of the Other remains so as much deprived of a solution, with the Other having not been elucidated for itself but serving alone to mark the limits for itself, either as unintelligible transcendence, or the mystical and the ethical, or the *outre-clôture* and writing, which belong to the Other as philosophy. The old antinomies of the judgement of humanity (still animal or already human? Political or religious? God or wolf? Individual or subject? and so on) have been reprised and reactivated under the form of new antinomies that belong to the judgement of alterity (Other-as-subject or the Other-of-the-subject? The Other-of-me or the Other-than-I? and so on). Everything around the philosopher becomes discontent and aporia, man and the rest. Everything around the Stranger has become for a second time still unsolvable.

One symptom of this difficulty is the very position of the problem as being the problem of the Other: Must we speak of the Other or rather the Stranger? In philosophy and its ontology, the problem of the Stranger is more or less rapidly reduced to the problem of the Other and treated like the Other. The Platonic 'great kind' of the Other belongs to ontology and the anonymity of its entities. Even though our perspective will neither be political nor the perspective of international relations, but a scientific perspective, we rather prefer to reduce the problem of the Other to the problem of the Stranger.

A problematic that wants itself to be human in priority, unlike philosophy, will substitute not the Other-Person [*Autrui*] who is still too close to the Other [*Autre*], but the Stranger who gives their radicality to the problem. The problematic will elucidate to what extent this concept still belongs to the sphere of transcendentals and the sphere of transcendentals of a somewhat new nature. It is time to abandon the terms of the Other and alterity that are still too neutral and anonymous. More than the Other, and alternatively more than the Other-Person, the Stranger is necessarily a human. Our goal is then to tear this concept from the solely political and ethnic field where the Stranger remains vague and undetermined and propose the outline of a genuine theory of the Stranger. It is time to make the Stranger enter into the sphere of scientific problems and to no longer be content with seeing the (Platonic) figure of the philosopher or the 'other philosopher' – the superior form of the Other man or the 'foreigner' in the ethnic sense of the term.

Touching on this classical antinomic situation of philosophy we make the following hypothesis that attempts to explain philosophy's powerlessness to recognise autonomy and positivity to the Stranger and extends its war with the I. It concerns a double gesture of devaluing and overvaluing the 'Other'. Indeed, through what operations is Ego-xeno-logical Difference and its work manifested on the material of 'spontaneous' political or social relations? Ego-xeno-logical Difference imposes a determination of the I and the Other through an assumed first decision or distance that is precisely determinant. These most general philosophical presuppositions are the presuppositions of the decision as the first essence or determination, a decision from the I to the Other – sometimes more or less inverted or 'against the grain' [*à rebours*] (Levinas) – and form the content of Ego-xeno-logical Difference which, in this way, doubles and splits the I through the Other and the Other through the I. It is important to identify at the basis of all philosophical solutions to the problem of the Other this assumed same or irreducible presupposition that is never clarified, simply varied and criticised, broken down or deconstructed: the system of the reversibility or convertibility of the I and the Other, the system of two I(s) and two Other(s) which form a dyad of terms that are given simultaneously with some near slippages or near differences, so that by dividing the Identity of each of them and soaring over these terms, hanging over this *de jure* and antagonist fraternal couple, philosophy cannot not set up the spectrum of tensions, conflict and war. Correlatively and through a second operation, a supplementary gesture extends the first, re-blending them a bit further and a bit otherwise. It is not the particular mixtures that interest us but their logic that tends to a division or a duality between one starting amphibology and another terminal and redistributed amphibology. It was only Levinas who, for non-Greek reasons drawn from Judaism, attempted to unilaterally break the more or less disjoint circle of convertibility of the I and the Other to the benefit of the Law (of the Face) and the Prohibition (of killing), but by putting the Other back (to) themselves, if we may say, as the 'Most-High', the Other thus loses any chance of getting back their human and intelligible identity.

Let us explain the content of Ego-xeno-logical Difference. Philosophy poses the problem of the Other in accordance with a very simple universal schema that it modifies and varies, by contrast, nearly infinitely, conserving it each time essentially: the universal schema of the reciprocal, even reversible, duality of the I and the Other, two face-to-face terms which the philosopher soars over and contemplates, the philosopher plays the duality between them and varies it in their relations. Hence, three characteristic 'effects':

1. There are exchanges between the I and the Other: the Other person is themselves an I – therefore another I (alter ego); reciprocally, the I is another for the Other-person. I am, perhaps, an alter ego in turn, but above all another Other. Each of the two terms ends by becoming their contrary. Finally, there are two I(s) and two Other(s) in complicated relations that can go as far as the dialectic or chiasmus. These four entangled entities – there is no Me without You and reciprocally – is the structure of Difference, of Intersubjectivity itself, in its greatest generality as a problematic.
2. It is important to note this division of the I and the Other (two I(s) and two Other(s)). The division is characteristic of philosophy that refuses the undivided Identity and only thinks the Real, the term, by dividing it. We shall return to this. However, we see right now that the I and the Other form a complex, softened antinomy, and hinder each other, impinge upon one another, and reciprocally withdraw themselves from reality. Hence, scarcity and war.
3. With some near nuances or processes that philosophy always takes care to note, if the I and the Other are reciprocal or convertible within one another, and if, to parody Leibniz, nothing is not truly an alter *ego* (or another *I*), is not truly an *alter* ego (an *other* I), there is a certain confusion (or 'amphibology') of Myself and the Stranger.

The unperceived symptom of this structure is indeed the old schema of the alter ego, the Other as the other I that does not stop haunting the philosophies of Intersubjectivity. Completed and described in all of its dimensions, the alter ego reciprocally acknowledges the I as an Other, understood no longer as an other-I but as an other-Other where the identity of the I is dissolved. This latter formula is inevitable and cannot remain hidden for a long time as soon as we have grasped that the relations of the I and the Other are traditionally presuppositions – even when it concerns the I – that inhabit transcendence or Exteriority, or precisely Distance. Two reciprocal I(s) or two reciprocal Other(s), or reversible in the best of cases, to wit: the I represents an Other (I) for (another) I. We can call this inscription, not only of the Other but of the I itself, within a transcendent or third element, an ether or common space of representation, their auto-position. Philosophy is the thought in which transcendence or distance is supposed determinant but where it is obviously threatened by a void or unreality and, therefore, must be realised by taking on the form of a redoubling, fold or refolding: an auto-position. Auto-position is the most general structure of the philosophical and its effects, making up a system with Ego-xeno-logical Distance.

On the basis of this mode of the givenness of the Other, some solution-types have been presupposed. Principally, they are the following that illustrate the whole antinomy of the I and the Stranger up to its extreme limits.

1. In priority, elementarily, the Other is given in the face of Myself as a quasi-object, a non-descript ontic presence – specularly as an other I (alter ego). The Other is thus given by their own fact or own authority, through themselves, bearing their right, their *de jure* and *de facto* givennesses. This is the solution of 'common sense', the least elaborated one, but it possesses a fundamental formal trait that philosophical solutions have in common of assuming to refine and modify it, make it 'indirect' or 'possibilise' it, and so on: the Other has an autonomy from itself of the same type as the I's autonomy, but it is the autonomy of the Other and therefore is a rival of the I. The Other as well, but as the opposite of the I, exists in the mode of their auto-position; the Other has its essence where it is or exists. This is the-Other, or again Theother: the effect or the double, the mirage or the specular image of the I. The I is then assumed in turn as coming through themselves and specularly divided: another Other (I is . . . and not I am).
2. The Other is always given in the face of the I and at the end of a distance but as partially autonomous and partially constituted by the distance that does not produce the Other *ex nihilo* as the Other I but that produces its sense of the other person for this I. The Other yields their autonomy to the I but always on the basis or presupposition of the Other's coming to the I through themselves and from their own auto-position. This auto-position of the 'other I' is broken down but not suppressed. It is the idealism (Fichte, Husserl) of the other I that is elsewhere, historically, the first discovery of the Other, the discovery of the subject as the Other, for the I identifies itself with the sense of the other-person with which the I clothes the other and contingent given.

3. The Other is no longer solely given in the face of the I as an object but 'in me without me' or outside-of-the-object by affecting the I from the interior and exterior, without the constitutive distance being really destroyed. Rather, it is exacerbated as extra-territoriality, an alterity that transcends me but I cannot transcend; the ensemble remains on the basis of this auto-position of the Other as (another) I (the correlative of the I as the other Other). This is the meaning of the formula 'I is an other' – is, and not am. This is the second discovery in the times of the Other, the post-modern times . . . where the Other is no longer I but the Other of the I.
4. The Other is given as the absolute non-I who inverts their relation and reduces the I 'to the state of the I-hostage' [*otage*]. Is the most general philosophical presupposition really levied? Probably not: the Dyad and its primacy remain in the state of a negative condition of this 'against-the-grain' experience of the Other.

In its generality, the philosophical antinomy of the Stranger implies that, from the I to the Other, there is the mediation of a relation, *rapport*, an intentional com-portment or transcendence in general. Every original relation, at least such that it is thought by philosophy as external or internal, in both cases as constitutive of the Real, is ultimately the 'dyad'-form, and emerges from a coupling of terms that thought gives itself the exorbitant right to soar over and therefore inscribe in the transcendence of the World, immediately abolishing any experience and any law of Identity. However, it is possible that there is no original social relation (at least as a constitutive title) – not more a human relation than a sexual relation – and that Intersubjectivity would be a false problem 'inflated' by philosophy, having become a symptom of its way of doing. This structure that we have already called the structure of the Stranger-as-the-I-in-the-last-instance, or the 'I who exists (as) Stranger' is reduced and dislocated on the Procrustes' bed of predicative judgement and its avatars, giving rise to antinomies of the judgement of humanity of which nothing, absolutely nothing, proves that it correctly describes the phenomenon of the essence of man. The I becomes subject, the Other becomes the attribute or, rigorously, alters the attribute that the Other supposes. We are not sure that the ontologico-predicative model with its different modes (the analytic mode: classical individual; the synthetic mode: the modern subject; the differential mode: the post-modern inhuman, and so on), and, in general, the relational and/or intentional schema, belongs to the phenomenon of the Ego and, to a lesser but more nuanced extent, to the phenomenon of the Stranger.

Philosophical Xenophobology and its Practical and Theoretical Difficulties

The ego-xeno-logical schema is apparently very satisfying and one that relieves guilt: I am also an Other and the Other is also an I. Realistically, this is disastrous on the practical and theoretical plane. On the practical plane, this is obvious: conceived on this schema of the I and the Other, the Stranger remains ordered and determined by relations that are relations of philosophical distribution or auto-positional difference. More precisely:

1. The determinant instance is by nature auto-positional. Therefore, it is an intrinsically hierarchical structure or an auto-domination, an identity blended with Being, with the position, therefore, having become auto-position and dominant itself. The philosophical I is a mode of the *Logos*, the Whole, the Centre, and Presence - we know this already - and the philosophical I is always a hierarchy for itself.
2. It is inevitable that this spirit of hierarchy radiates beyond it up to the Other and its relations with the Other. The Other participates in this general structure of auto-position at least as its residue or rather its contestation. The Other is also given in this mode of philosophical transcendence in which the Other excavates a supplementary transcendence that is their own. Divided and refolded onto themselves, though in a way less apparent than the Ego, the Other collects the crumbs of domination and participates in the hierarchy. However, the Other is the inferior instance and can always reverse the order, a possibility which the deconstructions and more reactive thoughts still exploit.
3. The effect of this general system of a thought through determinant transcendence is the reciprocal determination of instances, the tense struggle and conflict of the I and the Stranger (under the name of the Other). These instances are precisely two and the Two resolves the conflict of its duality and its simultaneity under the form of the hierarchy where the instances rival each other in sharing and appropriating a unique reality. It concerns one *de jure* structure or possibility: even peace is still 'precarious' or paralysed by the conflict.
4. In particular, the Other must share identity, which they lack *de jure*, with the I who is the owner of identity; the Other is condemned to tear identity from the I, to struggle for the recognition of their own identity, and to thus vanquish the I. On its side, the I is condemned to defend itself and consequently accentuate its domination and refuse the Other their

> autonomy. The Other is doomed to the serving and subaltern tasks of critique, decentring, dissemination and differe(a)nce. The Other represents a threat or a political danger, beckoning an allergy and repressed by the I. Philosophy elevates empirical or accidental war to the essence and makes it a state of law.

On the theoretical plane, precisely, Ego-xeno-logical Difference is a vicious 'explanation'. The schema of reversibility or convertibility does not have theoretical or rigorous scientific pertinence. It is the simple trace or reflection, with some near nuances, of what happens in common social historical and political reality, and is in no way a testable and inventive hypothesis. The grounds of our common experience is undoubtedly conflict, indeed war, and nothing avoids the form of the differend. However, an explanation that is somewhat rigorous for this experience cannot be the simple specular reflection of phenomena, for Ego-xeno-logical Difference only records the spontaneous experience of alterity which sees in the Other a dangerous and insidious alter ego without thinking this experience in itself, without testing its validity, interiorising or displacing it alone. Under the name 'difference' thought as such, it registers such politico-social conflicts, elevating this state of fact to the state of norm without really criticising it, the norm being the rule of undecidability, and so on, without seeing that it has begun to surrender to the claim of this Transcendent Other and this I by positing themselves. However, the authentic theory is not an image of experience; the theory of conflict is not itself conflictual; the explanation of war is not itself polemical, and if the contemporary philosophy of the Other in particular is a commentary on the real situation rather than its explanation, it adds its conflictedness to the conflict of things rather than transforming it into the meaning of peace. There has never been philosophical peace - but a war or guerilla warfare of philosophy - and a philosopher never fully recognises the autonomy and positivity of another, only reducing them, devaluing and overvaluing them.

Thus, the European philosophical tradition, be it classical or contemporary, imparts to us the universality of conflict between people and interpellates us in the goal to subjugate us. Becoming would be a universal or intense becoming-war, both its smoothening and extension. What is most real in situations of intersubjectivity or interhumanity would be the spirit of battle. From I to Myself, from I to the Other, from the Other to the Other, we have learned to detect the differend and the litigation in the unstable equilibrium of forces, ruse and war in the contract, and strategy in love. Therefore, with the philosophers, let us assume these descriptions are pertinent or adequate to the effective situation: Do they have less theoretical and explanatory value? The philosophers – not only Machiavelli, Hobbes, Nietzsche or Foucault – in general conclude – subject to some operation of displacement or reversal, 'critique' – on the philosophical description of facts with the theoretical pertinence of this description. By interpreting war among people, they believe to be able to really transform or change their relations. By modifying their thought or vision of these relations, they assume to modify their reality. Traditional philosophical practice transfers this situation from being-in-war of historical reality to its theory, reproducing it in its own explanation, eternalising or reflecting it, bringing it to the essence, and therefore forbidding itself from really transforming it. War is thus essential to philosophical thought, too fascinated by war to be in the posture to explain it.

These ultimate presuppositions that formulate the question of the Stranger therefore exclude any solution that would not install a permanent conflict. The tradition of the simultaneous unresolved tension, the front and rupture structure is extended to the Other and turns the Other into a 'question'. Rigorously, this conflict is displaced in the structure of a symptom: it 'shifts', in relation to its 'Heraclitean' form, in favour of the Other who is demarcated from it – but remains the assumed valid and constituent ultimate horizon of the being-stranger of the Stranger. This logic from simple interiorisation to the concept and Being, even if it were differe(a)nce, therefore commands as much the theory of the I as the theory of the Other, for example investing Cartesian egology and commanding the relation of the Ego with the Infinite. Despite its proximity to the radical immanence of the I, the Cartesian thesis still testifies to the transcendent or philosophical contemplation of the immanent Ego instead of the assumption of letting-be-given the absolute immanence as the guiding thread of any current thought. Ultimately, Descartes remains a meditating geometer, an Ego-(xeno)-logical geometer at the very moment where he appears to assure himself with the non-representative character of the Ego, and, however, he continues to objectivate this un-objective immanence. Precisely, the relation of the Ego and God, which could appear through many aspects (sometimes through the Ego, sometimes through God) is able to liquidate representation, but is still division, the ultimate dislocation of the identity-of-the-last-instance of the Ego and 'God' on the ego-xeno-logical cross. Through Descartes, thought can go either towards the absolute immanence of the Ego – but it then sacrifices the idea of the Infinite – or towards the radical transcendence of the Infinite – but it then sacrifices the autonomy of the Ego (unless Descartes himself would be the rigorous, coherent synthesis of these two positions, and a synthesis of these positions gathered as close as possible). For all that, the ego-xeno-logical structure would not be eliminated . . .

In the philosophy of the Ego, what has never been elucidated in its essence is not only, as Heidegger says concerning Descartes, the mode of the being of the *sum* and the *existo* in '*ego sum, ego existo*', or Being as the being of the Ego; nor even the mode of being of the Other as Other. However, more radically, in the very name of the complicitous omnipotence of Being or the Other, the constancy in absolute phenomenality, the constancy in the reality-One or the Identity of the question of Being itself and the spontaneous ontological thesis according to which the Ego is, or would have to be, its convertibility with Being; and the complementary thesis according to which the Ego on this basis would maintain a relation-with-the-Other. Ontology, but just as much the deconstructions of ontology, has passed the problem of the identity of the I and the identity of the Stranger, the non-reciprocal character of the Ego itself with Being and with the Other, under silence, or has only 'resolved' it under the obligated horizon of universal ontological representation. It is the totality of philosophy as structured by Ego-xeno-logical Difference that excludes this problem. It first keeps to its general conception of thought and its relation to the Real, to its initial conception of Identity. As always, philosophy takes on a double, indeed contradictory or 'aporetic' attitude towards the Other as towards any such object, and then seeks to unify these two perspectives. For example: (in Descartes, Leibniz, Husserl, and so on) it is ready to say that the I is an identity indivisible in itself, or a substance inherent to itself (the *res cogitans* of the classics) or an immanent I and an Ego called transcendental (in Husserl). However, philosophy never follows through in this idea and ends by implicitly recognising that the I is also divided, that it is also self-distant, that it is a blend of the unreflected and reflection, that it is not a subject without also being an object, and that it is represented to itself as soon as it thinks itself (*cogito me cogitare*). The philosopher begins by always setting the I at a distance from them - and even more so the Stranger - observing or overhanging the I, making the I an object again despite their promises that the philosopher places face-to-face with another thing. Finally, the philosopher distinguishes the philosopher's I and the I that they observe: a disinterested I (Husserl) and an I interested in the World; a 'We, philosophers' (Hegel) who seeks out meaning and truth, and a consciousness who naively struggles and blindly suffers in the World. The divided I loses its identity. There are several heterogeneous Is, and there are distinct and hierarchised functions that must reform an I of the synthesis or a reconciled I, and so on.

The Identity (of) the Stranger, first the identity (of) Myself, is thus never thematised for itself and distinguished from what they become in Being and its modes (*Physis*, *Kosmos*, *Polis*, and so on). We treat the I and the Other like the terms of a dyad that thought gives itself as first, but one that thought soars over or objectivates, opposing the terms, confronting them from a distance or a difference which is more or less reversible. Identity is immediately missing because it is posited in too broad a manner and beyond itself as a One-All, One-Being, One-Difference, One-Same; and the Other is just as missing because they are posited in a relation-with . . . and therefore in opposition-to . . . the I. This is an old thought that harbours the most dangerous prejudices. The ego-xeno-logical constitution of our dominant Western thought is of the order of an antinomic amphibology of Identity and the Other, Myself and the Stranger, preventing us from thinking their 'relation' correctly without having to assume it as already given under the empirical and transcendent form under which it is spontaneously announced.

Finally, the universality of this Difference allows us to demonstrate the grounds of egophobia and not only xenophobology that inhabits Greco-philosophical categories, and allows us to explain to what almost unfathomable depth our thought is inscribed by the hatred of the Stranger, not of this man assumed in our faces but in the face of Humanity – the superior form of racism, the anti-humanity that every philosophy shelters.

The Principal Theorem of a Science of People as Strangers

Without a really human science, there is no scientific continent of man, unless we can include and resolve the problem of the Stranger in order to install peace especially within thought. We must define and resolve the problems undoubtedly in accordance with the element where they appear as symptoms, where they are idealised from the universal social battle, as is the case in philosophy. However, because they are manifested in culture does not suffice: they must receive a solution in the framework of a thought that protects itself from reproducing them within itself and interiorising them: the thought of science. There have been responses to the question of the Stranger, responses that have only made the question more unsolvable, up to, perhaps, making it appear as more than simply a poorly posed question for any question is not good, and even more seriously, a question is perhaps a way of repressing a problem, of not posing the problem, of substituting the problem with the desperate escape into transcendence.

Let us say it again: the rigorous thought of the human battle must be a theory, and a true theory is not the specular reflection or double of its object. A discipline that would like to understand why there are conflicts and thus procure the means for their good use cannot be a mode of these phenomena; the knowledge of war is not itself polemological. If, therefore, philosophy interiorises war into the concept and makes the concept a superior war, if philosophy is war's sublimation and idealisation and cannot really transform it, only one science can 'objectively' treat human war without having to take part in it. We will not believe that the point is to utopically negate the reality of conflicts. To the contrary: only one science refuses to idealise and interpret them, to supersede or raise them, and so on, precisely because a science itself, in its essence and its humanity at least, is absolutely not by nature conflictive – without being a 'beautiful soul' . . .

If there is a rigorous thought of man as Stranger, this theory will therefore know how to eliminate from itself the antinomy of the judgement of alterity. The problem is first of the theoretical nature of concepts – the I and the Other – to elaborate according to identically scientific and philosophical laws before any always premature practical or political question. In particular and we know this already (see Chapter I), if philosophy rather has the tendency to think the difference of the Stranger, then a theoretical posture will strive to describe their identity. We will substitute Ego-xeno-logical Difference with a wholly other experience of the Other and especially the I, the Ego: and we will substitute philosophy with this other hypothesis: the hypothesis of a way of thinking which will no longer distinguish two Is in a hierarchical relation principally where the I of the thinker and the I that they speak of would rather be strictly identical. This thought is the thought of science as a unified theory, and it is by nature unreflected because the I no longer has the self-distance necessary for reflection. It is a strict identity without any division that is so coherent with itself that it neither objectivates nor alienates itself in the World or in an object. To elaborate a theoretical thought of stars, it is not necessary for the I to make itself a star and take pilgrimage in the *cosmos*. The I remains in itself. We will reprise the formula: the Ego is non-decisional and non-positional, I am a 'radical immanence' that does not represent itself; I am not a 'subject' but a real-of-the-last-instance. A consequence: I, man as Ego, cannot become Other than I – I cannot alienate myself; I cannot blend myself with the Other Person or be affected by them. It is this conception of the I, and therefore the conception of Man, that destroys Ego-xeno-logical Difference and, in general, the theories of alienation (legal alienation, not social alienation).

One such system of axioms implicitly defining the Ego as the Real Identity then allows us to posit the following theorem: *there is no alter Ego, nor is the Ego an Other, there is no specular game between I and the Other, for I and I alone can also be the Stranger – if there is one – and the Stranger is in-the-last-instance this I that I am.* If there is a Stranger, they are therefore not first who are what is presented in the face of Myself or in social, political, international struggle. The Stranger is first Myself. Let us say all of the following that this does not mean 'I is an other', but – this is entirely different – 'I (=Ego) am also an Other'. I and the Stranger do not form an Ego-xeno-logical Difference, a reciprocal duality, one held by philosophy itself; we are identical 'in-the-last-instance' alone. In particular, we must explain this latter nuance attached to Identity. This solution destroys the dyad of the I and the Other at the root of which the problematic of Intersubjectivity draws its insistence. The nuance consists in demonstrating that I am (*qua* the I that I am-nothing-but-I and not another-Other) also the Other itself (not another I, nor an alter ego). That the radically ego ego, the Ego, who does not become an alter ego nor is reversible with the alter ego, I am also an alter and that I am so *qua* an inalienable Ego or Ego-of-the-last-instance. This formula probably does not make philosophical sense nor has any philosophical receivability and perhaps we should say that it concerns this triviality 'I is an other'. However, 'I am an Other' means that I can only say that 'I am' and never 'I is'; and that the 'being' here is rigorously immanent and not a copula; that the Stranger is not here the predicate of the Ego but its original position such that it does not affect me. The Rimbaudian formula belongs to the system of Ego-xeno-logical Difference that claims to alienate me in the I-they mixture, namely in the I as an other-Other that floats in the neutral and undetermined element of transcendence. To sum up this solution of an undoubtedly still ambiguous formula that is perhaps subject to a misunderstanding: it is not the assumed given 'Other' who is another I, an alter ego, it is the I and the I alone who can also be an Other – a Stranger. It takes some nuances and some descriptions to strip the formula's appearance of being the simple inversion of the first. The theoretical labour that remains to be carried out consists in dissolving the philosophical amphibology and demonstrating this statement, the fundamental theorem of a science of Strangers: *I and the Other 'are' not the Same, 'we are' identical-in-the-last-instance.* Identity and Strangeness then cease being confounded – and their dyadic opposition belongs to their confusion and constitutes it. It is in-the-last-instance alone that they, I and the Stranger, are identical rather than different or the same.

The Stranger and the I are henceforth so little opposed, and the Stranger barely destroys Identity by giving it existence, that we propose rather to bring the Stranger back to the 'locale' that we elsewhere call the One and tear the Stranger from the attraction to Being and finally the 'Other'. The identity-of-the-last-instance of the Stranger assumes that they would have changed terrain, that the Other passes from the circular order of Being to the direct and immanent causality of the One. On its side, the I 'Other-exists', 'Stranger-exists' without being alienated in its existence: the I is not woven by a constitutive relation (either 'intentional' or 'against the grain') with this so-called Other given in the World, with it and in a regime of auto-position. I am also an Other (not, therefore, an other-I). I am not this Other that I find in the exteriority of the World or in the space of transcendence, or that I encounter by chance in society, with whom I identify my affliction or finitude. However, it is as the I that can always say I that I also exist as an Other – an absolute, first Other, but not an alter ego. I am, therefore, I (too) am an Other, not Other-than-I or an other-I; all of this with the slightest contradiction. Existing-as-a-Stranger neither annuls nor affects the I. To the contrary, this existing testifies to . . . and for . . . my identity – more exactly testifying to the Identity that makes up my reality.

'In-the-last-instance' opposes itself to the 'reciprocal' and to the 'same' and means that the I is the 'last instance' and the ultimate and definitive place where the Stranger is received, lived and experienced. No doubt, the Stranger experiences or knows themselves as a Stranger, but they know and do so in an I – it is an I (not a Stranger) which knows or experiences themselves as a Stranger without contradiction or antinomy. This is the only solution so that, on the one hand, I do not except myself from the status of the Stranger – this is the exigency of universal democracy – and so that, on the other hand, the Stranger would no longer be defined by exclusion and hatred in a negative and undetermined way; so that the Stranger as well has an identity and that they would not be doomed to flee and dissolve themselves in doubles and simulacra, not doomed to become the unending other-of-the-Other. Finally, this is done so that the philosophical anonymity of the Other yields the place to the humanity of the Stranger.

With the existence (of) the Stranger of the Ego such that we understand it, the point is not to return to existentialism. Here, the Ego precedes existence-as-Stranger and, moreover, it is not confused with it. It is not the Ego that is transcendent to existence, existence is transcendent to the Ego . . . Likewise, the point is not of Heidegger's 'being-in-the-World' because if this is undoubtedly a universal and necessary structure that is valid for any man without exception – therefore it is an *a priori* – it rests in-the-last-instance in the Ego and not in the World, resting in man himself and not in the anonymity of Being.

This solution – the only one to give its full, non-political concept to democracy – will seem either miraculous or contradictory in the philosophers' eyes, simply because philosophy is expressly made to not see the domain of this solution, inalienable Identity, namely 'Identity-of-the-last-instance', which forms the real grounds of the I. This Identity, with its own logic, the Determination-in-the-last-instance which declasses Ego-xeno-logical Difference, is an absolute non-philosophisable. It is this absolute non-philosophisable that we must describe in its status to resolve the problem that is otherwise unsolvable, the problem of the Stranger and the problem that we in full innocently call 'intersubjectivity'.

If the Ego, such that it must be thought *qua* Ego, is real before being, if the Ego escapes from the Greek being as much as from the Judaic Other, then the Ego is the chance of an experience of man as I and as Stranger that is neither Greek nor Jewish. Not more than the I is the Stranger accountable to the Greek - the Stranger is not the barbarian - or to the Jew - the Stranger is not the pagan or gentile. This is the meaning of an immediately human science that acquires a really universal concept of man as I and as Stranger: a non-Greek I without being anti-Greek and a non-Jewish Stranger without being anti-Semite. It is sufficiently universal to escape from this disjunction and, generally, from the antinomies of the judgement of humanity.

This apparent equality of treatment means that, in its order and in its own way which will have so fascinated our contemporary thought, Judaism represents a problem of the original Other but centred on the sole defence of man rather than on a science that would also integrate this defence, and finally without further theoretical value than the Greek and ontological treatment of the I and Identity. In both cases, it concerns an assumed autonomy of Transcendence: either the auto position of transcending under the form of Being and philosophy in general *qua* metaphysical; or a quasi-auto-position of the transcendent, or the Other, of an absolute, inverted 'position' adapted to the Other, and what involves suffering for this 'position'. Therefore, it belongs to the meaning of a human science to lift this auto-position as to the I and as to what subsists of it in the Other. I and the Stranger can be subtracted in this way from the ethno-religious traditions that could exclude the Stranger or, rather, reclaim the Stranger and announce them as their own possession. The realistic content of the Stranger and the I is their undivided force irreducible to decisions and prohibitions, refusing to dissolve themselves in the phantasms of Being or letting them be the hostage of the Law.

That one such science of man-as-Stranger represents a destruction of the presuppositions of Philosophy and the Human Sciences is seen from their postulates and the treatment that the science makes them undergo. The specificity of Ego-xeno-logical Difference is indeed to not be content with the postulate that would make either an infinite multitude of Strangers or an absence of Strangers correspond unilaterally or indifferently with the identity of Myself-as-the-last-instance; but it is content with adding to the I a second postulate which modifies the nature within the I and specifies that to any I corresponds henceforth reciprocally and constitutively one and one Stranger alone, thereby even instituting relations of war or rivalry between them and transforming the I into a Stranger for the Stranger and ready to declare war with them. The critique of the ego-xeno-logical construction of philosophy must therefore pass through the elucidation of these two postulates that determine every philosophy as to human relations, through the establishment of a 'theorem of democracy' which grounds, on the contrary, a theory of humans as Strangers *de jure* – a term that can only be said in the multiple. It is obviously to give 'political science' its genuine object. 'Political science' only has for the moment philosophical objects, phantasms and statuses issued from the transcendental illusion that feeds any philosophy. Political science will receive its object from this 'human first science' that provides it the rigorous concept of the Stranger. One of the effects of these investigations is to establish a political science that is grounded on the Given of man-as-Stranger(s); and, consequently, on a non-political given. Current political 'science' is essentially vicious or auto-positional: it is given already political objects – the Contract, the City, Power, Justice, the Rational Subject, the Prince, Proletariats, and so on . . . – and is thus content with making the philosophical circle revolve once more. By elaborating under identically transcendental and scientific conditions the non-political concept of the Stranger, by constituting the Stranger as the cornerstone of a non-political theory and pragmatics of democracy, we are given the means to constitute politics into an authentic science in turn: it is enough for it to treat this concept of the Stranger as the object of a theoretical and no longer philosophical hypothesis in accordance with the materialised provided by said 'political' philosophies which are realistically meta-human.

Demonstration of the Theorem of Being-Stranger

To demonstrate the theorem that says that the Ego as such is the 'Other' but in-the-last-instance alone and the only rigorously posited Other, we must proceed through several points, even if it means reflecting later on regarding the following method and the nature of the argument.

1. As an absolute given, we can posit that which, *par excellence*, may fulfil a function of a really first given without itself being defined in its essence by priority, and therefore without a philosophical-type of pre-supposition: the Ego as Real Identity, non-decisional in general, that is, as much non-positional as non-decisional. Here, the nature of the argumentation is already important. It cannot be a question of a philosophical type of given: it would already have the 'dyad' or 'coupling' form, it would be a givenness (an act or operation) as much as a given, a position as much as a posited, a mixture assuming it already divided and therefore not simply given, a 'first principle'. To the contrary, we posit the Ego as Identity simply given without more [*plus*] and without less [*reste*], given not only without position but without givenness. Therefore, it can only be a question of one term that is philosophically undefinable and

indemonstrable: the object of a hypothesis or an axiom (no doubt real, not logical) rather than a metaphysical-type of absolute or a philosophical notion in general. It is also a question of an axiom called 'real', or more exactly 'transcendental': if it posits the non-positional Ego in-self [*en soi*], it is itself second or determined-in-the-last-instance by the Ego (its 'object', see Chapter I).

Indeed, the *ego-logos* can do nothing but divide and lose the constitutive identity of the Ego. The Ego escapes from ego-xeno-logical alienation when it is left-being-given as non-decisional immanence and when it coherently is posited as an ontologically undefinable and indemonstrable notion, in a simple axiom, rather than as one of these half-absolutes of philosophy that are relative-absolute mixtures of the already divided given, an already alienated beginning, and an already lost origin. Here, the Ego is not posited with the status of the an-hypothetical hypothesis that is always the real content of the philosophical-type of absolute (even when philosophy claims to begin with an 'absolute' or apodictic fundament, it does nothing but sublate and interiorise presuppositions bound to the divided or decisional state of its beginning). On the contrary, the real identity necessarily fulfils the conditions to also be an absolute or first starting point this time in the sense where it is the object of a scientific-type hypothesis or axiom nevertheless determined-in-the-last-instance by its object and no longer in the sense of the absolute or apodictic fundament that refers to the previous philosophical and Aristotelian, onto-logical and intuitive form of the axiomatic. Rather, the *Ego sum* (is) given by a system of axioms, but by the axioms of a transcendental *mathesis* rather than by geometric-transcendent type axioms as Husserl objected to Descartes. The first axiom to posit is therefore the following: I (am) real before being [*Je (suis) réel avant d'être*]; that is, in meta-linguistic terms: the 'I', the 'Ego' 'is' real before saying 'I am' [*'Je', 'Ego' 'est' réel avant de dire 'Je suis'*]; and more rigorously in accordance with the things themselves: I or the Ego (am) (and not 'is') real before saying 'I am' and determines this saying [*Je ou Ego (suis) (et non 'est') réel avant de dire 'Je suis' et détermine ce dire*].

2. A methodological rule that concerns the use of the Ego and its status as a real axiomatic given rather than as a meta-linguistic term is drawn from this position of the problem. The greatest danger here awaits the transcendental thinker and it is the case in saying – this time against Husserl – that we are on the ridge line where everything can be lost. It serves nothing or nearly nothing, indeed, to posit the immanence of the Ego if it is to surreptitiously return, as has happened in certain 'philosophies of Immanence', to its objectivating and transcendent contemplation, to a still philosophical and meta-linguistic use of this Identity that one would once again confront with the Other or

with the World, reconstituting one of these dyads that the philosopher soars over, that he accompanies and dominates as a third term of synthesis. If the science of man is radically transcendental or immanent, if it is not an egology that immediately alienates the Ego within the *logos*, then the Ego must remain the unique point of view and guiding thread of all reasoning, precisely of all knowledge of man himself and consequently the Stranger that I am as known. What may I infer from the Ego, this is the problem, if I currently and in a 'performative' way put myself in Myself and if, ceasing to contemplate myself as a new foreign and unthinkable object (while I am nothing but ontologically indemonstrable and undefinable), I remain within the interior of myself and think myself without nevertheless leaving myself? To respect the law of this radical performativity, we thus write in that which follows, at risk of complicating the intent of the demonstration: I am able [*Je peux*] or the Ego is able; I am or the Ego am; and not 'I can', 'I must', 'I is', and so on . . . that is, we will again abandon the objectivating and meta-linguistic philosophical style, except to reprise it later on for reasons of the ease of reading.

3. Indeed, let us suppose that I or Ego, *qua* Ego and not *qua* the philosopher speaking of the Ego, asks myself how I am, which is my being, and how as well I am able to think myself, think this Identity that I (am) whereas, as an Identity that thinks, I am unable, by definition initially, to exit from myself, to alienate myself in an Other that would be assumed already-there? If I want to think (my) Ego, to think 'myself' whereas it is I alone who thinks, I must undoubtedly conclude that I am not able to objectivate or alienate myself, reflect myself or posit myself before myself and, this is the same thing, to necessarily conclude that 'my' thought is other-than-Ego. I am obliged certainly not to attribute myself with exterior properties like as to a subject, but to posit my thought or my representation of Myself as exterior, definitively displaced or shifted, unilateralised, in relation to Myself: as a non-One or non-Ego. If the Ego is, then the thought of the Ego is outside the Ego all by being thought from the Ego - therefore, probably without the Ego being the object of this thought. It is related to Myself without, for example, alienating myself there, without therefore it further being an accidental property reducible to an Ego-substance.

Let us take this up somewhat differently. Take the Ego *qua* philosophically indemonstrable, *qua* 'first term' which stops being a philosophical-type principle or postulate: What then results for the *cogitatio*? By virtue of the axioms of the Ego, it stops co-belonging or co-determining it. The problem will no longer truly be Husserl's transcendent and inessential problem: discovering a *cogitatum* well within the *cogitatio* without bringing back into question the final co-belonging or ultimate reciprocity of the Ego and *cogitatio*. After having discovered the un-objective Identity of-the-last-instance in the heart of the Ego, it will be on the contrary the dissolving of the classical amphibology of the Ego and the *cogitatio*, assuring the rejection of the *cogitatio* outside of the Self in order so that the thought of the Ego – the *cogitatio* that would take it as an object – would not be an objectivation of myself.

What is this argument that allows one to conclude from the 'Self' thus experienced from the exteriority of the *cogitatio* to the Myself? Or again (because the *cogitatio* will be intrinsically human as the Ego that I am), to conclude from the exteriority of the Other, from the Stranger (to) the Ego? This argument is simple: it is based, as we have seen, on the nature of Myself and never to be an object upon which we reflect, to be, on the contrary, myself the real or absolutely performative 'subject', that is the performed-of-the-last-instance as being the Real itself which 'thinks' without being doubled in this function by a philosopher. The resource of the argument is what we have called the radical immanence of Myself (and not of the I) [*de Moi (et non du Moi)*], the fact that I cannot alienate or exit from myself to reflect myself; or again, my performativity, or more exactly my being-performed-without-performance, that is, my always current 'presence' in the act of thinking. Indeed: if I am an Identity that remains in myself, it is enough that I also want, no doubt from the start for philosophical and/or empirical reasons, to think and represent myself, for example in my relation to the World or Society, or that I want to 'exist' so that this thought or representation would be rejected outside of Myself: as that which has never been Me, as this where I am not alienated, as the absolute Stranger (rather than relative to Myself). Therefore, I will say that I Myself, who by nature remains in-Myself, I do not concretely bring myself into existing except outside of myself or under the form of the Stranger who, of course nonetheless, I and I alone am – therefore in-the-last-instance – and the one who is my very Being or my Existence. I do not become an existent or Stranger, I am so; or more exactly: I am not existent or Stranger immediately, but I also am so, in a second time or in addition, to my real essence, of a supplementary and new structure where I will not fade away, but which is the mode upon which I probably exist – and I will examine this later on – in accordance with that which is exterior to me, the World, Society, Language, or the Representation that I receive of myself. The formulae advanced above for the Stranger – the '(non-)One' or '(non-)Ego' – indeed hides one ambiguity. We must distinguish between the fact that the thinking (of the Ego) appears as the Stranger themself, and the cause of this fact, which is the Ego, to think myself, being given my unreflected radical identity, without a constitutive representation, must reject or 'posit' this thinking (outside) of myself as Other(-than-Myself) – not to reject it as an exteriority and thus redouble it, but to posit it as this exteriority that it is as soon as it is no longer Myself.

We, Ego, rather – not the 'we, philosophers' who are still a transcendent and totalising 'we', a false first-person-plural that must be 'our' point of view here – the Ego sees finally appear the first possible form of the 'Other', the originary phenomenon of the Stranger, which I will conclude from Myself, that I have not taken or extracted from the exterior – even if the project of thinking the Ego presupposes an exterior or occasional cause – that I have not simply demarcated or ideally transferred from the Other-person-in-the-World. The Ego limits itself (= I limit myself . . .) here to carry out the only 'genesis' of the Other that would be possible to me under the form of an inference from the given of my Radical Identity. In reality, what the Ego will describe is as much the Being as the Thought of I (the of: objective genitive, insofar as this relation to I still exists under this form). This could mean (provided that I (am) independent of the am, the One independent of Being): being that I am, then I-also-am-a-Stranger. Better yet: being that I am, therefore I am able 'to be'; that is, very exactly (Being being here the Other of the One): I am able to also an Other (Stranger), for henceforth – one will measure the distance from Cartesian egology or another: *being that I, then I am able to be or I am eventually, and, if I am, I therefore am or exist as Stranger.*

This conclusion precisely derives from the absolute autonomy of I as a first term, independent of Being or the Other. Being, the am, is detached from the I, and passes with the Stranger 'on the other side' or is unilateralised by the Ego. However, this inference is conditional ('I am able to be') but it is not so for the Ego, which is not the object of an inference; rather it is for Being or the Stranger. Firstly, to be more rigorous or give less grip to philosophical and egological re-interpretation, it is suitable to suppress or limit the 'if . . . then' syntax that exists nevertheless as secondary, and to replace it with the 'being that . . . therefore', the 'being that' introduces the first term axiomatically posited rather than the philosophically auto-posited Being; the 'therefore' introduces the inference of Being or the 'am-Stranger'. This inference is this time non-circular or non-philosophical, remaining immanent and transcendental, not leaving the Ego when the Ego says: being that I, therefore I am able to think or Be. In all cases, the 'able to' records the conditional character of the inference that presupposes an occasional cause to go beyond the Ego and infer Being. It is at the level of the occasional cause that the 'if' intervenes: granted the Ego (real-One, performed-without-performance) if the Ego thinks now, then this thought of the Ego is Being or the Stranger (the 'am-Stranger').

It is decisive to note that Ego, when I think or speak, (is) not divided and rejected outside of myself (speaking, thinking, being and writing does not mean my death or my half-death); it is thinking and speaking that are dead, and come thereon after Me, without which, by definition, I would be divided. The Stranger, 'in' the instance of which the Ego is able to be said to exist, is not a scission of the Ego and an alienation. I elsewhere exist as-Other or as the thought (of) Myself that is neither Myself myself or the thought-of-Me, the representative thought of my thought, *cogito me cogitare.* There is no reflection in the Ego and, consequently, when the Ego thinks myself (= I think 'myself'), in reality thought is rejected outside of Me as an Other rather than present under the reflected form of the 'themself' and 'myself' [*du 'se' et du 'me'*]. I do not become other than myself. If I think 'myself' as I (if the Ego thinks myself as Ego), nothing but as Identity and not already as Other, then all eventual reflection is rejected into the *a priori* instance of the Other beyond the Ego. Being that I, therefore if I think ('myself') and in particular if I think myself as being, then I also exist or I also am in the mode of Being and therefore, here, in the mode of the Stranger.

Finally, the argument or inference holds to both a transcendental induction and deduction without it being an empirical induction (the Stranger is an aprioristico-transcendental structure) or a logical deduction (the Stranger is real). The Stranger presupposes themself beyond the simple Ego, presupposing themself in their essential structures which are not deducible from the Ego or reducible to it like an accident or a mode is to a substance – this is their relative autonomy. However, they are presupposed without auto-positing themself in the way in which finally a philosophical presupposition would do or tends to do: it is a position in itself relatively autonomous from the Ego and irreducible to it, but which is received or lived in-the-last-instance in-the-Ego where it receives its reality as an aprioristico-transcendental structure.

On the Theory of Strangers as *Mathesis Transcendentalis*: The Real Axiomatic Against Egology

The immanent domain of the argumentation or inference of the Stranger is what we call the Determination-in-the-last-instance, which is nothing other than the causality of which the most inalienable immanence is susceptible: being that the 'Ego' (in the meta-human or meta-egoic terms that we now reprise here) remains in its immanence without exiting itself to contemplate itself, what then results for the rest, for example, that which belongs to thinking the Ego? This causality breaks the inscription of causality within the transcendent horizon of Being; it prohibits transcendence from positing itself as its own element and prohibits it from claiming to draw the reality of this self-position from its unreality. Two fundamental and complementary traits characterise this theory: its immanence, and its deductive nature.

1. The heart of the argument is a transcendental inference within the most unreflected immanence or in the vision-in-One; a deduction, not a decision. The Ego thinks what it is (= the Ego thinks myself or thinks what I am . . . and so on) by using from exteriority, no doubt, for example the statements of Cartesian first egology, but without being grounded upon it; without treating itself as a new objective essence, without reflecting upon the Ego or upon egology, which is nothing but a meta-egoic discourse.

It is capital, as we have seen, to theoretically renounce the meta-linguistic point of view (we will henceforth return to it to simply the formulation), and being placed back in the vision-in-man, to stop considering immanence as a new objective entity that one surreptitiously worldifies [*mondanise*] or rejects into transcendence. It is obviously the condition for the representation (of) the Ego to be rejected outside and beyond it, unilateralised by the rigour of this immanence. If it thinks itself, then it exists as thought or as being (indifferently) without this Stranger-being keeping from themself the force to oppose themself to it, without it being of themself, independently of the Ego, other-than the Ego, being nothing but the Stranger because the Ego determines them thus in-the-last-instance and if at least the question of the Other is posed, for example, under the form: How does one think it? Then, it is only a matter of an occasional cause, because to say that the Ego exists (as) Stranger is not self-evident from the point of view of the most radical immanence (if not 'subjectivity') that renders any other cause simply occasional. Always and in the end, up to the Stranger, it is a matter of the radical performativity of the Ego.

Undoubtedly, I can always say: 'I am an Other' and even 'I is an Other', but these statements are ambiguous, and intra-philosophical most of the time. Here, it is no longer a question of the philosophical 'subject', the Ego of egology, the first person neutralised by their inscription in the universal horizon of transcendence ('I is . . .' or the Ego is X or Y . . ., and so on); but it is a question of the absolute first person and the immanence of their being-performed. If therefore one asks for such and such reason exterior to the Ego that which is and how it is constituted, that which it can think or be represented of it, this can only be pushed back outside itself as an 'Other', of which it sees itself that it can never be its continuous prolonging, but that it is posited as not belonging to it, as 'floating' outside of it in a relative autonomy. Therefore, it is a question of the form of the (non-)Ego or (non-)I.

The nerve of reasoning is obviously a philosophical paradox that volatilises the ego-xeno-logical matrix and its amphibology. This is only if the Ego is not alienated within an already-there Other, not blended with it in a mixture or a difference, or if the I thinks itself as being by essence nothing-but-Identity, or better: it is only if it is the Identity that I am who thinks (and who thinks 'myself' in the sense of: the one that thinks the I), that the I must also be thought as existent and, in general, as Other. The 'Other' or the 'Stranger' is not an already-there and already-given structure at first simultaneously with the identity of the Ego, and yet, it is rather the I that (is) the Other, that is, simply, it is I who am or who exists, therefore who exists-as-Other.

In addition, one will not see any relation of a new kind between the Ego on the one hand and the *sum* (or Being) and the Other on the other hand; but a causality through immanence grounded on the determination-in-the-last-instance alone. No longer 'I am . . . an Other'; but 'I . . . therefore I am or am able to be' or 'therefore I (am) an Other'. It is no longer a question of the traditional Philosophical Decision between 'Being' and 'Other', 'Ego' and 'Being', or the 'Ego' and the 'Other', but the non-egological break by which the Ego gives leave to the *sum* (to Being) and the Other assumed given, and requires, if the occasion forces it, that all of this now finds a new cause, of-the-last-instance, within the Ego. The whole relational structure, the entirety of this conjunctive philosophical web – sometimes Greek, sometimes Jewish – within which the Ego and the Other were enclosed, is rejected outside-of-the-Ego and stops claiming to invest its Identity. When I say – in this new sense –: 'I am an Other', no more will any ego-xeno-logical decision organise and mediate the I and the Stranger. It is now a question of an inference – a real, not logical, one – of the Stranger as a mode of the existence of the Ego where it is not alienated.

2. In the treatment of the problem of the Stranger and first of the Ego, we introduce some axiomatic-type rather than philosophical-type considerations that may nevertheless, for this reason, conserve the immanence of thought more rigorously than the philosophical decision. In first egology, the I and the Other form an indissoluble or amphibological mixture that itself and in each of its terms is at once, from the reasoning point of view, half-given and half-deduced. Let us recall that the very essence [*le propre*] of a human science, here as elsewhere, in the problem of Myself and the Other as in the problem of the One and Being, is to dissolve this confusion. On the one hand, against the mixture, a science requires the following exclusive disjunction: the I and the Other, each of them, either is given-without-being-deduced or is deduced-without-being-given. On the other hand, this alternative is not the entirety or the essence of science, but the effect of it, of its own 'logic', upon philosophical blends. This logic belongs to the unilateral order: being that I, therefore I am or I exist-as-Other. Of course, only one deep modification of the experience

of the Given, a rectification of the philosophical and phenomenological concept of 'givenness' can render necessary this real axiomatic. We must exercise it to dissolve the philosophical amphibology of the Ego and the *sum*, the Ego and the Alter, and so on, and not fall back into the logic of blends. The Other is the mode in which I exist; but, in its essence (of) I, I do not 'exist' or I am not alienated in existence. It is precisely by remaining the Identity-of-the-last-instance that the Ego also comes into existence or into being – into being the Stranger. On their side, the Stranger stops being of the subaltern order of an attribute as Being of the order of a predicate: they are now post-dicates, phenomena which are absolutely originary in their order, but which do not rise and are not said except after the Ego. The Stranger is not related to Myself except as the effect to a cause of-the-last-instance.

We have entered into a universal non-Cartesianism. It is from the *cogito ergo sum* that we retrieve the axiomatic yet transcendental kernel or the one determined in-the-last-instance by the Ego, therefore absolutely non-Cartesian, instead of refusing it as being necessarily of the geometric and regional type (Husserl) or as being precisely an axiom and a refusal to think (Heidegger). In the theory of humans, we neither return to the analytic individual, nor the synthetic and critical subject, nor to the differential superman, nor to their deconstructions (*Dasein*, and so on). Two complementary solutions are then excluded. The Stranger, insofar as they are conditionally or occasionally inferred from the I, but from the I as the-last-instance and through a transcendental rather than logical inference, is not an Other Person contingently found facing Me in the perfectly unintelligible way in which the Human Sciences find and exploit him (in this science of humans, the Other will serve only as an occasional material); however, they are furthermore not idealised and constituted as a mode of the Ego nor even as another Ego (the alter ego). It is useless to invert intentionality for the benefit of the Other for there is no intentionality in the sense that Husserl and his disciples could understand it. The inference is irreversible by definition: it goes from the Ego to the *sum* or *cogitatio*, but in no way in the opposite direction, all by taking the occasion of philosophical egology.

The real-axiomatic method therefore allows one to stop commenting on the *cogito ergo sum* and disengaging from Cartesianism the kernel of immanent phenomenal experience that is the content of what we describe as the Ego (I . . .) and as Stranger (think and therefore am). The theory of humans is a transcendental *mathesis* (theoretically and identically pragmatic) that excludes philosophical ontology and its egological avatar. It is even less than 'grey ontology', for if it defines being through (egological) knowledge that is taken up in it, the Ego-without-*logos* defines the Being itself (of the Ego) by determining-it-in-the-last-instance under the conditions of an absolutely immanent knowledge.

Therefore, here, the *sum* is no longer first in the metaphysical sense where it is in Descartes' first egology. It is not exactly the Ego *sum* that is, but rather the Ego in its being-Performed, while Being is second: I am not able to think myself as being except as Other-existent. Therefore, we will not say in Sartre's ontological style that existence precedes essence, but the Ego precedes its existence as Other-existing, and yet the Ego in its identity is no longer anything of a human nature or this residue of human nature that the transcendence of existence is.

Thus, the Ego itself determines how 'its' being, that is, Being, is torn from its metaphysical auto-position and ontology, and how it now enters into the vast sphere of the 'Other' as (non-)One or better yet of the Stranger. The radical destruction – that is, theoretical pragmatics – of onto-ego-logy assumes that the ontology of the Ego be lifted and liberates a being (of) the Ego, a *sum* inferred from it. Being no longer serves as a seat or a foundation of it and the I no longer is a mode of it in the way of the classical individual, the modern subject, or even *Dasein*. Being stops being blended with it just like a copula or an absolute predicate would ultimately be as it is in the philosophical thesis concerning Being. It is enough to posit Being as first given in the non-metaphysical mode – therefore outside of any egology – so that the *sum* stops being its predicate, the predicate of absolute position, and that it would be inferred as a second region of reality or experience after the Ego and unilateralised by it. The Ego is neither posited nor mediated by Being; it is Being that is 'posited' after the Ego as the main ingredient of this dimension of the Stranger that is added to it without it being alienated there. Rigorously, with Being philosophically being the 'absolute position', it cannot be posited once more in its own mode – this would be to return to philosophical auto-position or sufficiency. By contrast, it is determined in-the-last-instance by the I.

Therefore, not only the 'meaning-of-being' of the Cartesian *sum* but the *sum* itself ensues from the Ego, rather than the inverse. It is no longer even its meaning-of-being in general that is in question and that would remain unthought in the heart of the Cartesian *sum*, but rather of its real or non-donative phenomenal constancy. It is a globally non-Heideggerian solution: the real constancy of Being is not only shown indeed on the side of the *sum* rather than Being in general, but it only appears when the (I) am is determined in turn by the Ego and deduced from it, which eliminates all risk of metaphysical subjectivation of its meaning. The end of the convertibility of the Ego and Being to the benefit of the priority of the Ego has this effect that Being, the *sum*, becomes the Other – which is also human but in-the-last-instance – therefore the Ego, in the mode of which is the Ego rather than the foundation, itself unstable and divided, of the Ego. The Ego bears the absolute first mask of Being and only advances in the flesh of the Other. I cannot manifest myself on the edges of the World or philosophy, society or history except dressed as the Stranger. The Stranger is not so much the one who arrives facing Me than the way in which I arrive in the World.

The Stranger Within the Bounds of the Science of People

The proposed solution responds to no politico-ontological partisanship. It is pre-drawn within the restitution to man of his essence and acquired by a science and a pragmatics. Philosophical egology is only an idealisation of the unthought phenomena of humanity and alterity, certainly not a rigorous knowledge of man. It is content with registering raw or ontic data, only elaborating upon them through operations of reversal and displacement – of the *cogito* for example – which assure the reproduction of philosophical circularity and do not bring about to it any form of scientific-type of inference. The Determination-in-the-last-instance allows one to add the Other to the Ego without alienating the Ego, without claiming to constitute the Other. It suffices that I think myself as Identity-of-the-last-instance so that I also think myself as existent or as Stranger. If the destruction of Ego-xeno-logical Difference pursues no philosophical decision of a new style, it is the necessary effect of this rule: do not speak of man except in the strict extent where we may know something about him. Not: *What is man?* an insoluble question of all philosophical prejudices and mirages; but: *What may I, Myself, know of man?*

Therefore, it is no longer a question of a utopia without efficacy. It is not another World, one that is more pacified and dreamed of, that we substitute for a pitiless World. It is both simpler and more fruitful: we will only define the conditions of a rigorous and real thought of man as-I-and-as-Stranger. Perhaps here it is only a question of establishing a science of humans that would distinguish itself as much from the existing Human Sciences as philosophy. Together, they postulate that war belongs to the essence of man and even the knowledge of man. This is a mirror game, between them, and between them and their object, that the Stranger will unsettle. We transformed the question: *Which one is the Stranger?* into a problem, and the solution to this problem consists in saying: the Stranger as they are is especially not the Other encountered in the World under social, political divisions, and so on; it is I who I is in-the-last-instance the Stranger. On this basis, a democratic knowledge of man becomes possible.

Indeed, the most originary Stranger, the one who appears for the first time or under their phenomenal form, is not the idealised double of 'intersubjective' relations such that they have a place in the World. Undoubtedly, there are still now two forms of the Other, but in a new, non-specular distribution because their philosophical economy is entirely rejected onto one side alone, in the worldly Other which only serves as a material to elaborate the immanent phenomenon of the Stranger. The Stranger is not another I, an alter ego, a formula of which one sees that it does nothing but redouble the question of the I. One science fixes its task on the contrary to describe the first and definitive appearance of the Other; and it is not another I nor an other Other, because it is rather the I insofar as I am - therefore as I also am - the first and only Other. Only I am able to be the Stranger on this earth, and it is by essence that man is the Stranger in history but further than History, not by the coincidences of History. I alone - and not the Other that presents himself as the adversary and to which I alone deal with in the World. However, I am not able to automatically be a Stranger; there still must be the cause 'in general' of the World and I must come to be, not in-the-World but in accordance with the World and its occasion.

Rather, it is a matter of a founding theorem. If man is indeed this Identity who exists-as-Stranger, one really human science will consist in taking the concepts of the Human Sciences as simple data without human relevance, and to elaborate and rectify them in accordance with this theorem that says nothing of what happens in the World in fact to the Other, but that which by contrast conditions the knowledge that man can take of it. This theorem opposes the infinite philosophical guerilla war that the Stranger is an objective phenomenal structure or a state of things that defines the human complex, a specific sphere of reality of which philosophy has immediately 'forgotten' the identity. It is a scientific-type of discovery, rather than a new philosophical thesis. Far from otherwise being a *factum rationis*, the Stranger refers to the most internal essence of the Real, that is, man. We have 'assumed' to describe him, we have treated as absolutely given rather than 'assumed', man alone outside of his historical, social or other insertion: we have made him into a hypothesis and have inferred the Stranger from him. The Stranger is not a conceptualised or interpreted 'fact'. Philosophy, the Human Sciences and Judaic thought as well, which takes them 'against the grain' [*à rebours*], do not dispose of a human concept of man except through appearance and perhaps through lying. It does not suffice to speak of man to 'think man'. His experience is the experience of images or representations that they manipulate - above all the first two - to their benefit. What they are dealing with is a supposed human, a transcendent thing alienable by themselves and for their benefit, and traced from the data of alterity. To be a Stranger can and must be said to the contrary of any individual beyond ethnic and political cleavings: it is a transcendental trait that is nevertheless of-the-last-instance, that is, here, of the scientific-type. In philosophy, the I partially becomes a Stranger (for another I), but it exempts itself and essentially makes an exception for this status, while the universality of the founding theorem of democracy says that the reconciliation of the two worlds, their identity, cannot be done except in-the-last-instance, that is, that it is actual under this form and determines the future.

The Identity of the Stranger

Which one is the Stranger? 'Stranger-Existing' – only one tenant, existence being the Other itself, in flesh and bone – what does this concretely or descriptively mean?

1. The Stranger is not first and of themself, by auto-position, a transcendent absolute, an Other-than-I; it cannot be a matter of this 'First Other' apparently found in the World and which is the counterpart to the First Ego of egology: the Other is inferred as Other (of) Myself, that is, from Myself. Yet, without either being diminished or reduced by the former, constituted by the I, being of a relatively autonomous essence. The Stranger's being-inferred is precisely that which assures their autonomy and specific reality against the philosophical attempts at their constitution. To think myself as Other is to sufficiently think myself as the Other itself and as such, as the Other than I. Stranger-existence is neither a mode nor an attribute, nor a property, of the Ego.
2. Yet, it is rather I who, far from escaping alterity and the status of the Stranger, is this Stranger. No double, I am only the Stranger in-the-last-instance – this nuance saves my Identity. The Ego is the place where I see the Stranger who is not the Ego. I therefore do not think myself as Identity and in an antinomic way as Other. First, it is the identity that (itself, or myself) thinks 'in' myself, and it is the one that in-the-last-instance thinks (itself, or myself) as Stranger. The Stranger is not an attribute or a predicate taken from the exteriority of Society. Even if the doing of Other-existing does not affect the identity of the Ego itself, it is rather I and I alone who is also this Stranger.

A double impossibility within which philosophy is enclosed and ego-logy is responsible for directing is thus lifted:

1. The I would be nothing but I without being, also, an Other. In this case, the I is reduced to being affected by the Other, limited and unsettled by

it from within and without as if the Other was . . . another, the Other-of-the-Other. The I not being also itself and in-the-last-instance the Other, it is therefore at war with it. The true solipsism, more profound than the solipsism of Descartes or Husserl, is here - where it touches all philosophy - within an I who, susceptible to becoming Other by identifying itself with a transcendent Other, is never of itself, *de jure* and radically, this Other. Solipsism and war are complementary; solipsism is not the lack of the Other - it is not missing because it wages war with solipsism - it is the refusal of the Ego to consider itself also as Other - 'also', that is, 'in the second instance', otherwise being the 'last instance' of the Other.

2. The Stranger would have no identity because they are required and cynically requisitioned by philosophy in the subaltern functions of affecting, hindering and breaking the I, that is, a certain identity itself transcendent. The philosophical I has two complementary attitudes towards the Other. Either it refuses the Other its own identity, or it gives it one but not in-the-last-instance: immediately or through representation and delegation, always by force (the 'alter ego'). Either it excludes it from itself and makes it into its enemy; or reduces it specularly and subjugating it - dividing it into the Other-of-the-Other, making it lose its simplicity. Philosophy oscillates in this dyad, describes this invariant, nuancing or redividing it; redistributing the terms within this confrontation that it is occupied with managing like an interminable war. We need the most immanent Human I to save the Other from the secondary tasks for which philosophy requisitions it (social, political or textual critique, philosophical deconstruction, and so on) without granting it an identity, even if it were in-the-last-instance; to save it from its philosophical counter-employment, from its ontological mis-use.

The cause of the Other - for there is now a cause of the Stranger in all senses of cause, it is the condition of their non-subordination to the I and peace - is no longer auto-position, but the Identity-of-the-last-instance. Because the Other would have a cause does not mean that it is nothing but a part, member or a fragment of the cause. The determination-in-the-last-instance is the only cause that lets-the-Stranger-be as Stranger. It is a matter of a phenomenal Stranger, their phenomenon that constitutes their real 'in-itself' alone, their inalienable identity, so that it is lived in-the-last-instance by the I no longer as aggressive and dangerous or as the agent of the Gift or the Call, but in its qualitative and specific being. It is by force to divide and redouble them, to receive them a second time, that common sense and philosophy experience the Stranger as good or dangerous, by force of redoubling and magnifying their transcendence. A human science *a priori* dissolves the amphibology of alterity and danger – or goodness – and receives the Stranger just once. Social, political or ethnic causes justify this confusion or equation: the Same is the Other and Enemy, the Other and Friend. By contrast, all theoretical reasons campaign for the identity (of) these terms in-the-last-instance and prove that any man is universally a Stranger, that all people belong, as such, to a relative autonomy to the I, and not relative to one another as 'Selves' [*des 'Moi'*].

It is to the restrained and 'blended' xenophilia that belongs to ethics that we will oppose generalised xenophilia outside of any onto-logical limitation. The I and the I alone is filled with a self(-)*jouissance* of the Other, the self(-) enjoying Other 'in' I. This is the element of democracy, as barely Greek as possible, the 'natal' element of heretics and minoritarians. It is worth the pain to note that we do not replace ego-xeno-logical difference with a contrary xenocentrism that is just as poorly thought. The I and the I-existent-Stranger are the two structures whose order – order, rather than hierarchy – must break any 'centrism' and instantiate rather, for example, a 'generalised fractal' conception within human relationships.

Thus, between the Other posited by philosophical excess of intelligibility or constituted by the I and therefore not autonomous or alienated, and the Other posited by Judaic excess of unintelligibility or transcendence that suddenly alienates the I into an I-hostage, science does not have to choose. It undoes – at least for its 'theoretical' account, not in the phenomena themselves – the complementarity of this double excess, their variously proportioned blend. One of the great benefits of this theory is that the multiplicity of Strangers (as we will see, it is *de jure*) is one with their primitiveness and solitude: the Stranger appears only once, in an absolute unicity, compatible with its multiplicity, but never twice simultaneously. The Stranger is definitively Other without indefinitely or continuously being so, without being the-Other-of-the-Other. Appearing to knowledge one-time-each-time without entangling and doubling itself mutually with others, the Ego does not produce the Stranger and the Stranger does not alienate the Ego. The specular philosophical structure of the-Other-of-the-Other that flees such an imaginary (the flight of the Other) exists, but it is now a simple material that can no longer make up the law for the rigorous knowledge of man. The Stranger becomes – in the theoretical order at least, but this is the only chance to transform the World – a positive phenomenal given, more positive still that a phenomenological egology could not think them. They are lived and received – as Stranger – by themself in their identity and in the phenomenal mode of it, but in-the-last-instance: that is, without confusion. It is rather the Stranger who is received or given as they are; but they are not first given in their specific mode to that of the Stranger, and even less given twice like the philosophical Ego. The science of Strangers stops any attempt of an idealism of the Other, that is, as well, a realism, by auto-position, of the Other.

Undoubtedly, the reality of the Stranger is not independent from the reality of the I, yet it is not constituted by the reality of the I. It forms a phenomenally original, relatively autonomous region of the real and it suffices to describe to refute Philosophical Idealism. As the cause is of 'the-last-instance', it is not self-objectivating and does not hinder the reality of the Other, it also conserves the benefit of a position like Levinas': the Other is given as is before and outside of any ontological constitution or givenness; the Other escapes from Being and contributes towards disarming it. However, without this, one would be obliged to subjugate the Other to the Law or make it into the Face: the Stranger is thinkable in the wake of the One (of the Ego) and perhaps as this wake that they leave across the World. In relation to the purest Judaic solution to this problem, it apparently is a matter of an inversion. Instead of the One-I only existing as the hostage of the Other (a 'constitution against the grain', if you will . . .), it is the Other who is not certainly given as a simple effect of the I, but as the autonomous sphere of existence of the I. Instead of the One being the correlate of the first Other, the Other is the correlate of the One – but in-the-last-instance – because the One is real precisely before being first. We need to rectify in priority the description of the phenomenal experience of the Ego, its mode of being-given-without-givenness, to tear the Other from Being as much as from the Law, from humanist constructions in general, whether of the 'subject' or the 'Other Man'. Thus, we conserve the essential benefit of the Judaic solution – saving the phenomenon of the Other by discovering a mode of the given so radical that it precedes any operation of thought yet without being obliged to renounce any intelligibility and confide in the opacity of the 'Most-High'. This is to avoid the ontologico-idealist reduction of the Other by representation at the same time as the absolute transcendence (of) the Interdict, the affect (of) the Unintelligible or Unrepresentable. Man is the only 'being' who may say 'I am the one who is, therefore I am as Other'. Man is the only 'being' who can destroy the ontology that destroys him when he knows himself as the 'One-who-is' or the one who is in-the-last-instance One. The Parmenidean matrix is reduced to the state of a symptom for a non-Parmenidean problem: I and the Stranger are not the Same, we are identical-in-the-last-instance.

The Two Concepts of the Stranger and the Dissolution of their Amphibology

The I and the Stranger no longer designate here two empirical individuals or individuals taken from transcendence and virtually quarrelling, who profile one another as a threat, but two ordered structures who are exactly valid for each-and-every-one [*tout-un-chacun*]. This is why they are no longer *de jure* in struggle nor preventing one another: without a doubt, only I am able to be a Stranger; but I alone am able to conserve the autonomy and reality of the Stranger, no longer claiming to constitute it as philosophical idealism (Husserl) still does but by letting-it-be-given. Inversely, the Stranger is no longer where the I loses itself. The unified theory of man is nothing but a treaty of universal peace between the I and the Other; it is between us a treaty-less peace, a pre-established peace which alone is capable of acting upon the World.

This solution undoes the amphibology of the I and the Other, their convertibility, and even their reversibility. It assures each region of reality their autonomy: absolute for the Ego which is nothing but Ego, and not the Other still; and relative for the Other or for the Ego as-existent or as-being. It forbids the I represent an Other for another I: it is I who is in-the-last-instance the Other. This radical and solitary I, if it is itself also the Other, destroys within its unthought foundations the problem of solipsism, which has no other reality but the reality of philosophy and not more reality than it.

We can certainly still say that we are strangers to one another and for one another. However, this reciprocity is here nothing more than a secondary or occasional phenomenon. We no longer hold onto our reality from this war that sometimes tears us from one another as philosophy sub-tends, from an originary polemo-logical relation, but from our Identity. We do not receive our status as Stranger from outside, through force and as a malediction of history, or even from on high and as through a reflection of glorious divine alterity: we directly enjoy ourselves by enjoying the Stranger that we are in flesh and bone. Man is the only being who, through his radical self(-)identity, has no contraries, but may be by contrast, directly and through himself, a Stranger. To be a Stranger, far from being a malediction or even a benediction, simply defines the being of man and his specific dignity.

This means that the Stranger is not the philosophical and conceptual double, the idealised figure of the phenomena of foreignness and marginality, adversity and goodness, that we encounter in the World. The rigorous concept of the Stranger cannot be a specular reflection or image of the social ordinary. The concept of the Stranger is not itself 'strange', what does this mean? Let us think about philosophy for a moment: it sees a being who presents themself as 'foreign' [*étranger*] and aims for the Stranger through them; philosophy divides and redoubles them by their concept or idea; there are two of them at the same time as there is only one or at the same time as it wants to realise their unity. Here, by contrast, the Stranger appears only once and not twice simultaneously (yet they are multiple, a multiple that is not calculable or not deducible from the Two). Because the Stranger is a unique identity, because they are not an Other-of-the-Other, it is possible to tell them: 'You are welcome' [*Sois le bienvenu*]. How could this peace formula welcome a being who presented themselves twice or under two divided and conflicting forms by ruse or strategy, both by effraction and sublimation?

The philosophical aporias of the Stranger have the same causes as the aporias of the Ego: they come from the position of the problem in terms of a determinant decision, distance or dyad. The Other is first found or assumed given under the form of the empirical phenomena of alterity (the invisible of perception; the signifying difference of language; conflicts of social existence; marginalities, foreignness or resistances of all kinds; and so on). Then, these phenomena are in turn doubled by an instance of a more universal Other no doubt, but which globally protects the same status as these phenomena: the state of blending, reciprocity and conflicting hierarchy with that which is otherwise assumed given as the ego, the self, the centre, and so on. What matters is that these two dimensions of the Other are outfits for the Same, either the second simply extends the first by idealising it ontologically; or, in a more altering, more extra-territorialising way, it is announced in its deconstructive efficacy by the specific operations of reversal and displacement of hierarchy, with the Other being re-marked and extracted from its occultation, and then buried again in a new hierarchy. Despite their force of heterogeneity and dissemination, these operations continue in assuming the first, ontological state of the Other and remain prisoners of the Same, that is, philosophical invariants.

Consequently, we do not call 'Stranger' the Other person such that they are announced or profiled in front of us in social, political or national life: this would be to return to the philosophical situation that contemplates the I and the Other in their confrontation, and which is finally given or assumed given the Other without clarifying its mode of givenness. From this point of view, that of the relation to Society and the World, the Stranger will be I insofar as I also exist or represent myself in accordance with the interrogations of the World as an occasional cause. This nuance is important: the Society which arrives before me with its auto-positional transcendence is not that which gives me my status of Stranger. Society is only the occasional cause of which the I extracts, that indicates and overdetermines this phenomenal dimension of the Stranger or Existence. In the World, it is obvious that there are many phenomena of foreignness, alterity, marginality, conflict and war, but the I has its seat in-itself and not in the World, and it is not even first being-in-the-World. However, being-in-the-World is not totally excluded: it is simply only an occasional, not the main, cause of the emergence, between I and the World, of my existence, that is, my being-Stranger. Philosophers would here say that we defend an 'occasionalist' conception of political and social life. Man in his Identity is real or absolutely autonomous before sinking into the effectivity of social life and receiving the being-Stranger on the occasion of it.

Therefore, there is one essence of the Stranger, the object of one possible rigorous discipline. This is a philosophical paradox: the Stranger is no longer here other-than . . . or the other-of . . .; the Stranger is not relative-to . . . I, like an empirically given and found alterity; the Stranger is now absolute in their order. This important distinction is between a philosophical egology and a rigorous science of the Ego. The first is crossed by the antinomy of the judgement of alterity: the Greek Other and the Jewish Other, or the absolute Other and the Other-in-the-symptom, or the Other of the subject and the Other-outside-of-the-subject, and so on, precisely because it establishes a continuity between an empirical Other and an idealised Other assumed 'in itself'. The second puts an end to these antinomies and the judgement of alterity in general because it discovers that the Other does not belong to the order of a difference, of a *heteros* positing itself, but of a radical phenomenon, before any judgement, received in the mode of the One and that it liberates from the phantasmatic procedure of auto-position. Describing the Other as it is given or in its phenomenon grasped on the basis of its radical identity is the task that is fixed to fulfil the first hallmarks of a science of Strangers.

We have opposed this experience of the Stranger as Other-in-auto-position and therefore twice transcendent with the Other who only appears one time each time and for the first time. It is necessary to more precisely describe this Stranger by comparing them systematically with their philosophical double.

1. The Stranger does not have a raw and empirical, sociological or other first form in the worldly phenomena of alterity or foreignness. Generally (and this trait distinguishes them profoundly from the philosophical or religious Other), the Stranger has nothing of a thing, either a being or Being or a mode of Being. Nothing of a thing or a fact: the model of any fact, even rational and philosophical, is the auto-position of transcendence. Philosophy factualises or fetishises the Other in the-Other-of-the-Other, but what we call the Stranger is absolutely de-factualised, 'simplified' of all auto-position, the simple existence of man as he is. This is why, rather than about the Other, which remains too objective and anonymous, and rather than the Other person, who remains still despite everything a 'category' marked by religiosity, a science of people describes both as Strangers. The Stranger is the revealed as is, without ever being a social or psychological thing of the World nor even an ontico-ontological event. They are within themself, beyond their reality of the Ego, a genuine aprioristico-transcendental structure.

For its reality, this structure is rooted no doubt in the Ego alone rather than in the World or Society; it is an autonomous order or a (lived, human or immanent, non-metaphysical) essence; a sphere of reality distinct from the attributes of the World (society, history, psychology, and so on). However, this does not obviously mean that the structure maintains no relation with it – it is not abstract or transcendent – but simply that, in its human essence-of-the-last-instance, it is not co-determined by the World. By contrast, unlike the 'simple' Ego, the Stranger could not appear phenomenally except on the occasion of the World or its attributes, which here only play the role of an occasional, non-determinant but only over-determinant cause of their specific structure of the Stranger.

2. Therefore, the Stranger is manifest or given – as much as possible – on the basis of social conflict, marginality and alterity that haunt the World: however, they do not interiorise conflict even in their essence as philosophy wants. As an object of science – the Stranger is not an enemy – I am this Stranger – and yet they are not simply confused with me, this confusion precisely being the source of conflictedness. Far from being the philosophical auto-position and idealisation of small ego-xeno-logical differences that form the background of the war of existence, the Stranger prevents the ego-xeno-logical tangle from even going to philosophical sufficiency through which it believes to be able to viciously conclude from itself to the essence of the Other, from its existence to the nature of the Stranger; and it is included in the bounds of this science as simple material.
3. Even if the autonomy of the Stranger in relation to 'my' identity is relative alone (this 'mineness' is not limited to it: I am also this Stranger and in any case I do not possess them but I am so without anything further, that is . . . without 'being' so), one cannot say that they would be relative-to . . . the Stranger in the sense at least where philosophy would think this relativity and relationality as an Other more or less especially exterior to I, an Other-of . . . or an Other-than . . . even an Otherwise-than . . . I . . . From the Stranger to Myself, there is rather a relativity – it is the correlate or effect of the determination-in-the-last-instance, but no relational structure, for example intentional, objectivating and constitutive, and furthermore no 'relation against the grain' of affection, call or prohibition will double this relativity of the effect insofar as it would imply an auto-position. This relativity from the Other to Myself does not itself have the form of an auto-position; inversely, the priority of the I over the Stranger does not mean a primacy or a domination. The Stranger is a specific structure but their identity-of-the-last-instance prohibits them to be auto-positional and relational. The Stranger is an absolutely simple transcendence without folding – we will

describe this later on – they are not given a first time empirically and then a second time essentially; they do not have their place or reality in themself, that is, in the infinite opening and displacement of a circle, but within the One. Other-Existence and Stranger-Existing (and not the 'other' experience . . .) stops being relative-to . . . Myself as to an Other. I am not an Other for the Stranger (that I am) and the Stranger is not relative to Me as one would be for another: but relative-to . . . an identity-of-the-last-instance.

4. The last-instance is the only means to guarantee the autonomy of the Stranger as a phenomenon in their own right, distinct by their structure or quality from the Ego and which we must describe without blending the Stranger with the Ego. The Stranger conceived by philosophy only has a false autonomy and the violence of transcendence or exteriority referred to themselves. It is always possible to dissolve itself in the disorder of ontico-ontological events and regularities to the benefit of Ego-xeno-logical Difference, which, as a Difference that craves itself, craves the reciprocal combat and ruin of the I as much as the Stranger – of man in general. The determination-in-the-last-instance refuses any blend of the structures of the I and the Stranger, prohibiting their mutual dissolution, for example the contemporary form of their convertibility such as their entanglement, exchange and mutual 'dis-appropriation': here, there is only a play within the invariant limits of philosophy, and this is always the case, the Universal Master or Authority of authorities that, throughout Ego-xeno-logical Difference, draws a benefit of a so-called 'appropriation' and its displacements. More generally, if philosophy redoubles, fetishises or factualises the Other, philosophy makes it into an adversary. As if there were not already enough conflicts in the World, philosophy magnifies them with its own existence, for it knows that the Master is nothing but the master through the controlling of conflicts (for example, peace as metastable equilibrium). The de-fetishisation of the Stranger passes through the description of a structure of existence, as we have said, that would be non(-)self-positional; this does not mean without position or without transcendence, and so on, but without the fold towards dividing/redoubling it, to make the Stranger infinitely deep and threatening and to institute it into an instance of 'soaring over', the enemy-who-arrives-from-nowhere or infinite debt. Even if ego-xeno-logical difference will withdraw itself, this does not diminish this fetishisation, but only appears to attack it to reinforce and re-affirm the 'unavoidable' power of the *xenologos*. Only science can *a priori* suspend its pretension or 'validity' and reduce it to the state of necessary data or phenomena undoubtedly, but which it does not reflect nor interiorise through interpretation, reversal and displacement, and so on.

The Body (of) the Stranger as a Subjective Body in-the-Last-Instance and Organon of the Ego

We have chosen to no longer define 'man' in the way of a metaphysical entity and with a philosophical argumentation. The latter takes a foothold upon empirical givens that it continuously idealises (the unitary concept). Among these givens, and this definition, the body-form is certainly fundamental, and it oscillates between the object-body and the body proper. There is no philosophy or Human Science that investigates a unitary concept of man as a body, where the idealised body - image, form, surveilled or contemplated concept - appears to exhaust human reality as a whole. Thus, there can be no question of proceeding within a science of humans and interiorising once again the imaginary paradigm of man as a transcendent 'body' whether objective, subjective or both at once - or any other distribution - depending on the variable yet each time definite proportions. However, let us suppose that we still define the specific essence of man, the sphere of Being or the Stranger, by the 'body' in order to give a body to the Stranger. On the one hand, the non-positional and non-donative Ego is not itself this body, but rather the cause of the body, its subjectivity-of-the-last-instance. This sphere of the body (of) the Stranger is, truly speaking, de-realised. On the other hand, regarding this transcendental body that is real-in-the-last-instance alone, there is no unitary concept that mixes the empirical givens (including the 'object-body') and their idealisation within a mixture, but a non-auto-positional and non-auto-donative objective essence specified and determined by the variable knowledges produced concerning it.

What we will call, as well, the body of man will therefore no longer be a physiological, anatomical, social, economic entity, and so on, idealised from elsewhere; a regional entity finally identifiable on the basis of empirical givens. However, the body of man is a universal aprioristico-transcendental, supra-regional structure independent of any empirical givens, even if it were natural and biological, but whose knowledge will depend on these givens depending on a relation defined as 'occasional'.

Therefore, we must change hypothesis: instead of thinking the body from itself, through the auto-position of empirical givens, and to attribute a folding upon itself and a sufficiency - a Principle of the Sufficient Body - that re-establishes philosophy in its laws, we will infer the body (as the Stranger) from the real cause, from the Human-Ego-of-the-last-instance, except to then determine it in accordance with its knowledge. This is the only means to tear the 'totality' of the human from the soul/body metaphysical hierarchy, which phenomenology (Husserl, Merleau-Ponty, Heidegger) did not know how to really renounce like a poisoned heritage, and which we know that it is turned back or inverted at will from Descartes to Nietzsche; and to re-establish it within the Ego which gives its radical subjectivity to this body (of) the Stranger, an 'objective' body that is itself not an object.

Therefore, it is through the body – understood no doubt in this transcendental yet non-ontological sense – as determined-in-the-last-instance by the Ego – that we completely exist as Stranger. If the universal, non-political democracy (in the sense that we understand this 'non-') wants to be a democracy that is fully human rather than a supplementary abstraction or a political generality, one of the universals of 'political science', it must be able to provide an absolutely subjective though in-the-last-instance alone concept of the Stranger or their body, and especially reconcile these two determinations by tearing one from biology and the other from politics or history. The identity-in-Ego of the body and Stranger-being is only paradoxical for the philosophical distributions of reality, but it is understood from the point of view of a universal science of humans, of which we see it entirely exceeds, through its scientific-type of generality, the famous Nietzschean 'disciplines' and the production of the modern body by the machines of micro-politics. These remain taken up within the distribution of domination or Authority, in this spirit of hierarchy which philosophy will not have spared man.

A certain number of antinomies and amphibologies of the judgement of corporeality are dissolved. The philosophical interpretations of the body are readied according to a spectrum whose extreme poles are obviously the invariants of the 'subject' and 'object' inscribed within Being *qua* auto-position. Sometimes the objective character bears it, but as worldly or precisely as the object-body (the amphibology of objectivity and object); and sometimes the subjective character bears it, though precisely as subject-body (the amphibology of the subjective-of-the-last-instance and the 'subject'). In both cases, transcendence folded upon itself, auto-positional transcendence, is not only the universal element of the body, but its reality (the amphibology of the real and the objective). It is only the concept of the cause as an absolutely subjective and non-positional last-instance that can make the body avoid this philosophical drowning. Another amphibology must obviously be dissolved as well: the amphibology of the ideal or unreal body and its biologico-social determinations, the specular model of the body in general. The immanent phenomenon of the body is not reduced to the body proper but furthermore not reduced to the immanent Ego: there must be a reserve of the last-instance that changes its concept. The heterogeneity of the body lived-in-One and transcendent – 'subjective' as much as 'objective' – determinations can be affirmed on the basis of the immanent Ego, which assures it of its uncreated, non-produced or non-constituted character, and consequently its emergence in relation to that which rather emerges from its biologico-psychological conditions of existence. This universal body forms a dimension that is not only meta-physical but rather meta-biological that precedes its specific content or its conditions of existence to which the Human Sciences attach themselves. However, 'meta-biological' does not mean that it transcends these ultimate conditions from them or that it 'goes beyond' them by passing beyond themselves, but that it only supersedes them because it constitutes an autonomous order of non-auto-positional objectivity and universality that in some way comes before these empirical conditions by starting from the Ego where it is rooted; it is an *a priori* order which is not however obtained through a process of abstraction.

The body in its essence is rather the Ego, yet outside of any Platonic *ascesis*: it is the Stranger alone that we may be, the only way in which we exist. There is no rejection of the body by the soul; at most, the heretical affect of absolute autonomy of the Ego and the relative autonomy of the body as the Stranger which we are as well assures our relation to the World. The Stranger that we are justifies the World and protects this relation. It is the Stranger, rather than the Ego, who regulates [*enregistre*] the existence of the World and its conditional or occasional signification for the Ego. This is the true significance of the Stranger: the Stranger is the solution to the problem of the I insofar as the I acts through the Stranger upon History and Society, upon their external bounds, that is, posited by science, or insofar as it maintains a finally theoretico-pragmatic relation and no longer a practical violence with them. The Stranger is in some way the transcendental organon of the Ego, its possible acting.

How do we concretely comprehend the body now that we have stopped positing it as first, the first body of philosophical anthropology, even when it seems to want to make the soul dominant? How do we know this rather, know the Stranger precisely insofar as they are no longer first in this sense, but rather second though autonomous in relation to the Ego? It is up to us to give a positive content to the body as Other-existing, having it hitherto defined above all in relation to philosophy.

The Stranger as Void, Law and '*Multitudo Transcendentalis*': The Concept of 'Human Multitudes'

1. A democratic or universal conception of the body as the very dimension of the Stranger can do nothing but empty it of its empirical and regional, in general ontic givens. It identifies it as an abstract dimension, but not obtained through abstraction from the empirical. The void, above all the void that is the

body, however, as we will say it again, is not at all and cannot be confused with a metaphysical and 'Eastern' void. It is the specificity of the Stranger to bring the void where they are, to institute the void around them, to invalidate the empirical norms and constraints, to 'sterilise' the conditions of social, political and psychological existence even if it means retrieving them afterwards but otherwise. Unlike philosophy, the point is not to say that the Stranger inhabits a prior void that they go beyond, or even, rigorously, that they are co-extensive with it – void of margins, dysfunctions, vacuities, illegalities, and so on – but rather it is the Stranger, as the non(-)self-positional and non(-) self-donative body that installs a no-man's land from the Ego to the World. It is not at all a margin, an interval, a differe(a)nce for a peripheral or interstitial minority, but the full and positive void, an abstract dimension which has never been the insistent remainder of a triumphant plenitude.

Therefore, it is not the Stranger who enters by effraction into a centred and closed World; it is the World that is from the outset reduced to the state of a simple occasional cause for the givenness of the Stranger. It is not the State nor politics that forms a body relevant to physics or biology, encompassing the Stranger and integrating them with more or less force and success; rather, it is the Stranger who has since always displaced, as unilateralised from their void, the State, reduced to 'resisting'. It is not the body that occupies a physical or social void; rather, the body is what makes its non-auto-positional void the measure of all things: the Stranger is *index sui* – undoubtedly less than the Ego – and the measure of the State as they are the measure of the universal democratic discourse and, thereby, political discourse. Rather than a 'marginal' conception of the Stranger, it is a question of an 'occasionalist' conception of Society, the City and the State. Rather than a sought democracy that exalts crushed yet resistant Minorities, it is a question of a positive democracy that utilises secondarised Authorities.

2. The Stranger not only brings about a void of reality and a void of objects; it also brings about a void of the Ego, on the one hand, which is in-the-last-instance alone, and a void of the political and social object on the other hand, that it simplifies or de-auto-positionalises. This void possesses one specific content without ever ceasing to be a void: precisely the content of the specific objectivity, universality and necessity of the Stranger – which are all non-auto-positional and non-donative. A universal democracy cannot make the Stranger a risk, an exception or a 'difference', it must make the Stranger, rather, the 'norm'. More exactly, since this dimension is also void of norms like any transcendent object, the dimension is the very element of the law, not the power or custom to obey laws, the doublet of the-law-of-the-law, but

the very body of the law as the non-auto-positional body (or law), the law's essence (of) the law, its ultimate identity. A statement about the Stranger being the identity (of) the law, that is, the law itself in flesh and bone, the humanity of the law, would make no philosophical or political sense, but it has a scientific pertinence and constitutes the only solid basis of democracy: there is no (philosophical) law of the law, no political meta-language of the law, as man-as-Stranger brings it about with him. The power of the Stranger is to dissolve the amphibology of the essence of the law and empirically constituted laws and comprehend the essence of the law as the law's essence (of) the law; it is also to distinguish between the objectivity of democracy and its political or other objects, the formal or politically indifferent being of the law and its social, economic and political conditions of existence. The Stranger brings about with their existence this unilateralising cleaving that passes within all objects of 'political science' and does not let itself be identified by them.

The dimension of the Stranger is particularly rigorous: the Stranger is the emergence and existence of transcendence itself, and yet they are a transcendence without a secret or a fold, without auto-position or auto-justification, and consequently without a model or paradigm. The Stranger is the law without being its own cause, the pure form of the law, but one that does not posit itself. It is impossible to treat the Stranger, unless through a circle, as an idealisation of the phenomena of exteriority and marginality, as their 'remarking' and nuancing at the limits of the social and political body. It is impossible to subsume them under the State, to include/exclude them from pre-existing wholes. The Stranger is not a simple de-limitation of onto-socio-centrism, onto-polito-centrism or ego-xeno-centrism, and requisitionable for these ends. If the Stranger is the essence, the transcendental structure of humanity rather than an exception or a case, they prohibit there being a 'centre', if not at the subaltern level of its phenomena of existence and their auto-interpretation. The Stranger is the universal democratic element, the identity of the democratic, and cannot give rise to a simple political strategy. There exists the equivalent of a categorial intuition of the Stranger, a non-political and non-ethnological intuition because it is grounded in-the-last-instance in the vision-in-man. It is this intuition that theoretically uses – within the 'non-political' science of humans – idealisations and strategies of the integration or exclusion of Foreigners [*Étrangers*], these people who suffer just because they are only half-Strangers, still too 'national' and too 'integrated' elsewhere.

3. The specific content of this void can be described a bit more precisely: the Stranger is the multiple by definition. Already within 'Intersubjectivity' and political philosophy, the singularity extreme and the multiplicity extreme are

said of them; this is true under a still circular or mixed form. However, man appears in his radical multiplicity only when he is considered as Stranger and not only as Ego. The Ego is only the condition of reality or immanence that we must posit, like a first term or rather a hypothesis, to explain and criticise anthropological representations and to elaborate knowledges adequate to the human essence. However, the Stranger is the very existence of man and this existence is *de jure* multiple; this is the real phenomenal content of the old concept *multitudo transcendentalis*. On the one hand, if the Ego is the Real itself, the Stranger is the transcendental that is rooted within it and who is valid for any social or political phenomenon. On the other hand, this transcendental defines humanity as a *de jure* multiple. Why? For the same reasons that the Ego is called One, the Stranger is called Multiple. However, neither in one case nor in the other is it a question of a quantitative or quantifiable determination, but a phenomenal or qualitative determination. Transcendental multiplicities are inconsistent yet more radically than the mathematical and set-theoretical concept of the multiple, which is content with grounding inconsistency on the simple repression of the set-form upon which it continues to depend. The pure transcendental concept of the multiple *a priori* excludes the 'set' without remainder as much as the more meta-physical forms of unity. Finally, as a third determination, as it is a matter of humans and not things (atoms, parts, elements, and so on), it is better to speak of multitudes rather than multiplicities. The Stranger is in the state of transcendental multitudes.

With human multitudes, there can therefore be no question of a multiple under 'Unity', this restrictive conception of the multiple that makes it into a gradient of Unity. Furthermore, there is no philosophical inversion of this hierarchy: to invert the One/Multiple hierarchy for the benefit of either a Multiple/One thesis, or an affirmation of Multiplicities as that which happens between the One and the Multiple, is not to leave things in tact, but to still conserve the anti-democratic spirit of hierarchy, primacy or domination belonging to philosophy. It is to reflect once more the conditions of the political existence of the Stranger within the essence of the Stranger and reinsert human multitudes by force into an authoritarian or pre-existent body or under a unitary horizon, within an onto-polito-logical teleology. The Stranger disqualifies that its multiplicity - precisely because the multiplicity is transcendental, yet in-the-last-instance seen-in-man, therefore radical - interiorise empirical cleavings (nation/people, nation/race, group/individual, state/civil society, subject/sovereign, proletariat/capitalist, and so on). None of these distinctions can institute by definition the identity (of-the-last-instance) of multitudes as the formal being of the Stranger or as the way in which humans are 'in-one-body' [*en-corps*]. This means that they are not the result of any distribution, that this type of multiple is not obtained through division or a prior identity, but that humans *qua* Strangers *de jure* exist-as-multiple in full positivity. Humans do not inhabit a space too great for them and consequently empty in excess, but they are immediately, as multiples, this void. Humans refuse to interiorise transcendent (mathematical, physical, ontological, sociological) models of the multiple; they are not multiple by accident or by history, but by radical reality. This state of things means that they condemn to *de jure* inexistence the political or other forms-of-unity that would claim to be constitutive; the forms of liaison and synthesis: there is no originary social relation in the sense, at least, of the unitary or the reciprocal, binding separated terms. More exactly perhaps, the Stranger implies that man does not exist except as absolutely relational, not as a semi-relation and a semi-term, a relation that is already a semi-unity or semi-unified by its terms, or a term that is already a semi-distance; rather, man exists as the phenomenal identity of any relation (the unilateral duality) and the phenomenon of the multiple (human multitudes). Only the multiple in this sense is absolutely relational and stops being semi-relation as the relation in varying philosophical senses of the word is. The phenomenon of relation is the unilateral duality rather than the bilateral one. Consequently, the problem of a relation to establish and conserve, a social bond, indeed a social contract to maintain and affirm among individuals assumed as atoms, parts or elements ultimately of a 'communicational' structure to operate in order to assure the constitution and reproduction of the social body is a problem that makes no human theoretical sense and is nothing but a philosophical 'question', that is, a problem specific to the State. If human multitudes are *de jure* multiple, solitary yet not solipsistic, and if they ignore in their essence, at least, the requirement of the social bond, the problem of their originary communication is already regulated by their very essence as Strangers. The only 'bond' is the Multitude and exists only as non-social (barring redefining the social through this level of reality), and one will learn within this science to dissociate the amphibologies of the multiple and the forms of unity, humans and the social body, and the being-man-as-multitude-of-Strangers and Robinson. There is no Robinsonade, no anarchism within these concepts which have a theoretical rather than politico-metaphysical validity. On the contrary: if man exists only in the state of the multitude, the reign without distribution of the aporias of political philosophy has ended.

The Stranger as Specifically Human Being

1. The Subject as Subject (of) the Stranger

Before pursuing the description and completing this conception of Multitudes that would otherwise remain abstract a little more, here are some remarks concerning the possibility of a science of people. It is impossible to know this dimension of the Stranger, otherwise relatively autonomous and original, with the immanent Ego alone, without this material – the philosophical or ego-xeno-logical conception – being given, utilised and explained. It is entirely obvious that it is a question of a mixture, as is the case with 'difference' and the Philosophical Decision in general. The problem belongs to the treatment of this mixture in the vision-in-man; of what subsists of this amphibology from the hypothesis of the immanence of the Ego.

Regarding this instance that we call the Stranger, we may say that, seen-in-Ego, their real identity is nothing but 'in-the-last-instance'. However, it directly possesses a proper residual identity that is furthermore not a philosophical synthesis assured by a third and dominant instance. Truly, it is a question of a residue obtained by the unilateralisation (suspension) and unidentification (the givenness of identity) of this ego-xeno-logical mixture-form. This double operation of the Ego is really conditioned by it, but it is not its direct work. What we call the Determination-in-the-last-instance is the Stranger themself since the Ego – of which the Stranger is the 'force' – acts only under the supposition of the Stranger = X as the still undetermined *a priori* trait (which we must not confused with its object, the philosophical mixture, and furthermore not with its completely determined form that is extracted from it). Therefore, to be determined in their own essence and this essence being known, the Stranger presupposes a philosophical material whose givenness and reality cannot otherwise be recognised except in the sphere of the Stranger, not in the sphere of the simple Ego.

What is therefore the specific content of this residue that must complete what we know of the Stranger? We draw the conclusions from these givens that form the real situation of knowledge: on the one hand, the Stranger-in-the-Ego, and on the other hand, the ego-xeno-logical amphibology. Indeed, this residue cannot be constituted by pure transcendence alone assumed empirically abstract from the mixture and opposed to the immanence of the Ego; and on the xenological side alone separated from the egological side, abstracted from it as if the mixture was absolutely and suddenly dissolved, as if it had no specific reality. We do not make a new meta-physical and idealist use of the Ego, and consequently we do not only say that it involves the remainder-less dissolution of the amphibology between the Ego and *Xenos*. We make a scientific-type of hypothesis of the Ego; consequently, we correlatively treat the mixture as having a positive reality that, in a sense, is indestructible, and which we must always take account of in a science. We do not give ourselves the definitive and sufficient right to separate the mixture into its two sides in the pure state: the immanence of the Ego, the transcendence of the *Xenos*. More exactly: only the 'side' of the Ego can and must be 'pure' or radical, an immanence without any transcendence, but the side of the *Xenos* cannot be reduced – unless as the essence (of) the Stranger = X – to pure transcendence even in the sense of the non-metaphysical, the non(-)self-positional and appeals to a certain knowledge and determination from knowledge. Undoubtedly, one can still call this second sphere 'transcendence'; recognising even that it constitutes a void or unreal, and that the specific content of this void is a transcendental multitude. However, this is the specific essence of the Stranger, not yet the knowledge of which they are susceptible to be the object.

So, firstly, what does it mean that the mixture is 'unilateralised' under the presupposition of the Stranger = X? That which is dissolved is not the mixture understood as the proper imbrication of two dimensions like a unity-of-contraries without reality, an abstract and purely syntactic concept; but what is dissolved is the mixture as spontaneous or assumed 'sufficient'. Rigorously, this distinction is furthermore not the nevertheless transcendent distinction between the mixture-form and its content or diversity of dimensions. The point is not to suspend within the mixture its syntactic form and conserve the assumed isolated terms; rather, the point is to suspend its sufficient or philosophical use and discern the residue-of-the-mixture such, at least, that it is then lived-in-Ego or related to the One (of) the Ego. The One (of) the Ego, left to itself, would obviously form 'the void' or be absolutely indifferent to the ego-xeno-logical mixture; however, the point of a science, as we have said, cannot make up the economy of the reality of the material (at least occasional), not more than it can transform the hypothesis of the Ego into a new ontological thesis, but must conceive it as Ego-of-the-last-instance.

In these conditions, it is impossible to be content with the radically non-consistent Multiple to define the Stranger. The Stranger also possesses a concrete body or a flesh: not an empirico-metaphysical one, but defined within a science in terms of knowledge and by the knowledges that are related to it. The two dimensions of the mixture are conserved yet profoundly transformed. Therefore, if they are no longer identified in the mode of philosophical auto-position, they are identified in the mode of this transcendence = X of the Multiple, which still tolerates, differently than the Ego, a certain subsistence of the material. We will not confuse the specific dimension of the Multiple = X, which is *de jure* a non-auto-positional objectivity, therefore unimaginable or unrepresentable (but which is a question of precisely knowing) and the residue left by the mixture. These two things nevertheless unite in their own way, which is: (1) simple, not split or redoubled like auto-position, with the residue specifying the body = X of the Stranger, that is, the Multiple; (2) assured by the Multiple itself that informs and determines this residue; (3) a use (to specify the Multiple) of these terms which are immanence and transcendence, or let us say schematically the 'point' and 'distance', obviously transformed in their definition and not only in their relation; and (4) naturally lived-in-the-Ego in-the-last-instance.

One may call 'flesh' the Transcendental Multitudes = X as they are specified now by the radical identity-in-the-last-instance of the term and relation in the state of multitudes. They are not semi-individual, semi-relational complexes, once more blends or mixtures, but rather identities of the 'point' (and) 'distance', such that they are no longer precisely relative to one another and enchained by their opposing functions (for example, in 'difference'); rather, they are absolutely dispersed, deprived of any form of philosophical or even scientific-regional consistency. A unified-theoretical determination of the essence of man, even if it utilises philosophical concepts, is no longer philosophically intelligible, and it is no longer accessible to the transcendental imagination. This is the case of these entities that form the content and flesh of the void or the body = X. Concretely, Strangers are not persons, individuals or subjects in the transcendent philosophical sense of these words; rather, in any case, they are radical subjectivities nevertheless in-the-last-instance; and that which takes the place of the body - of the body transfixed by this subjectivity - belongs to the order of these entities without difference and woven within the transcendence of the void.

These entities indeed associate two traits as closely as possible, without syntax or articulation, so to speak by way of superimposition or transparency. They are points (of) exteriority, not in any case 'individuals' or 'subjects', nor empirico-ideal bodies that are always divisible, nor '*Dasein*', but rather phenomena lived in-the-last-instance from the exteriority of the Multitudes-state. In addition, they are undivided particles that are distinguished from the Ego itself because they are in the Multiple-state and, without strictly floating within a transcendence too broad for them because they are this transcendence, because they are unilateralised by the Stranger = X and as beyond them, in the same way that the Stranger is beyond the Ego, but without this beyond once more and in turn having the thus redoubled form of transcendence (as is the case of individuals and subjects, and their fold). Strangers are states or 'modes' of transcendence as the autonomous sphere consequently outside-of-the-Ego, constituting an instance other than it. We have repeated it enough: these two things must not be confused - the transcendence or the element of the Stranger is relatively autonomous, but at the same time it is unilateralised as outside-of-the-Ego without it thereby being split/redoubled by its 'unilateralised' state which, well to the contrary, 'simplifies' it.

Moreover, it is suitable to distinguish them as we now find - these long preparations allow us to draw this fundamental conclusion - two very different concepts of subjective identity: (1) the radical subjectivity of-the-last-instance or the Ego; and (2) belonging to the Stranger as an organon of the Ego, a subjectivity in the Multitudes state, an *a priori* structure extracted from the ego-xeno-logical material that nevertheless specifies and is specific to the Stranger and consequently belongs to the sphere of the 'Other' as its own identity, no longer belonging to the Ego; in some way, it is a specific Ego of the Stranger and one that belongs to the determination that specifies their body. Like the rest, the subject is determined-in-the-last-instance by the Ego, but it is the mode under which now the Stranger is presented or given.

2. The Identity Of-the-Last-Instance of the Fundamental and Regional

One last determination of the body (of the) Stranger is still missing. Through the non-consistent Multiple and even through that which it informs from the ego-xeno-logical residue as we will specify it under the idea of the 'subject (of) the Stranger', the body is sufficiently determined, not completely determined. No doubt, these determinations, from the effective or complete human point of view, are not abstract, as if authentic human experience would only begin beyond science: science (here, the Human Sciences) is the first region that intervenes within 'non-philosophy' as a unified theory. However, it is only one region – not a foundation – and there are therefore other ones of which we must now deploy their possibility. They are human, and twice over. On the one hand, science such that its 'non-philosophical' theory may know it has its cause in man: the cause of the Stranger is the same as the cause of science – and it is 'of-the-last-instance'; in a sense, there is hitherto perfect correspondence between these two sciences, and the unified theory of science is identically a unified theory of man. On the other hand, the ego-xeno-logical material of the Human Sciences assures us of the necessary regional reference, but this reference requires being completely explicated if the being of man must be able to explain a series of activities that entirely exceed science towards other regions. The opening upon the World and the recognition of its reality is not exhausted by science, but encompasses technics, ethics, aesthetics, and so on. The science of the essence of man, of the man who precisely has his essence within the Stranger, is more vast or more complex than the science of the essence of science. It posits the same human invariants, but it must posit them in a necessary way to achieve 'building a bridge' between the Ego-without-the-world and the World. The point is not to negate the objectives of theory and its own type of non-philosophical rigour, nor is it to open a dimension that would finally belong to concrete man. On this basis, it is impossible to understand a biologico-metaphysical or psychological, cultural, and so on, determination that is assumed given as 'human' by philosophy and the Human Sciences in the way of an eternal determination that fixes man, and would be but one of the universals of anthropology. A theory of the essence of man, precisely because it is identically a science and a philosophy, proposes to know this essence and can therefore only be given determinations that are indefinitely rectifiable in accordance with phenomena that are themselves constantly renewed by virtue of their contingency, such as the phenomena of technics, ethics, politics, legality, aesthetics, and others still like psychology or social life that presuppose man-at-work. Therefore, if the point is to not list out regions 'more human' than others, it remains to assure in its generality of essence the necessary reference of any unified theory of man to any such region in general in order to explain the identity of the Stranger = X and their specification, what we have previously posed. This science does not possess a general part, but an incomplete one, described previously, and a special part that would complete it, man then becoming an object-of-science only across some of his works. On the contrary, a unified theory assures us of the identity nevertheless of-the-instance of the fundamental and the regional, the philosophical and the scientific, the technical, and so on. Here again and to initially limit ourselves, this character is itself grasped within a certain generality that prohibits us from utilising as material the phenomena provided by such and such Human Sciences as we will do in the following chapter. It is however important to posit as *a priori* of experience the aprioristic reference of the philosophical to the regional. It is explained by the fact that both are reduced precisely as modes of the Stranger, who is not only the object that we must now determine, but the agent or organon of their own knowledge and the one who requires therefore this identification on their own model – but only of-the-last-instance.

With this theory of Strangers elaborated in its broad strokes, what remains is to implement it on the privileged case of psychoanalysis. Here again, it will only be a matter of a scientific-character outline or 'ration', and it is in no way exhaustive and closed, yet it is formed by rectifiable concepts and knowledges.

Chapter III

Principles of Non-Psychoanalysis as the Unified Theory of Philosophy and Psychoanalysis

First Section: The Stakes of Non-Psychoanalysis

First Terms and Algorithm of Non-Analysis

To procure a first serviceable schema of the discipline that we will call 'non-analysis',[1] we can give it a sort of algorithm and some preliminary definitions. Let us recall that, unlike philosophy, which is given man only once but divided in his identity by the structure of objectivation and its derived modes (splitting, difference, dissemination, and so on . . .), a unified theory of man, whether of a political or analytic origin, is given man under two or three identities which are absolutely heterogeneous or organised in 'unilateral dualities'. Firstly, as non-positional and non-donative Ego-in-Ego, which is in general non-decisional, lived (of) identity anterior to any scission or transcendence: this is the instance of the Real, the real cause (of) non-analysis. However, to create an original non-analytic terminological register, with new 'first terms', we must start from psychoanalysis. Thus, we will call the Ego-in-Ego or the Real, defined by its radical immanence, the '*Joui*' and then dually or absolutely distinguish the instance of the *Joui* from *Jouissance* itself. Secondly, as the *datum* of man effectively sundered by Being or the Other or the Unconscious (regardless of the mode of this division, whether it be philosophical or analytic) even if this givenness does not in turn give man as 'object' (he is already given) but as *datum* required by non-analysis in a mode that is no longer of objectivation, but rather of identity. This is only

[1] Another version of non-psychoanalysis with material other than the Lacanian ones that we use here is in the process of elaboration by Tony Brachet, psychoanalyst and philosopher. [Translator's note: The reader may find a version of Brachet's non-psychoanalysis in both *La décision philosophique* 7 (January 1989), 93–110, and Non-Philosophie, le Collectif, *Discipline hérétique: esthétique, psychanalyse, rêligion* (Paris: Éditions Kimé, 1998), 103–112.]

the content of that which is then given in this second mode, which may be the dyad of the Subject-Object, or Conscious and Unconscious, Signifier and Signified, Metaphor and Metonymy, and so on. We will call philosophico-analytic mixture or complex the content of this *datum*, and this *datum* is itself the instance of the symptom. And, thirdly, in the mode of a transcendental and *a priori* structure (in the new sense of these words), a structure which is non-real yet rooted in the Real and which is the phenomenal content of the Unconscious that non-analysis proposes to describe. It is a structure that parallels what we previously, in a context of philosophy and of politics, called the Stranger. This is the place and realisation of the Determination-in-the-last-instance as the causality of which the real-Ego or the *Joui* is susceptible. We will call it '*Jouissance*', distinguishing it from the *Joui* and distinguishing these two concepts from the analytic concept of '*jouissance*' that therefore emerges from the philosophico-analytic mixture.

If we utilise the following acronyms: DLI for Determination-in-the-last-instance, E for Ego-in-Ego, E' for Stranger, Ji for *Joui*, Jo for *Jouissance*, PAC for Philosophico-Analytic Complex, M for Man in the philosophico-analytic sense, S, O, Cs, Ucs, Sr and sd, for Subject, Object, Conscious, Unconscious, Signifier and Signified, the algorithm of this science would be the following:

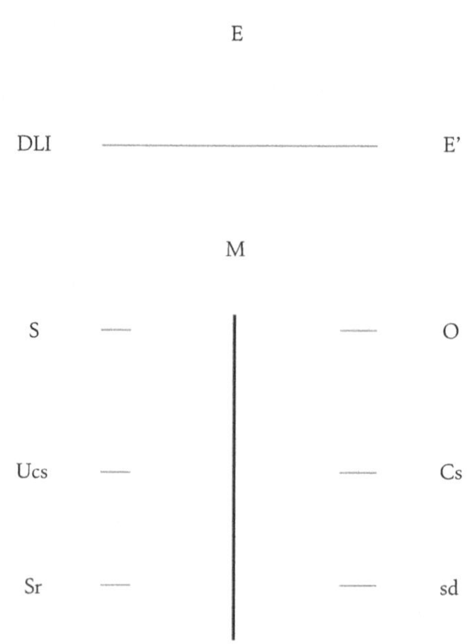

Or, more precisely:

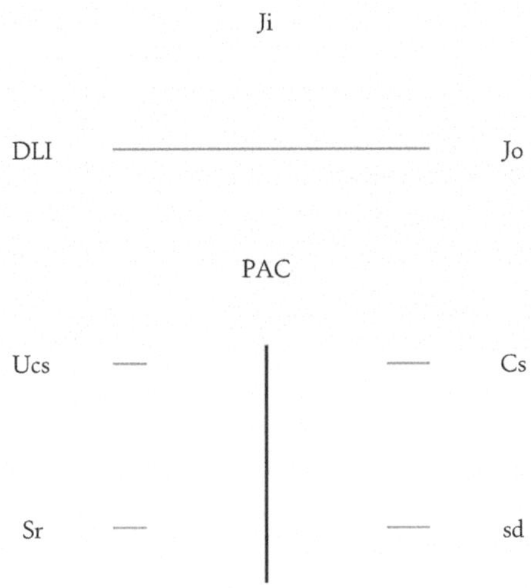

The distinction of the two types of barring is fundamental. The vertical bars indicate philosophical or unitary types of dualities, split identities of the type of Being or Consciousness, but also split by the Other because the distinction between Being and the Other is no longer, here at least, pertinent. The horizontal lines, by contrast, are precisely no longer bars or operations of scission, division, of transcendence in general and hierarchy, but rather the indication of a radical, static and structural duality that does not derive from the scission of an identity and is not destined to return to scission: this is the 'unilateral duality' grounded in the immanence of the One or the *Joui*, equivalent to the DLI. It is a duality characteristic of *Jouissance* and the phenomenal content of the Unconscious, which we will speak about later.

The proposed algorithm will appear necessarily too simple if it is compared to the discursivity it generates. It is nevertheless more complex than Lacan's algorithm: (S1 — S2)/S, and it could only be complexified by what we already said about it, namely the reciprocal determination of the two terms that make man (M) barred or split, a reciprocity within which we must now include from the perspective of this more universal problematic the phenomena of bordering, in-between, folding, lack and hole, even *différance* or dissemination, which are content with negating it without really destroying it.

In that which follows and above all in the following two sections, we use some conventions: (1) 'Real', '*Jouissance*' and 'Unconscious' with capital letters designate their non-analytic concepts, not their philosophico-analytic concepts. They are first names (= proper names + first terms) that will be explained in the second section. (2) We call 'privational' or even 'auto-privational ontology' that which sustains Freudianism and above all Lacanianism, and which is oriented upon an affect of the Real as lack or depriveness. (3) The 'PA Complex' designates the indissoluble mixture of philosophy and analysis, the very material of non-analysis because it is demonstrated as the 'unified theory' of philosophy and analysis. A 'unified theory of the Unconscious' or *Jouissance* takes the correlation – otherwise traditionally recognised in an empirical fashion – of philosophy and analysis as its object.

Non-analysis therefore includes the following instances:

1. First and foremost, the Real as Ego-without-givenness, without an object consequently, an absolutely immanent lived experience which is not found in-the-World but 'in-Ego'. The Real as radical immanence does not have *jouissance* for its phenomenal content, but the *Joui* that is neither impossible nor transcendental; the *Joui* is the real 'substance' of the Ego-in-Ego or vision-in-man, the phenomenal content of the instance of the Real in the 'perspective' or 'attribute' of psychoanalysis insofar as it is now our new material.
2. The symptom, here the transcendental appearance that man is in the World or in analytico-philosophical mixtures such as the Subject/Object, Conscious/Unconscious, Signifier/Signified, and so on. These two instances, the Real and the symptom, are no longer simultaneously presented in a unitary structure like the structure of analysis. Here, the symptom is a simple given (of science) that is necessarily contingent, which does not in turn contribute in determining the specific *essence* of *Jouissance* or the Unconscious and even less the *Joui*. It is the whole system of the unitary aporias as the transcendental imaginary – no longer empirical and psychological, but of a philosophical or analytic form – that is abandoned, not consequently as the object of a science, but as that which would also claim to ground it. Indeed, the antinomies of the Subject and Object, the Conscious and Unconscious, the Signified and the Signifier, this is the Transcendental Appearance that testifies to the worldly, social, and so on, existence of man. Nevertheless, the conditions of objective existence of non-analysis are no longer at the same time as that which should ground – that is, as it happens, as much to ruin or forbid – a science of man.
3. Finally, from these two givens is inferred the instance parallel to the Stranger, that is, *Jouissance* and its mode, the Unconscious, that finds its place in this betweenness and whose structure of unilateral duality is the phenomenal content of the signifier as inconsistent heterogeneity or the 'unary trait'.

One such static duality is that which, even more than *Dasein*, deserves being called 'human reality'. The Unconscious as Stranger or *Jouissance* is the relation that 'reconciles' these two givens without unitary violence.

To specify it somewhat otherwise, rather than a unique-and-divided subject, man is made from the radical identity of heterogeneous phenomenalities that come in pairs without confusion, each time as original, through their mode of phenomenalisation. On the one hand, the *Joui* (of) the Ego, the radically immanent phenomenon of '*jouissance*', is distinct from the conscious and the unconscious. From this point of view or through its cause, non-analysis is an avatar neither of the conscious nor the unconscious, nor of their heterogeneous types of reality: rather, it is non(-)self-decisional and non(-)self-positional. On the other hand, the subjugated split subject of the Philosophical Decision or rather the split subject of the unconscious, even if it were in this case more divided than unified. Finally, the aprioristico-transcendental structure that we call *Jouissance* and no longer the *Joui*, but *Jouissance* as it is inferred in priority from the Real as *Joui* and the occasional cause, the philosophico-analytic symptom. As the organon of the *Joui*, *Jouissance* is the cause-of-the-last-instance of the Unconscious, something, if you will (although we must rectify this expression), like the 'energy' that makes it function. Such dualities that are irreducible though undivided albeit in-the-last-instance make non-analysis a 'dualysis'.

Finally, it is important to specify the theoretical style of non-analysis. The Ego-in-Ego or the *Joui* above the horizontal bar does not function like a 'unitary horizon' or an 'overhang', like a philosophical thesis in the way of that which is 'under' the bar. This algorithm is rather one of a system of axioms capable of inferring theorems. The current, already completed, suspension of transcendence as auto-position (Being, Other) is the work of the *Joui* insofar as its structure of immanence, indeed, can be described by a system of statements or axioms whose terms are taken undoubtedly from psychoanalysis and philosophy, but are implicitly defined by this system and rectified to be capable of validating its radical immanence. The language (of) the Ego or the *Joui*, the language of the Stranger or the Unconscious, is taken from the meta-language of analysis and philosophy, but is no longer, in non-analytic use, a meta-language. It is a production where analysis is required yet to be inserted into a use grounded on the rules of the formation of axioms, the induction and deduction of theorems that ensue from the hypothesis of the Ego-in-Ego, the *Joui* as the radical phenomenon that *Jouissance* elsewhere inhabits.

The new concepts that we will introduce without precautions, bracketing their genealogy, are indeed first terms of axioms rather than philosophical 'concepts' in becoming. Hence, their 'free' position each time by decision, even if they are withdrawn from the conceptual stock of philosophy and analysis, and their indivisible mixture. They are not the equivalent of the letters of the algebraic technique of Lacanianism, but the equivalent of symbols of a conceptual nature taken mainly from Lacanian analysis but analytically or 'Lacanianly' undefinable and indemonstrable. It is obvious that what remains for the systems of axioms and the theorem of non-analysis is for them to generate as a theorem said of *Jouissance*, to give a specific 'non-analytic' meaning.

The following paragraphs belong rather to the order of old argumentations: 'commentaries', 'explanations', 'programme', 'defence' and 'critique'. It is with the second section of this chapter, the term-by-term explanation of the transcendental theorem of *Jouissance* as determination-in-the-last-instance of the Unconscious by the *Joui*, that the coherence of the non-analytic programme will have some chance of appearing. One may immediately refer to it first for a more precise comprehension of the relations of the unilateral duality between the Real or the *Joui* (*-sans-jouissance*) and *Jouissance*, the unilateral duality of *Jouissance* and the 'dual' or generalised Unconscious, and lastly the unilateral duality of the Unconscious and the philosophico-analytic symptom.

The Non-Analytic Generalisation of Psychoanalysis: A *Mathesis Transcendentalis* of the Unconscious

We are not certain that the future of psychoanalysis, its future as a human discipline among science and philosophy, is limited to its conflicting relations as always with philosophy and even with science, nor to its exchanges and its blends with them; nor are we sure that it is even limited to a generalised 'intercession' or again a reciprocal 'deconstruction'. Let us suppose that we will, to speak too brutally, 'break the history of psychoanalysis in half': if this project can no longer rigorously belong to philosophy or science separated exclusively or inclusively, how would it not belong to a discipline of human identity? If the past of analysis is in its relations with philosophy and science separately and in a conflicted way, could its future not be within new relations to non-philosophy as a unified theory? In addition, if it sometimes objects that it is already by itself a philosophy, and sometimes that it is a science, we respond: it is rather an artefact-of-science or an artificially transferred science that does not genuinely bear on its object for philosophical reasons; and it is rather an artefact-of-philosophy that, for reasons of transcendent use of the science of the unconscious and its other concepts, does not render justice to man as such and does not reach the Real – it is rather a meta-science or a meta-human discipline. A real bifurcation within the history of analysis is possible to imagine on the side of a more rigorous reformulation better adapted to its object, a science of people as Ego-in-Ego and as Stranger, as *Joui* and the unconscious *Jouissance*, entirely distinct from the Human Sciences. How one integrates analysis into this new scientific continent, the one that the being-human of man should give rise to, is the problem. Let us assume that we are capable of 'theorising' and describing this most human science, which would also be, in its capacity to relate itself to the Real, the true successor of philosophy; what would then probably ensue is the possibility of a new 'fate' or use of analysis. It is a use that would no longer by definition represent a supplementary philosophical attempt at appropriation or dis-appropriation; which would be at once identically a relation of theoretical generalisation to this discipline and its connection to the radical real of man. Integrating analysis into a more universal theory and a more universal pragmatics of man, of which it would henceforth represent a particular case, a given or model of interpretation, would be to renounce these abstract and transcendent generalisations that are either philosophical, or logico-linguistic, or linguistico-mathematic, and to distinguish its radical or 'unified' universalisation. Indeed, they are perhaps practices of generalisation separated *toto caelo* but that the philosophers, always unitary, want to confuse in the name of epistemology. We will call 'non-psychoanalysis' this 'scientific pragmatics' of analysis thus generalised within the bounds of a really human science and to distinguish it from the 'restrained' or Freudian analysis and its Lacanian avatars. This science will no longer confuse its object – the human-essence-in-the-last-instance of the Unconscious – with its anthropo-logical forms or philosophical modes, so that following the ontologico-analytic war or complex, following the interminability of a conflict which makes adversaries advance in power rather than in the real knowledge of man, would succeed a true peace.

There are some great possible types of 'generalisation' of psychoanalysis: (1) a cultural generalisation, of the 'psychoanalysis-as-a-Whole' [*Tout-psychanalyse*] type, which implicitly or *de facto* presupposes its non-pertinence as to the Real and science and, therefore, is without any interest other than ideological; (2) a philosophical generalisation, through the reciprocal appropriation and dis-appropriation of the unconscious and consciousness (or of Being); the philosophical strategies with regards to psychoanalysis are in reality as diverse as philosophies themselves; like them, however, they obey invariants that are possible to identify, the main one being the 'idealist triad' which implies this reciprocity, sometimes convertibility and sometimes reversibility, of the One and the Real and the unconscious or the Other; from this point of view, schizoanalysis and even 'textual' deconstruction can still pass for ultimate generalisations, the former being super-analytic, the latter ultra-analytic, of the mixtures of the unconscious and consciousness; (3) a scientific generalisation, through the rearrangement of its foundations and the transference of quasi-scientific techniques (Lacan's 'structural' analysis); and (4) a 'non-philosophical' generalisation, or through the transformation of analysis into a material for a dualysis or a discipline more universal than it. Science already does not generalise theories in the way of philosophy as philosophy naturally believes; and the unified theory universalises nevertheless otherwise, identically *a priori* and in the mode of a rectifiable theory and pragmatics which is related in-the-last-instance to its 'real object' (the essence of man as identical to the Real). The point is to constitute a non-analysis as the *mathesis transcendentalis* of the Unconscious *Jouissance*. The philosophical-type of universal – to which even the scientific generalisation of analysis is ordered – is always teleologically closed, in any case associated to the mixture of a generality and a totality, to a teleology (*Logos*, Reason, Being, Power, Desire, Language, Unconscious, Communication, and so on); it is a folded and redoubled universal, or self(-)positional. Even when it is opened to or by the Other, affected by breakage or splitting, it remains intrinsically closed for the more or less long term. It is a unitary space (subordination, subsumption, supersumption, integration, foundation, and so on) of the idealisation, reduction and dissolution of the reality of analysis itself. By contrast, the non-philosophical or unified-theoretical universal is absolutely deprived of norms (rational or other) assumed constitutive and of one such teleological fold. It is a quasi-empty space of philosophical forms, first decisions, teloi, topologies, and so on, and, precisely because of this universality, it is capable of really transforming a more restrained theory like Freudian analysis into a given-of-knowledge to which it removes nothing of its pertinence and whose scientific point is not blunted. The philosophical and unitary model of the interlocking [*emboîtement*] of theories by the hierarchisation of the particular and the general, by an always hierarchising decision, still functions within schizoanalysis and deconstruction, in the multiplicities of 'desiring forces' (partial objects/flow/full body), but also 'textual forces'. We distinguish from this model a non-hierarchical model, a non-auto-decisional and non-auto-positional model, simply 'unified' of the articulation of theories which presuppose them with a use of an occasional cause alone and a model. There is a pragmatics of philosophy and sciences immanent to the non-philosophical or unified-theoretical posture. From this point of view, a science of people, far from fading or finally dissolving the virulence and rigour of analysis in arbitrary philosophical teleologies and decisions, conserves them in any case except to delimit them within their own 'absolute' point of view, their universal human 'pretension'. If analysis takes its greatest force of claiming to be a science rather than a cultural 'great invasion' on Western soil, only one other scientific-type of discipline can gather it without 'resisting' it. Because, for 'ideological' reasons, one confuses both of them, because one has not accessed the human use of science as that which brings with it an opening without an ecstatic-horizontal doublet in general yet intrinsically and actually open, one maintains the epistemological illusion that resides within the confusion or amphibology between objects of science and objects of philosophy, and their universality as well.

Therefore, the point is no longer to constitute it despite everything into the guardian of analytic innocence threatened by the returns of the metaphysical repressed. In any case, it belongs to science alone to 'protect' science, and it belongs to the unified theory to validate against any particular theory a more universal space that is nevertheless, by definition, not measured by the capacity to accumulate the objects and magnify theories by one another. This way of 'saving' science from philosophical control, under the form of a radical universalisation turned against all its restrained forms (including its forms in the mode of 'totalisation'), is equivalent to a generalised analysis or transforms it into a non-analysis. Non-analysis is nothing other than the science of people specified and overdetermined by the 'restrained' analytic material (by the PA complex).

Perhaps one will object that an intrinsic mathematisation of the unconscious is the only possible solution that is left (otherwise itself very variable among logic, combinatorics and set theory) as the renunciation of its hermeneutic interpretations; it is the means to precisely avoid letting it return under the authority of the Human Sciences. This is nothing of the case: this type of hard yet local or limited mathematisation (if total, it would simply dissolve psychoanalysis) is specific to the Human Sciences and it is almost like going from Charybdis to Scylla, or let us say to Scylla to Charybdis, than it is to abandon hermeneutics for the matheme if it is reprised within a gesture of auto-position or, as is the case of Lacanianism, in a gesture of auto-depriveness. The proposed solution is of an entirely different nature: the becoming-science of analysis does not necessarily pass through a mathematisation, which is certainly always possible, but through its insertion under the conditions of a unified theory of science and man, which would have the Ego (the *Joui*) as its cause and the Strangers (the Radical Unconscious) as its object – therefore, a transcendental *mathesis* of *Jouissance*. The good generalisation of analytic theory and practice cannot in any case find its necessary condition in mathematics: it would need at first, in full rigour, to have elucidated the essence that makes mathematics a science adequate to the man-object and to his specific being, rather than having decreed, as philosophers do, that it is the model and necessary instrument of any possible science. This elucidation necessarily refers to an essence of science whose thematisation and description form the main object of a unified theory of science and philosophy, wherein the science of people is a privileged mode. The universalisation of analysis assumes to submerge it as is – without dismembering and without interpreting it – into this discipline. The point is to acquire the concept of a really universal and void Unconscious, freed of the matheme itself after having been freed of philosophical teleologies and humanisms, but not at all void of all human phenomenality. As we have said, the point is to dualyse rather than mathematicise it. This is obviously the only means to no longer claim to effectively intervene from outside into analytic practice in the name of local and regional theories or knowledges that we will have once more, in a hasty and premature way, philosophically instituted into the essence of science and therefore the science of man.

The scientific generalisation of an existing discipline cannot indeed have the form that philosophers imagine, the form of the amphibology of a constituted science or a particular knowledge with the essence of science, which is nevertheless an entirely different thing. The real movement of scientific generalisation is inverse: instead of transferring a regional knowledge into the essence of science, a regional science is constituted on the real base of the essence of science and starts from it. We must stop reflecting a constituted discipline – for example, set theoretical mathematics or topology – within another, in the goal of constituting the latter into a science. To acquire, for example, the concept of a science of man in its greatest generality, it is suitable to start from the essence of science – given within a unified theory – and the type of generality that is specific to it, outlined, for example, concerning the universality of the Unconscious. Any other procedure is circular, vicious, and dissolves within the philosophical possible the reality of science that one would like to institute. Rendering psychoanalysis fully scientific and at the same time adequate to its human object is to think it under the conditions of this generalisation of knowledge that is without common measure with the doublet of 'generality' and 'totality' proper to the philosophical style. Thus, one will integrate analysis into the continent of a science of people, on the generality of which it can draw a necessary trait for its existence. One such science does not programme particular applications, even though it utilises – but only, as we have seen, as material or occasion – all existing Human Sciences. Only one such science can, for example, let-psychoanalysis-be without resisting it through its philosophical objectivation, nor believe to transform it into a rigorous discipline through the importation of regional mathematical means into it in an arbitrary way, and which are imposed upon it by a philosophical forcing. Psychoanalysis must arrive where man is as the cause (of) science.

Finally, non-analysis is neither a super-analysis (in Deleuze's and, in a sense, Wittgenstein's way), nor a meta-analysis, nor a hetero-analysis nor a deconstruction, which are philosophical generalisations and, therefore, always restrained or restrictive by definition. Non-analysis derives from the autonomous human cause (of) thought as unified theory; it does not derive from the auto-position, to the nearest difference, of analysis itself de-magnifying, redoubling or even deconstructing itself. It considers restrained analysis as a simple given, a function required by the science of humans, so that what distinguishes it absolutely from this restrained analysis delivered unto itself is because from the outset it suspends the pretension of it, reducing its assumed validity to the state of a simple belief and brackets the *Principle of Sufficient Analysis*. While super-analysis, schizo-analysis, hetero-analysis, and so on, begin by admitting the validity of what restrained analysis postulates as the essence of man and does not denounce its illusion except by still assuming it constitutive of the being of man despite everything, non-analysis assumes it from the outset without a value for this being itself, for the cause (of) science, and confines it within the functions of 'objective givens'. Non-analysis marks the end of analytic Authorities that schizo-analysis, as a super-analysis, was missing. Freud's discovery had been simply interiorised in the concept and sublated, or intensified, or even deferred/differed and carried on, but always on the basis of this belief in its humanly unavoidable character, which is precisely what non-analysis strives to deracinate without any possible return.

From this point of view, even though analysis generalised into the 'non-' presents the appearances of a 'return to man' and, worse yet, of a return to humanism, it is obviously not a matter of a 'humanist' revenge against the unconscious that would, for example, have deprived us of the Copernican subject. There is no return here to Freud or to an opposing humanism; rather, it is a departure from the Unconscious within the vision-in-man and within *Jouissance*, within the cause (of) science that is the end of all humanist pretension and the givenness to science of its real object. This intrinsic, non-teleological 'humanification' [*humanification*] of analysis is its real transformation: no consequent return to the *psychē* – rather, it is a unified theory of analysis as meta-psychic and philosophy; and the destruction of any psychological point of view pairs with the destruction of meta-psychology to the benefit of the Radical *Jouissance* issued from the *Joui*. The Freudian unconscious and its avatars somewhat remain of the order of a meta-psychical imagery; the Generalised or Abstract, de-logicised and even de-philosophised, Unconscious is the object of a discovery that carves out an entirely new pathway for analysis.

The Forgetting of the Real or the *Joui*

1. The Greco-Judaic Antinomy of Psychoanalysis

For the moment, the One is a Greco-metaphysical ideal or a Judeo-religious passion. As One-in-One, or destined to renew the problem of '*jouissance*' and the 'real', the One is still 'in front of us'. Whether some psychoanalysts, in general the ones dedicated to guiding the Lacanian tradition, implement it – even if from afar, indirectly concerning '*jouissance*', and directly the 'One-signifier', and finally the constitution of an 'impossible' science of man under the form of a theory of the subject – is the sign both that thought in some of them has awoken from its Greek dream and that it is prepared for a possible renewal, but it remains imprisoned by the old prejudices despite everything. Besides, we now finally denounce in a motivated and argumentative way the poor consistency of Heidegger's unfortunate formula – but how little surprising for those who still think from Greek prejudices: 'science does not think (like philosophy)', and one suggests that science is also 'connected' to the One, no doubt secondarily still, and to the Other above all, therefore 'connected' to the highest instances of thought. The problem is to determine how one understands this 'otherwise' that, in Heidegger, means that in reality, it does not truly think, but that should now make analysis and science in general enter here into a complete and autonomous thought. To this end, what we propose is very different from Lacanianism: science assumed already constituted does not only use the One in general; rather, the One is the instance that gives science the power of thought. The One and the unified theory that ensues from it are perhaps no longer on the side of the 'Unconscious' and the 'Other' as they are not on the side of the 'Conscious' and 'Being', but they define another instance of the real and therefore of *jouissance* and are found to be 'the-last-instance' *par excellence*, a concept that should unsettle even up to the unconscious. However, this kind of attempt – which forms a conjuncture – is for us precious, at least as the 'symptom' of an abandonment of the indefinitely narcissistic games of philosophy for the problems of a really human science. Who could doubt that the tasks of an elucidation of the essence of the intrinsic unity of man, philosophy and science, in the name of the One would be, in all respects, less flippant than the 'question of Being' which will have been a new attempt to obscure them?

The multiplicity of the ways in which the One is traditionally said, or the modes of its efficacy, is probably not re-interiorisable within a unique history. Not only do we distinguish between these modes of the One its immanence of radical immanence insofar as its denegation is the condition of the exercise of philosophical belief; but well within these codes, the biblical

One, for example, is obviously foreign to the Greek One as the One (of) the Other - or the One of the signifier - is to the One (of) the Same. It does not let itself be re-appropriated by the ontological style of the Greeks, but rather de-constructs it. Some analysts or mathematicians, who are sometimes the same but all post-Lacanian, explore this other One, the One of set theory, from which they draw unprecedented effects that sometimes belong to the order of the unconscious and the letter, and sometimes form the order of the set-theoretical ontology of the Void. Rather than an extension, it is a question of a differenciation and an inversion, undoubtedly a 'breaking point', within the theory of the One where it would traditionally dominate the Multiple that henceforth represses it on its periphery. One extends the scope of set theory, conceiving this extension as a 'transference' or rather as ontology *par excellence* and which inverts the hierarchy to the benefit of the Multiple at the expense of the One. One describes a heterogeneity of logics and theories, sometimes even a pure or inconsistent multiple having become the content of Being, and one no longer evokes the One except under the form of their overlappings, entanglements, 'blends', except as a real yet finally secondary phenomenon. The post-Lacanian analyst makes the dreamwork [*le travail du rêve*] and a certain chaos of languages - theoretical or ordinary languages - resonate. Thus, they dispense with [*pratique*] the One, but in all scenarios as One (of) the Other or the Signifier, and more or less ordered to the latter or the Multiple. They do not summarily apply mathematics to the 'subject', but they make us experience the improbable communication of orders, affecting us with the undecidable, and sometimes make the One that which renders possible science from its own impossibility. They strive to 'partialise' or disperse the unconscious, bringing it to the limits of the void. In their own way, which is entirely mathematical and sensible, full of language and affect, they deconstruct in the name of the void or the multiple, or their identity, a Freudo-Lacanian orthodoxy that was content with passing from a still homogenous and substantialist conception of the unconscious to another one, substituting a logico-linguistic identity with its old biologico-mechanistic identity. Yet in all cases, there is a fall or lapse of the old Greco-metaphysical 'One' to the benefit of the ascending hegemony of the Multiple, a hegemony that makes up the era or conjecture, but consummates the forgetting of the essence of the real-One.

What can I know of man? It is to this still inapparent question as such to the eyes of philosophy and perhaps even - though in a lesser extent - of psychoanalysis, we cannot attempt to respond in a way grounded in (human) reality and (scientific) rigour except through the transcendental position or hypothesis of the real as One-in-One, rather than as One-of-the-Other or One-of-the-Multiple: that is, as One (of) the *Joui*, rather than as One of the unconscious. The expansion [*conquête*] of this theoretical basis should allow us to elaborate a positive relation, of use rather than critique, with attempts like the ones we will examine. Whether psychoanalysis, for example, does not exhaust the essence of man, whether not more than philosophy it does not reach it, being made to reach other targets, is one of the effects of the expansion of the essence of the Real or the *Joui* as radical immanence.

In philosophy and psychoanalysis, the One in its multiple meanings is therefore at stake. However, they all have in common being mixed or transcendent uses that efface its identity. Take, for example, these definitive formulae of a mathematician analyst that all come down to combining the One and the Other in undecidable mixtures, even systems, and reducing the One to the role of the signifier's trait: '[A set theory therefore starts] from a "Universe" U that is *the* One [*le Un*]: the whole of sets in question, connected among them by the play of the relation of belonging'; '[it appears that] the logic of the One [*l'Un*] passes through the Other and inversely', in such a way that it is their complex entanglement that is to be thought; 'mathematics [is] . . . the spirit of the Letter searching for the effects of the One in the real'. Or even: 'in human groups, the one that each one believes to form is bored [*troué*] by *the* One [*le Un*] that carries all their language and brings it towards its silent point'.[2] Thus, this is what one speaks of the One: as 'set-theoretical'. Nearly nothing here, though some Judaic nuances, distinguishes philosophy and psychoanalysis in the denegation of the *Joui*, both are inscribed within the most constant invariants of Greek thought. What are these invariants if not the 'confusion' of the One and Being, then the One and the Other or the Signifier to the extent that division or transcendence render themselves irreducible and tending towards 'depriveness' and 'lack'? What are they if not the reduction of the One to the functions of synthesis and totalisation, analysis and de-totalisation, and then dissemination and alteration, unicity and existence of the signifier, that is, reducing it to the subaltern functions that presuppose as unelucidated its own essence? What are they if not this immemorial 'entanglement', this undecidable knot of the One with the Other? What are they if not the division of the Real into the One of *jouissance*, the One of the unconscious and the metaphysical One on the one hand, and the empirical and 'human' real on the other hand? And lastly, what are these invariants if not this necessary passage from the One through language, a passage that is sometimes called 'philosophy' and other times called 'psychoanalysis'?

[2] Translator's note: The following quotes are from Daniel Sibony, 'Remarques sur science et inconscient', in *La décision philosophique* 7 (January 1989), 23–31.

Thus, armed with the Letter and the Tradition together, assisted by all the confused forces of the 'One', 'Being' and the 'Other' – to a near inversion of their hierarchy – thrown together into battle, post-Lacanianism pursues Freud's work and carves man, the Real and *Jouissance* into pieces in the name of recasting, flaw and deviation, *différance*, the pure multiple and set theory. There subsists some residua including an equivocal and transcendent concept of *jouissance* that cannot succeed in detaching itself from 'energy'. This levelling by the universal crumbling, this desired loss of the intrinsic identity of the Real, is the most interesting one of the analytic affair: it is a symptom of a global refusal to think, in defect of 'symbolising' it, *Jouissance* in the name of the new good conscience of the 'Other' supposed to exhaust the unconscious, the hubris of transcendence – the tension towards the old philosophical authorities urgently called back to the front. The philosophers, with the deconstructors in the vanguard, do not react otherwise, do not fear this vicious and miraculous reasoning of invoking the existence, and therefore the authority, of philosophy as the ultimate legitimation of its 'reality'. The philosophers cling to philosophy and analysts to analysis like Baron Munchausen: it is nothing but normal in this refusal to 'lose grip', but it is simply one such authoritarian refusal that has never stopped, elsewhere and in others, the freedom and necessity to think without a miracle through phenomena alone.

Obviously, all these traits form a system and their assumed pertinence is fed by the 'forgetting' of the essence of the One. The One, the '*Joui*', perhaps does not need a support like Being or like the Signifier to be the Real itself; nor does it need to be divided and magnified in amphibological concepts to be this Real; nor, even, does it need to fulfil the directing functions outside of itself, as if the Real itself should act technologically and continuously upon exteriority (*Jouissance*, the 'motor' or 'efficient cause' of unconscious labour). Philosophy and analysis are not the accidental 'fall' of the One to Being or the Other, at least it does not derive from them, because they are this continuous fall itself: they correspond to another experience than the experience of the One or the Real. The One-Ego and the Stranger, the *Joui* and the unconscious *jouissance* are in reality given radically, that is, in their own essence, rather than in essences of substitution and anonymous essences like 'Being' and the 'Other'; they are as included within the immanence of the human posture in general and in the ultimate experience – not simply assumed – that man is the 'last-instance' of knowledge that he can acquire by touching his being. The One is the experience of that which, of the-One-itself, is nothing but given; it is the embrace and self(-)*jouissance* – the *Joui*'-before-any-*jouissance*, the phenomenal content of analytic '*jouissance*' – before being touched by any such transcendence in the form of representation and divided on the model of psychic energy in exterior forms. A science of man is that which protects this One against its sacrifice in the vapours of Being or in the embarrassed speech of the Other. It protects the Ego-in-Ego, not the Cartesian subject, as the only real instance, as the true concept of *jouissance* when it is phenomenally and no longer energetically understood; it manifests it as the 'last-instance' that does not need to be humanised through its entry into the politico-philosophical order or in the symbolic order, but which determines in-the-last-instance alone the labour of the Unconscious, and no longer in an efficient way. This One allows one to welcome the Other without negating or dissolving it somewhat more, while the Other or 'first' unconscious cannot respond to the nothing-but-One except through a crumbling and a formalism, an exterior relation of the affect and the letter, *jouissance* and the unconscious, which results in a global effect of non-receiving. The human generosity of these 'instases' - the One, Being, the Other - is measured by their minimality, not of their 'withdrawal', but of their immanence or identity which leaves a free place - an em-placement - for the effects of the signifier, as an example.

The analysts cannot complain to not be understood here because a unified theory admits, without discussing it - it is not its object as the theoretical, practical and affective pertinence of their way of doing without denying it in any way (except in its transcendental sufficiency) - greets within analysis, above all Lacanian analysis, the finally serious existence of a theory of the subject. Yet, what is essential to what we say of the One-in-One, they cannot however admit it: to the point that they do not even see what we tell them. We do not speak of the same One nor of the same *Jouissance*. More exactly, they speak of the One of the metaphysical tradition to reduce it to an operation or a simple limit, to negate its being, invert its primacy to the benefit of the Other or the Multiple, indeed, to reduce it to the arithmetical One, whereas we speak of the still unelucidated essence of this One and its uses, even analytic uses; we speak of the amphibology of the *Joui* and *Jouissance* which still philosophically restricts psychoanalysis. In resistance and hastiness, they have a tendency to falsify what a general science of man must understand by the equation One = Real = *Joui-sans-jouissance*, and to give it a globally metaphysical interpretation. For example, they assume in the most traditional way that either the One is transmitted by language, or that the signifier cannot transmit it: in both cases, it is the thesis of language, here the language of the signifier, as *logos*, as constitutive of the essence or reality of the One. This is because we formally discard this Greek (and perhaps Judaic) thesis as to the essence of the One: language does nothing but transmit representations of the One, not the One or the Real itself which is non(-)self-decisional and non(-)self-lingual immanence; yet, it is neither capable of transmitting it, which is another metaphysical thesis.

Through a congenital empiricism, philosophy believes that the One does not stop being said in language, language determines its essence and even fails to determine it. The ruin of this hallucinatory belief is the rock of non-analysis. The essence of man is the human-vision-in-man and not divino-lingual or theological. Thus, we will take the measure of that which is engaged here as the resistance within the 'conflict' of psychoanalysis and a science of people: the true *Aufklärer* is we who affirm the intrinsic radical finitude of man-in-man, rather than his 'transfinitude' or his splitting as a 'subject' by an unconscious or first unintelligible signifier (the phallus). The 'synthesis' of psychoanalysis and philosophy, the tripod of Being, the Other and the One as the One-of-Being and the One-of-the-Other, is what is most constant in thought in the philosophical mode and it is this Greco-Judaic legitimacy that we attempt to delimit in an utterly somewhat rigorous way. In the same way that metaphysics speaks (of) Being without being interrogated on its essence, it now and more and more speaks (of) the Other and (of) the One without ever taking the time to elucidate the essence of these entities that are, within it, purely functional and rotting.

The somewhat more shaken up or confused reprisal of the single and split Greco-Judaic tradition is therefore not the concern of non-analysis. Even as 'supple' and 'plastic' as its contemporary forms are, which make it communicate with philosophy and even other knowledges, the situation that analysis aims for by lacking it is perhaps a bit more complicated still: there is not a disseminated givenness but two givennesses of man wherein one determines this dissemination, and the problem is to articulate them. Retorting with a psychoanalysis of the *Joui-sans-jouissance* or the One-in-One as a phantasy or a mirage, somewhat in the way of the famous '*jouissance* of the Other', is nothing as well except strategically normal because we ourselves suggest to the analysts that they are taken up in a transcendental illusion and an amphibology. Simply put, there must very well be between analysis and non-analysis a real and no longer strategic difference: it is precisely in the way of treating . . . the Other; of receiving and cherishing man rather than the Other as First, and as Stranger rather than with these anonymous concepts such as *jouissance*-energy and the unconscious-signifier. This difference in the posture and reaction is a sign that hardly deceives and upon which we must reflect for the future of the theory of man.

2. Psychoanalysis as Restrained Analysis

Measured to this new position of the problem of the sciences of man, psychoanalysis could very well appear as the greatest failed attempt of one such science. It has necessarily failed in one sense not without reason: our problem is not to carry out its critique in favour of a competing analysis. It will cry out with some correctness that 'man' has never been in its intention and that the man of which it speaks is defined in its own way under its epistemological conditions, rather than letting itself be defined by him. This is indubitable and not what is being questioned. However, it is not up to it alone to fix the criterion of the Real, and if another thought fixes it in a way that would be more radical than its own, it cannot either aim for it at least in the mode of avoidance. This is so that, therefore, the Human Sciences appear as not having posed the question of the 'real object' *qua* 'real', a transcendental question *par excellence* and, here, in a new and inalienable sense of the term. They have not perceived that there needs to be a special science for the question of reality, that is, the question of the essence of *Jouissance*, whereas philosophy is only the place of the question of possibility (even if it were also 'real'). It is not shocking that philosophy and the Human Sciences, psychoanalysis included, programme the dissolution of human reality within the possible and violent exaltation of superhuman 'possibilities' or in an absent and 'impossible' real. There is a superior racism that philosophy - above all philosophy, with psychoanalysis here partially functioning as a rampart - conveys erected against man. There is no paradox in saying that the Human Sciences have not known man and allow themselves to be led astray by Greek prejudices. They make of man and science 'vicious' or ready-made representations, abstracted each time from the reality of their process, blending them prematurely without digging into the Radical Identity of the being-immanent that assures the indestructible reality of man, science and their connection. They are content with exploiting them to their benefit, without knowing it in accordance with its essence and properties by which it could be imposed as a scientific object. At best, they also correspond to an inflation of knowledges, to the abstraction of a certain theoretico-mathematical, combinatorial and set-theoretical labour in the best of cases, applied to ready-made and assumed given representations of man, but which are nothing but abstract because it is not related to man as to its real-of-the-last-instance. We make the complementary hypothesis that these sciences are neither really human nor scientific; that they are still massively philosophical transcendent auto-interpretations that ignore themselves as such at the same time as they ignore their condition of possibility is within the denegation of their object. They are meta-languages of man. They are content with a certain premature theoretical formation of givens that are not really human but emerge from unitary attributes with which philosophy has always confused man himself: Power, Desire, Language, Knowledge, Labour, and so on. They could not yet have given a theoretical explanation of the ensemble of human phenomena; at least they do not place themselves in the posture that would allow one to give it, that is, to unveil in its original type of reality and its type of rigour, the new scientific continent. Nor could they have wanted to relate these phenomena to their real object, but rather have dissolved it within the multiplicity of local knowledges and vicious auto-interpretations. When they have, however, wanted to relate them to their object, it was always under the unitary-philosophical form of a transcendent man, reconstituted from outside with universal attributes, and opposed to this multiplicity as a synthetic unity: a 'man-horizon'. A humanist nostalgia haunts the most sober Human Sciences which dream, despite everything, of integration and recollection, when it is not totalisation and hegemony – they dream of a 'pilot-science'.

However reworked in its foundations it may be, psychoanalysis conserves the same presuppositions as those of its birth. It can neither want to interrogate itself on the meaning of being, here the reality, that is, the mode of phenomenal givenness of the Unconscious and *Jouissance*, but ask itself how – once the existence of both of them admit without anything more from their uncontrollable energetic effects or references – to interpret and conceptualise them, how to render the scientific knowledge of it all by maintaining these presuppositions. It presupposes their concept, that is, their connection to man, and the concept of science that it fabricates with odds and ends. For example, it assumes in Lacanian terms that language and its combinatorics structure the subject or, better, that the subject determines man or that *Jouissance* is a neighbour of energy: theses which it receives from a risky history under the too often empiricist pretext of the 'clinic'. The problem of the intrinsic reality of the Unconscious means: To what extent do the Unconscious and its logico-combinatory or set-theoretical structures – they function, that is not the question – relate to the specific reality of man and how do the analysts know it? The response to these questions is wrongly assumed to be sufficiently grounded by the simple clinical recording and treatment of effectivity, undoubtedly specific, of certain phenomena having common characteristics that one identifies, such as the unconscious and its effects. However, this problem of the real constancy of the unconscious (and moreover *jouissance*) is absolutely not ruled out when one has admitted the specificity of these phenomena not, without a doubt, in simple opposition to the old 'consciousness' or Being, but as that which neither is nor is not – as that which is absent. Regardless of the conscious and the unconscious, if the Other as One-of-the-heterogeneous and beyond as lack represents a superseding of 'negative magnitudes', it is always assumed in an arbitrary and connected way, with the subject on one hand and *jouissance* on the other, to a 'human' out of pure convenience. One cannot obviously deduce the unconscious from the conscious, nor make its genealogy from consciousness such that philosophy, for example idealist philosophy, has elaborated its structure. The unconscious represents a specific discovery whose practice and clinic demonstrate originality and irreducibility. However, the problem of the human reality of *jouissance* and the unconscious - which is precisely no longer the philosophical problem of possibility, of possibilisation and even impossibility of the Real - is not resolved by the clinic, nor, theoretically, by the call to a 'decision' other than the philosophical and Greek decision, for example a Judaic-type decision, or an experience of loss and advanced lack without which its relation to the Real, without which the Real itself, of course, would be pursued even in its ultimate retrenchments. Therefore, it is not a surplus-philosophical objection that we make to psychoanalysis, for philosophy could tell us the same thing: like psychoanalysis, it is always given human reality and reality *tout court* in an arbitrary and utilitarian way. Both presuppose it in a mode of auto-positional exteriority and transcendence and, by this very fact the givenness that they carry out is excepted from the given and superadded to it, completed by blurring the identity of the Real. One gives it in the mode of Being and its fetishes (*cosmos*, *physis*, *polis*, reason, consciousness, language, inconsistent multiple, and so on), the second in the mode of a strain [*épreuve*] of the Other received from external traditions which cannot be equivalent to a thought and even less to a science. The human object cannot be postulated from the outside by a discipline that relates itself to it, even if it were as to a simple 'subject'; nor can it be technologically constituted by motley pieces and fragments from sampling, abstraction, analogy and transference. It must be given with and for science of which it is the specific object, at the same time that it is first - but this trait exceeds the science of man - the unobjectivable cause (of) this science. The point is not to negate the unconscious, but to make it into the concept adequate to the inalienable, that is, incontestable, essence of man.

What is the specific real that analysis recognises in the unconscious if it is not man himself as One-in-One? It is the Other, thus inevitably as first or self-positional even in its essence of lack or absence. Therefore, it is more profoundly still the One of the *heteros*, the One prey to exteriority and accusing transcendence. It is not the One-as-the-Other which would still be Greco-metaphysical, but the Other-as-One, the signifier and its unary trait that marks it with heterogeneity, for if the One is the Other, it is on the condition that the Other would also and first be Other-than-Being; but this Other-than-Being is not nothing, it acts within Being itself, this Other is the One insofar as it is withdrawn, absented or missing in Being. Led back to its quasi-Judaic strain, psychoanalysis is an experience of the Other beyond Being and non-Being, but is this response better than the philosophical response which says that we have no experience except of the One-that-is - even when it is said 'to not be'? In all scenarios, the One is abstract and dependent, in one capacity or another, of Being. Therefore, there would be no experience nor autonomous thought of the One, but it must be associated with an always transcendent support or situation, sometimes Being, and sometimes the Other (which is not). These analytico-philosophical arguments at most admit the constancy of the One, its necessary yet unelucidated presence in the foundation of all thought; for the rest, they sink into a radicalised Greco-Judaic aporia or antinomy of which a science of man precisely should escape, for is the secret of this so unanimously invoked One a thing other than man, a man here split into *jouissance* and the subject?

The reasons of the impossible presence of the One in arrangements with Being or the Other therefore do not hold to Greco-metaphysical reasons, to the historiality of an '*envoi*' in relation to which we will be late, 'missing' and irresponsible heirs, but more simply to this fact of all facts that the One-*qua*-One, the heart of *Jouissance*, is the Real itself, the absolutely and not the assumed given; the one that is independent of all ontology or philosophical givenness but which cannot be *thought* independently of them. Neither ontology nor psychoanalysis can assure us of the Real - as it happens, man - unless they rather have the task of repressing by dividing him. The One is the instance required by them each time in heterogeneous, perhaps irreconcilable, modes, if not in their common foreclosure of the Real. We must elaborate a new theory - non-analysis precisely - to think that which is no longer an analogy nor a univocity: the very theory of a science that finds 'before it', to inscribe them within a universal space as henceforth contingent givens, philosophy and psychoanalysis with their multiple uses of the One.

Measured by the One-in-One which it believes, despite everything, to aim for and which only aims for it through the prism of the Other - this is the unary trait - psychoanalysis bears the same stigmata of decisive arbitrariness as philosophy: the One or the Real is enslaved to transcendence having become radical, functionally requisitioned for the secondary tasks of the dispersion of the signifier after having been requisitioned for the secondary tasks of the philosophical unity-of-contraries. Instead of being ordered to a synthesis, to an Other-under-identity, the One is now ordered to an Other-without-identity; it is no longer identitarian, but it is still unitary, being submitted to an instance other than itself, communicating its reality with that which has none or which has a reality of a secondary type and still other than its own. Instead of serving Being, the Real now serves Difference, gap, delay and lapse as the syntax of the unconscious. From this point of view, psychoanalysis' latent Judaism since Freud will have fortunately renewed the affects and forms of philosophy without, however, destroying the philosophical decision itself, combining itself rather with it depending on improbable modes at the limits of coherence. This struggle is nothing but interesting: it is not scientific and has no importance that it imagines for a science of people. There is struggle precisely because the adversaries place themselves outside of the Real itself and within representation even when they combat each other concerning the One and the Other after having battled around Being. Therefore, the authentic Real, the One, is rejected as 'impossible'. The Real, if it is the specificity of man, cannot obviously be the 'impossible'. The impossible is at best the transcendent real as it is delimited, for example, by philosophy. For the science of people, the Real is immanent and cause-of-the-last-instance, and it is the possible or the signifier, the unconscious, that is unreal, which does not mean that it would be nothing. Indeed, the One-*qua*-One, as the identity (of) the *Joui* that knows itself non-positionally and non-donatively, is that which gives its lack of reality, but its phenomenal reality of-the-last-instance, to the Other (insofar as it is not) as much as to Being (insofar as it veers towards phantasy and unlimited appearance) and, finally, to the Unconscious. It is with the means that its radical immanence can provide that we must describe its specific reality and the effects of it upon the philosophical and analytic imaginary.

The idealist triad analysed above has some analytic avatars: the imaginary triad (mother/child/phallus); the symbolic triad; need, demand, desire, and so on. Every recent critique of psychoanalysis (Deleuze, Derrida, Foucault and Henry) has denounced these triads, but being most often content with differenciating or de-magnifying them – it remains a 'critique'. This critique must be done in a more immanent way through a re-elaboration of the essence of the Unconscious, which, instead of being posited as first, cannot not henceforth have man as a cause, of course, 'of-the-last-instance'. Psychoanalysis and philosophy never stop their conflict but finally join hands against the science of humans. The triadic procedure that triumphs in philosophy and psychoanalysis is the means of this resistance, and it is this resistance that we must globally suspend in the elucidation of the theory of the Unconscious. The Unconscious no longer passes through a philosophical-type of foundation nor through a deconstruction of this foundation, the 'Human Sciences/philosophy' problem is certainly not what we oppose to the analysts. We substitute the traditional demarcation line that places philosophy and man as the Cartesian-type subject together to oppose them to science and analysis with another demarcation line: it places man on the side of the Real or the Cause, and we distinguish them together from philosophy and psychoanalysis in their spontaneous exercise.

We must dare this hypothesis: this demarcation line saves man from his so-called scientific 'objectivation' and his subjugation by the unconscious which, in reality, are nothing but an effect of the spontaneous idealism of philosophy.

However, they do not belong to the essence of the unified theory, nor are they tolerable by the unified theory of man as the distinction between, in general, philosophical auto-objectivation and the non(-)self-positional objectivity of Strangers has shown. Man is not an object of a science – as Universal Humanity or Strangers – unless he is first its cause-as-Ego-of-the-last-instance which never itself has the form of objectivation and, more generally, position. It is on this basis of man as Ego-without-object that he can also be an 'object', that is, an objectivity that is now non(-)self-positional – undoubtedly the real content of the Unconscious. The primitive, absolutely originary unity of man (and) analysis, which is not decided by philosophy nor analysis but is determined by man, is the absolute soil of any non-analytic thought. Analysis, or what it becomes, stops being a simple possibility of the Philosophical Decision (of Being, *Logos*, Reason) to a near variation as the philosophers would love to believe, as it can no longer be turned against man from whom it holds its reality. It finally stops being this alienation, this dogmatic thought that the philosophers cannot not want it to secretly be. This approach requires the abandonment of the epistemological procedure: instead of being given an Idea or a Fact of the sciences and, in particular, of psychoanalysis and already posited by philosophical decision, to then be asked how to describe and found them and thus pass from the fact to the law, one immediately lets-themselves-be-given the Real of the *Joui* as Given-without-Givenness (neither fact nor law) and, on this basis, one elaborates the knowledge of humans as they are, that is, as Strangers, under the entirely 'occasional' condition of psychoanalytic material.

The analysts will object: the 'radical' or the 'Real' is either a metaphysical phantasy or an impossibility, but this is not because philosophy and psychoanalysis are constructed to repress it or made to resist it, or simply to experience it as inaccessible or impossible, that the radical is unfindable. This is precisely because man as *index sui* is the one who has already found within himself as himself or as inalienable Ego – the vision-in-Ego. 'Radical' means nothing other than 'inalienable' or 'of-the-last-instance': a non-Cartesian Ego, and it is not accessible to an analytic critique like the Cartesian Ego.

The question of the reality of a science, of its relation to its 'real object', is not extrinsic as philosophy wants it nor hesitant and indirect as psychoanalysis wants it. It is a question to which a unified theory, making use of analysis when, at least, an idealist or positivist philosopher is not present to dissolve its reality, responds immanently rather than metaphysically or through an appeal to an extrinsic or devalorising ontological foundation. Analysis as it is 'saved' in a unified theory is not more submitted to the Other than to Being; it is transcendental in a new sense, and finds itself in this context or element able to think and govern itself.

Non-analysis is a psychoanalysis generalised under the conditions of the radically immanent Ego such that it determines the Unconscious. It is distinguished from a psychoanalysis simply broadened by philosophy and that would on this point neither appear more nor less valid – on the plane of principles and rigour – than one of these mixtures that we combat. It falls into the approximate and concepts of the communicative that are theoretically unverifiable ('instinct', 'interest', 'interesting', 'dialogue' and 'network' between the philosophical and analytic, and so on). Thus, the condition of human and technical sensibility of an analytic practice that only asks to be understood, in no way its '*de jure*' relation with its object – and to which object (the in?human unconscious or man-as-unconscious?) – is described to us and it is an entirely different question. Metaphysical scepticism will smile at these types of questions that it will call . . . metaphysical; psychoanalysis will see it as the work of desire; and intellectual vulgarity will believe to rule out the problem by speaking of 'theoreticism'. Nevertheless, it is rather through these types of problems that we intend to distinguish ourselves from the interminable conflict between analysis and philosophy and restart work on the essence (in a new sense: the theoretical use) of psychoanalysis against all the metaphysical dissolvents with which the contemporaries cleanse man of the dead [*font sur l'homme la toilette des morts*].

Therefore, the problem is not to make philosophy and psychoanalysis 'communicate' in a transfinite network, of beginning again once more with a mixture of the Greek and the Jew, which is decidedly the new philosophical common sense (analysis as the Other of philosophy . . .). Rather, it is to put them back in their place defined by the Ego-in-Ego and the Stranger. Of course, it is inevitable to posit the Ego, the cause of the Identity of man and analysis, 'in advance'. Here, the analysts are tempted to denounce a philosophical *habitus*. They forget that even the 'Other', the 'signifier', the 'deviation' or 'unexpected', and so on, are posited in advance and even auto-posited *qua* first 'structure', even if it were at the same time deprived of the real. Yet the point is to go further: one will not make us believe in an empiricism *ex nihilo*, one will no longer unitarily confuse the thing and the effect of the thing, for example man and the fact that he speaks, nor the real and the effects of the real, nor the truth and the effects of truth. There is a positivism of the signifier, the effect, the indirect, deviation and return, the interval, *différance*, the pure multiple, a positivism and a dogmatism of the Other or the unconscious – poorly corrected by the Freudian idea of the auto-perception of the id and the drives – which, in the contemporaries, has replaced the metaphysical positivism of the attribute or predicate and responds to the same – simply displaced – unitary ideal of the confusion of man and a universal and transcendent instance. This amphibology of the unconscious and an auto-positional transcendence is what one human science should precisely suspend . . .

Man is not submitted more to the Other than to Being, more to the signifying interval or difference than to metaphysical or logocentric identity – man determines, nevertheless in-the-last-instance, his unconscious. Analysts are tempted with asking regarding what we advance as being the essence of man: How do you know in advance that . . .? It would be easy to give them the same ball: they know in advance, no doubt they have learned it in the Old Testament, that man is prey to the Other. If there is always something in advance (the *a priori*? the presupposed? the tradition? philosophical theses or 'first terms' and 'axioms'?), the problem, therefore, is rather to posit the least 'advance' possible but the most radical advance, to find the 'given in advance' [*donné d'avance*] whose being-given is not determined by its being-in-advance, a given first-without-primacy. It appeared to us that it was the One as Given-without-Givenness rather than the Other or Being; the human multiple of Strangers, rather than the multiple of Being or the signifier. This prior recognition, and it alone, which is no longer a philosophical presupposition but the order of a transcendental or 'real' axiomatic, grounds a directly human science, that is, the only somewhat new and serious 'stake' which will take the pain of looking at once again, but from afar, on the side of psychoanalysis.

The unified theory that we speak of that can give analysis a human usage is as much distinguished from the 'science of Being' (from metaphysics to philosophy-as-rigorous-science) as the One-in-One is distinguished from Being and, consequently, as the Stranger is distinguished from the 'subject of the unconscious'. The science of Being is a true metaphysics and analysis is a problematic science that cannot do without philosophy. We definitely and definitively aim for an 'empirical' (but not empiricist) theory of man that possesses a 'science' side, but that is transcendentally related to the real of man. We do not deny that analysis includes something other than principles – for example, the local sequences of knowledge (of) the Real, even the very fragments of the Real. Yet the Real is not given, as a hypothesis of the Given-without-Givenness, except in-the-last-instance than at the end of a deviation or in the 'midpoint' of the deviation, through fragments or as the impasse of the unconscious. Yet, anterior to the possibilisation or 'impossibilisation' of psychoanalysis, there is not its realisation but its reality, its constancy of humanity. Indeed, the problem is not only the scientific-type of labour done to these sequences of knowledge. Non-analysis begins when one is asked how the partial objects of the body and the unconscious knowledge are related to the real objects and finally to a Real that is not the impossible. Therefore, it seems to us 'slight and, to put it bluntly, metaphysical'[3] to not posit under its radical form the question (the unified theory is the response to this question which, as a response, precedes this question): Why is there some analysis rather than nothing, or rather than only some philosophy? Better yet, what real use is to be made from analysis, because there is some analysis but we do not know if it is human? The positivism that watches over one such forgetting is not discarded by the analytic care to make the One speak as the Other.

The theory proposed on the basis of the One as *Joui* – let us say all that follows to predict one misunderstanding – does not deny the slippages of the 'real', the leaps or events upon which analysis is grounded, and furthermore not the 'real' that is the hole or lack, the partialisation of the 'real' and the 'symbolic'. Rather, it responds to a question forgotten by philosophy and psychoanalysis: they are the ones that speak and ceaselessly use the One as a trait of totality or as a trait of the unicity of the signifier, the ones who know that it is the slippage and the partial which make up singularity and which make up the unity once more, but where do they take hold of this One that they cannot not speak of and use? Despite what they say, they are also given the One at the same time (this is the problem) as Being and the Other – they are given them all at once . . . Their One is taken from traditions – the Bible and the Presocratics – but it is not a discovery, just a belief and a rumour; a barely creative, a barely interesting response because it is authoritarian, a response through transcendence rather than an immanent and scientific hypothesis. It is not as a reader but as the cause (of) science that man 'receives' himself or lets-himself-be-self(-)given as *Joui*-of-the-last-instance. Beyond that, nothing allows us to think biblical and Jewish language would be more open to the truth than philosophical and Greek language: both assume given the One and Being, the One as the One-of-Being. They are simply given a lot to assure themselves of the 'real', but what they are given exceeds the Given-without-Givenness and is nothing but the supposed real. To the contrary, the very thing that non-analysis postulates in the hypothesis and axioms of the *Joui* and the Unconscious, their 'dual' and 'unilateral' distinction, can only first be the Real-outside-presence, outside-intuition, the One-without-Being, even if thought or the hypothesis-form gives it (back) or makes the already-Given a givenness. Lacking these distinctions, the Real no longer radically precedes representation, or is once more and at best the 'impossible' of representation. There is once again a vicious circle, rather than a rigorous explanation through induction and deduction.

[3] Translator's note: This quote is an allusion to Descartes' Third Meditation in *Meditations on First Philosophy*.

One of the founding appearances of philosophy is believing that Being can give or the Multiple refuse its reality to the One or the Other to divide it, as if this unreal buttress, this transcendent support could be equivalent to an intrinsic reality. This belief obviously has a vicious form because the One must then give its reality or its essence and because, repressed by the Multiple, it continues to condition it or because it is necessary as the trait nevertheless to assure the multiple of the signifier. It is to these feats worthy of Baron Munchausen that philosophy and psychoanalysis are suspended, in lack of a specific elucidation of the essence of the One and its (non-)relation with Being. This means that to posit the equivalence or communication of the One, Being and the Other, or, to the contrary, posit their incompatibility, does not move the problem an inch such that the thought of the One is not clarified and is content with registers what the double Greco-Judaic tradition is willing to concede to it in an authoritarian way. The very contemporary art of 'connecting' or 'networking', generalised communication, the tinkering of pieces taken from the oldest machines of humanity, can certainly pass for philosophy – for it is one – but not for another thing. How could the One not have, as its ultimate content, the non(-)self-decisional *Jouissance*, the *Joui* itself rather than *Jouissance*, if it must also be eaten away at the core by the Other?

Among other things, the 'ordinary man' or the Stranger means that one does not have to be 'informed' or a 'scholar' [*savant*] to know that the One excludes division or that it non(-)self-donatively and non(-)self-positionally 'enjoys'. Even less, in any case, than it is to know that division and indivision communicate, which is a necessarily more complex and more derived thesis. It is enough to admit – every man is confused with this premise – the minimum of the real given and not simply assumed given at the end of a transcendence, to be able to take the immanence of the nothing-but-One, the *Joui*-of-the-last-instance, as the guiding thread. By contrast, one must have read Parmenides and the Bible – one must have already posited communication in-itself viciously – to believe that division and indivision, Being and One, and the Other and One communicate. Decidedly, no agreement will ever be possible between thinkers who exercise the human liberty of thought and the thinkers who postulate the authority of texts.

It is poor and in any case barely effective to want to cover up this gap with the galloping ideology of dialogue and communication, because every communication, and even to the nearest Other, is a triviality, a quasi-tautology and a narcissism. Communication merits being thought when something – it turns out it can only be the being of man – not only refuses to communicate, but has never entered into the vicious circle of universal communication. Likewise, it is not because the One is said in several ways that these ways belong or determine it: this belief is also philosophy although it is nothing but one belief and a rumour. A 'thought of the One' like non-analysis has interest only if it can finally interrupt, at least on account of thought, these circular reasonings by which the philosophers and analysts claim to make themselves the masters of the real itself through 'communication' and, with the authority of the old texts in hand, pronounce the exclusion against any attempt to think otherwise than as Greeks and Jews together.

The Universal Unconscious and the Phenomenon of Unilateral Loss

'Non-psychoanalysis' is the science of Universal Humanity or people-as-Strangers, but specified and overdetermined by psychoanalysis, which serves it as a condition of existence, material or model. As a generalisation of an identically aprioristic and scientific type of analysis, non-psychoanalysis definitively tears psychoanalysis from the sphere of culture. After the Ego-in-Ego and under the name Strangers, the science of people possesses as we have seen a purely immanent, non-redoubled experience of the transcendence (of) the Other as unilateral duality. After the *Joui* as the Real, it is a matter of a new concept of the Unconscious as a henceforth aprioristico-scientific hypothesis. Indeed, it is constituted *a priori* – this concept is no longer philosophical here – an *a priori* non-decisional and non-positional affect (of) alterity, position, and so on. To re-insert restrained analysis in its generalised form, it is then enough to elaborate upon the signifier (for example) its mathematico-linguistic concept, which remains self(-)decisional and self(-)positional to the nearest lack or depriveness, depending on the new experience of the Other or the syntax of unilateral duality. It is a qualitatively new extension. This Unconscious is the consequent identity of *Jouissance* and transcendence or exteriority, but which is itself 'not' or which is not a second time transcendent like the restrained or 'signifying' unconscious. A science that finds its cause in the immanent being-human of man can thus introduce psychoanalysis to the experience of the most irrecusable unconscious and give it its real object, which, far from being culturally or religiously determined, or mechanically and biologically determined, or even linguistically and logically determined, is now determined in the mode of a finally transcendental or absolutely immanent *Jouissance*. The phenomenal, non-empirical or non-metaphysical concept of the unconscious is the effect of this power exercised by the *Joui* upon the restrictive forms of the unconscious and surrounding 'concepts'. Their unilateralisation is equivalent to an irreversible indifferenciation, to a rejection of the restrained as unreal and transcendent, to a neutralising reduction through indifference.

Let us start once more from the restrained unconscious. It is an affect of absence and lack, more exactly of loss, neither being nor simple non-being. However, it is an affect of loss that loses itself, that divides and redoubles itself to give itself reality, to give it back to itself or reproduce itself, yet sink into indetermination. We will define the immanent ontology of analysis as an auto-privational ontology. Analysis can only reach up to demi-loss, as it will only reach half-retrieval. By contrast, the unilateral dualysation, an operation of non-analysis, contributes towards finally determining (it remains undetermined) and 'minimalising' the phenomenon of the Unconscious: it is an absolute loss or loss as it is, even if it is not reduced to this loss which is but one of its 'sides'. It is Absolute: because it loses the Absolute itself, the real-One (of) the *Joui* or the cause (of) science, which is not an object, what in reality it does not lose as one may have lost an object. As (non-Ego) or (non-)*Joui*, the Unconscious is also the Ego albeit in-the-last-instance-alone; as the loss of the Absolute, it is also the absolute (of) loss; in some way, it is the transcendental identity or *Jouissance* (of) loss, that which does not lose itself again nor is it retrieved. The Universal Unconscious is this *a priori* yet immanent phenomenon (of) a loss without object nor being lost. It is a lived or enjoyed loss as it is yet in-the-last-instance by the Ego rather than a loss affecting a 'subject' or an 'Ego' posited as transcendent. And if loss is a relatively autonomous and positive affect where 'nothing', no object nor world, no being nor Being [*aucun étant ni être*] is lost and will limit loss, it means that there is nothing to retrieve or make a return: this is the identity (of) desire, which has nothing to do with the desire of identity. There is *jouissance*-in-the-last-instance of loss, everything is suspended without having to return, everything is lived immanently conforming to what there is specifically within the essence of man. This is why the varying heterogeneous forms of return – the return of the lost object, the return of the repressed, transference itself – all by remaining what they are in the effectivity of psychoanalysis will be treated here as positive hallucinations or consistent appearances. The loss that is nothing but loss without nothing being lost, neither a signifier nor '*objet a*', like a transference which is nothing but transference without nothing being thereby transferred, are immanent lived experiences, not *jouissances* of the Ego; rather, they are modes of the *Joui*-in-the-last-instance. The *Joui* is not affected by loss, by contrast, and it is the same thing, it protects it from any filling in. Therefore, it is because loss also possesses an entirely positive reality.

The passage from restrained analysis to its generalised form has two effects. The first is that the unconscious specified in biological, physical or linguistic terms definitively loses its first transcendence, its hierarchical- and metaphysical-type of priority over consciousness of which it still assumes the concept valid, its determinant causality is too close to the causality of Being for example and a philosophical-type of hierarchy. It becomes second because, even though constituted by an absolute Other, by the first phenomenon of the Other (rather than a first Other), the unconscious is no longer determined by a simply repressed consciousness or Being, but the *Joui* as a non-donative and non-decisional cause. There can be no question of depriving the Unconscious of its transcendence, at least of that which remains redoubled or folded, of its philosophical massiveness (and not only biological or linguistic massiveness) unless it is to posit always in a constitutive relation with Consciousness, which one would conserve despite everything: this would be a simple analytic reversal of philosophy, undoubtedly followed by a displacement, but Consciousness would then remain ultimately constitutive. It is only in relation to man in his essence-of-One, which is no longer the conscious but the strain of the non(-)self-decisional *Joui* that remains on its inalienable reserve of the 'last-instance', that the unconscious is de-posited and constrained to become the ordinally second instance that 'suits' the Other (the signifier, and so on).

The dogmatism and transcendent realism of psychoanalysis are definitively liquidated by this inference of the 'emptiest' Unconscious through the Ego as *Joui*, which, determining it in-the-last-instance alone, by this very fact assuring it an autonomy and identity that psychoanalysis refuses, spontaneously preventing the folding-back-upon-itself of philosophical transcendence. Of course, the Unconscious cannot be called 'determined' unless it is determined by another cause than the cause through which it acts, a cause without an equivalent in psychism, the social or life. Therefore, we cannot confuse this entirely 'passive' causality of man upon the Unconscious with that of the conscious or philosophical in general. It gives rise to a hypothesis and operations of induction and deduction, rather than to a 'foundation' of the Unconscious. Non-analysis has no foundation, but it has one cause.

The second effect of this generalisation is that the Unconscious is itself universalised in a transcendental mode as identity of the theoretical and the pragmatic, and no longer in the necessarily restrained philosophical mode (Being, the logico-linguistic Signifier, *Différance*, Desiring Machines, and so on, are all 'restrained' variations). Hitherto, it will have not been purged of its mechanistic imagery except to be filled up, by philosophers disguised as analysts, by a mathematico-linguistic and topological imagery. These empirical contents, abstract transcendent models, drawn from local knowledges taken in reality from the process of science, function as artefacts by which restrained analysis covers, to avoid it, the unbearability of absolute loss. When generalised in accordance with the cause (of) its unified theory, it is finally void of its local contents, of its cultural and imaginary representations like its topologies. Continuing to fill it up and ballasting it with the logico-linguistic rather than with the biologico-mechanistic, with difference as such rather than with signifying difference (schizoanalysis), is to remain within a divided/doubled concept of the Unconscious and not reach its simplest and most abstract universality, its most actual infinity, its status of unilateral duality. It is not familialism and Œdipalisation that we must extirpate from the Unconscious; it was the 'philosophism' itself and in its greatest extension. What is the point of de-Œdipalising desire if it is still to machinate it, to fold it upon the ultimate restriction of desiring machines or again to the last fold of 'differe(a)nce'? This combat within philosophy does not respond to the scientific safeguard of analysis and its real object. If the Unconscious does not know contradiction or logic, it will not either know philosophy, which is a construction interiorising upon logic and inseparable from it. Neither formal logic, nor combinatory logic, nor the *logos* or the onto-logical: the Unconscious is 'desperately' void because it is 'full' of multitudes of the Strangers that we are. There is no question of filling it once more with substitutes, the 'imaginary' or the 'sociocultural', the 'mathematical' or 'topological'. Rather than the last wound, the wound in-the-last-instance or the real wound, and it is not the wound that the Unconscious inflicts on the conscious, it is rather what the *Joui* and *Jouissance* inflict upon this unconscious still too full of metaphysical ersatz and artefacts, inflicting upon the residual philosophical narcissism of psychoanalysis.

The Unified Theory of the Unconscious as Non(-)Self-Signifying: From Analysis to Dualysis

Correlatively to this change in content, the Unconscious changes in theoretical and practical status. If its specific nature is thus deeply modified, its relation to the empirical is as well, here the already-divided man or the philosophico-analytic 'subject'. Instead of philosophically re-blending it with Being – its withdrawal, its reserve, its difference, or its set-theoretical multiplicity – we have extricated its real kernel now over-determined, but no longer determined by this matrix. Instead of the unconscious as a deviation, a reserve, a flaw, breakage, part, slippage, *différance*, and so on, all determinations which remain inserted between auto-decision and position, non-analysis manifests and describes the affect (of) an absolutely non(-)self-decisional and non(-)self-positional Other. The restrained analytic material then carries out not only as a simple given for science, which 'extracts' from it this type of *a priori* (this is the 'dualysis' of the Unconscious), but also as that which necessarily overdetermines it and forms its condition of existence.

This articulation of the real object of non-analysis and its data is worthy of an explanation: it implements the theoretical nature of the concept of the Unconscious. Let us start again from what the analysts call 'the Other'. This is not a precise concept except in appearance: analysis confuses through amphibology what it signifies, a certain heterogeneity, and its precision as a concept; the thing with the word; and more rigorously: the empirical content with the essence. It is from this constant indetermination of the call upon the Other, upon its . . . nevertheless unitary heterogeneity, that – from our point of view, and from it alone, no doubt – Lacanian and post-Lacanian discourse suffers, accumulating Heideggerian indetermination and a quasi-Judaic depriveness. All our effort is to give back a content of real identity to the singularities that science investigates: we do not at all believe that the real content of the singularities would be the Other, the signifier, or the partial. Furthermore, is it not necessarily the One as Real Identity, not logico-real, of the '*Joui*', that is still anterior to the Other of which analysis makes the fold of the transcendent and transcendence? This has nothing to do with the false immanence of phenomenology ('to the things themselves') and Heidegger's thought, which has lacked, still in excess of transcendence, the really 'hidden' or invisible essence of the phenomenon, that is, the phenomenon's essence (of) the invisible. A great, typically contemporary illusion is to believe that dissemination, breakage, the partial, the magnification of the flaw, the delay, differe(a)nce, and even the Pure Set-Theoretical Multiple, would be the only possible real destruction of the metaphysical One and moreover the One that would like to present itself to the contrary as thought from its essence. This is to believe that it is enough to profess [*pratiquer*] the multiple and diversion, even depriveness, to have done everything that is really possible to do with metaphysics, whereas one does nothing but substitute or co-ordinate the Other with Being, conserving the same invariants of thought. This agitation of the Other makes us believe that thought is made, this non-comprehension of the One (of) *jouissance* confused with metaphysical Unity under the title '*jouissance* of the Other', is the most constant trait of the 'post-modern' and not only under its analytic form. It is also an attempt at intimidation or a magic trick that this philosophical, non-founded universalisation because it is still too empirical, is of the Other. The cause of science is the *Joui*-of-the-last-instance, not Being or the One taken at the 'letters' or the 'calls' of the human, taken at the signifier and language; it is the One as non(-)self-decisional immanence. It is obvious that there is also 'Being' in non-analysis; yet we must rethink it in turn from the One instead of wanting to co-ordinate or connect everything 'on the surface' and slip from one to the other: the point is to dualyse, not only analyse. What do we mean by this?

The One (of) the Ego is obviously not the Unique nor otherwise the Multiple – this disjunction is only valid for *Jouissance*, not the *Joui*: still, it is struck with the transcendental identity of *Jouissance* precisely. It is important that not only would the One (of) the *Joui* also be the Multiple – for example, the set-theoretical multiple as Being or multiplicities as desiring (the thesis of schizo-analysis) – but it would be the cause-of-the-last-instance of the most inconsistent Multiple, the Multiple of the Unconscious whose 'unilateral duality' is the essence and origin of this Multiple. The non-deconstructive dimension of the radical duality (for example, the *Joui* and *Jouissance*) completes by squashing the metaphysical and the unitary pretensions of the Other itself when it is, as it seems in analysis, the dominant point of view over the One and Being. There is obviously not a unique concept of the multiple, but there are at least two: the first 'derives' from the One itself, *Jouissance*, finding in the unilateral duality its essence, the essence of the Radical Multiple or the Unconscious non(-)self-signifying; the second is the analytic 'Other', for example the signifier, and it is still ultimately consistent. A really general science of man does not speak of man and his 'deviations' in a globally unitary way as the analysts do. However, it speaks of a double givenness of man: his essence (of) the *Joui*, where there are no diversions, no alterity; the philosophico-analytic symptom or the transcendental appearance of analysis is where diversion makes the law. An 'eased' or 'broadened' psychoanalysis by means of the Other or signifier remains, from our point of view, a unitary or philosophical enterprise. The magnification of the effects (of) the Other is not enough, as, for example, Deconstruction still believes in the extension of analysis, in liquidating the fantasies of metaphysics or really deconstructing them, but only to disperse them. The whole non-analytic enterprise precisely resides within the first distinction, without return – within dualysis – between the *Joui* and philosophico-analytic effectivity. In addition, Being, even the Other, the flaw, and *différance* belong, from our point of view, to this broadened concept of effectivity. More than an economic distribution, this unilateral duality is the rock of a definitively non-metaphysical science of man, whereas psychoanalysis and deconstruction cling to metaphysics to simply wound it. The non(-)self-positional Unconscious – what we must call the non(-)self-signifying Unconscious – even if it would be invisible to analysis, is not a bar upon the field of knowledge or the subject. It is not internal/external to the field of the analytic decision, it is absolutely external to it albeit as the immanent cause. We must thoroughly invent a new paradigm of thought if one wants to re-found analytic theory to render it adequate to its new object. Therefore, we can rigorously speak of an epistemic (not epistemological) break within analysis, on condition of apprehending that this break is an effect of the posture of *Jouissance* assumed in-the-last-instance by the Ego, that is, that it is a unilateral duality, that it does not pass within analysis – a new decision more altering and 'unconscious' than the other ones – but this is entirely different: it is a unilateral duality between the Principle of Sufficient Analysis (sufficient to man) and the analytic material conserved as a reservoir of 'terms' necessary for the formation of non-analytic axioms.

Not more than 'Being' the Stranger, the Generalised Unconscious as non(-)self-signifying does not entirely take the place of the old unconscious. They respond to a 'unified' rather than blended discovery and invention (semi-psychological, semi-ethno-religious, semi-philosophical). Non-analysis does not transform analysis from inside and outside, but only from outside. It is as much a new science as a new use-of-thought of a meta-science in view of knowing the scientific continent of man. The inner and outer Other was philosophy itself to a near nuance, for example, the deconstructions where it would only affect its convertibility with Being by being convertible still with the One. Contemporary analysis gives rise to this attempt of an empirico-(linguistico-)transcendental unconscious, of which we will not say that it is monstrous, but rather that it manifests the monstrously impossible character of philosophy that prefers to think man as Other rather than really annihilating itself before him. The Stranger or the Generalised Unconscious does not give rise to a supplementary deconstruction, but a science that occasionally contains the non-Freudian generalisation of Freud, the non-Lacanian generalisation of Lacan, and so on. A non-philosophy in general, if it contains deconstruction, only uses it locally without being defined by this practice. Whether it is also a non-deconstruction, the proof is that it takes existing deconstructions as simple models of interpretation of its own statements. Far from taking analysis for what it is given and what it wants to be – for the Real itself or, to the contrary, as deprived of the Real, it is always the pretension of a tradition to constitute the reality of man – it rather suspends this sufficiency and reduces analysis to the functions of occasion, material and 'axiomatic' model of its knowledge.

Science-thought in general, what we can call thus, above all the one that takes man as an object precisely because he is a First Given and not retro-anticipated, is not that which has taken place; the *Joui* is not a possibility of the tradition to elucidate, comment on and deconstruct. The *Joui* is more than a past, more than a forgetting or, even, more than a repressed object of philosophy and which would like to make it into a symptom. If being foreclosed by analysis apparently defines it as an Other, it is because of its positive constitution, whereby it is not first an Other but the full-identity of the Ego, even more other than the Other at the point of it ceasing to be an 'Other'. The science of man does not first think him as a transcendence, but rather as the radical immanence of a *Joui*. By contrast, in relation of this instance to analysis, the representation of the *Joui* is defined as *Jouissance* or as the non(-)self-signifying unconscious that 'corresponds' to the Other of deconstructions or the restrained unconscious, but in such a way to a 'degree' higher or in a superior power.

A Transcendental Pragmatics of Psychoanalysis as *a priori* of Experience

Finally, what is to be done with psychoanalysis, the object of many lusts? And why is it a question in any case of continuing to practise it across its insertion in a science that would no longer be a by-product of philosophy? To avoid any misunderstanding about what preceded, to define us in relation as well to philosophical localities, let us somewhat otherwise redesign the overall project that we call 'non-analysis' or 'non-Freudian' analysis.

The critique of the Human Sciences and psychoanalysis is a vain task if it remains a simple 'critique'. Through its empirical dimension, non-analysis uses analytic material; it is a transcendental pragmatics, undoubtedly not related to the objects of analysis, but it is related to analysis itself. Here, 'transcendental' is said of the unilateral relation of transcendence to the Real, which it is not, and to the empirical, which it is furthermore not. Therefore, the Human Sciences are necessary enterprises within their contingent order, but susceptible to a new use that now consists in re-including them within the transcendental procedures that the real-determination-in-the-last-instance explains. This operation is equivalent to a transcendental induction and deduction carried out upon these sciences. The most human science culminates in a pragmatics that is not added to it as a supplement, but which exits from its immanence and takes the existing knowledges of man as its object. The point is not to re-organise them from outside in a style of philosophical and transcendent re-unification, but to go and seek out man in his ultimate seat, to be placed back in it and treat, on this basis, the existing sciences as a simple meta-language and material. Rather than a horizon or a lost paradigm, man is the 'first' point of departure (in an axiomatic sense), the real basis of a science that bears on the givens which already belongs to knowledge. This emplacement, this givenness of a place of contingency means that the newly recognised scientific continent integrates other knowledges, which would occupy and claim to exhaust it, now as simple data.

Regarding the approach of analysts and above all Lacanians, we of course have nothing to object to from the point of view of psychoanalytic logic and the relation to man such that it has assumed it – this is not our problem. Well within this limit, Lacanianism introduces a specific generalisation of analysis, an opening, a heterogeneity, and an effervescence that renews the problematic and prevents it from veering into a simple successor of philosophy all by suddenly making appear better what it ultimately and in any case owes to philosophy. Yet we must go further still and posit as the *de jure* principle of universal extension of psychoanalysis as the *a priori* of all possible experience. Everything that is interpretable by it must be; and even everything that is interpretable in general, 'human phenomena', must be at least 'once' by psychoanalysis and not only by philosophy. However, with this principle of posited universal validity – and it cannot be so by analysis itself – subsists the problem of its limitation and legitimation by a more powerful science such that we draw it from another principle. The givens of this science are phenomena of auto-interpretation, which it would be more or less specular as in philosophy or differed/deferred by the signifier. However, non-analysis universalises analysis by positing beyond undecidable mixtures of facts and theories, phenomena and interpretations, the identity of psychoanalysis and the most expansive experience, an identity that transforms the concept of it. It posits that the Unconscious does not exist in itself, that psychoanalysis 'creates' its own phenomena or, more exactly, exists in an indissociable way with the Unconscious, unified with it in the immanence of the cure. Outside of the unified theory as non-analysis, which is neither circular nor even founded on undecidability, which does not make any type of circle with its givens, which therefore eliminates from its relationship with them any objectivation, there are no givens except theoretico-factual mixtures that it brings to the state of identity without amphibological confusion. We do not here deny the theoretico-factual effectivity of analysis, even its function as a meta-language for the human sciences, but only this restriction that is its auto-interpretation (were it through the depriveness of the real). This total given undecidable of psychoanalysis and symptoms stops being valid for science, its claim in this sense is suspended, and it is reduced to the state of an undecided identity (among others, sociological, economic, ethical, and so on) – non-analysis is not their totalisation or globalisation. Besides, a science neither totalises nor de-totalises its phenomena or its 'objects'. Its first task, but not the only one, is rather to reduce to the state of simple aprioristic givens that which presents itself first as essences, the philosophical type of *a priori*, universal determinations, totalities, and so on. From this point of view, science individuates or determines-in-identity these objects, that is, these universal knowledges, it posits by right their radical universality *for* human experience. Thus is inhibited analytic sufficiency such that it is thought and spontaneously practised on a transcendent basis. Therefore, human phenomena are never raw, they are in any case absolutely primitive mixtures of mathematisable facts and philosophical interpretations or decisions, but to which non-analysis gives a new scope.

Non-analysis is the science that in some way takes as its material meta-psychical discourses and its goal the knowledge of the *psychē's* essence (of) the *psychē*. It implies a radical, non-auto-positional extension of the 'psycho-analysable' such that it is classically defined. Analysis as meta-psychology (in our sense) delimits it in all its contents (unconscious, subject, cure, imaginary, and so on) through a system of decisions, landmarks, distributions and procedures that all amount to excluding a non-analysable (even a psychoanalysis of psychoanalysis must reserve the right of a non-analysable in the sense of a Real-that-is-impossible-to-analyse and finally an un-analysable analysis). An analysis generalised under the conditions of a non-philosophical Real re-introduces into the sphere of the analysable, yet in the new sense of this word, necessarily everything that was excluded from it, therefore psychoanalysis itself as such, with the ensemble of its own decisions of 'non-analysability' – even if it does not re-introduce the Real (of) the *Joui* that 'falls' outside it. Non-analysis is not an auto-analysis, its auto-position, the analysis of analysis, but rather the dualysis of psychoanalysis itself as meta-psychology. It alone can generalise the symptom-form that is necessarily auto-/hetero-limitative and substitute it with the material-form on the one hand and the objectivity-form on the other hand, both this time being non-auto-positional. They are delivered from the internal limitations of the 'symptom' and therefore can now contain psychoanalysis itself without the least 'reserve', 'margin' or 'withdrawal', all that still affects the symptom from within and outside. Thus everything enters back – with psychoanalysis itself – into an *a priori* universal materiality. No longer is the symptom the form of that which is analysable, it is this very form that constitutes the new material of non-analysis. Therefore, non-analysis is not a refusal or a negation of psychoanalysis, but only the philosophical, if not the metaphysical limits that it is given to itself as a meta-science. The closure of the unconscious by the symptom-form falls in turn into the Transcendental Unconscious and this symptom-form (as well as other 'forms') is no longer the object of a displacement and a restrained analysis, but an emplacement by the Universal Unconscious and a dualysis that transforms it into a simple material. Thus, everything is dualysable, even psychoanalysis: simply put, dualysis is an operation that is no longer first like analysis was, but second and ordered by the *Joui*, which, as the last-instance, does not truly 'fall' outside of non-analysis, but precedes or conditions it absolutely.

The principle that 'everything' – with exception to the identity of science (and) man – is philosophisable or (auto-)interpretable, equally psychoanalysable, is not an unhealthy extension of knowledge unless it precisely suspends the 'everything' of experience and conceives that it is henceforth psychoanalysis itself that is our *a priori* experience. Therefore, psychoanalysis is for us only one representation necessarily 'accompanying' the self(-)signifying unconscious, one represented and well-founded in the empirical limits of the undecidable mixture that it forms with it and in the aprioristic bounds that non-analysis fixes for it. Its relevance does not go beyond its theoretical limits.

Hence the concept, or task, of 'non-psychoanalysis'. It is neither a matter of a negation of psychoanalysis, nor a psychoanalysis of the non-, but of the rigorous and real knowledge (according to man-of-the-last-instance) of the psychoanalytic material and its practical transformation within the bounds of this science that is simultaneously – by virtue of its pre-supposeds and its mode of constitution, but we cannot demonstrate it here – theoretical and practical: it is the only pragmatics which immanently ensues from the identity of science (and) man and does not exceed these limits. Therefore, 'non-analysis' describes the pragmatics that one such science acquires from psychoanalysis itself when it uses it under conditions that no longer circularly belong to psychoanalysis itself, but belong to the real instance that is man. The real essence of man is the cause *for* analysis and the cause *of* non-analysis. Thus, non-analysis is not a post-analytic or post-Freudian practice, it is the specification, by any such analytic material (classical or already post-Lacanian), of the unified theory of man; a specification that does not determine the essence of man but only the knowledge of man with the help of its conditions of transcendent exercise.

The proposed generalisation does not above all result in the abandonment of its current practice and theorisation. Both must be pursued, although in the limits of the suspension of analytic sufficiency, within the bracketing of its claim to be a 'pilot' human science, the most adequate one to its object. It is not in the intention of non-analysis to limit it, but rather – this is the contrary of limiting – to deliver it (thanks to a limitation of a new type, a transcendental limitation or through *Jouissance*) from its internal limitation by a belief that emerges rather (as we have seen when the essence of man – the *Joui* – has been elucidated for itself) from a transcendental appearance. Thus, a human science does not invalidate analysis in the sense where a philosophy is always tempted to do so (resisting it, blunting it, hierarchically legitimating it, founding it, substituting its real object with a philosophical object that is always of knowledge or a crystalised decision, and so on).

In addition, from this point of view, the reconstitution is definitively impossible by right or for man, of a mixture of a so-called new type under the form of networks, interconnections, intercessions, with rupturing blows or *différance*, between philosophy and analysis, as the analysts, despite everything, are always tempted to resolve to give credit to the good will of alterity of contemporary philosophies. Making from these blends something other than an occasion for a science, once more yielding to the unitary drive which dreams of transforming these givens into the essence of science and thus constituting them into the theoretical conditions of knowledge themselves, all demonstrate at most the force of the Principle of Sufficient Philosophy and the offspring that it begets: the Principle of Sufficient Analysis (sufficient for man).

The Philosophico-Analytic Appearance of Psychoanalysis: The Non-Analyst as Analyst-of-the-Last-Instance

The confusion of the essences distinguished previously, the 'dual' essences, the two-by-two confusion, even in analysis which posits the question of the subject, this is what produces the philosophical amphibologies of analysis – the Philosophico-Analytic Appearance. For example, the Human Sciences stumble upon an ambiguity that, for reasons which hold to their investment by philosophy rather than in their lack of philosophy, they do not succeed in eliminating: it is the same man, they say, who is the subject and object of these sciences. This formula shelters an essentially philosophical aporia, the aporia of the Same as divided or sundered identity, the circular simultaneity of the One and the Dyad. The culture of this aporia is philosophy or, in the best of cases – Lacanianism and the ontology of depriveness or lack – psychoanalysis, which can do nothing but de-magnify and aggravate the aporia to render it more tolerable and theoretically fruitful.

We then understand that psychoanalysis would be grounded on the functional requisition of transcendent entities because they are abstract, directly auto-positional or so in a repressed way: the conscious, the signifier, energy, the unconscious, the Ego [*le Moi*], the Other, and so on, without which it would never be asked how such entities are received and lived, undoubtedly in-the-last-instance, by the Ego in the mode of the *Joui-sans-jouissance*. It is presupposed under a globally transcendent form: it is a technology of the unconscious, rather than a science of it. Hence, to the contrary, the project of an immanent pragmatics by the lone cause (of) science, in opposition to this transcendent pragmatics of the unconscious which analysis currently is. It is not a scientific hypothesis, being ultimately founded by philosophical authority alone, even if it were contested: it is the Principle of Sufficient Consciousness, the sufficiency of the conscious supposed to co-determine the essence of man. Even if the Unconscious and its subject do not derive from a simple negation of the conscious but of its 'alteration', as depriveness, they form a system with it or with Being, and endorse their claim to constitute the Real. *Jouissance* as the non-analytic cause (of) science deracinates this pretension and sends it back to unessentiality, as it sends back the conscious and 'restrained' unconscious to the contingency of simple givens. The science of people can only be established on the reduction of this aporia as a phenomenon of meta-language to the state of contingent given from which it seeks to produce an explanation grounded in rigour and reality. The dissolution of this unitary amphibology, of what philosophy designates in a hasty way as 'the same' man, is done within the prior recognition of that which a scientific posture, rather than a philosophical decision, is in the right of requiring.

Such amphibologies – and we will detect a certain number of them later on – obviously create an objective appearance of the unconscious under its transcendent and dogmatic form, an objective psychoanalytic appearance. Within it is grounded restrained analytic practice, being deeper than any psychological, anthropological, sociological re-appropriation, and so on, of analysis. From this point of view, the equivalent of the *factum* or the mixed fact, the empirico-rational doublet that the philosophers are given by presupposing their own transcendent existence, are here the symptoms as productions of the unconscious within the conscious or again in the 'subject'. They are utilised in accordance with this objective analytic appearance. Confused with it, they are supposed to contain – to a near interpretation or privation – the science of themselves, at least virtually and 'in a broken line' [*en pointillé*]. Neither the position of the analyst as representative of the *objet a* nor transference nor the lack that can break or differ/defer any duell [*duelle*] or specular relation are enough to oblige analysis to renounce this mythical identity, this sameness of the symptom and the science of the symptom. By contrast, a science of humans (as Strangers) and the non-analysis that ensues from it completes by dualysing without return the symptom and its science. It is rooted within *Jouissance* as cause-(of)-science rather than in the subject-of-the-symptom, here simply reduced to the state of a given becoming 'analytically' inert or sterile. The cause (of) science is the genuine 'analyst' – now 'of-the-last-instance', and there is no non-analysis unless it is 'identified' with the *Joui* and the immanent posture of *Jouissance*. As to the symptom or the subjugated subject barred by the restrained analytic decision, it has to instead come upon this Universal Unconscious that we are able to define in another context as the specific void of Humanity or Strangers. This is all the Unconscious can still provide once it has been purged by science of its transcendent ends and contents and once it is generalised or has become the immanent affect (of) an absolute loss, or again the *Jouissance* (of) what we call a 'uni-lateralisation'.

Which One Resists? Indifference and Resistance

Re-introducing as we do the 'Ego' and 'man' on the basis of a science will appear to psychoanalysis, despite the new meaning of these old names, like a provocation of an impardonable naivety after the Freudian and Lacanian reduction of the

Cartesian subject, a new attempt of revenge of philosophy against the unconscious. Yet if analysts read us as a subspecies of metaphysics, it is because they cannot understand the non-analytic use of the old names of philosophy as 'first terms' and lead us back to a subjectivist and narcissistic metaphysics that psychoanalysis has obviously sealed off. This attempt is to displace and even 'emplace' both: to finally put them back in their place in accordance with the unilateral duality henceforth of the *Joui* and the Unconscious. In a sense, being fetishists of language and the signifier, it is enough to write the word 'Ego' so that they accuse us of 'consciousness' and '*logos*' punishable with analysis or deconstruction. However, this would be to forget that we proceed in our own way to an 'analysis' or 'deconstruction' – a dualysis, rather – of the Ego, but that it is not grounded on language but on the 'thing' itself or the Real, that is, in *Jouissance* as cause-of-the-last-instance of science. It is curious yet inevitable – this is its own resistance – that analysis leads the One back, such that it is given as lived-in-One before Being, towards unitary narcissism, and it is always surprising to hear oneself object to what one has put all their care into, forging the necessary tools, to reduce or suspend. Psychoanalysis and deconstruction are obviously accustomed to this procedure.

We cannot speak of the narcissism concerning the 'self(-)enjoying' Ego which, or better yet the one who [*qui*], is *Joui-sans-jouissance* except on condition of falsifying it *a priori* on the basis of one resistance; of confusing the fully non-thetic One with the One of metaphysics. It is somewhat like if one confused Heidegger's 'Being itself' with the Being of metaphysics. This pure and simple denegation of that which is in question consists in projecting a transcendent or ontological image of the One-in-One, nevertheless defined by the lone non(-)self-decisional immanence of the *Joui*, therefore outside of the criteria of ontology. Deconstruction and psychoanalysis say that narcissism is invincible or unavoidable, but this thesis does not make sense unless within their most general presuppositions, which are very exterior and unelucidated because they belong to auto-positional transcendence. They take their own auto-limitation or their own narcissism as universal and want to spread it everywhere, even up to the heart of man and science. Where we attempt to place non-unitary, radically open dualities, they will undoubtedly see in the contemporary way connections or interlacings. Placing deconstruction and non-philosophy or non-psychoanalysis on the same plane is a very complex form of humour, and the post-Lacanian analysts are decidedly closer to Derridean deconstruction correctly understood than non-philosophy.

The transcendental point of view – albeit in a 'non-philosophical' sense – as Kant and Husserl have remarked it without being given however the means of liquidating the empirico-transcendental doublet, is often poorly understood, interpreted as a judgement or an effective intervention in the field of experience where it then becomes, for example, the adversary of psychoanalysis. One such philosophical intervention into psychoanalysis is obviously not our problem, which is rather of use by man as *Jouissance* of the strains of the Unconscious and statements of psychoanalysis. Non-analysis is everything except the effective, immediate negation of psychoanalysis. A unified theory does not negate or mitigate the virulence of it even less as philosophy always does to the contrary, than it is to consider it as the only authentic theory of the subject that would be born on the terrain of the Human Sciences, even if it estimates that it still concedes too much to philosophy as to its conception of the 'subject' of which it has not perceived the real phenomenal content. Unlike philosophy, psychoanalysis is the discovery of the care of the Other as subjugating the subject, and the Real as lack, but it also wants man to do his part as soon as it treats him sometimes as a subspecies of the Other (man) and sometimes as the Subject subjugated by science, while the Archimedean point would rather here be the radical identity of man, and therefore of science and philosophy. The new discipline can do nothing but accept the somewhat Judaic radicalisation of the Other that philosophy would tolerate with recognition, and without philosophically combating it. However, its posture is more of a science for basic reasons: it considers psychoanalysis itself (in the broad sense of a theoretico-factual mixture) as a new material called on to be not only known but transformed by and within the limits of this knowledge. An effective material to take up within the integrality of its claims, if it is not upon the point of its illusory 'access' to man, it is a relation that is still other than what it believes and that this science will begin by suspending to examine and faithfully describe the 'psychoanalysis' phenomenon. As we have said, the point is to define an immanent posture, rather than a strategy and a teleology; a posture of absolute, non-objectivating respect, of the irreducibility and interpretive force of analysis, rather than resistance or even the immediate aggravation of the alterity of the Unconscious.

Therefore, let us distinguish between a philosophical resistance to any science, consequently to analysis as a particular case of science; and a non-philosophising, non-idealising reduction, a 'realising' rather than 'materialising' reduction, of a more restrained theory by a more general theory. This reduction (to the state of given or material) no longer proceeds through 'difference', but through the suspension or transcendental indifferenciation of the spontaneous theories that then become inert or sterile, not from their point of view, but from the sole point of view of this more general theoretical use within which it now enters as an 'occasional' material-of-knowledge. There is a general power of indifferenciation by the Real-of-the-last-instance of empirical or given theories, and whose analytic 'neutrality' is a particular or restrained case. We will distinguish between: (1) a philosophical resistance to analysis: it is resistance to science alone, if at least analysis does not want to be an inessential phenomenon bound to a conflict of cultural forces, a hypothesis which we exclude here as without real importance; (2) analytic neutrality, a means against (philosophical or other) resistance, but in turn a resistance to a generalised analysis; it is a resistance somewhat distinct from the philosophical resistance because it is founded within an indifference no doubt, but still too restrained because of its inevitable philosophical overdetermination; (3) a 'generalising' transcendental indifference of an origin that is itself real and absolutely foreign to resistance; this is not even a 'resistance to resistance' (for example of philosophy); it has no traits of resistance that is always of an other-than-real and other-than-scientific origin; this is the 'Equivalency Principle'; and (4) finally, it belongs to the new science of people to define a broadened or generalised concept of resistance, such that 'classical' analysis, which we must more rigorously call 'restrained', still falls into because of its transcendent presuppositions. The affect of the 'absolute' or first Other, which is the content of the unconscious (and its entanglements with the conscious), is undoubtedly not entirely one such transcendent or auto-positional presupposition, but it is necessarily one with a philosophical-type of transcendence (re-divided and re-doubled, transcendence-in-transcendence, and so on) and sometimes, in certain somewhat rigorous interpretations of analysis, is simply cultural and technological. It is impossible for a philosophical decision to renounce this combat and return to the strain of the non-auto-positional Other or in the bounds of simple humanity. Only one science can demonstrate that the hardest concept of the unconscious still contains a transcendent and therefore arbitrary determination; it is efficacious in its own way no doubt, but without rigour nor real foundation; it is an efficacy still techno-cultural in another turn, which has nothing to do with the real transformation of effectivity that the unified theory can do. Hitherto, man has only been interpreted or analysed by psychoanalysis; the point now is to know him in reality and in rigour, and to transform that which of him can be transformed within the simple limits of his knowledge.

Second Section: Explanation of the Theorem of Non-Analysis

The Real or the *Joui-sans-Jouissance*

We strive to explain the founding theorem of non-analysis – without demonstrating it, its demonstration being of the same type of demonstration as the Stranger – by taking it up in each of its terms. Let us recall: the Real or the *Joui-sans-jouissance* determines-in-the-last-instance, that is, through the organon of *Jouissance*, the Unconscious as the dualysis of the Transcendental Appearance which is the philosophico-psychoanalytic symptom. It is a matter of an explanation, not a commentary. We renounce the rhetorical and discursive precautions to use by way of the lapidary style of the dictionary or the axiom. The terms put forward are 'first names' and axioms made to function, with some indications to elaborate and rectify, as simple yet poorly carved stones awaiting a construction. Let us add that this theorem and explanation take Lacanianism as a material because Lacanianism forms a conjuncture for us. It is a matter of a 'standard' and simple Lacanianism, and our concern is not to refine and nuance it; rather, to transform it.

1. The analytic concept of '*jouissance*' is an amphibology of a philosophical nature, the mixture of the *Joui-sans-jouissance* and the operation of *jouissance*. It is a unitary generality that makes psychoanalysis a 'neighbour' of philosophy.

This mixture cannot be destroyed or annihilated as such, but only dualysed on the basis of the absolute autonomy of the *Joui* as being the Real. The *Joui* implicates outside itself, on the one hand, the dissociation of the *Joui* and *Jouissance* as two heterogeneous natures, abusively yet necessarily blended by philosophy; and, on the other hand, the determination-in-the-last-instance of the second by itself. As to the mixture, it is treated as the philosophico-analytic complex and conserved as a symptomatic material that non-analysis takes as its object.

2. The *Joui*-that-is-nothing-but-*Joui* is not the result or product of the transcendent operation of *jouissance*, it is *Joui-en-Joui* or self(-)immanent rather than immanent to the *jouissance* that would give or constitute it. Its reality is a phenomenal (radical) type, not a transcendent (empirico-ideal) type. It is the concrete essence of radical immanence, not yet divided between joy and suffering, nor by the other distributions of affectivity. As lived experience (of) the lived or the lived-before-life, the *Joui*-before-*Jouissance* is the real essence of man and it is within him that non-analysis must be rooted in priority if it wants to be able to relate psychoanalysis to its real object, man.

The *Joui* is foreign to the Philosophical Ego, to the 'subject' as to the 'individual', which are always divided, eventually distributed by *jouissance* in its philosophico-analytic (hereon = PA) concept. It does not enter within the bounds of such transcendent forms (the ego-form, the subject-form, the substance-form, the partial-object-form, and the flux-form, the signifier-form, and so on), being nothing but self(-)immanent, never the attribute of a psychic or physical subject already constituted within transcendence. In particular, it excludes the 'auto-perception' (of the id) which is nothing but intuitive, ergo objectivating, auto-positional and transcendent. The *Joui* being given without *jouissance* has nothing of an affective intuition or an intuition of drives, which would be theoretically disastrous concepts with the return to the worst Greco-Western presuppositions of philosophy. *Jouissance* itself will not be intuitive in the sense of an auto-position, but, rigorously, a simple intuition or objectivation, without a folding, refolding or doublet.

However, it is possible - this is our axiomatic liberty - to identify the *Joui* and another 'first name', the 'Ego', if the latter is then defined as Ego-in-Ego: this is not to re-insert analysis, on the contrary, in a psycho-metaphysical context. Generally, the *Joui* is the first name - the first name of the Real - and the type of the real that explains that, if there is an ('unconscious') thought commanded by it, it will proceed through philosophically and analytically undefinable and indemonstrable 'first names', like the real (of the) *Joui* itself which is 'ontologically' or phenomenally first, absolutely autonomous and precedes, by definition, Being, non-Being, *Jouissance*, the Unconscious, and so on.

3. We can form the following axioms regarding the model of the two Lacanian axioms of the One: (1) there is some *Joui* [*Il y a du* Joui]; but (2) the *Joui* is not.[4] Provided by their object and above all the way in which the One is included there as the One (of) the *Joui* or the Real, it is excluded that they still have a non-descript Lacanian meaning. The first means that 'there is some *Joui* as given-without-*jouissance*, a phenomenal given that precedes the operation of *jouissance*'. The second means: 'The *Joui* is the Real-without-being; it is real, because it is the *Joui*, rather than because it is or it is not.' These two formulations also contain the critique of psychoanalysis and its ultimate presupposition that is assembled in the two axioms of the One. To not be experienced as One-in-One is indeed then experienced as the old transcendent One of philosophy that has been simply 'sobered' [*dégraissée*] or emptied of Being and led back to the locality of the Other, as the contemporaries do, who are in general 'deconstructors' and substitute the convertibility of the One and Being with the 'post-modern' convertibility of the One and Other. To not be experienced as cause, it is held liable [*mis en cause*] in an ultimately philosophical way through the confusion with Being. To not be experienced as the Real, it is rejected on the side of the signifier (the unary trait, the One-as-*heteros*; the One identical to difference and multiplicity). All of this forms a system: the philo-analytic resistance to the

[4] Translator's note: Laruelle is alluding to Lacan's formulations present in Seminar XIX. The reader is recommended to refer to *The Seminar of Jacques Lacan, Book XIX: . . . or Worse*, translated by A. R. Price (Cambridge: Polity, 2018).

Joui is identically the resistance to the One-in-One and the Real, the alienation of the One to the Other (rather than to Being), the rejection of the Real on the side of the Other and even beyond the Other. Non-analysis begins with the equivalency of the One (nevertheless as in-One), the *Joui* (nevertheless as without-*jouissance*), and the Real (nevertheless as non-convertible with Being, being, and the Other).

4. With the absolute autonomy of the *Joui*, whose essence excludes Being and Totality, and their modes – the 'subject' and the 'individual', but also '*Dasein*' – non-analysis finally inserts analysis into the human real by excluding both the subjectivist-philosophical reduction to the conscious but also to the unconscious, which, when it is not ordered by the *Joui*, is posited as 'first' and sinks into the most unreal transcendence and, finally, into a substantialisation of lack that postulates, simply to truncate it, the most substantial Being. The *Joui*, as that which determines the Unconscious in-the-last-instance, is the surest guarantee of the non-substantialisation of the Unconscious, either positive and metaphysical or by lack and absence, by the ultimate fetishisation of the 'signifier'.

5. The real (of the) *Joui* is not accessible or inaccessible, possible or impossible – this is a question of a transcendent disjunction that represses its essence – it is given-without-givenness or lived-without-*jouissance*. Any other comprehension of the Real submits it to philosophical amphibologies and antinomies, even if it then means to push it away into the extreme transcendence and alienation, into the external limits of philosophy, the very exterior of the Dyad or Decision, beyond the being/non-being couple, towards the impossible, absence and lack, and so on, which continue to presuppose the real pertinence of philosophy even up to the heart of psychoanalysis. This is to confuse the Real, defined by its radical immanence, with its philosophical and analytic (= PA) image or representation. The procedure of non-analysis is more than the inverse: instead of opposing or apposing the Real with the philosophical and even analytic prism at risk of contradictions which result in a destiny of aberration for the Real, it lets-itself-be-given the *Joui* and as a consequence modifies the theoretical field of analysis more deeply than any 'reshuffling' of its 'foundations'.

Non-analysis also recognises its limit within the Real, but it is not an inaccessible, unrealisable real, the lure of an incestuous-type of absolute *jouissance* – therefore, non-real and transcendent. On the contrary, it is because it is absolutely immanent that the Real is outside of the alternative between the accessible and inaccessible, the possible and the impossible. This latter problem is not posited – except within thought where transcendence is determinant: it is that which associates analysis with the philosophical, since the Real determines-in-the-last-instance the thought or Unconscious within which they are and made to manifest themselves the desire proper to analysis of an impossible real as hallucinatory desire. It is not the '*jouissance* of the Other' that appears to us as inaccessible and subject to the lure; it is, in analysis itself, its confusion of the Real and *Jouissance*. Whether the Unconscious would be, as *Jouissance*, determined-in-the-last-instance by the real (of) the *Joui* is the internal or real, not simply transcendent, limit of non-analysis and, moreover, of analysis. The limit of non-analytic knowledge is therefore not that there is no signifier or relation to 'symbolise' or 'know' *Jouissance*; it is that the *Joui* has no need for this symbolisation, the Real by essence and positively excluding the signifier and in general the Unconscious; and it is because *Jouissance*, of which we will say that it is the organon of the *Joui* and intrinsically identical to the Unconscious, does not have need more than the Unconscious of the symbolic relation, but an articulation-without-'relation': we must describe this.

6. The *Joui* excludes the alternative or antinomy of the symptom as the suffering of the subject or as satisfaction or solace for the unconscious. It desensitises the most transcendent sensitivity as it de-energises energy, and it has nothing to do with orgasmic pleasure, for example. What we mean by this is that we must stop conceiving the *Joui* as a super-idealised or subtilised form of sensitivity and energy, that it is the undivided heart of the Real-One and that, as such, no distinction of the suffering/joy, pain/pleasure, tension/relaxation, and so on, can happen within it. Non-analysis is one way of thinking – as we have incessantly said some words about – that requires us to learn to withdraw from the givens of analysis as an intuitive and naive discipline first terms, that is, terms whose radical identity of their object is analytically undefinable and indemonstrable. The *Joui* is therefore not a more radical form of auto-affection, a more immanent form of sorrow and joy, tension and relaxation. It is the undivided lived experience (of) pain – pain does not determine it – as the undivided lived experience of joy, but in no way their synthesis, however immanent, their becoming or passage from one into the other that would then reconstitute the philosophical triad at the heart of the Real.

7. Following Freud and radicalising the specific affect of analysis, Lacan invented a special form of non-metaphysical ontology but within the bounds of philosophy, an experience of Being as lack, neither Being-substance nor an opposing non-Being, but, as he says, as 'not-yet-realised' or an 'impossible to realise', consequently avoiding this metaphysical alternative. This ontology

is accompanied by new affects, surprising theoretical means (what we will call a certain form - there could be other ones - of real algebra). In a certain way, it is distinguished from all already existent philosophical ontologies constructed on the experiences of 'non-being', 'nothingness', substantialist and classical 'depriveness', 'negation', 'real opposition', 'dialectical negation', and phenomenological 'givenness' and 'non-givenness'. It is an ontology of active depriveness, of loss as that which is withdrawn or removed from us, of the hole as that which is dug, and so on. An already subtractive, yet what we call 'privational', ontology (rather than 'donative' or 'negational', and so on) and that is probably or could be (no matter, what only matters is the conjuncture or symptom) the ontology adequate to the Freudian discovery. It is rather a matter of an ontology in the broad sense or a philosophy in that which it bears upon a transcendent real - even if it does not confuse it with Being. It is to metaphysics, rather than ontology, that it is opposed to Heidegger's following. Therefore, it remains taken up 'in' the limits of philosophy, thus binding once more psychoanalysis and philosophy in a complex or a mixture that is one of the objects of non-analysis. However, with this thesis, non-analysis is not a new philosophical interpretation of psychoanalysis (Wittgenstein, Deleuze, Ricœur, Derrida, and so on), and it is precisely opposed to such philosophical reductions as soon as it posits, as it does so here, the inseparability of philosophy and analysis at the same time as their distinction (the affect of depriveness) within the philosophico-analytic (=PA) complex.

8. The *Joui* unilaterally commands non-analysis, it cannot immediately, that is, reciprocally, be the real object upon which bears non-analysis, contrarily to analysis which also bears - by failing - on *jouissance*. As absolute lived experience, independent of 'life' itself, it commands the identically theoretical and pragmatic style of non-analysis. The summary and transcendent alternative of the mathematisation (algebra/topology) of the unconscious or the return to the 'lived' (under the vulgar form that we now oppose to Lacan but to which he gives sway) is displaced outside of the lived (of) the *Joui* and, through it, towards the symptom alone. This is why non-analysis is the 'unified theory' or transcendental identity of the *mathesis universalis* and the lived experience (in the new sense of *Jouissance* determined by the *Joui*), a more radically subjective or human lived experience than the one of psychology. This unification does not have its secret within itself, but within the essence of the lived-as-Real. The *Joui*, therefore, is that which imposes in-the-last-instance the theoretico-pragmatic style of a transcendental *mathesis* towards 'unconscious' thought or the dualysis that is its organon: there is no philosophical decision or position, more or less arbitrary, here.

9. Of the *Joui* and with the *Joui* alone, non-analysis can say 'nothing' or cannot say anything except to assume given or constituted the other phenomenal orders: *Jouissance* (which provides the organon for it), the Unconscious (which provides the 'syntax' of its language), and finally the philosophico-analytic Symptom (which provides its material and language). Said otherwise, the *Joui* must be 'surpassed' towards . . . (but not alienated in . . .) another order, '*Jouissance*' itself – we have not yet posited it – with the emergence of that which is finally posited, the problem of the causality of the *Joui* or what it can do. *Qua Joui*, it cannot do anything for non-analysis and even less for analysis – it is for them *de jure* as absolutely indifferent as the Real is able to be. The Real is not the impossible, it is the absolute indifference (towards . . .). By contrast, it is across *Jouissance* that it acts (upon) the Unconscious. The crucial problem that is too quickly ruled out by analysis of what *jouissance* can do to the unconscious and their articulation is what non-analysis makes into its central theme. If analysis posits within transcendence this articulation or 'tinkering' by connecting these two instances, non-analysis posits them in immanence or in accordance with the 'syntax' that the *Joui* can tolerate.

10. The substitution of an axiomatic style with the algebraic style is undoubtedly explained by the difference of 'ontologies' – a term debatable in both cases – between analysis and non-analysis. The notions that theorise the unconscious when it is affected by a real as lack, the unconscious knowledge when it is *de jure* holed out and lacunary even deprived of any metaphysical identity, they are constructed by means of literal substitutes, letters designating the unknown or impossible that discourse elaborates. The notions that theorise an unconscious, on the contrary, determined by a real as One-in-One, as Viewed-without-Vision or *Joui-sans-jouissance* determinant in-the-last-instance of thought, and not co-determined by it, rather function as first terms or names allowing for the construction of a theory or a hypothesis. The two conceptions of the '*sans*' or 'without' – one as a 'privational' type', the other 'donative', as we will see – are so distinct by the 'ontology' that they presuppose that one requires a real algebra, the other a real axiomatic.

In a general way, this type of first terms, when it is a matter of non-analysis or any other 'unified theory', means that they are quasi-first names. Therefore, they are formed from the past participle, rather than the present participle in order to thereby indicate the being-given-without-givenness, not that of the 'terms' themselves under their linguistic aspect, but that of their object-of-the-last-instance, this use of symbolism applied to concepts themselves being determined-in-the-last-instance by the Real or the *Joui*. Here as elsewhere, it is allowed to use resources of the old names and, instead of suffering them like a paleonomic destiny, forge them into a neonomic use, a use of discovery and invention that treats them as what we call first names. We do not above all confuse the analytic refusal to define and measure *jouissance* and pleasure with their treatment as analytically undefinable first names as we will see: there is no negative physics of the unconscious, no negative energetics.

11. This is perhaps a progression within the intelligence of analytic phenomena than it is to pass from a substance-*jouissance* to a loss-*jouissance* and thus designate the limits of the ineffable, even to 'algebrise' and 'topologise' them. Yet how does one confuse the passage from a substantial ontology to a privational ontology, a passage that is helped by a requisition of new mathematical means, with a passage within the sciences and a real critique of the presuppositions of philosophy? The first Lacanian innovation is in 'depriveness' as an ontological *a priori* and not as a simple local experience, in depriveness as a new affect in relation to the existing affects of philosophy but which can entirely insert itself into philosophy. The second is in the requisition of the new mathematical means to prop it up, to describe it and give it a consistency (ancient ontology already has 'its' mathematics). However, this encounter leaves unchanged the most general invariants of philosophy, for it is towards them that non-analysis attacks, rather than the 'main *pathos*' of depriveness as schizo-analysis does. The illusion of philosophical transcendence, of the supposed determinant decision of the Real, rather oozes out re-enforced by this proof of lack or lets one believe that it is the real critique of philosophy. It now takes the form of a mystical sphere of the unfathomable real beyond the limits and the possible, a sphere described from outside by mathematical language but which, repelling the occult character of the unconscious further, in no way abolishes it.

Non-analysis does more than invert this flight into transcendence. It opposes the unfathomable with the Real as *Joui-en-Joui* and gives it an intrinsic intelligibility. It defines it as '*sans-Jouissance*', making the '*sans*' an effect of the immanence of the *Joui*, rather than an assumed constitutive depriveness of the Real. It nominates the Real of a first name (first term + proper name) that it can insert into a real-axiomatic-in-the-last-instance, therefore into a *mathesis transcendentalis* wherein *Jouissance* is the organon or immanent operator, simultaneously theoretical and pragmatic. If *jouissance* is a 'mysticism' beyond limits, the *Joui* is intrinsically mystical, a phenomenon of immanence which does not pass through limits destined to phenomenalise it or through algebras destined to algorithmise it. Finally, as to *Jouissance*, it could draw a positive meaning from Lacan's confession: 'there is no sexual relationship, an understatement:

formulable in a structure',[5] and posit that there is rather a sexual relationship of an unprecedented kind that, if it is not formulable in a thought through structure, is entirely formulable in thought through the first names of non-analysis.

Jouissance

1. As Organon of the Real

1. The dualysation of '*jouissance*' as a unitary generality of analysis makes a second instance beside the *Joui* appear: we will precisely call it with the first name '*Jouissance*'. It possesses an original qualitative structure in relation to the *Joui* – it is a structure of transcendence (which is nevertheless not itself transcendent or auto-positional) and not of immanence, but just as radical in its order as it. By contrast, its phenomenal and functional autonomy is nothing but relative . . . relative to the real (of the) *Joui* in relation to which it is solely second and by which it is determined as by a cause (from) immanence. The *Joui* is the cause-of-the-last-instance of the non-analytic cure, *Jouissance* is its organon – still a thing other than what the metaphor of the 'motor of the cure' restrains.

Finally, it itself determines the Unconscious, not by a driving [*motrice*] and in some way efficient causality, but by a determination-in-the-last-instance. The Unconscious of non-analysis is not so much a concrete effectuation and a modalisation of *Jouissance* than its syntactic aspect of side. Far from being amorphous like the analytic 'real' that is only structured in a physico-energetic and transcendent way, then obliged to invest the signifying differences of the body where it is alienated, it is from the outset structured by the 'dual syntax' or 'unilateral duality' that is the Unconscious in a radical sense, that is, by the real kernel of the 'signifier'. We will examine this in the following paragraph. We reprise these different points.

Dualysis is the very method of non-analysis applied to analytic material, here to the philosophico-unitary concept of *jouissance*. If dualysation is determined by the *Joui* in-the-last-instance, it liberates from this unitary generality the utterly specific original content of *Jouissance*, distinct from the *Joui*, and explains the otherwise unintelligible articulation of the *Joui* and the Unconscious. Qualitatively, *Jouissance* is absolutely original: it is transcendence itself such that it is presupposed independently of the radical immanence of the

[5] Translator's note: Quoted from Jacques Lacan, *Autres écrits* (Paris: Éditions du Seuil, 2001), 413. This work has not been translated yet, and thus the translator has to rely on a certain familiarity with Lacanian psychoanalysis.

Joui. Its specific essence, distinct from its forms taken from psychic energy and which rather repress it, is indeed radical transcendence or which is nothing but exteriority. It is not limited by the space/time/horizon/signifying/differe(a)nce/set-forms, and so on, by which such and such philosophy strives to separate it from itself and from what it can do. More generally, it is not divided, split and refolded by auto-position or any such doublet as is the case in analysis. It is transcendence itself, its identity in person, rather than a transcendent entity. It is thus, in its essence, not in its investment of the Unconscious, a non-auto-positional position, even less than an ontological position as one would attempt to imagine it 'simplified': for example, it is not 'power-desiring', which is at the heart of Being itself according to Heidegger. It is a power reduced to its strict internal identity or to its performativity, which neither exceeds nor is withdrawn from itself. Psychoanalysis is necessarily 'lacking' this problem of the identity of *Jouissance* after having lacked the problem of the *Joui* or the Real.

However, it also lacks, for the same reason, its real constancy. If the qualitative nature of *Jouissance* does not belong to the *Joui* and is absolutely heterogeneous to it, if from this point of view it presupposes itself or is presupposed 'beside' the *Joui* as soon as there is non-analysis, then by contrast from the phenomenal point of view it does not posit itself however – as analysis believes by making it thus into a transcendent principle for the exercise of the unconscious (beside another one, the Phallus) and a sort of hinterworld of the unconscious – its phenomenal reality – that is, its real content –; it holds it from the *Joui* where it is received and lived in the very mode of the *Joui. Jouissance* does not penetrate within the phenomenon of the *Joui*; rather, it is an 'operation' that is itself 'enjoyed' [*jouie*] without being a real part of the *Joui*, which nonetheless does not tolerate it. Whether *Jouissance* is 'enjoyed' in-the-last-instance is not a tautology – the heterogeneity of structures prohibits this –; it is the real condition of its non-analytic efficacy.

2. We will summarise these relations – this is their syntax – by the definition of *Jouissance* as an organon of the *Joui.* Through its absolutely phenomenal essence, the *Joui* cannot be alienated in *Jouissance*, it cannot be lost there or divided by it. On its side, *Jouissance* holds its own inalienable identity of the *Joui*, but it is an identity which is said now of a thing other than the Real or the *Joui*: of this transcendence that is *Jouissance.* Therefore, it is a transcendental identity or one that prohibits *Jouissance* from being distributed according to transcendent distinctions, not only the 'generic' and analytic ones, but rather the philosophical ones themselves. We call this articulation of an absolute autonomy and a relative autonomy, an articulation without synthesis but through the identity (of)

a duality of structures, the determination-in-the-last-instance. Thus is broken not aprioristically by a distinction of thought or reason, but by a real distinction or still more rigorously by the very identity (of) the Real, the amphibological generality of 'the-*jouissance*'. It is dualysed to the benefit of, on the one hand, an undivided identity between the *Joui* and *Jouissance* without synthesis; and, on the other hand, their duality, also without synthesis, an irreducible duality which involves the qualitative autonomy of *Jouissance.*

The causality of the *Joui* 'within' the Unconscious is now rendered intelligible by its very immanence and stops being a 'theoretico-clinical' bricolage of massively metaphysical entities. The *Joui* is the cause (of) immanence of *Jouissance*, and *Jouissance* is its simple, unique organon without a doublet and therefore without an 'instrumental' or technological 'circuit' at the heart of the Unconscious. *Jouissance* does not determine the *Joui* and it is not determined, at least in its qualitative essence and above all in its phenomenal identity, by the Unconscious like the transcendence of the 'signifier', or even determined by the impossibility of this signifying difference, as much as analysis posits it.

The problems of causality, treated in a hesitant or amphibological way by analysis, are finally ruled on in the following way. Whereas analysis 'forgets' the original causality of the Real, of the immanence (of the) *Joui*, to substitute it with a divided, empirico-transcendental causality, with the doublet of the energetic and lack, non-analysis restores it as absolutely original, distinct from the four metaphysical forms of causality. Whereas analysis attributes the material and ideal causality to the signifier or the unconscious, the efficient causality to this real divided by the energetico-ontological doublet, and perhaps final causality to the imaginary, non-analysis dispossesses the Real of the efficient or driving causality and gives *Jouissance* the identity which gathers ontological reality in an interior way distributed between the four forms of transcendent or metaphysical causality and, therefore, gives it by making it into a non-auto-positional organon. One could believe that the latter marks in this way the technical achievement of metaphysics in non-analysis; this is nothing of the case: thanks to the *Joui*, *Jouissance* is a non-technological organon of the Real and, at least in its essence, does not carry any aspect of finality, formality, efficiency or materiality.

3. The analytic concept of *jouissance* is transferred [*décalqué*] from psychic energy and from a transcendent physical model that their transformations are not enough to totally eliminate to carve a space for a specific or transcendental concept of *Jouissance.* The energetic-type of phenomena: discharge, expenditure, conservation, repression, tension, overstimulation [*suractivation*] - graspable on the level of lapses, dreams and symptoms - are not only foreign to the *Joui*,

which is no longer an energetic and economic concept, but, under the analytic form, to *Jouissance* itself, which however – as we have demonstrated incessantly – possesses phenomenal characters capable of explaining the ones belonging to the energy called psychic. The same goes for the neighbouring concepts of general, 'an-economic' expenditure, 'without reserve', insofar as they generalise concepts of an economic origin. In a general way, the Lacanian path of abstraction and theorisation of Freud's psycho-physical models and metaphors (as much in the real as in *jouissance*, the unconscious, language, and so on) is an admirable symptom of the desperate hopes of psychoanalysis to extract itself from the sciences from the locality where it is born, to be specified by an original object and conquer its autonomy as a science. They are desperate attempts because the flight into a poorer and poorer and more and more minimal transcendence 'sobered' of its metaphysical substance is the symptom both of the attraction exercised by the immanence (of the) Real and the refusal or impossibility of reaching it otherwise than through the lack or absence that disguises the invisibility, the being-given-without-givenness of the *Joui*.

It goes without saying that Lacan distinguishes *jouissance* and energy, but in an insufficient way for non-analysis, and a distinction that has never been analysed radically, that is, dualysed. Whether *jouissance* is not mathematisable is not enough to think it in its absolute autonomy and in its effects – this is to once more condemn it to the irrational. The *Joui* (and *a fortiori Jouissance*) is nevertheless not foreign to any knowledge, but only to the forms mediating knowledge through representation. Likewise, pleasure is not of the order of the feeling of consciousness and *Jouissance* of the order of the unconscious. It is a matter of a unilateral duality (*Joui*/*Jouissance*, *Joui*/Pleasure, *Jouissance*/Pleasure), in no way a dyad or a transcendent distinction where the *Joui* is always threatened with being re-absorbed into *Jouissance* as the Real is in the Unconscious and, finally, the Unconscious in the Conscious. Non-analysis stops thinking *Jouissance* according to the old model of hubris, as a limit or rupturing phenomenon of consciousness, thought and their continuum, that is, as that which would distinguish it from pleasure and pain. It is a feeble distinction that cannot really tear the Unconscious from its differential conception, even if it goes towards '*différance*'. In the same gesture, another question must then be eliminated: there is no space and time of the non-analytic process, they cannot serve it as a referential even if it were softened, broadened beyond perception, because the heart of non-analysis is the *Joui*, whose mode of being-given excludes time, space, their ontological mixture, and its topological forms. By contrast, *Jouissance* begins by maintaining a certain relation that we will call 'occasional' with the time and space of the PA complex, that is, with that which now emerges from its conditions of transcendent (yet necessary) exercise.

Of course, Lacan neither more nor less than Freud 'forgot' from the outset – this is the very foundation of the sufficiency of spontaneous analysis – the *Joui*. He only achieves by inscribing analysis in a globally philosophical horizon nevertheless implicit in Freud because he simply and solely proposes to tear it from its psycho-energetic origins and to give it, through this unitary transference, another form, yet which is still a mixed form, the mathematico-philosophical mixture, changing its internal form without changing its real object and without first linking it to its real cause: Lacan's theory is a 'unitary theory', not a 'unified theory'. Under the name '*jouissance*', this is how the *Joui* is affected by a transcendent tripartition drawn from the energetic model: 'phallic *jouissance*', 'surplus-enjoyment', and the '*jouissance* of the Other'. This alienating dismembering of the identity (of the) *Joui* and even *Jouissance* is typical of philosophical bricolage in general, and a typically structuralist bricolage in particular.

2. As Jouissance *(of) the Other or Intrinsically Unconscious*

It should be possible to retrieve within the *Jouissance*-organon the traits that, abstracted from it and projected into auto-positional transcendence, have given rise to the three types of *jouissance* distinguished by analysis and the possibility of their co-determination by the physico-energetic model.

1. 'Surplus-enjoyment' [*plus-de-jouir*], the intensification and *jouissance* of internal psychic tension, precisely corresponds nevertheless under a transcendental or intelligible form, without a metaphor both of qualitative and quantitative growth or growth in energetic intensity, to the essence of internal identity of *Jouissance*, which it holds immanently from the *Joui* and escapes from the external/internal variations, transcendent ones in any case, of the 'surplus-(or scarce)-enjoyment'. This latter expression aims towards an energetic mode at the essence (of the) *Joui* or the self(-)experience of *Jouissance* and does not manage to make it into anything but a property of it among others, an extrinsic character which completes in dismembering its transcendental identity. In particular, by falsifying it in the prism of the philosophico-analytic imaginary, it aims for the essence of the actuality and performativity of *Jouissance*, which it transforms, as philosophy does with Being or its essence, into the 'fading'-type of event that is only 'identifiable' at the limits or shores of life. 'Surplus-enjoyment' marks a certain acquisition on the side of the 'verbal', subjective and internal character of *Jouissance*, but it was necessary to infer the essence of *Jouissance* within a transcendental theorem, rather than in a circular argumentation viciously moving between physical energetics and transcendent identity.

2. 'Phallic *jouissance*' or discharge regulated by the phallus corresponds – insofar as it reciprocally presupposes the determination of the unconscious by the energy of *jouissance* – to the proper causality of *Jouissance* (structured according to the unilateral duality, not according to the 'signifier') 'upon' the Unconscious as a concrete modality specified by the organon. *Jouissance* and the Unconscious are not two entities exterior to one another – even in analysis where the latter invests the former, and the former negatively structures the latter – but are no longer either connected, depending on a 'motor' energetic causality. *Jouissance* is the first or transcendental drive invested within and regulated by the 'unilateral duality' (the kernel of 'signifying difference'). It is not amorphous, but it is no longer alienated within an assumed transcendent unconscious because it rather brings about this syntax. On the other hand, whether this regulation is absolutely intrinsic and not extrinsic also means that there is no globally signifying transcendent instance of the Unconscious as the Phallus is – neither a 'full body' nor 'phallus', *Jouissance* never invests a 'body' in the philosophico-analytic sense, a whole-instance or a residue of this instance. Not being born within organs or in 'partial objects' (see schizoanalysis), it furthermore does not invest a transcendent body as the complement of partial organs. There is undoubtedly an immanent body of *Jouissance*, but it is co-extensive with its radical and simple opening, without a refolding or an ecstatic-horizontal structure, and, in any case, it has nothing to do with the transcendent 'body'-form ('object body', 'body proper', 'full body'). It is a subjective body, or a body enjoyed-in-the-last-instance, consequently delivered from any plenitude as from any lack: neither a 'full body' nor a 'phallus', this disjunction rather belongs to Analytic Appearance. By contrast, a certain regulation of *Jouissance* is done by the mediation of the Unconscious when the Unconscious, which 'effectuates' *Jouissance*, no doubt, albeit through the dualysis of the PA Appearance, brings about a specification extracted from it for it. The Unconscious overdetermines *Jouissance* from what it transforms of the material of the mixture, but even under this relatively exterior form, the regulation of *Jouissance* is not done in the transcendent way as psychoanalysis imagines.

Finally, if *Jouissance* is limited, it is from within, by its immanent cause itself (the *Joui*) and because it is a transcendental instance alone, rather than the Real. Therefore, it does not need an external limitation by a signifier, the phallus, and by a transcendent and inaccessible real as '*jouissance* of the Other' would. If there are limitation phenomena, they are rather represented by the very existence of the PA complex and the 'restrained' way in which it spontaneously understands *Jouissance* – this limitation is therefore itself a transcendental appearance. As to the non-analytic cure, the specification with which it proceeds from the Unconscious through what it extracts from the PA complex, it is not a limitation: the former remains universal, the latter is limited to make it exist concretely. The Unconscious is not 'that being, in speaking, enjoys' (Lacan),[6] for it 'enjoys' before speaking, or, more exactly, it is the *Joui* that precedes the enjoyment (of) speaking and, consequently it enjoys (= *Jouissance*) on the *occasion* of speaking. Speaking is only one occasional cause of the unconscious *Jouissance*, in no way a cause of the *Joui*.

3. Finally, '*jouissance* of the Other' – renowned to be so paradoxical and so contradictory that it would remain imaginary and impossible because it would amount to consuming a full and substantial relation with the Other that would be lack and absence – corresponds to this double trait of Transcendental *Jouissance*: (1) indeed, there is no *jouissance* of the Other (2) because it is *Jouissance* (of) the Other. What explains these two traits is that the Other as simple, non-auto-positional exteriority, is the immanent 'body' of *Jouissance*, its givenness or manifestation, what it has always already invested, being rigorously co-extensive with it. This radical identity of *Jouissance* and the Other excludes what the Other – which is transcendence itself – would be, as analysis wants, taken from . . . transcendence, inserted into it as the folding [*la pliure*] of its fold, as much as it is still the case of the Other as the place of signifiers and relatively external to *jouissance*. As *Jouissance* is to be no longer confused with the *Joui*, it is 'opened' not up to the Other that would affect it, but intrinsically as the Other itself, which does not affect it, but structures it, that is, as the 'unilateral duality' itself. Provided this internal uni-relation that inhabits *Jouissance*, it cannot indeed bear on an absent Other or lacking Other, but it cannot do so for reasons that, no longer belonging to Lacanian analysis noted above, 'invalidate' the analytic schema and argument themselves, displacing them in the symptom or Appearance. If, therefore, it would satisfy the Lacanian thesis by another argument, it as well negates this thesis and posits that there is a *Jouissance* (of) the Other and that it is thereby its specific or qualitative essence, rather than one of its types besides two others. This is so on the condition of suspending the (of) that marks intentionality and the fold articulating, or dis-articulating, both *jouissance* and the Other. It is obviously less than saying that there is a major signifier, the phallus, not of *jouissance* but regulating and signalling [*balisant*] it; and it is more than saying that it is despite everything circumscribed by signifying (orificial) differences of the body that would thus only surround it in an exterior

[6] Translator's note: Laruelle is alluding to Lacan's formulations present in Seminar XX. The reader is recommended to refer to *The Seminar of Jacques Lacan, Book XX: Encore*, translated by Bruce Fink (New York: W. W. Norton and Company, 1999).

way. The thesis according to which the signifier does not know *jouissance* cannot be the thesis of non-analysis. *Jouissance* is enjoyed, that is, self(-)experienced-in-the-last-instance and is the self(-)knowledge or self(-)manifestation itself, without ever having this knowledge take a transcendent signifying and moreover auto-reflexive form, or a form regulated by a big dominant signifier.

Rather, we will consider this major thesis of Lacanianism, undoubtedly authentically analytic, as the sign of the repression by analysis of the very essence of *Jouissance* in the name of a 'prohibition of incest' whose social pertinence is not identically a human pertinence and cannot be auto-posited as the essence of man or the Real. However, it is necessary to correctly understand *Jouissance* to not return, on the side of the acquisitions of analysis, towards a substantialist and naturalist conception of the Other. *Jouissance* is distinguished from the *Joui* as Radical Other, in flesh and bone, and is distinguished from radical immanence. No doubt, it is lived-*en-Joui* and this without there being a *jouissance* of *jouissance* or self-*jouissance*, with the *Joui* being non-positional and non-donative in general, yet purely phenomenal. Nevertheless, the Other that it is without distance does not participate in the undivided identity of the *Joui* except by receiving it as transcendental identity. It is the same identity as the identity that makes the *Joui* yet, henceforth, with a support and therefore a different status. *Jouissance* is not one intermediary between the *Joui* and the Other. Everything that is possible to affirm is that the transcendental identity does not come from the Other but falls upon it from the exterior precisely because it is strictly immanent. Therefore, it is not *Jouissance* that would arrive from the outside to the Other, arousing the aporias within which analysis interminably debates, but it emerges as soon as there is the Other and that the Other, necessarily so, is lived-*en-Joui*.

4. Let us then take the Lacanian axiom: there is no sexual relationship. This is one of these false axioms, the philosophical mixture of a thesis and an axiom, a unitary generality that emerges from the Philosophico-Analytic Appearance and that must dualysed as the 'axiom' of the (impossible) *jouissance* of the Other. For its own account, non-analysis globally refuses relating from transcendent exteriority the terms here equivalent to that of 'sexual *jouissance*' and 'signifying relationship'. It therefore as well refuses the whole idea of the 'sexual relationship' but equally refuses the reason that analysis may give of this refusal. By contrast, it posits the internal co-extension of *Jouissance* and the 'relationship' and, in this sense, not only there is 'some' sexual relationship [*il y a 'du' rapport sexuel*] but (Sexual) *Jouissance* is intrinsically a relationship (and then specified by the 'sexual' discourse of the philosophico-analytic symptom). However, this formulation is incomprehensible and seems to simply

contradict the analytic thesis, such that the point is not made regarding the 'relationship's' essence (of) relationship.

Analysis transfers its experience of relationship from a transcendent ontological model, that of bilaterality (convertibility, reciprocity, reversibility). It refines it, and precisely dis-applies it of substantial Being to determine it as the signifying and phonematic relation. However, it does not destroy its ontological and philosophical presuppositions that also coincide with the most banal and most vulgar idea of the relationship. The signifier most watered down of all substance, the most negative, oppositional, differential signifier, simply reconstitutes, to some near nuances that non-analysis cannot judge pertinent, a substance in the negative and does nothing but destroy the oldest and most metaphysical forms of philosophy, in no way the essence of it. The articulation that makes the signifier and the unconscious remain a 'syntax' is therefore a transcendent order-form - not the immanent order-form of transcendence, which is, rather, a 'uni-tax', an order issued from identity of the One (of the) *Joui*, so that the analysis most remodelled in its foundations still reconstitutes the philosophical circle in the Other, subject to some topological variations upon which non-analysis cannot melt away. Indeed, this uni-tax is the unilateral duality, one of the sides of the Determination-in-the-last-instance. Because there is the Other or transcendence in *Jouissance* there, it receives the order-form of this duality. It is therefore no longer a relation but a unilateral relation - rigorously, a uni-lation, rather than a re-lation. On one side, it receives from the *Joui* as its essence the already evoked transcendental identity; on the other side, it receives an object or term that is readied with a relative autonomy. To tear the 'relationship' or 'relation' from their onto-logico-philosophical and therefore analytic context, it is necessary to dualyse them; to first understand them as being re-rations [*ré-apports*], then to extract from them their identity as *ration-without-relation* [apport-sans-rapport]. The rationing of an autonomous term presupposes a uni-lation, no longer a relation, precisely, but a uni-ration [*uni-apport*]. The uni-ration is the phenomenal kernel of the Other or the Unconscious, the order-form internal to *Jouissance*, with which it is structured and determines the Unconscious as a specification of *Jouissance*. Finally, we will therefore posit, rather than Lacan's unilaterally negative axiom and which sounds like a prohibition, the following already more positive formula: 'the sexual relationship is not a relationship', or, again, 'there is rather a sexual relation, but it is a ration-without-relation, in the precise sense of a uni-lation, a duality without reciprocity, and constituted by an undivided identity and simple ration'.

We do not trivially say, using analysis to contradict it, that 'the Unconscious enjoys', but it is *Jouissance* itself. It does not enjoy like a subject behind it or one produced by it would do so, like an unconscious behind the Unconscious: the Unconscious is fully or phenomenally *Jouissance*. This is because there is no 'subject' of the Unconscious, the master subject or subjugated subject, and because the signifier that we will call 'dual' rather than 'differential' is not accompanied by a subject that it 'would represent'. By contrast, it is rather the Unconscious or the Other that enjoys (the) *Jouissance* or that is absolutely co-extensive with it. Correlatively, far from being an amorphous beyond of the Unconscious, *Jouissance* is enjoyed by it without there being indeed any such signifier *for* . . . it: not signified, but intrinsically identical to the Unconscious, and therefore signified in an internal way through and within any dual signifying. The id [*Ça*] does not enjoy within the ego [*moi*], without the ego being a transcendent *jouissance*. The *Joui*, not *Jouissance*, fills the Ego, but it is the Ego that enjoys in-the-last-instance – not as a psycho-philosophical subject – of *Jouissance* or the Unconscious which is not, but which is inferred from it.

The Philosophico-Analytic Complex as a Symptom for Non-Analysis

1. The philosophico-analytic experience to which non-analysis relates itself presents *par excellence* the form of the symptom or conjuncture: it magnifies the symptom-form by the mixture-form, the mixture-form including the symptom-form, and the symptom-form originally modulating the mixture-form. Regardless of the so-called autonomy of analysis in relation to philosophical presuppositions, the problem indeed is not to know what Freud or Lacan *de facto*, historically and doctrinally, had to do with the philosophers, but to note that these *de facto* blends are nothing but the content of a structure *de jure* required by non-analysis, and which is the mixture-form (Dyad + One = Triad) or again the auto-position-form, within which philosophy and analysis communicate and proceed towards exchanges. This mixture-form is the form of all content and the true material of a unified theory of philosophy and psychoanalysis or, again, as it is the same thing, a non-analysis, only having existence in a certain relation of analysis with philosophy, even if it were at the start a relation of rejection, critique, deconstruction, interpretation, and so on. The philosophico-analytic (= PA) symptom therefore integrates, one into the other, the analytic concept of the symptom and the structure of the mixture that serves as essence. This integration would be difficult to think or elaborate in its factuality, no doubt, but non-analysis requires it *de jure* or posits it, and it is rather this *de jure* integration that should be elaborated to simply be able to then be dualysed or reduced by the Unconscious that we call 'universal' or transcendental, which is identical to *Jouissance*. The PA complex

is an object of superior complexity in relation to the dream, lapse, stumbling speech, the 'primary' analytic symptom, and, in general, individual discourse, the discourse of the individual given in worldly transcendence (social, psychological, perceptive-philosophical). The goal of non-analysis is not to explain or analytically integrate the 'formations of the unconscious', but to explain under real (and not meta-analytic) conditions analysis itself as a philosophico-analytic mixture. Finally, the PA symptom does not mean a state of illness of philosophy, analysis or their relations – this is an interpretation in exteriority through isolated terms assumed 'in themselves' – but takes on the meaning and function of *Jouissance* that includes and transforms it into the Universal Unconscious.

2. One PA symptom presents several traits:

a. As an auto-positional structure, it is self-interpreted in philosophical or even analytical terms, or again philosophico-analytic terms – in the three cases, it is thought under an explicit or latent antinomic form. This auto-interpretation testifies to the philosophico-analytic sufficiency and must be eliminated in priority by *Jouissance* to be able to contribute to the constitution of the Generalised Unconscious. For the use that non-analysis makes of it, analysis is not an 'infantile theory', but it is necessarily *de jure* accompanied by an infantile sufficiency and an auto-interpretation 'deprived' of its causes. This auto-legitimation of analysis, this meta-analytic *telos* with a philosophical essence cannot be destroyed or excluded as being without reality or signification; it belongs to the PA symptom and must be simply rendered theoretically-and-pragmatically inefficacious. The theories of analysis, the search for its foundations or, to the contrary, its deconstruction, make up the wealth and complexity of the symptom and its conjuncture, too.
b. It is no doubt auto-limited, drawing up for itself certain boundaries or pronouncements of refusals. Some of these refusals are more significant than others (than, for example, the rejections of philosophy) because they take as its object the denied One, the Real or the *Joui* and, in general, the structure of non-analysis. It is not because analysis does not explicitly know it that it does not know this refusal. We must nuance: (1) in the same way that the Real or the *Joui* is given-without-givenness, we must postulate that the analytic resistance to the *Joui*, that is, resistance to the cause of non-analysis, is as well given or *de jure*, that it is an absolute resistance to the Real and that it simply asks to be thought as it is as the foreclosure of the Real; (2) by contrast, unlike the Real itself, in the same way that

> *Jouissance* is given through givenness in its own essence and its analytic specification (not in the manifestation-*en-Joui* of this essence), likewise the analytic resistance to the non-analytic theory is this time pronounced and speaks for itself explicitly even within the discourse of analysis (such as the Lacanian axioms of the One: 'the One is not', 'there is some One', and above all the way in which analysis may understand them).

Non-analysis identifies (manifests as it is already, but cannot manifest it as such without co-determining it, at least to specify it, that is, to incarnate it in a knowledge taken from the PA symptom) the Universal Unconscious as the point where the PA symptom does not fail or stumble as speech would, but loses its pertinence or its so-called weight of the real and floats in a suspension and an indifference, a beyond that goes in front of it rather than it superseding or transcending it. *Jouissance* has no place in a breakage or a circuit rupture with speech like analytic *jouissance*, but rather in its transcendental identity and its co-extension with the transcendence which suspends the PA symptom (a symptom that is here always more complex than speech or the elementary objects of analysis). In a certain way, if it historically comes after analysis, non-analysis maintains with it an *a priori* relationship of knowledge and use and therefore, in this sense, precedes it without there being reversibility or a circle of a compensation between these two movements: the vector of non-analysis goes from *Jouissance* and the Universal Unconscious towards analysis as to a field of phenomena or properties of objects. This auto-limitation of analysis in refusal or exclusion of non-analysis therefore takes on a meaning as well through and in it, and it must be 'interpreted' with its means.

Therefore, the non-analyst is not the recipient of the PA symptom precisely because they are already, rather, on the side of the cause and because he cannot have any such confusion of the cause and recipient, the circle of the analytic or 'restrained' unconscious thus being broken in the principle. It is only within its resistance that analysis can apprehend the non-analyst as a subject-supposed-to-know and make itself a philosophical and teleological use of the sign (address or refusal, and so on) to the address of the non-analysis in order to escape from the theoretical use of which they make use. Whether it thinks the 'sign' (representing something for someone) or 'signifier' (representing a subject for another signifier), analysis will spontaneously think its relationship with non-analysis in the encompassing terms of representation, as representing a cause (symptom or unconscious, it does not matter), and even a 'material' for the persona of the non-analyst, regardless of whether they are conceived as the Other individual or as the signifying Other. Non-analysis begins its labour through the suspension of this representation for a subject-supposed-to-know, even for a supposed-analyst-subject. This general triple procedure of the supposition of the subject and representation is excluded by non-analysis in the name of the Given-without-Givenness, but it includes it in the symptom such that it comprehends it and, under this form and with this limitation, attributes to it a certain predisposition, even if it were through this very resistance, to accept to enter into the non-analytic process where, in any case, it does not depend on it to enter into it or not.

c. Finally, the PA Symptom, when related to the non-analytic posture, is not more solitary than the intra-analytic symptom. More radically even than the latter, which does not postulate another unconscious or the inclusion of analysis and the analyst in a common or encompassing unconscious, it postulates the existence of a Universal Unconscious in the multiple state or in the state of which, in the previous chapter, we called a *multitudo transcendentalis*. In its auto-interpretation, it is obviously thought in accordance with the mixture of the empirico-transcendental one and/or the multiple of philosophy or as the circulation of one unique unconscious between analysand and analyst; or, moreover, as the blend of these two models. However, non-analysis does not empirically transfer the multiplicity of the Unconscious from the auto-presented content of the symptom. It distinguishes (1) the multiplicity as it is first given empirically, a *de facto* multiplicity of philosophico-analytic combinations which then become a *de jure* multiplicity into how non-analysis transforms it or which is the form under which it requires it; (2) it is given otherwise transcendentally as intrinsic multiplicity of the Universal Unconscious, what it is in its essence of unilateral duality, what it still remains as specified by these philosophico-analytic experiences of multiplicity. There is a solitude of the Real, but there is no solipsism of the Unconscious, which is nothing but universal in the state of multitude. The non-analyst exists in the state of transcendental, non-empirical multiplicity, and these non-analytic multitudes exclude the analysand-analyst doublet, as generalised as it is in Lacanianism as constitutive of the unconscious, and displaces it within the symptom itself but in the functions as material.

3. Thus are identified in their formal characters the typical statements of the PA symptom, that is, the non-analytic material. It is not a matter of dreams, lapses, jokes, and so on, assumed in themselves as is the case in analysis; nor is it a matter of any such discourse, but of all already realised combinations or again in the state of the possible combinations, reclaimed as such or denying the philosophical element, of psychoanalysis and philosophy. However, this is

but one empirically given starting point, regardless if it is necessary, and it is what non-analysis transforms. In a general way, analysis assumes as existing in itself and, in this sense, consequently, outside of itself, these entities such as the 'dream', 'lapse', 'symptom' insofar as they specify discourse or individual speech, even if it means admitting that the unconscious only exists in the immanence of the cure. Again, to avoid idealism, if it does not want to assume a reality in itself of the unconscious, it must finally admit one such reality of the psychoanalytic cure and act and therefore posit it in an auto-position that is supposed to give its reality to analysis and assure it a grip upon the Real. From our point of view, this solution through the immanence of the psychoanalytic act, of its enactment, continues to belong to one objective transcendental appearance, a consistent appearance of the real which motivates it and assures it with an objective semblant of existence. By definition, non-analysis renounces all philosophical types of hypothesis or substitutes-of-philosophy with an essence in self, that is, auto-positional essence, even if it belongs to a speech, an act, a practice, or a clinic. 'In self' does not designate the substantial 'in-itself' opposed by common sense to philosophy, but globally the philosophical act itself presupposing itself (giving and positing itself) as absolutely autonomous or real, for non-analysis, because it lets-itself-be-given the Real under the form of a radical phenomenal immanence and no longer a transcendence, renounces any extra-phenomenal hypothesis or any hypothesis which would not be phenomenal-in-the-last-instance. The real (of the) *Joui*, precisely because of its immanence, 'falls' in some way, if we may say, 'outside' or 'before' the non-analytic cure. Identical to *Jouissance* as organon of the *Joui*, the cure then defines a transcendental immanence within which not only takes place the Universal Unconscious as the 'Other' of which it is capable but, to a certain extent, the PA symptom previously described.

Thus, non-analysis excludes in a general way – or said in prediction of the elaboration of the theoretical and practical status of the Unconscious – the philosophical antinomy of existence (of the material, the cure, the unconscious, and so on) as immanent (interior . . .) or as transcendent (exterior . . .) to the cure; it avoids the alternative between metaphysical idealism and dogmatic realism or materialism. *Jouissance* is an immanence that is not metaphysical and abstract, but transcendental, consequently furnishing its own theoretical means and relating itself to its own objectivity whose concept is not provided to it from outside by philosophy and the sciences. The content of the symptom is certainly contingent, but the symptom-form under which the mixture of analysis with philosophy presents itself is already – at least with the characteristics which we have described – the effect of a first relationship of a transcendental origin of *Jouissance* with this material, and a first elaboration – which is undoubtedly still insufficient – of the non-analytic concept of the symptom. These combinations are therefore given with a facticity that records *Jouissance* that is grasped to interpret it according to its theoretical and practical criteria. These criteria constitute the Unconscious called 'Universal', which we must now exposit the internal constitution of in relation to the restrained unconscious of analysis.

First Aspect of *Jouissance*: Non-Platonic Desire and the Solution to the Analytic Antinomy of *'jouissance'* and 'Desire'

We were able to identify the Real, *Jouissance* and the essence of the Unconscious without ever speaking once about 'desire'. It is not because we disclose it from non-analysis, it is because we do nothing but disclose the form under which it is received at the heart of analysis as a massive metaphysical entity hardly refined and 'elaborated', often as a residue of the theory of faculties (faculty of desiring, Kant), a mixture of psychology and biology, and what rationalist philosophy delimits. In turn, rather than transferred empirically from instinct, wish, force and energy, it must be elaborated under rigorous real and transcendental conditions. Making desire the simple metonymic flow of referral or passage from one signifier to another in the subject, or the flow from one partial object to another (schizo-analysis), is undoubtedly to de-substantialise it, even to de-globalise and de-specify it. However– we reprise a general argument of the limitation of analysis – this is to reconstitute the equivalent of a new substance, a new body, a new whole, and so on, over the critique and ruin of representation, not to propose to it a new essence or origin capable of eradicating the congenital Platonism of theory. This Platonism still stimulates analysis: it is the thesis of desire that, with some obstacle or differe(a)nce which would be opposed to it, is produced and always consummated as the desire-of-desire, self-desiring, and even the desire of the desire of the Other. At the heart of desire or as beyond its horizon and as its simply repressed yet always efficacious underside, there is therefore one auto-position: desire as the 'transcendental' principle in the philosophical sense of this word, immanent and transcendent simultaneously, sometimes the real itself, and sometimes the search for the real. Regardless of the effort to differ/defer the flow, to metonymise it or even delay it constitutively, the PA desire Platonises in excess or in defect. It is understood as an aiming-for . . . Being, the Other, an intentionality of the object and its variants. This aim is more or less *de facto* fulfilled, yet it is a *de jure* structure and functions as meta-empirical and meta-physical, that is, as folded and redoubled by a clear or instituted auto-position. Platonism has two nearly identical ways of introducing itself into analysis: by philosophy and by desire, by the power-to-desire which is still a desire of desire. Hence, desire is sometimes an eternal return and topological flow, sometimes a truncated circle, depending on whether it is the auto-position of the real or the disclosure of the real and the distanced real from it as impossible.

Non-analysis dualyses this PA desire through several operations. It firstly identifies it not at the heart of the *Joui* – this is obvious – but of *Jouissance*. Far from separating them in an external and transcendent way as if by a prohibiting bar or simple difference or *différance*, that is, remaining within their amphibology, non-analysis finds the essence of desire in reality or transcendence which is the specific essence of *Jouissance*, whereas the Unconscious will be the 'syntactic' side of *Jouissance*, the latter adding, if you will, or assuming added to these two things, the transcendental identity. The internal form of desire, its originary and minimal form, under which it appears for the first time, in an ante-Platonising way, is the simple, non-auto-positional transcendence, structured by the unilateral duality itself or by the uni-lation of which we already spoke. Regarding desire, we will say the same thing as *Jouissance* (of) the Other: desire is desire (of) the Other, without any other intentionality except the intentionality of the simple unilateral duality, void of folding and transcendent objectivity, that of the object or even that of Being, even the Other assumed as a 'separate' entity.

Lacanianism does not fail to dig the gap of *jouissance* (aspiring for accomplishment) and desire (doomed to failure), with the latter limiting the former. This opposition is not better than the amphibological confusion of desire and *jouissance* to which it is opposed and would rather emerge from the philosophical imaginary. This antinomy between *jouissance* and desire is suppressed [*levée*] by the duality of the *Joui* and *Jouissance* and by the identity-without-synthesis of *Jouissance* and desire. *Jouissance*, and that of *Jouissance* (of) the Other, is not a hubris or an imaginary ideal, and it does not have to be limited by the misadventures of a supposed 'meta-physical' desire. To really resolve the antinomy, it is necessary and suffices to elaborate the universal transcendental concept of *Jouissance* and abandon the Platonism of desire by inserting it into *Jouissance* as one of its structural moments. In reality, it is the one in which analysis charges the symptom and phallic *jouissance* on the one hand, the phantasy and surplus-enjoyment on the other: avoiding the *jouissance* of the Other is the global problem of analysis – avoiding the experience of *Jouissance* (of) the Other radically understood finally. However, measured to non-analysis, one cannot say that it is satisfied with a 'partial' *jouissance*, but simply that it aspires to a restrained *jouissance*.

For reasons regarding terminological clarity and above all the style of 'dualysis', we must here speak of the essence of desire, or better yet: 'desire's Essence (of) desire' rather than the generality 'desire', and reserve the term 'phantasmatic desire' for what this essence extracts or manifests, as a mode of this essence, from the philosophico-analytic experience of desire described above as the desire-of-desire. Therefore, desire appears a second or a third time (if one includes its philosophico-analytic concept and its varieties) as what this ultimate experience 'becomes' when it is dualysed from *Jouissance* and the Essence (of) desire that is included. What non-analytic labour makes appear or manifests is obviously neither the Essence (of) desire itself nor PA desire, both given, but phantasmatic desire as a concrete modality of the first extracted from the second. In a general way, non-analysis is not a metaphysics and does not use concepts and entities assumed 'in themselves', but it is a use elaborated by such concepts, which transforms and dualyses them, which magnifies them in a heterogeneous way each time instead of doubling them by themselves or others. These denominations are undoubtedly very unsatisfactory and risk being interpreted intra-philosophically and/or analytically, while they are said of heterogeneous uses or statuses of the term 'desire'.

Second Aspect of *Jouissance*: The Universal or Transcendental Unconscious as *Jouissance* (of the) Void

1. If *Jouissance* is, as we have said, the non-analytic posture itself, to what extent does the Unconscious exist without being once more an auto-positional hypothesis participating in philosophical sufficiency as much as in scientific objectivity, blending these two types of hypotheses? The Unconscious called universal or transcendental is (1) less a structure in general, auto-positional and doomed to idealism, than a syntax that depends on the Real, therefore non-auto-positional; (2) it is less a formal syntax, having its content or 'semantics' relatively outside itself, than a syntax identical not to the Real itself but to the specific reality of *Jouissance* – precisely desire or the Essence (of) desire, which is not the Real; the *Joui* itself being without distinction between syntax and semantics, 'real' and 'structure', it identifies yet beyond it, within *Jouissance*, the proper phenomenal reality of it, desire, and its syntax which is the Unconscious strictly speaking such that non-analysis is able to think it; and finally (3) less a syntax than a 'uni-tax', the order of a unilateral duality or what we call a 'uni-lation', rather than a relation. These traits define the essence of the Unconscious or again the Universal Unconscious' Essence (of) the unconscious.

Despite certain appearances, the Unconscious is a fundamental moment of non-analysis besides the *Joui*, even if *Jouissance* appears theoretically before it. *Jouissance* is the identity of the reality (of desire) and the syntax yet precisely, as we have already suggested, not as two sides or two principles more or less exterior and to be connected, but as their transcendental identity, one which ensues from the Real in its relation with PA effectivity or the relation of the PA to it. The Unconscious is outside of the Real in the sense that it does not constitute the essence of the Real, but it is determined by it and represents the form of causality of which it is capable. This causality is concretely exercised as *Jouissance* (and not by it) but the Unconscious is the original syntactic content of it. Therefore, the Real, *Jouissance* and the Unconscious are no longer 'principles' confronting each other, forming a dyad for a new form of analysis and then appealing to a superior synthesis within a third term which would, for example, be *Jouissance*. If *Jouissance* is not the synthesis of the Real and 'syntax', it is by contrast the undivided identity of its own type of reality (the essence (of) transcendence or the essence (of) the Other in classical terms, the Essence (of) desire rather as non(-)self-auto-positional) and the 'uni-tax'. This is why the Unconscious is always one concrete side of *Jouissance* (it enjoys-*en-Jouissance* without leaving its transcendental immanence and not from an exterior *jouissance*), not an empty-formal syntax, doomed to the type of ontic reality of the linguistic, logical and mathematical form; it is empty by contrast and more generally of auto-position. Therefore, being related on one side to the Real, on the other side to being [*Étant*] (the PA *datum*), constituting with *Jouissance* the sphere of Being and the Other, it is empty of this trait of auto-position whose absence implies as much a new matter (desire) as a new form (uni-tax).

As for uni-tax, it is the order of the unilateral duality insofar as it is determined by the Real. Measured to it, a syntax, a syntax of the signifier or not, is by definition an auto-positional *taxis* that claims to be freed from the side of identity and constitutes with the duality of its basic elements alone a new synthesis or a so-called real or autonomous triad (the idealism of any syntax). From this point of view, the Lacanian labour of minimalisation and derealisation of the unconscious across the linguistic, logical and mathematical reduction to the signifier is one of these fundamental types of acquisitions against which the holders of the primitive forms of a doctrine always rebel, to which the theory inspires the fear of their own powerlessness. However, this reduction of the substance-unconscious remains, as we have said, the feat of the empirico-transcendental interiorisation of regional scientific models, a procedure denounced further under the name of the 'idealist triad', and results in the authoritarian idea of a 'pilot-science'.

The most radical de-realisation of the Unconscious consists in depriving it, on the one hand, of the Real (of the *Joui* yet precisely not of *Jouissance* and desire), and on the other hand not of being or Being [*l'Etant ou l'Etre*], which would be absurd, but the auto-positional forms of these spheres or types of reality. The logico-formal void, even the void of the inconsistent or set-theoretical multiple, is never anything more than a half-void: it is void of the particularity of being, even of being itself (this thesis is perhaps questionable), but it is content with repressing auto-position, which is simply brutally truncated or forbidden, yet which continues to give birth to transcendent offspring within the transcendental immanence of the Unconscious.

2. Let us therefore assume that, conserving as a 'first name' the term 'signifier' already broadened by Lacan outside of the linguistic sphere, we universalise it even more to characterise the Essence (of) the unconscious and we seek within it the phenomenal kernel, that is, what we will call the Essence (of) the signifier. We substitute the differential or restrained conception of the signifier with its dual conception (= unilateral duality). What are the characteristics of it? The first and most apparent characteristic is that a 'signifying' statement in the non-analytic sense does not belong to the order of the lapse, the breakage (of the circuit of speech), the flash, joke and fading away, in general the order of that which would be manifested in its very disappearance. This schema (Heidegger, Lacan, Derrida, and theories of the event) are valid to the sphere of the primary or regional objects belonging to analysis; they are not valid for the sphere of the Transcendental Unconscious whose manifestation responds to other phenomenal criteria. The alterity that they express does not belong to difference accessible to a topology; it is an alterity (of) *Jouissance*, therefore an affect (of) simple alterity, precisely without a doublet or fold. Yet to be an affect, and simple or identical, this alterity is not amorphous, irrational nor without a theoretical scope: *Jouissance* is an un-reflected knowing, it is precisely, as we have previously said, the identity of an affect and a uni-tax, the identity of a certain type of 'relation' with the PA material which serves as the material for non-analytic statements. This concrete and lived uni-tax (of which we have already prepared its description) assures non-analytic statements to be identically 'enjoyed' in-the-last-instance and to be theoretically irreducible to the most general structure of the PA statements. It is no longer a matter of 'clumsiness', 'failure', 'slippage' and the 'unpredictable' – these empirico-ideal categories must be replaced by the *Jouissance* of an alterity 'syntactically' irreducible to these events or dis-articulations of speech and everyday life. Consequently, once produced, such statements are unintelligible to analytic intelligence, exceeding any 'interpretation' through the circle of the differential

unconscious and do not enter into the symptom of which this unconscious is capable. They in particular exclude any subject-supposed-to-know to the point of even excluding the analytic exclusion of a supposition issued from the analysand and a construction issued from the analyst, which are, as excluded by the signifier in the analytic sense alone, still PA suppositions. Regarding the dual signifier, the object of an intrinsic and absolutely simple *jouissance* in the sense where it is not reversible or auto-positional, we must say that it is in one sense absolute. Regarding the differential, material-type of the signifier and the 'one' (= unary trait), we undoubtedly say that it too is, that it is manifested outside of all meaning or explanation, or that it functions outside of any teleology. However, it remains structured by a doublet or an auto-position that testifies to the ultimate presence of a *logos* and an amphibology of Being and *Logos*, therefore of a meaning or a *telos* animating this unconscious and restraining it (it is present still in schizoanalysis and even, as otherwise broken, in the deconstruction of Lacanianism). By contrast, the non-auto-positional simplicity of the dual signifier completes by emptying any non-analytic statement of a meaning re-appropriable by the PA system. The Universal Unconscious is rather a knowledge, a knowledge-without-*logos*, or, rigorously, a *logos*-without-auto-position.

The Essence (of) the Unconscious: The Dual or the Non(-)Self-Signifying Signifier

1. *Jouissance* is constituted: (a) by an ingredient of transcendence or alterity, and even the essence of radical transcendence: an exteriority or 'distance' not blended with immanence, purely qualitative and phenomenal; (b) by the syntax (the uni-tax) of the unilateral duality, which is distinct from it but in some way 'informs' it from within and gives the Other precisely an absolutely simple structure or a non-auto-positional identity. Above all if it is grasped by its 'unitactic' side, this set constitutes the Essence (of) the unconscious, that is, a signifier under the dual and no longer differential form. We see that the dual (a) always presupposes a contingent given that it presents for the first and unique time, which is therefore not re-presented or redoubled, but rather deprived of representation; (b) it presents or allocates it absolutely without representing it for . . . whether some signifier (the sign) or another signifier (the signifier): the Universal Unconscious is non(-)self-signifying. The dual signifier is the first emergence, without destination towards its own phenomenality or givenness (not to the phenomenon or the *Joui*), of the Other itself and all that which is susceptible of filling or defining it. It is also emptied of all teleology, not only external, but internal. The rationing trait of that which is thus rationed means that it finds nothing in front of it or in a bilateral

face-to-face, above all not the *Joui*. The *Joui* does not emerge from objectivity, therefore it is neither full presence nor lack. As a phenomenon not only invisible but (of) the invisible, it escapes from this alternative, so that the ration does not relate the *Joui* to the rationed and that it absolutely emerges for the first time, thus conserving a relative autonomy. *Jouissance* does not relate the PA complex to the *Joui* but rather 'transmits' the Real, transmits the Real without alienating it, to the PA data. No idealism . . . of the Real, no realism as the confusion of phenomenal orders that would strive to reduce analysis in this operation by which the Unconscious allocates or brings to transcendent analytic discourse.

At least at this level, we must therefore abandon the restrained unconscious, restrained by signitive or signifying representation, and acquire the concept of a Universal Unconscious that is non(-)self-consistent and non(-)self-signifying. The Unconscious is identical to an absolutely non-consistent multiple – this is what the conception of a 'literal' materiality and heterogeneity 'aims for' without reaching it and reaching something other. However, the 'letter' is a new form of the fetishisation of the Essence (of) the unconscious and a mixed inference of it through the empirico-transcendental interiorisation of language, and it is in no way the inference of the Unconscious through that which is given or the phenomenon (with and without givenness). Hence, the 'repetition' or again 'electric news strips' [*bande des annonces lumineuses*] (Lacan)[7] to which analysis subscribes. The Universal Unconscious is the emergence *par excellence*, the non-relation, the identity of the discovery (of a given which emerges within phenomenality or givenness for the first time) and the invention (this given is reduced to the state of a ration, delivered from its auto-position or its folding structure). There is no relation of *Jouissance*, but a ration that makes *Jouissance* the organon of all discovery and invention. There is rather an automatism that makes up the Essence (of) the unconscious, an *automaton transcendentalis* if you will, which is *Jouissance* itself, but there is no repetition in the sense at least of a transcendent form of it or a circle. Analysis shows a philosophical fascination and no respect for phenomena as such when it erects the Unconscious on the amphibology of an already made or already given automatism or repetition, when it infers from energetico-dynamic phenomena and when it adds to *jouissance* transferred from energy an unconscious transferred from the model of the motor and the mobile, force

[7] Translator's note: This is in reference to Lacan's 'Seminar on "The Purloined Letter"'. Please refer to *Écrits: The First Complete Edition in English*, translated by Bruce Fink (New York: W. W. Norton & Company, 2006), 21.

and effect. There is no repetition – even if it were only distended and convergent *ad infinitum* – within the essence of the Unconscious but first the phenomenal and qualitative, entirely internal infinity of an opening without horizon or circle, and which must be thought in order to be able to render intelligible on a new, unified-theoretical mode, the PA system itself and its forms of closure. Of course, what we have called above the Essence (of) desire and what we have defined through uni-lation rather than through the sexual relation or relationship is nothing other than this infinity or phenomenal kernel of repetition: the unilateral petition, or 'repetition', in the primitive state of identity.

However, how do we conceive of the operation or givenness of this given that is *Jouissance*? Both as the Essence (of) desire and the Essence (of) the unconscious, *Jouissance* neither functions nor interprets, it is a presentation that cannot be grasped in a representation, an original, non-reflected phenomenality, without being the radical unreflected of the *Joui*; it is therefore the uni-flected and only repeats or uni-flects as the presentation that it is. This presentation is the *Jouissance*-subject itself, where one does not accompany the other to regulate or exceed it.

2. Therefore, it belongs to the unilateral signifier to no longer be defined in relation to another signifier nor to represent X (the subject) for another signifier. The universal structure of representation, and not only the structure of the sign being excluded, it liberates a *de jure* multiplicity of the signifier, a multiplicity of which we know that being of the phenomenal and qualitative and therefore radical order, it cannot be quantifiable and countable, that it even excludes inconsistency as a simple repression or prohibition of the One proper to the set-form. Being absolutely non-consistent, it refers to the symptom the unary trait (the One of the signifier, one-signifier-among-others, therefore the One tolerated by the Other or the One convertible with the Other), but just as much the One of the set-form that subsists, yet simply repressed, within the heart of the multiple-of-multiples in a conception of Being with a set-theoretical and post-Lacanian origin. The equation signifier = unconscious or the one that radicalises and completes it, mathematics = ontology, emerges from the PA complex and its idealist functioning, and it consequently remains within a system of representation simply truncated or prohibited, in no way reaching a positive and emergent conception of the essence of the Unconscious. Once the structure of representation, that is, auto-position, is positively excluded and rendered non-constitutive, the Unconscious and consequently desire necessarily exist as a radical multitude compatible with the non-synthetic identity that transits the duality and prohibits its return to the 'dyad' state. The non(-)self-signifying signifiers are not for

one another. There is no alterity internal to the Other itself that is simple and therefore radically multiple, without a structure of referral as a residue of the old teleologies, of the referral, the circle and repetition. Lacan has stated that there is no Other of the Other but he did not have the theoretical means to hold one such statement, simply repressing an ultimate auto-position within the heart of the Other as the motor of the automatism of repetition.

More generally, the dual signifier is characterised by its transcendental identity 'ensuing' from the *Joui*, an identity of a non-auto-positionality, while the differential signifier is characterised by a trait (of) the One, by a unary mark that is imprinted upon the Other itself as an ultimate residue of the assumed convertibility of the One and transcendence (sometimes Being, sometimes the Other). Compared to the transcendental One of the dual signifier, this transcendent One must be evaluated in its origins and its environment (philosophical auto-position), in the necessary philosophical operations to obtain it (the repression of the substance-Being outside of the One to the benefit of the Other), in its functions (preventing the dislocation of the Other within an absolutely radical, ultra-signifying multiplicity, and therefore the dis-location of analysis itself); in its final degradation (the guardian of the transcendent identity of analysis, in the service of the authoritarian tasks of analysis); and finally in the relays that it prepares (its ultimate arithmetical degradation as a number, as the One of the set or the 'count' rejected outside of the multiple or overthrown by it).

The heart of the argument, where everything ensues and which explains the 'restrained' character of analysis, is that it remains a discourse, not only individual but 'private' discourse of the analysand, a 'private' discourse because the philosophical multiple is never radical and remains associated to the Transcendent One, even if it were repressed. To add the analyst here essentially changes nothing, which is that it is held up by transcendent unconsciouses, by an unconscious circulation assumed in itself by an ultimate philosophical-type of hypothesis. It rests upon the confusion of the Other and auto-positional transcendence, and this confusion renders nearly inoperant the distinction between an individual unconscious and an unconscious of collective circulation. The Unconscious and desire are neither individual nor collective and even less intersubjective – which are as much identities taken from social and psychological transcendence – they are universals beyond any generality, globality or specificity of this type, and consequently intrinsically multiple, though non-countable. Without being 'unique' as totalising and encompassing, each of them is intrinsically unique, as a transcendental identity that is 'said' of the freest or most inconsistent multiple. Consequently, if their complete concepts contain other concepts taken from the PA system, they will do nothing but serve as the material for the specification of their essence and will only affect the transcendent forms of their functioning, which are identically their concrete knowledge and their conditions of existence. It is only at this level that, for example, the problem of a distinction between the signifier each time manifest or 'One' and the other signifiers called 'virtual' or not yet actualised is posited. Analysis does not reach the universality that is the universality of the non-analytic discourse. It appears as a 'particular case' of a not more philosophically 'encompassing' theory, one that is more total or global, but more universal – that which allows it the theoretical mastery of philosophy as much as analysis. It is at this level of transcendental depth, in no way through the always summary comparison of the unconscious with the conscious, that psychoanalysis demonstrates its ultimate belonging, although not its substantial identification, to philosophy and its most invariant mechanisms.

The Dual Logic of the Unconscious

1. Compared to the differential signifier, the dual signifier presents two essential traits:

a. It seems close to amorphism or asyntactic though this is because its own 'structure' is not the modification of a syn-tax or a difference, but it is absolutely original. One cannot recognise here two terms whose assumed common property (oppositional, negative, differential) would make them elements of a set. There are neither elements nor a correlative set, neither parts nor whole, and so on, objects of a soaring-over, but a duality without reciprocity, without co-relation or even re-lation, and moreover without dis-ference. This is the duality of the ration of the rationed or manifested term and the transcendental identity. The first rationed term is transcendence's Essence (of) transcendence, the simple exteriority or radical distance, the element of reality or desire constitutive of *Jouissance*. As we have said, it is always already given or is itself presupposed yet only as 'rationed', yet without being posited or re-posited itself. Transcendental identity gives it or requires this simplicity from it. In a certain way, there are apparently three terms (the identity and doubled transcendences), but they are not only two: the one assumes two statuses and they do not make up a synthesis. On the one hand, the identity is not a synthesis, a third term itself split within the two terms of a dyad because, on the other hand, transcendence plays two roles yet it is not itself divided/refolded/auto-posited. And if it intervenes undoubtedly once as a PA *datum* or material and once as the ration-form, the former does not redouble the latter, it is rejected outside of it, and it does not essentially co-determine it, but only 'occasionally'.

However, reduced to its essence, and far from existing in itself as an abstraction, the Unconscious does not exist however, albeit phenomenally. It therefore appeals to a specific operation of givenness or manifestation, one that implements the PA complex. The dual signifier is dependent on the differential signifier or the PA unconscious from the point of view of its discovery or its emergence, its auto-manifestation or knowledge, but independent of it from the point of view of its real or phenomenal manifestation as enjoyed-in-the-last-instance. It is given as the specific sphere within the relation that it maintains with the PA data and it is through the occasion of this relation, a relation which has the form of a ration and which does not make it relative to . . ., which it is deployed as a radical multiplicity or a multiplicity of a dual origin. The minimal structure of the Dual Unconscious implies therefore that there are three instances but that do not make up a triad and closed circular system, which rather form unilateral dualities two-by-two.

b. From the point of view that one can generally call 'ontological' and no longer syntactic, the dual signifier is furthermore not a modification of 'privative' ontology, a supplementary refinement rationed to the classical transcendence of the real or its accentuation. The mode of the being-given of the *Joui* excludes depriveness, impossibility, withdrawal and subtraction, without speaking of negation or opposition. These are all second operations proper to the PA complex and carried out upon the already-given-given [*donné-déjà-donné*], the supposed empirical given as firstly pertinent; and are carried out upon the typically magical givennesses that are supposed to make arise or emerge the given or the Real and which, *de facto*, rather reduce it [*rabattent*] to the empirical. This is how the One is experienced analytically as it is given under the kinds of the hole or the lack, as a negative (or 'privative') image of the full One-Being of metaphysics. Yet like nothingness, the hole is always a determined hole and finally resolved, once more, within the borders, wakes, the lips of the empirical real – the lack itself is manifested with the help from what it is withdrawn, the subject which is the object of depriveness.

By contrast, the *Joui* as given-without-givenness is the Real that precedes subtraction and retraction and cannot ever be given by them and even as them (as the supposed identity of the given and givenness). This is more than an inversion: it is an entirely different experience of the Real and therefore of thought. The dual signifier not being doubled by the logic of lack, that which presents the rationed (the PA complex) cannot be a whole and it does not reciprocally affect the ration with a being-towards-lack. The formulation of this situation is difficult: the rationed, the unilateralised term, is the only one given-by-givenness or the only presented term; there are no other ones. Facing it, there is nothing, not even 'something-confronting-it' [*un 'en-face-de-lui'*] because it is the only 'face' or 'side', the only object that, objectivated, cannot be so through a subject alienating or mirroring itself in it as in its work or identifying itself with it as in a mirror. To avoid negative descriptions, we will say that the rationed is the object as the unique unilateral being: there is no subject that would be, as in philosophy, another one, a second or a first object, or the superior form of the object. The object is absolutely unique and, in particular, it assumes for itself an *a priori* residue of the PA subject, a subject which manifests *Jouissance* and which it attributes, under certain conditions, to the Universal Unconscious. We will therefore say that the dual signifier presents as ration any such *datum* taken from the PA complex, among other things the residual phenomenal kernel of the 'subject of the unconscious', that is, the supposit [*suppôt*] or substance or that which remains of it after the 'passing' from the differential signifier: that which subsists of the PA 'subject' when it comes upon the place of the Unconscious and enters into the order of *Jouissance*.

2. The phenomenon (of the) *Joui* is defined by a certain invisibility towards transcendence, but it is first positive and intrinsic, possessing therefore its own mode of 'visibility'. Here, there is nothing of the hole or lack, but the phenomenal character of self(-)immanence even more radical or simpler than lack is. Yet the true problem is that this type of comparison of PA thought and non-analytic thought makes no sense term by term, statement by statement, thesis by thesis, if one remains without perceiving it within the PA style of thought. Non-analysis precisely excludes such bi-univocal correspondences, proceeding through 'first names' rather than by 'concepts' or 'signifiers' and 'letters'; it dualyses or unilateralises the PA symptom, rather than splitting and folding it once again. Thus, the *Joui* can be called a Visible or a Viewed-without-Vision on condition that it is here a matter of a use of first names, rather than concepts. On its side, *Jouissance* can be called that which presents a 'subject' or a 'ration' in an absolute or originary way, that is, without a background relation or horizon with a 'subject' or a transcendent 'world', belonging to a set or simply to another signifier. However, this is so on condition that the without-relation is here understood also as a first name, and as designating not a hole or an absence, and so on, but the unique, simple, non-split phenomenality of the object of the Unconscious; therefore also as being . . . without relation with the absence

of the predicate 'absence' or 'lack'. In this order of thought, it is self-evident that the 'subject' rationed as the simple or unique object cannot give rise to any topology and that the 'hole' is rejected into the PA material where it is the neighbour of the philosophical circle, of which it is an ultimate mode.

3. While within the differential unconscious, the old metaphysical One convertible with Being is hollowed out by the Other (the hole, the lack) and rejected to the external periphery of the signifying chain that produces it and exteriorises itself within it through connection and substitution, through identity and alternating. This is a wholly other One, a One-without-Being and without-Other that is now said of the Other (of transcendence). If the One of the signifier is produced as already-there (the redoubling of one signifier within the One of the signifier) or exits from the immanence of the signifying chain, the One (of) transcendental identity is received one time each time from outside, that is, from the *Joui* as the immanent cause of *Jouissance*. If the analytic One makes a place or topography [*topique*] in the sense whereby the signifier stops being virtual and becomes actual or ex-istent, the transcendental identity does not ex-ist but manifests the Unconscious *en-Joui* alone. The Unconscious is a relatively autonomous structure that, corresponding, if you will, to ex-istence, does not result from a process of ex-istence or a topological exit, an alienation of the Real, or a quasi-totalising auto-limitation (the set) of signifiers, or again a productive lack of a supplement, a hole generating a place of actual existence. The non-analytic topography is absolutely static, ungenerable [*inengendrable*] of these ways, and no virtual/actual, chain/place type of distinction affects it: it is fully actual or performative (performational), yet requires being manifested as it is, by the *Joui* on the one hand and by its knowledge and relation of use to the PA complex on the other hand. Said otherwise, the distinction of 'repressed representations' or the repression and the 'return of the repressed' is done otherwise and happens elsewhere. It no longer corresponds with the distinction between the virtual and the actual, the chain and the One in the place of ex-istence, but corresponds with the distinction of the Essence (of) the unconscious as it is, not yet manifested as such, and the PA complex. The real and theoretical kernel of the being-repressed of representations is their already actual and performational existence as by right relevant to the Essence (of) the unconscious as it is and not yet manifested with the help of these representations, while the return of the repressed is their state or belonging to this essence when it is manifested as such.

4. Immanence, radicalised as the *Joui*, allows one to dualyse another one of Lacan's statements: 'there is no metalanguage'. Under this metaphysical form,

he also proves that there is one (itself) and that these two statements form an antinomy – there are therefore effects of metalanguage in sum and in any case. It would be suitable to say: non-analysis is so barely an attempt of metalinguistic foundation, legitimation and regulation of analysis that it and it alone can make analysis rather manifest itself as a metalanguage, as a 'negative' metalanguage of the essence of man or the Real and the theory that takes them as its object. Precisely, the PA symptom claims, under the impact of non-analysis, to envelop and comprehend it and finally interpret it according to its criteria what it has already denounced without expecting, in some way aprioristically, as the typical sufficiency of a metalinguistic ambition. How can a theory that affirms the unconscious structured like a language, therefore in any case on the transcendent model of it, not secretly dream, perhaps without knowing it, of a function of metalanguage? The Universal Unconscious is barely structured like a language that it displaces language, structure and the risks of metalanguage in the symptom to dualyse. Language and *langue* only belong to the occasional cause of non-analysis and will serve in specifying the Universal Unconscious. The restitution of the Essence (of) the unconscious, whose 'forgetting' or 'repression' is necessary for the constitution of analysis, is identically that which dooms it to become in turn the object of a unified theory. The being-performed of the *Joui* and the performation of *Jouissance* definitively tear the Unconscious from the occult entities whose type is provided by auto-position and by the biologico-energetico-signifying contents of it. That which is occult indeed in all analytical conceptions of the unconscious is not the transcendence (of) the Other: this is because this transcendence would have the mixed-form of an auto-position or would be deprived of an immanent transcendental identity. The Unconscious must be inferred concretely or within lived experiences – rather than 'produced' through fetishised models – within the immanence of *Jouissance*, an immanence that in no way prevents it from being deployed as transcendence, but as simple and belonging to only one tenant.

Jouissance and Subject

1. The 'Subject of the Unconscious' as Absolute Subjectivity

Touching on the problematic of the 'subject', the first operation of non-analysis is to be able to demonstrate the co-belonging of the philosophical subject and the psychoanalytic subject under the Lacanian title 'the subject of the unconscious'.

1. Let us reprise the schematic description (it does not suffice for us here) of the philosophical forms then the analytic forms of the triad. What is the subject not according to such and such philosophy, but the subject of the philosophical

triad itself? Is it the subject-function cut out by the PA triad on its own body? We distinguish a 'subject'-type function undoubtedly on the side of the One assuring the reprisal and synthesis of the Dyad. It is a question of a place or an invariant function of which, one may doubt, each given philosophy varies it in its own way. However, the 'subject' is in reality always split as the empirico-transcendental or productive-produced or objective-subjective subject – entirely rigorously, the subject is: rather (empirico-)transcendental and rather empirico-(transcendental).

The first form of the subject is rather transcendental, that is, transcendent and immanent to the dyad, productive and objective – this is the One as the productive synthesis, as a Unity that is not solitary but capable of a transcendental linkage, or *de jure* associated to one such liaison or connection, and so on, assuming that it comes from elsewhere. We can call this One *de jure* convertible with Being but more deeply and more universally still with the Other which is the power of alterity and transcendence, indeed the break, of Being, in quasi-Kantian terms, not even the 'transcendental *a priori*' (= the Other-as-One) but the transcendental insofar as it makes the *a priori* its organon (the One-as-Other). This is the first, complex form of the subject, and we will keep ourselves from reducing it, precisely under the effect of a truncated and falsifying comprehension of a vulgarised Kantianism, to a solitary unity, a solitary 'I think' or a solitary 'Ego'. The true subject is a subject-objectivation, an objectivating subject (otherwise 'object' or even 'objectivity'). In many ways, this subject is as 'objective' as 'subjective' in the exterior and empirical sense of these words, but it is suitable to call it rather 'objective'.

The second form is the correlate of the first, its ultimate effect when it is reduced to the Dyad (empirical or aprioristic, or empirico-aprioristic) of experience and what the entirety of a philosophical system sets in operation. The One traces two circles that overlap or loop each other when it is submitted to the conditions of the Dyad. These two circles overlap because they have the same centre, the same radius, but different directions [*sens*] of these radii, the one rather transcendental, the other rather empirical. A first exterior and large circle soars over the Dyad, making a circle around it, enveloping or re-enveloping it into a 'system'; a second, limited to the conditions imposed by the Dyad to this One that, as transcendental, must also be immanent to it: a circle with a break or a disjunction that affects the Dyad. The One itself is divided and begun by the Dyad. This is not because it would be intrinsically divided and destroyed: it is also divided, and its division is associated with its indivision. The residue of the One cut and isolated by the Dyad and also belonging to it constitutes the second, rather empirical form of the subject, its residual and 'subjective' form, that which remains of the Dyad or what it becomes under the effect of these two circles or in their common part.

This first axiomatisation of philosophy - the 'Philosophical Decision' - remains within the bounds of philosophical sufficiency, but makes one perceive the split nature of the subject, its nature as an empirico-transcendental doublet. There is a subject of philosophy, a subject-towards-philosophy, which therefore is no longer the conception that such and such philosophy, for example what Cartesian or Kantian philosophy made 'of' the subject, but the subject who consummates the activity of the philosophical process and enjoys from its production and reproduction. One comparison regarding this formal depth with the 'subject of the unconscious' becomes possible, in view of constituting a whole section of the PA complex - which is also a task, even if it were preliminary, of non-analysis. From this point of view, the specific difference that the 'subject of the unconscious' adds to the subjugated subject of the Philosophical Decision holds to that which affects the residual substantial nature of the latter of a lack that digs the 'natural' gap of the Dyad and is reproduced as the One-of-the-lack or the auto-privational 'hole', the typical triad of the unitary style remains more than ever operational in analysis. This is what we now attempt to demonstrate.

2. The 'logic of the signifier' is just as much a philosophy of the signifier: it is structured by a dyad and a triad that brings a 'subject' into play. Indeed, we distinguish three levels that organise themselves hierarchically. They deny the formalism of the structure and prove that it is a question of one form of transcendental logic:

i. the empirical level of the signifier in its reference to a concrete event of speech or life, its 'sign' side of representation - *for* someone;
ii. the aprioristic level of the signifier as formal structure or the dyad of two signifiers in an oppositional relation, a relation of negation and difference; its side of representation-*for* another signifier; the genuine dyad constitutive of the Philosophical Decision is indeed always locatable at the level of the *a priori* and the *a priori* is here obtained by the reversal of the signified/signifying hierarchy for the benefit of a signifier having become universal or self-signifying;
iii. the transcendental level of the signifier, its side of the One or the 'unary trait' by which any signifier is 'one' and therefore 'multiple', either being one is related to the multiple and re-affirms its multiplicity as such, therefore as a set, or it re-affirms the unconscious as such; this side harbours the 'subject of the unconscious' that itself is in reality split as the unary subject and as the imaginary subject or as 'I'.

The set of these three levels holds within the subject-supposed-to-speak or within the immanence of the speech act. There is a new and profound triad: the subject, the signifier, and the act of speaking or stating. The subject participates in speech, therefore it exists, empirical and concrete; but the speech act is exercised as signifier; therefore, it is formal, then an apriorico-transcendental subject or unary trait. The speech act reconciles the concrete 'we, speaking beings' and the subject as submitting to the signifier, fading away as a pure form.

Because the unconscious would be nothing but structured *like* a language is a philosophical understatement is to say that the signifier is in reality interiorised, supported [*pris en charge*] and sublated [*relevé*] by the unsurpassable invariant of the 'Philosophical Decision': Lacan makes the Freudian identification of the I with the distinctive trait of the object pass into the state of the *a priori*. One understands empirically (therefore abstract and metaphysically) the thesis of the 'subject of the unconscious' when one interprets in a structuralist way without deploying its full philosophical (and therefore transcendental) meaning and in believing that structuralism does not necessarily make use of the *a priori* and the transcendental; and one understands the transcendental in a restrictive way when one interprets it in a Kantian way as a 'transcendental subject'. Better yet: the subject of the unconscious, the 'unary trait', is rather a transcendental subject even if it is not the Kantian subject. The subject of the unconscious is indeed not an abstract or transcendent entity = separated from the play of signifiers. On the one hand, it is involved within the relationship of two signifiers or is immanent to them; it is even one particular signifier taken from the set. On the other hand, it is extracted outside of this set to fulfil a unique role. Therefore, it is not a simple signifier, but a One-signifier which relates itself, thanks to its situation of extra-territoriality, and relates the others to the empiricism [*empirie*] of events called 'signifying' (the lapse, the dream, and so on). This is why, very naturally, this One-signifier is called 'subject' and marks the empirical subject or the speech event. The philosophical-type of subject indeed is always the inevitable identity of the One and experience – and it is divided into these two sides – across the mediation of the constitutive relation of the *a priori* (here the signifier as the relation with another signifier). If the subject is the matter or unique object of analytic *praxis*, this is because the One is related to any such empirical events or speech experiences [*vécus de parole*] that signal and define the belonging of any such element to the status of the signifier and the set of signifiers. The 'unary trait' itself can be treated empirically as an invariable 'significative detail' subject to repetition, and one that 'gathers' the elements, but this is an interpretation which is itself empiricist and inductive. In reality, it is a matter of a genuine transcendental function (or, rigorously, a matter of a mathematico-transcendental set of signifiers) which, far from being abstract, determines the belonging of the lived experience or the empirical subject with the unconscious as such. Because the I is identified with a distinctive trait of the object or the subject with a particular yet objective signifier, it is the very structure of the One or the subject as a transcendental (and not 'transcendent') function. To be fully philosophically rigorous, the 'subject of the unconscious' is the synthesis or mixture of a pure relation (the *a priori* of the signifier) and the One; the signifying difference as One or as trait. One will have recognised in the unary trait the highest instance of the Philosophical Decision, the transcendental or real *a priori*, that is, the One such that philosophy can conceive it and make it into a universal function of all thought. One will have also recognised within the 'division' or 'splitting' of the subject one mode of the empirico-transcendental doublet of the subject.

3. Yet what remains is the strictly analytic specification of this function. If the essence of the unary trait or the subject of the unconscious is not specifically analytic, its 'Lacanian' realisation, by contrast, defines the specificity of analysis. As we have seen, the transcendental One is at once immanent and transcendent at the level of the *a priori* or on the order of pure signifiers. Yet this double relation cannot be conceived substantially nor even functionally, but in the very mode of depriveness. Freud still empirically treats the loss of the lost object as an affect that despite everything remains, if we may say, contingent, despite its generality. By contrast, Lacan gives it a universal structuring function, a transcendental function by which it transits the very concepts of theory and not only its objects or some of its objects. This is why the One, without stopping so that it can be functionally transcendental and therefore 'real' as philosophy wants it, loses its substantial nature to acquire the nature of the hole or the lack, and it is as One (of) the hole or One (of) lack (otherwise as lack of the One), even as One-towards-lack, that it assumes the determinant role of a transcendental *a priori*. The object is not only lost, it is loss that becomes objective or constitutive, with being-lost ceasing to be an attribute to become the real essence of the unconscious, that which determines or constitutes it. It is a completely philosophical rigour that requires a signifier to be extracted from the set, to make it defective and put it into the spot of the One – this is the universal transcendental function, the One as immanent and transcendent to the set – but this signifier is still, thus defined, ontologically 'void', its being-of-signifier must be specified. This is so through its inseparability no longer from a substantial being but from a lack, from a quasi-substantial being-of-lack, that gives it this trait . . . of the 'trait' that is both exterior and constituent, so that the scarce-One [*l'Un-en-moins*] or the counted

One is necessarily, even as lack, a surplus-One [*Un-en-plus*]; the subject of the unconscious is not only scarce of a concrete existence but as well with surplus: the subtraction of the One is the supplement of the One. Even depriveness or lack do not split each other only into the symbolic and imaginary, but they more essentially or more structurally at the heart of the real split each other up as (scarce-)lack [*manque (en) moins*] or scarce(-lack) [*moins (du) manque*] and as (surplus-)lack [*manque (en) plus*] or surplus-(lack) [*plus (du) manque*]. This is why the unary trait is undoubtedly interpretable in terms of absence or depriveness, withdrawal, yet on condition that withdrawal itself is understood as divided, and therefore equally as surplus [*en-plus*] or as sur-trait [*sur-trait*].

As we know, this structure is not only the structure of the symbolic, the symbolic identification of the subject of the unconscious. It is reflected or split into the imaginary identification of the I with images – this is the third instance of the ideal of the ego – and in sexual identification, if you will – the third instance of the phallus. Each of these instances fulfil and specify the function of the transcendental *a priori* – for example, the phallus must be called the transcendental *a priori* of the set of the different modes of sexuality.

We are apparently far from psychoanalysis; in fact, we are in its most secret heart, the one by which it is interiorly inseparable from philosophy though distinct from it. As one of the hypotheses of non-analysis and the point of departure of their unified theory, philosophy and analysis are given it in any case and at least as obeying without contradiction both the law of continuity and the principle of indiscernibles.

4. If the first operation of non-analysis consists in demonstrating this co-belonging, the second one draws the ultimate meaning of the co-belonging from the actual question of the subject. In the same way that Heidegger detects 'absolute subjectivity' as the completed form of metaphysics, one can consider the produced PA body as another form of 'absolute subjectivity', the completed form of metaphysics, where psychoanalysis is also included. However, this is on the double condition that analysis will be pursued in its ultimate requisites and that the absoluteness of its subjectivity would be understood as auto-position and this will be defined by non-analysis rather than, too restrictively, by the 'thought of Being'. The theory of the 'subject of the unconscious' is not a critique of the Cartesian subject except on the grounds of a more intimate and vaster belonging to this formation of 'absolute subjectivity', that is, auto-positional, where it rations its 'privational' modality, so that the 'subject of the unconscious' should be by and for us understood as the universal *a priori* of experience. Indeed, non-analysis is not content with reprising a Heideggerian-type of description of metaphysics to

affect it with a 'withdrawal'. It treats the PA mixture as such rather than from 'metaphysics' alone, which is for it a too narrow concept, and finally treats it as a universal *a priori* of all experience, an *a priori* of which it posits identity as effect of *Jouissance*, thus affirming the 'pragmatic' style of non-analysis.

2. Jouissance *as Subject (of) the Unconscious*

1. Finally, non-analysis evidently refuses for its own account this Freudo-Lacanian thesis of the lost or missing subject opposed to the present or substantial subject of Cartesianism and, if it treats it as a simple given or a material, it is in order to dismember this triad according to its style that requires the Real to be the Real of immanence and the 'syntax' that it determines, the 'syntax' of the unilateral duality. The 'subject of the unconscious' is the indication of an unresolved problem or one poorly posed by analysis: if there must not be a variant or a simple substitute of the philosophical subject, then it cannot simply be determined by a real of the lack that it co-constitutes in turn but must itself be absolutely precedent and determined by the Real of radical immanence, a human - not transcendental, but fully real - individual. If one subject is possible in the sense that the PA would aim for, and missing it, it corresponds strictly to the organon of *Jouissance* - otherwise the PA subject itself is not anything other than a 'transcendental' organon but one that is wrongly posited as the Real and attempts to usurp its place. The identity of the real and the possible or the *a priori* is, in general, the essence of the subject as organon, although it is obvious that this identity in turn takes up in philosophy the form of a synthesis or a triad by which it is auto-posited; whereas it takes up in non-philosophy the form of a simple transcendental identity of one real (which is no longer the Real itself but the desire proper to *Jouissance*) and an *a priori* which is the unilateral duality. Far from auto-positing itself as the ultimate instance of the Real, this identity of the Subject is determined-in-the-last-instance by the Real. As *Jouissance* or the Subject (of) the Unconscious, the 'subject' is now disclosed from the Real itself, yet constitutes an original and relatively autonomous region of phenomenality, distinct as much from the Real as the PA symptom. Here, Cartesianism is vanquished on the terrain of the subject because non-analysis posits the problem of the latter elsewhere than from this terrain and substance-Being, yet it is also the Freudo-Lacanian critique of the Cartesian subject which is demonstrated to be one with its adversary and which is thus limited in its reach.

2. *Jouissance* is the Subject, but the Subject is not behind Desire or the Unconscious, or on their margins, on their periphery; it is identically desire and the

(dual) signifier. It is not only formalism that is refused by the existence of the Subject, but the disjunction of reality and syntax characteristic of the PA complex. Indeed, formalism is not fought within analysis except through the return to the empirical, even to the empirico-aprioristic of the 'we, speaking beings' (see above: the 'we, philosophers'), for the subject-supposed-to-speak, which nourishes the amphibology of the Real and language, so that the subject, with speech, the demand and desire, remains opposed to *jouissance.* Yet the global PA illusion is fought within non-analysis by the 'return' to the identity of *Jouissance*: where *Jouissance* is, so too the Subject, and yet there is no metaphysical confusion here, but rather the condition of the dissolution of PA confusions. *Jouissance* is the Subject as it appears for the first time, in an originary or phenomenal way, as undivided though 'spread out' on transcendence. It is indeed identical to the transcendental condition of representation, yet if this condition is itself not representation, it is undoubtedly a simple position or nevertheless absolute or originary presentation following the *Joui*, which is not even presentation. The Subject is the uni-flected presentation that never forms a chain or circle, so that it is not represented (by a signifier) and does not lack the Other not more than it exceeds it as One. Neither a scarce-subject, nor surplus-subject, it is strictly co-extensive (with) the Other: it is the Subject (of) the Other or (with) the Other.

3. Therefore, the Subject does not have to become aphanised [*s'aphaniser*]: it is from the outset reduced to the 'minimum' tolerated by the Real and the Unconscious. By contrast, because it is co-extensive (with) the Other or (with) the Universal Unconscious, it nevertheless 'aphanises', if you will, albeit unilaterally, that which subsists no longer of the substantial, but of the auto-positional within the PA subject. Said otherwise, the Subject (of) *Jouissance* obviously does not have to recognise its limits, its exterior and interior limits. Not being castrated yet identical to intrinsically finite *Jouissance*, it is rather that which imposes a new form of castration (see later) upon the transcendent and objectivated 'subject' such that the PA complex presents it, and which is not the phenomenal subject. With *Jouissance* being intrinsically phallic, with a non-transcendent phallus (we will demonstrate this later), the problem is no longer posited for the Subject of having or not having, being or not being the phallus, to be submitted to it or not: its radical finitude excludes depriveness as much as substantialisation.

The antinomy of being and non-being was only partially eliminated by depriveness, for being was then understood in a restrictive way as substance and not in its auto-positional universality from which the problematic escapes the analysis enveloped within it. Lacking a radical analysis of the requisites of philosophy, Lacan confused desubstantialisation and deontologisation – of the subject among other things – and believed to have avoided the alternative between being and non-being, but he conserves the representation-form – reduced and localised to the signifier – as the empty shell or negative of substance, and he substitutes for the opposition and correlation of being and non-being the opposition and correlation of the One and the Other, the place and the chain, the actual signifier and the virtual signifiers – new antinomies. There is a gain in distinguishing the real and being, albeit insufficiently, and one must rule out the problem of the Real within the ontological horizon of which non-analysis, to the contrary, posits that it absolutely excludes it and that it is not content with excluding the mere possible or the mere signifying. Whether representation would be de-substantialised there nonetheless remains representation or circularity – whether enriching topological models or not, this does not matter – and thus subsists in the heart of the subject that does not efface itself in the chain except to conserve itself as One or represented as One and reciprocally, or that it does not identify itself except by disidentifying itself (the subject does not disappear, it fades away, and aphanisis is structural). The division – and therefore the auto-position – of the subject was already realised by classical ontology; this is in any case the essence of its philosophical concept. Being content with placing it elsewhere, under other conditions, produces other effects, but it does not change anything for this comprehension of the subject as auto-positional. Even by renewing the antinomy of the philosophical subject, the subject-not-supposed-to-know hardly is better than the subject-supposed-to-know: it is always supposed, even at best subtracted from auto-position and not in its very essence outside of any auto-position and identical to mere position.

4. Finally, the PA triad, which posits and divides the subject, is dualysed or reduced to a unilateral duality that, to the contrary, preserves its radical identity. Let us take the problem under the lens of the arithmetico-logical model that stokes Lacanianism. We know that the zero is defined by its duplicity, designating an impossible or non-self-identical object (like the subject excluded from the signifying chain), yet it participates in the number line, taking a precise place in the numerical succession (like the subject represented by a signifier and therefore immanent to the calculation). In its place and function, the zero conditions or renders possible the number line, while the subject as lack assures the circulation of signifiers: one passes from arithmetics to its transcendental or so-called 'real' use. Thus, the zero receives a mixed transcendental use by which it can become the transcendent model of the subject. By contrast, non-analysis, abandoning any mathematism philosophically fetishised and transcendent for an immanent transcendental *mathesis*,

stops conceiving the One and the Subject on the model of the zero. On the one hand, the One-in-One excludes any reference to number, either to the substantial, arithmetico-metaphysical One of the Greeks, or the scarce/surplus and divided One like the axiomatico-transcendental zero of the contemporaries. At most, the zero deprives the One (which interiorises the 1 precisely) of the 1 or the number of identity and instals duplicity there, but it does not liberate it from the arithmetico-transcendental mixture with which it remains confused. By contrast, *jouissance*-Subject, at least *qua* One, no longer falling into Being or the Other, is therefore not much more 'excluded' from the Other or the signifier to be then included in them. On the other hand, it is not reduced to the One-in-One that, as such, is never subject, but exceeds the One, without alienating it, by *Jouissance*, the only possible subject of non-analysis. Thus, the duplicity of the arithmetical-type zero is deprived of all transcendental use or 'real' pretension and replaced (serving us as PA material here) by the unilateral duality of the One and the Subject, the *Joui* and *Jouissance*, a duality which would aim at the mirror of arithmetical representation. Non-analysis sees-the-Real-and-the-Subject-without-seeing [*voit-sans-voir le Réel et le Sujet*] utterly in person, or sees them as viewed-without-vision.

Thus, non-analysis can absolutely use the One and the zero, tearing them from their mathematico-transcendental context and transforming them into 'first names' of a purely transcendental axiomatic. We can use the zero, after the One, as a first name designating *Jouissance qua* organon or pure exteriority void of objects but also void of the One or the Real. In general, the posture of non-analysis is mathematical, taking hold of *mathesis* on its axiomatic and universal side, rather than its algebraic and topological side. It freely 'nominates' in the sense where it deduces from analysis terms then treated as 'first'. Nevertheless, it is a real axiomatic determined by the *Joui*-in-the-last-instance and identical to *Jouissance*, an axiomatic of proper names - they are indeed said of the Subject (or respectively of the Stranger) - and it is in this element of proper-names-in-the-last-instance rather than in the element of individual discourse and speech that *Jouissance* is deployed, rejecting the lingual condition, even if it were the maternal 'tongue', into its 'occasional' conditions or its 'external' conditions of existence.

3. The 'Subject of the Unconscious' as the Foreclosure of Jouissance

The operations of non-analysis upon the 'subject' allow for us to elaborate a positive or real critique of the thesis of the 'subject of the unconscious' and demonstrate that, consubstantial with the PA complex, it rests on a genuine foreclosure of the Real and *Jouissance*.

1. Several breaks punctuate the history of the subject, for example: (1) the subject-substance, the identity of the One-subject and Being, therefore the identity of Being and Thought, of the I with itself, the I of the enunciation with the I of the enunciated; this identity of the subject is the identity of a representation which reflects or posits itself; (2) the depriveness-subject, the identity of the One-subject and the Other or signifying difference, the subject and a signifying representation which is therefore not reflected in the substantial and auto-representative mode, but which nevertheless makes up a chain and conserves within the Other itself the form of self-referral, of a purely signifying or void reflexivity. The subject is no longer co-extensive with the looping upon itself of representation, but it still accompanies the signifying looping which it elsewhere excludes and affects it, and which it neither knows nor constitutes, or of which it is not a real part. If it makes the signifier exit from the authority of the substantial subject, analysis does not exit from the authority of representation and does not reach a non-auto-positional presentation that is simply uni-positional or uni-flected. The subject is no longer represented for self or for itself, but for another signifier or for the Other that it is not related: it exists outside the chain but through it, in relation to it. Representation is solely unreflected for the subject, but it remains a re-flection for, within, and by the Other; the subject is necessarily associated to it in a heteronomous way without understanding nothing of it. In contrast with any substantial identity, the subject is therefore divided by signifying representation, by the Other and its discourse. Hence, a duplicity of the subject that the signifier represents but, because it does not represent it for itself, it makes it if not totally disappear, at least continuously fade away. This ultimate circularity of the void or the hole, this impossible identity of the One, this duplicity of the subject is the foreclosure of the uni-flection of *Jouissance*; it is one objective transcendental appearance which gives birth to the immanent 'fascination' of the identity of the Real or the identity of *Jouissance* and its absolute, constitutional rejection by the PA complex.

2. There is another form of circularity and foreclosure of identity: the reversibility of the hole of the signifier and the signifier of the hole. Analysis, above all Lacanian analysis, is constantly threatened with veering towards a 'negative psychoanalysis' that poorly hides a style of algebraic unknowns yet that annuls a certain tendency towards the reversibility of concepts, with the ensemble resulting in a *pathos* of antinomy or aporia, impasse or impossibility. Let us take the triad: the substance of *jouissance*, the hole of sexuality, and the synthesis of the signifier or the subject that it conveys, a subject represented both on the edge solely of sexuality by the hole of its non-knowledge and on

the edge solely of *jouissance* by the insatisfaction of its desire. The subject is at the crossroads of the Other where a lack of the signifier is instituted, and sex that it does not know; the subject is at the impossible intersecting point of the signifier and sex. The impossibilities proliferate and the negations multiply: there is some signifier 'for' the subject, but there is not one for sexuality; it represents or signifies the subject, it is absent from sexuality which is not signifiable. Yet if the subject is representable and if sexuality is not, the subject does not know and sexuality is a hole; or the subject is missing and the sex is non-known. The subject is represented as One, they are known without being knowledge; and sexuality is not even represented, it is therefore not 'One' [*Un(e)*];[8] it is announced, more radically than as non-knowledge, as a hole or absence of the sexual 'relationship', and so on.

Nevertheless, save for renouncing all thought and giving into occult entities adjoined by algebraic representations, it is necessary that the subject is announced or manifested, that it becomes a phenomenon in one way or another, even if it is not specifically in the mode of the Real and even less of substantial representation. It is necessary that sex is also made into a phenomenon, the phenomenon of the hole cannot be an ultimate, absolute hole of the phenomenon. Even if sex has no signifier, or is not known strictly speaking, if the essence of sexuality is not self-signifying, analysis is condemned – this is its status of transcendental appearance – to giving these formulae a positive and intelligible reason, something consequently like an identity otherwise foreclosed as such. Once non-analysis is acquired, it reveals that the hole of sexuality aims and disguises the phenomenon *par excellence*, the *Joui*, that is, the cause (of-the-last-instance) of desire. In addition, we must dualyse the analytic concept of sexuality; turning this concept back into the material or symptom of non-analysis by distinguishing the *Joui* as its real non-sexual essence and thus dissolve the amphibology which would harbour the analytic concept of sexuality. The attempt is spontaneous and inevitable to 'positivise' lack, inventing in some way a concept of 'privative magnitudes', transforming loss and defect of signifying positive elements (phonemes) into a new signifier, with the hole no longer only being marked by one signifier but itself becoming a signifier or producing signifiers as substitutes. Yet, precisely, there is nothing more here than the exercise of the auto-positional circularity that is

8 Translator's note: It may be inferred that the remark that sexuality not being represented and it not being 'One' is an allusion to the work of Luce Irigaray, most notable for the text, *This Sex Which is Not One* [*Ce sexe qui n'en est pas un*], translated by Catherine Porter and Carolyn Burke (Ithaca, NY: Cornell University Press, 1985).

itself the ultimate expression of the analytic foreclosure of the Real. For non-analysis, it is the real (of the) *Joui* that is foreclosed by analysis itself or that makes up the object of an absolute forgetting. Through these compensating procedures, the PA complex attempts to assure its actuality or performativity, but refuses at the same time the means of its realisation.

3. Finally, another form of the foreclosure of identity can be detected at the deepest level of the structure of any triad. Like philosophy, although in its mode to it, it is remarkable that analysis postulates a point of identity of the subject or the One and the signifier, the subject under such and such signifier or saying. The signifier does not make an effect (of the subject) except in speaking being; so, it is the stating act which is the identity of the subject and the signifying chain, the subject and representation. The saying or stating act makes itself pass for this identity; in reality, it envelops and actualises it, supposing it and dissimulating it. This is a magical solution, a skeleton key solution. The structure of the triad would appear resolved in a certain supposed performativity, an amphibology between the two 'natures' nevertheless without a common nature: the subject and language, the One and the Other or again the Other-in-One and the Other-in-Being. However, the solution of this antinomy, the aphanisis of the subject - even if it were within and through the Other - is nothing but too reminiscent of the philosophical model of fading away, the flash, the solution of continuity proper to the post-moderns. Because the subject is suspended, divided and effaced in the signifying chain is one possible becoming of the subject, yet it does not rule out the fundamental question upon which philosophy stumbles as the foreclosure of the radical identity of the One-in-One.

Otherwise, if therefore the Other or the signifier in the subject is at stake [*il y va*], this stake, which is itself not elucidated in its possibility of affecting and dividing the subject, implies that there is no metalanguage of the subject, that analysis is not this metalanguage. Nevertheless, the thesis or amphibology of the subject-supposed-to-speak - for it is rather this that is in question, whether speaking would be a substantial essence or an Other-essence of man - in turn serves as metalanguage for a fully 'human' science, therefore on the synthetic horizon assumed valid for one identity: analysis is a meta-science, rather than a science.

The problem of contemporary philosophy and analysis is that the relentlessness to destroy identity in the name of the Other bears only on the substantial identity of metaphysics, but rests within the foreclosure of a more radical identity, within the anguish that grasps them before a 'One' without Being or Other. This is not to inscribe the subject outside of itself and into the field of the Other, as if it was constituted by the Big Subject which the Other is, that the zone of magical opacity of their point of identity or connection is dissipated. Yet it is there where they withdraw themselves and where they envelop in secret the occult entities that make them into a mystery . . . a transcendental 'black box'.

The Philosophical Triangulation of Psychoanalysis

Let us summarise the previous investigations very schematically: *Jouissance*, the organon of the Real or the *Joui*, is the transcendental identity constitutive of the Universal Unconscious whose two strictly 'fused' components are the Essence (of) desire and the Essence (of) the signifier or the 'dual' signifier. We may now gather under the heading 'philosophical triangulation' of the Unconscious and the Real what non-analysis must eliminate from analysis and of which it must carry out the real or universal critique.

1. On the syntactic plane, the analytic use of the signifier is inspired both by linguistics and set theory, and it superimposes upon it a certain structure, yet neither one can explain the deep transformations, of the typically philosophical order, which makes them suffer and which make the linguistic signifier pass towards a certain 'logic' of the signifier. This use proceeds with a dyad from the mathematical extraction, the element and the set, but instead of mathematically binding the properties of both, it binds them philosophically through a synthesis or a third term of which it makes an otherwise special use. This term can be nothing other than the One – a withdrawn or subtracted element from others to be positioned on the edge or on the exterior limit. Others (from within) are therefore supposed to be identified with it and it is supposed to be identified with them; but the set is also identified with it, so that the element and the set, furnished by mathematics, are extracted from it, placed in a confrontational [*face à face*] relation, a relation of opposition and a correlation of contraries, a philosophical-type relation; and synthesised in the third term of the One to which both participate. The dyad has become a triad, more exactly a matrix with 2/3 terms. Another formulation would say that the One is the synthesis of two opposed and connected effects, the hole in the set in which it is extracted and the supplement of which it makes up the limit or edge to ensure the consistency of the set.

Let us note the philosophical phenomenon of the fold, the lining, or redoubling: (a) the 'unary' hole redoubles the existent gap of supposed multiple terms or the gap that is already the signifier; (b) the One in the posture of exteriority or ex-istence redoubles the limit or consistency already postulated by the existence 'in-itself' of the supposed given set; and (c) finally, the One is redoubled itself by assuming, as 1 element, the functioning of the one-set. The two simultaneous functions of the One – subtracted from elements or lesser, added to their set or greater – do not only signify that the One only exists by dint of redoublings and under the form of doublets that testify to a psychoanalyst *ex machina* – this is the 'normal' status of the analyst – but that it itself exists divided and de-magnified in its simultaneous functions (lesser and greater) and that thus the Real (of the) *Joui* undergoes full force operations *ex machina* that, we must say, send it back to the philosophical quarters [*décors*] of analysis. These fabricated doublets with the terms of the basic mathematical dyad sufficiently indicate a philosophical use, the passage towards an empirico-transcendental doublet and the abandonment of mathematical exigencies. It is all the more obvious that one post-Lacanian philosopher (Alain Badiou) has returned to the exploitation of the mathematical properties of the relations between elements or multiple-terms and the One. The terms are then posited as multiples-of-multiples without, at least, the apparent risk of forming a circle like the Lacanian unconscious; and the One has fallen from its status of transcendental synthesis and has been reduced to the state of the one-of-the-count. Hence, a materialist-type of ontology read directly by set theory and one that is opposed to the style of the empirico-transcendental triad, rejected elsewhere. However, from our point of view, this solution assumes the former is valid or pertinent to simply prohibit or truncate it.

2. These two solutions finally refuse to be characterised as philosophy: the first is a 'psychoanalysis', the second is an 'ontology', and ontology, as it happens, does not arise from philosophical activity. Yet what, in psychoanalysis, beyond the triad, which is already one of philosophy's criteria, seems to prohibit philosophy at the very heart of philosophy? It is materiality or the type of real, the ontology of this triad, yet even on this plane of the reality of the unconscious, philosophy remains dominant. Far from being positive and ontologically full or 'substantial' (for example the fulfilments of *jouissance*), signifying relations are negative in the active mode of retraction or subtraction. Far from being manifested as substance, the Real manifests itself as a strong absence of the 'lack' or 'depriveness' type. And 'loss' is not one mode of 'negative magnitudes', despite all 'positive' ones as we know, but rather the positive itself or the Real – in some way a 'privative magnitude'. Like in all of philosophy, the dyad, that is, finally, the hole or a 'partial' mode of the hole, is the determinant essence of the unconscious as a set, that which gives it its energy, for the essence or determination resides within the dyad, the One being the side of domination which assures the closure of the unconscious

as a system. The true dyad is therefore the one of the element and the real, the signifying element and the partial hole of that which is deduced from it. Here, we retrieve the structure of 'phenomenological distance': loss is the loss of an 'object' and the hole that makes up this loss is at the same time the necessary condition so that the One is related to the elements. The objectivating phenomenological distance, the condition of Being and its auto-position, is now given in a new experience, not of distance or nothingness in general, but of the hole as depriveness; it is as if all positive phenomenology of givenness became a phenomenology of depriveness. The being of the signifier, the one that gives its breadth to its predicates (oppositional, negative, differential) is being-deprived-of and not being-given. Another description of the logic of the signifier as a philosophical triad is possible, and makes one even understand this privative ontology. It consists in identifying the elements as ontic terms, the diversity of the ontic real; the set as the universal plane or the *a priori*, ontological horizon for the ontic diversity; and finally the One as a being subtracted from others and identified with Being of which it assumes the functions, so that the One is the supreme cause-being which causes through depriveness – like an onto-theo-logy, not 'negative', but 'privative'. This new description confirms that mathematics is a rapidly sublated, doubled starting point of an ontology of depriveness or subtraction that remains of a philosophical essence.

Let us summarise. Syntactically, the disjunction of the real and the symbolic, *jouissance* and the Other or the unconscious, the sexual and the 'relationship' – this disjunction can be carried out in the name of lack and representing the type of articulation of which a privational ontology is capable: it nonetheless remains an ultimately philosophical structure. Semantically, if you will, *jouissance*, body and sexuality are deprived of a symbolic relation or knowledge. They are rejected into an unintelligible and transcendent ineffability, through a typically philosophical flight into transcendence, doomed to opacity beyond the signifier and the logico-mathematical, as if they would constitute a meta-unconscious sphere, a new form of metaphysics: a metapsychics or perhaps a meta-analysis, an arbitrary and uncontrollable one, made from transcendent hypotheses on the in-itself of psychism. Of course, this is not a philosophical critique of analysis but the ascertainment that this type of 'human' discipline co-belongs, beyond any particular theme, to the Philosophical Decision and maintains, like it, on deciding on the Real, dividing it, tracing a line of demarcation between regions of being, between conscious and unconscious. It is also constrained to stop this haemorrhaging or to close this wound, to repeat this empirico-aprioristic gesture within a second gesture, to pose an aprioristic-transcendental distinction and correlation between the unconscious and the meta-unconscious real (here a hole that is, beyond the effects which are attributed to it, endowed with a transcendental-real function). One of the most massive and philosophical presuppositions of analysis is that of desire as desire first of one whole, as appropriation and incestuous parasitism at the place of the body of the Other. That lack comes to institute this global or total identification is its second presupposition. Finally, that the identification is utterly made to the phallus as to the symbol of lack and what can fill this lack is the third, the synthesis of the previous terms.

3. Hence, a style of proliferating triads that borrow terms from each other and cover each other: the hole, the One, the set; the surplus-enjoyment, phallic *jouissance*, *jouissance* of the Other; need, demand, desire; the *objet a*, the semblant, interpretation; child, mother, phallus; dyads which only ask to give triads: the two axes of speech, substitution (paradigmatic) and succession (syntagmatic); the double articulation of the signifier/signified hierarchy and its bar of repression; desire as metonymy from one signifier to the other and paternal metaphor. Or again: the empirical trace, the effacement of the trace, its marking through another signifier (substitution) which is a remarking (condensation) and the authentic trace – then the cycle begins again by force of substituting and identifying, condensing one signifier with the other.

More profoundly, the triadic style implies that the registers of the symbolic, the energetic, the corporeal, and practice (the cure) respond to each other and finally come to overdetermine the ontology of lack. It produces, regardless of the asymmetry of the two disjointed sides, explicit or hidden bilateral exchanges between the real, the symbolic and the imaginary, a whole specular circuit of homologies and analogies, certainly blocked and prohibited, but which necessarily rises like a repressed of the Philosophico-Analytic refusal of the identity-without-synthesis of *Jouissance* and the Other under pretext that this would be a substantial identity and would bear on what we name the *Joui*. The mirror stage, having been insufficiently analysed as a cause of biologico-philosophical presuppositions, has not made the object of a real critique or a dualysis, and invests the psychoanalytic apparatus itself, inseparable from a mirror structure which disjoins and objectivates the 'real' and the 'symbolic', the 'symbolic' and the 'imaginary' under the invariant form of a double reflection or two images mirroring the one in the other. The auto-privational ontology that forms the substructure of psychoanalysis arises from a broadened or generalised 'mirror stage' that non-analysis can manifest. It is from this circular triadic structure indeed and all of the others of the same type – they are numerous – that it wants to detach itself to think otherwise. One will not end with analytic triangulation save to elaborate a simpler theoretical schema that is definitively distinct from this PA armature.

4. The Lacanian and post-Lacanian doctrines have never abandoned the idea of an order of the syn-tactic type, made from two basic elements undoubtedly in a state of opposition, negation or difference, indeed multiples-of-multiples, but invariably reciprocal (to two proximal terms) or reversible (to a proximal infinity or a proximal multiple). This order, doomed more or less without delay to circularity, has been critiqued in the context of 'Deconstruction', but it is content with truncating and breaking the circle by leaving it to subsist sporadically without getting through in instantiating a genuine uni-tax typical of the Unconscious and its alterity in relation to the PA mixture.

On the plane of the Real, analysis attempts to further straighten out philosophical ontology but this is to assume the contemporary forms of what we must call the ontology of the Other. On Lacan's side, for example, the apparently extended triads in a space of juxtaposition are in reality intensive triads even if lack prevents them from being so as much as those of schizoanalysis. For example, *jouissance* is articulated according to the classically contemporary model, the *nec plus ultra* of post-modern thought, the One-of-the-extremes, of the immediate tension of opposites and voided of any representative buffer, of the event as the rupture and emergence of an alterity which is manifested by a continuum, so that the maximum of tension, the surplus-*jouissance*, is a maximal loss, an aneconomic expenditure; hence its predisposition to invest the topological edges, furrows, curves and bodies; likewise the power of the Other is lived as impossible, as the limit or ideal phenomenon, death, madness, the peak of beatitude, and so on. Analysis attempts to save its reality by reclaiming different types of immanence or what it believes to be of this order: the immanence of the act or the analytic enactment, the cure, the clinic, intersubjective discourse, the dyad of the analyst and the analysand, the field of observations, and so on. All of these forms of immanence nevertheless are transcendental in appearance, they always combine immanence and transcendence simultaneously or reciprocally and are therefore of a philosophical essence. Hence, the sometimes idealist, sometimes realist affirmations of the reality of the unconscious.

While Deconstruction (Derrida) has made a 'critique' of analysis or has deconstructed analysis through an excess of transcendence, a certain progress in authentic immanence has been made on two sides. On the side of schizo-analysis (Deleuze), which has emphasised the immanence of desire, desiring production and its syntax of difference (desiring machines, flows/partial objects), and finally privileging the functioning and production at the expense of interpretation and meaning. This becoming-immanent of analysis, this reversion of the unconscious, is obviously accompanied by a critique of the transcendent structure of Œdipus, the Lacanian triads, familialism and the ideology of 'lack' and the 'phallus'. However, this attempt is but one brilliant revenge of philosophy against analysis, a re-affirmation of Spinoza and Nietzsche against Freud and Lacan and consequently a reduction of the auto-positional type of analysis, a reduction to philosophical desire as auto-position and towards the amphibological, even 'differenciated' confusion, of the real and desire. The auto-position of desire leads to a reversibility of immanence and transcendence, at best by a parallelism finally re-established of philosophy and analysis, but sacrifices what there is of the original proof both of immanence and transcendence in analysis and philosophy by submitting them to the form of auto-position, which, from our point of view, is simply a transcendental appearance. Schizo-analysis substituted a triangulation through global or specific terms a triangulation through differential terms.

Then, on the side of a philosophy of radical immanence understood as 'life' and 'affectivity' (Henry). However, the emphasis of immanence is here done surreptitiously within an ultimately philosophical and quasi-intuitive framework, the Immanent Ego being treated still in fact here as a quasi-object and within a quasi-intuitivity, as auto-affection obtained by a simple 'crushing' of philosophy, this idealism injures the immanence (of) the Real or (of) the *Joui* and, as a complement, leads to a pure and simple negation, a refusal and a non-use of psychoanalysis. On the other hand, a non-analysis should be able to render justice to analysis if it conceives it as excluded from the immanence (of) the Real because it is determinable in-the-last-instance by the Real and thus receives, through this dualysis without auto-position, a theoretico-practical immanence that avoids the auto-position proper to the 'cure' or the 'act', which are crossed by the most classical philosophical antinomies. The actuality of analysis is proven through an act and discourse broken away from a transcendence to which the doublet of the analysand and the analyst changes nothing. The actuality of non-analysis assumes to the contrary in-the-last-instance the performativity of *Jouissance* and more profoundly the being-performed-without-the-performation-(of)-the-*Joui* – a solution which is neither that of a return to a subjectivity of consciousness nor the regular and disastrous confusion of the Unconscious and a transcendence of the auto-positional type. There is therefore no sense in making the antinomy of hypotheses play on an in-self of the Unconscious as if we have to decide if it is exterior or rather simply interior to non-analysis.

5. The most profound triangulation and familialism of psychoanalysis are in no way in Œdipus, which is but one mode. They are, on the one hand, in the invariant philosophical schema of triangulation and, on the other hand, in Familia-logical Difference, which is an essential mode of it, in the experience of man as a child, the child is supposed to be the origin, and therefore the

essence, of man. On the one hand, the triangulation of the Unconscious is not the fact of Œdipus. Under Œdipal triangulation there is a more general syntactic triangulation with the auto-positional and 'real' ambitions through its absolute universality, of all of the forms of analysis, schizoanalysis included, which substitutes for the dyad of signifiers that of 'desiring machines' (flow/ partial object) and for familialism a simple 'anti-Œdipus' that bears witness at most to a revenge of philosophy over analysis, in no way a *displacement* of it on another terrain. The true triangulation of the Unconscious is not 'Œdipal' but philosophical, nothing-but-philosophical. Led back to this level, Lacan's 'privational' ontology remains taken within the mesh of auto-position, for to deprive the unconscious of auto-position (its holing [*mise-en-trou*] if not . . . 'putting in a hole' [*mise . . . au trou*]) is not to deliver it or reject it from outside of it. On the other hand, that man would be an assumed child, non-analysis must also deliver itself from this 'regional' prejudice or this entirely empirical because of the historical essence of man. Schizoanalysis itself does not exit from the doublet of the infantile and the adult, from the child/adult/schizoanalyst triad. One will ask to what extent what we call 'child' is not still an infantile prejudice, and if the theory of the child, of the identity of the child, is made by psychoanalysis. Measured by a unified theory of man and woman, psychoanalysis could rather be but one superior infantile sexual theory, technically elaborated but interiorising of the infantile, all-too-infantile 'foundations' and practices of sexuality.

6. However, radical de-triangulation is not only a critique: it is a new use of triangulation, and it is precisely dualysis which can effectuate it and render it universal. It is enough, for example, to return from the triad, from the philosophical dyad, towards a unilateral duality therefore without dyad, to invalidate the transcendent and restrained models of analysis, the biologico-energetic, linguistico-logical, topological and algebraic models, and renounce these PA mixtures which are symptoms claiming to interpret themselves. It is from this transcendental illusion that non-analysis strives to 'cure' analysis, to cure its 'transcendental' deliriums or its hallucinations of the Real under the form of a real-as-lack.

The existence of triangulation is undoubtedly enigmatic but not more enigmatic than representation. This is representation itself, the dyad or the circle of the *for* (a signifier represents an X for another signifier). In reality, there is no response to this question: *Why is there some dyad, some re-presentation or something* for . . . *rather than only some One?* except to revive this question in the mode of the dyad. Likewise, 'depriveness' is a great Freudian and Lacanian invention in ontology, having become 'privative' or 'privational', without which obviously a positive response could be provided to the question: Who or what makes a hole in the signifier itself, who or what deprives it of the substantial being-given? And even less the ultimate question: Who or what gives depriveness that is the Real to the signifier? How is depriveness itself given? It is useless to respond that analysis does not interrogate itself on its philosophical borders for it is very well in philosophy itself that, by definition, is not interrogated in its mode of the ultimate being-given and in the mode of the being-given of the Real. Very obviously, the schizoanalytic critique of lack in the name of difference and the 'full body' further does not interrogate itself on these ultimate givens. Thought is therefore condemned to this: there is some dyad, something *for*, some representation, there is some signifier for the signifier. The problem is then of what can be done through another hypothesis that will suffice for us to know how to think adequately: there is some *Jouissance*, some Desire, some Unconscious, and so on, all of which are non(-)self-signifying. This hypothesis can, on the one hand, explain in a quasi-scientific sense the previous property of representation or the signifier *for* itself, explaining it without which it would be a new hypothesis of the representational type or bearing on the essence or the in-itself of representation; and only, on the other hand, explains it in this direction by positing it solely as the foreclosure of the Real and *Jouissance*, by limiting itself consequently to this real but non-philosophical type of hypothesis. Non-analysis refuses to interpret or function: it is not the labour of the 'signifying' or 'machinic' unconscious. Non-analysis 'dualyses', and it is an identically theoretical and pragmatic labour. That *jouissance* would be unconscious, more than pleasure; that the 'subject of the unconscious' would therefore be excluded or that it would be incommensurable with *jouissance*, that it 'enjoys' in us without us or even with us but not through us, are at most the indications that we must not extend but dualyse and more than invert. The point is to substitute a dual and unilateral unconscious functioning 'towards' identity for a triangulated, differential and machinic unconscious functioning 'towards' synthesis. The point is to place dualities irreducible where analysis places specular reciprocities, circles, holes and sometimes full bodies, amphibologies and antinomies, and to de-triangulate analysis we must posit a first duality, that of the *Joui* and *Jouissance*, with their identity-of-the-last-instance; we must then posit a duality internal to *Jouissance* with its identity to the Other or the Unconscious.

From *objet a to objet m*: The Unilateral Concept of Loss

1. By extending philosophical logic, analysis distinguishes two, split and more or less distanciated, concepts of the Other nevertheless close to making up a doublet: the Other as symbolic, unconscious, the place of the signifier, and the other – called the *objet a* – which emerges less from the symbolic than from

the real and the imaginary. This new dyad is a place of splitting and correspondence in echoes: between the partialisation of the essence of the symbolic and the detachment of the phantasmatic object, between the hole of the symbolic and the hole as the real orifice traversed by *jouissance*. Lack firstly belongs to the structure and is defined in the order of the signifier, and is then secondly realised in the phantasmatic and imaginary modes, and even the real. The same amphibology affects its correlate: the One of the signifier necessarily responds to a One of the detachable and lost object. The One of the signifier exceeds and doubles the real from within; and the empirical real exceeds and doubles the symbolic from the outside itself even if otherwise the symbolic order is supposed to produce this excess or surplus of the *objet a*.

One perhaps will object that we make the *objet a* into an organicist conception. On the one hand, this organicism belongs to the order of an interiorised, idealised and 'sublated' empirical model within the global structure of analysis; it is conformal, on the other hand, with the signifying partialisation, with the signifier as real gap and detachment; and, finally, the thesis according to which the genuine *objet a* is the hole itself of lack as invested by surplus-enjoyment, whereas the *objets a* are masks or 'semblants of being' for this hole of *jouissance*, with this thesis precisely confirming the organicist model within its generality and complexity. The hole is the complement or correlate of partial objects, a hole-body, precisely not a 'full body' but the body such that a privational ontology can conceive it. However, this does not matter: what is essential is the restrained character of partialisation of loss and dyadic schema, not only the signifier or the holed element/set, but the hole/organ or partial loss/surplus-enjoyment. In any case, organicism is deeper still and refers to a certain type of philosophy. Indeed, in the analytic concept of the lost object, one will sporadically distinguish the remarking by the lack of a philosophical distinction called 'real distinction', frequent in Leibniz, Nietzsche and now Deleuze: two things are distinct yet inseparable, the synthesis of the law of continuity and the principle of indiscernibles. Among other things, Lacan says: 'these detachable pieces [are] nevertheless innately bound to the body'.[9] Of course, the ontology of the first lack or the constitutive hole implies that the distinction becomes a detachment. This detachment is real, while the distinction would not be, but the reality of the distinction changes concept or makes the object with another experience such that the hole deprives it of nearly all blend with inseparability. This is why we say that analysis remains suspended at the internal and external limits of philosophy without being able to detach itself from these limits, even if it shed a good part of its metaphysical content.

9 Translator's note: As quoted from *Le séminaire XIV: la logique du fantasme* (Paris: Éditions Seuil, 2023).

2. One of the theoretical and quasi-'ethical' tasks of non-analysis is to simplify these mixtures; not by diminishing the quantity of terms (it is the same, or it is superior to it) but by radically differenciating, by dualysing as we say, the functions or uses of the sides of the amphibology which sometimes have the same lingual support. We have substituted the determinant dyads of the signifier and the signified, the Other and the other (*objet a*), and truly speaking the *de facto* existence of two or three unconsciouses with a new theoretico-pragmatic model, the unilateral duality. Invested within the material-problem of *objet a*, it involves the duality (without synthesis, therefore non-dyadic) (1) of the Other or the Universal Unconscious inscribed within *Jouissance* and identical to it (the identity of the phenomenal and the uni-tactic order), consequently indivisible between the symbolic and the real, the symbolic and the imaginary, and the symbolic and the phantasmatic; and (2) the object of *Jouissance*, what we call elsewhere the material of its unconscious elaboration, constituted (from the point of view of its content) by the PA complex. This duality within which the material is nothing more than the occasional non-determinant cause of the Essence (of) the unconscious prohibits circular, reciprocal and assumed determinant exchanges and finally the splitting by a 'Big Other' into a 'small other' or the simply differe(a)nt transference from the latter by the former. This radical clarification rationed within the ambiguities that make up the fabric of analysis does not mean that they have no function or are vain, but that their pertinence must be limited: they are only valid for the relationship of man with the world (with social structures, with Œdipus, and so on), not the essence of man.

Therefore, for its own account, non-analysis clarifies this situation and distinguishes 'its' *objet a* within the material as a function that the non-analytic elaboration traces. The *objet a* is here that which remains of the PA complex under the effect of the Universal Unconscious that dualyses it. In some way, it is the underside of the ration-form to which the material must be folded to make up the object of *Jouissance*, that which precisely 'falls' in order to be unilaterally 'suspended' by the Unconscious, outside of *Jouissance*, even though it cannot be a question of an absolute exteriority because it is precisely *Jouissance* that makes it fall (outside of it) under the form of its unilateralising suspension or bracketing. Precisely, the mode of the being-lost of the lost object is no longer 'detachment' with its partialising and differenciating context and its double antithetical horizon of global lack or the hole, or even the full body. The lost object is not more lost in-lack than in-full: the being-lost is a unilateral loss. This term means, on the one hand, that the object is lost for and by *Jouissance* identically, a loss that has its cause of the last-instance within *Jouissance*, within the transcendental identity or non-auto-positional simplicity of the Unconscious rather than in the attractive/expulsive effect of a hole. On the other hand, it is because it is an absolute loss, without return, without remedial or possible compensation as lack would still allow; it is a unilateral loss whose mourning is in some way already done. This theory of the *objet a* therefore also mobilises the instances of the Real, *Jouissance* or the Unconscious, and the Transcendental Appearance albeit under the form where non-analysis knows them, without blending them or making them intervene in a simultaneous and hierarchical way within the definition and position of the *objet a*. The being-lost is in-the-last-instance the effect of the being-given (of the) *Joui*; and it is the effect of givenness (of and by) *Jouissance*, so that the lost object is the effect of the object of love, in no way its opposite capable of affecting it in return as analysis posits it, which identifies them within the horizon of its problematic of narcissism.

3. How do we define that which is lost, that is, that which cannot be the object of *Jouissance* or be presented in an originary way (the ration) within the proper phenomenality of the Unconscious? Analysis proceeds empirically on this point as on the others and then attempts to formulate 'principles' that remain co-determined by this starting point: it enumerates examples and the kinds of *objet a* (the breast, sex, excrement, the voice, the gaze, and so on) assumed both detachable from the body and belonging to it (hence its mixed concept of the lost object), then it generalises this organic-transcendent starting point by resorting to the structure (the three concepts of the lost object: imaginary, phantasmatic real, symbolic) and its ontology of lack. Under these motley conditions, organs and secretions of another type, through dualysis, one more univocal and less motley, is possible, positing the lost object as an *a priori* of non-analysis. Its unique content is then the mixture-form typical of the PA complex. The *objet a* is no longer an image, a phantasy or a symbolic trait; it is neither more nor less than a 'principle' – the Principle of Sufficient Philosophy and Analysis, that is, the 'mixture-form' as the formal or ontological trait of the object *qua* object within the PA element. That which is lost is the auto-positional objectivity that the object receives within the PA element under the form of the mixture. This trait, which is not 'objective', but a trait of objectivity, completes by universalising loss beyond such and such organ or secretion of the transcendent body. If analysis loses 'objects', organs or identifiable products despite everything within the horizon of the transcendent human body, it is analysis itself, at least analytic sufficiency, that non-analysis treats as the lost object *par excellence*. The *objet a* then designates a formal *a priori* trait of the PA complex and it is truly speaking the concept of the *objet a*, specifically of analysis, that is now treated among other things as absolutely

or unilaterally lost . . . We must therefore, in turn, abandon or 'lose' the *a* that refers to the other, to the splitting of the Other and a dyad. Because it is a matter of the mixture, we will write *objet m* to designate this mode of the analytic being-given that makes up the object of this loss.

What we will describe as the *objet m* is in some way the essence of the lost object, the '*objet a*'s essence (of) *a*' [*essence (d') a de l'objet a*], but this essence is never given 'as discovered' or 'completely dry'. It is specified and individuated each time, like the Essence (of) the unconscious itself, by such and such conceptual entity of analysis. They must both, without exception, make up the object of the experience of this loss of their analytic mode of being-given, without which *Jouissance* would not realise its work and which is perhaps the only 'curing' of which non-analysis can authorise in place of analysis.

4. The loss of the *objet m* is not, like the loss of the *objet a*, an assumed real event, that is, effective, producing itself within the element of auto-positional transcendence or the World, social life, and so on. In a sense, after its phenomenal essence that it takes hold of from *Jouissance*, the being-lost is a being given in the mode of *Jouissance*, already given as 'being' (it is not the being that is lost . . .) and non-analysis only intervenes within the manifestation of this phenomenon. If the *Joui* does not need to be manifested, *Jouissance*, the Unconscious and the being-lost need to be manifested, and yet only insofar as it is a matter of this manifestation on the side that emerges from their knowledge, not on the side that emerges from the *Joui*. Otherwise, the classical vector from the 'subject' (who loses) to the (lost) 'object' is in some way inverted. While the 'subject of the unconscious' loses the *objet a* 'passively' and while the motor of loss is the anonymous and transcendent signifier (the speech of demand), it is *Jouissance* as the true 'subject' or organon of non-analysis which 'loses' in a new sense of the term – in the sense where it leads it to its loss – the *objet m*. The *objet m* is therefore not only torn from the subject, and above all not torn by an auto-positional transcendent instance, the *jouissance* of this loss not only happens elsewhere than within it albeit in a transcendent way in relation to it. If it is *Jouissance* that enjoys the unilateral loss that it makes it undergo, tearing its sufficiency from the PA complex, then this cause of loss is rather immanent though heteronomous in effect to the 'subject' that is the PA complex; better yet: it is cause through immanence of this loss.

5. The labour upon the PA material can still go further and be more precise. The *objet a*, as analyses have signalled without perceiving the philosophical triad still at work and without generalising this description in the PA mode, requires a rather imaginary condition, yet not only, of the relief and flow,

salience and protuberance; a rather symbolic condition, yet not only, of the break, partialisation and detachments pretraced under the form of wakes, signifying edges, and so on, inscribed within the body; and finally a condition of synthesis just as imaginary and symbolic as the previous ones, of synthesis and exchange, a function, for example, fulfilled by a 'full body' or by the immanence of reciprocity, for example dialogue (mother-child or other). It objectivates this syntax of the lost object outside of the previous individual conditions, generalising it with the dimensions of the whole, thus completing by tearing it from the individual body and redistributing the lost object to the limits of the full body as the object of an objective hallucination. We thus describe a philosophical invariant of analysis, but what analysis, by the very fact of its fundamental theoretical conditions or its experience of the real as impossible, of Being as lack and the signifier as partialisation and detachment, cannot perceive as that which conditions it. However, this is of little importance: it is a matter of a first universalisation of the conditions of obtaining the *objet a* and we only produce it for the services, as PA material, that it can procure for us on the condition of apprehending it under non-analytic conditions, and therefore conditions of identity. Indeed, we will say that the conditions of obtaining the *objet m* (as unilaterally lost) are the following: (1) the *m*-form (= mixture) as identity is that which gives the PA contents their 'salient' or 'imaginary' allure, their allure of auto-positional relief, their *a priori* form of flow (no longer consequently the empirical or schizoanalytical concept of the 'flow' but its concept generalised for non-analysis, which is henceforth valid for the mode of the being-given of the schizoanalytic concept of the flow itself – we must repeat the same operation over other traits of the being-given of the *objet m* and which must make up the object of loss); (2) the *m*-form also gives PA contents their external limits or their 'symbolic' allure, their *a priori* form of partial break and prepares for their loss; this means that these relative-absolute, internal-external limits are now treated 'in the gaze' of non-analysis as uniquely external and valid for the experience of the breaks that schizoanalysis gives; and (3) precisely, the *m*-form as *m* or as such is presented as the synthesis of the two previous traits, it is that which gives the PA content their aspect of the indivisible 'whole', the 'full body' if you will (a full body that will henceforth be the mode of the being-given, and therefore lost, of the schizo-analytic concept of the 'full body') more universal than the restrained and transcendent body and which completes by detaching the PA concepts to inscribe them in a vaster immanence as hallucinated objects. What we call the *objet m*, the mixture-form of the PA complex, thus itself functions as the triple 'imaginary', 'symbolic' and 'total-synthetic' condition for obtaining the lost object such that non-analysis conceives it.

The Constitution of 'Phantasmatic Desire'

1. Above, we distinguished between (1) desire's Essence (of) desire, intrinsic to the Universal Unconscious, a type of phenomenal reality identical to the moment of the unilateral duality or uni-lation; consequently, included within *Jouissance* (which is *jouissance* through its cause, the *Joui*), which nevertheless possesses this proper type of phenomenal reality where it is desire; (2) desire such that the PA complex can conceive it under the varied forms nevertheless susceptible to invariance, essentially 'imaginary' desire-of-desire, included within the transcendental appearance that is the PA element, a transcendental appearance entirely 'objective' and efficacious; and (3) finally a phantasmatic desire that results from the specification of the first through what it extracts from the determination of the second as its conditions of existence. We will summarise the relations of these three heterogeneous kinds of desire as thus: the Essence (of) desire as the desire (of) the Other is the cause of the last-instance *for*... but not *of*, the desire-of-desire; and it is the cause of phantasmatic desire. It in any case animates from within it, but the problem begins with its effect upon PA desire: first with the suspension of the auto-positional form of this desire (the *objet m*); and, second, with the conserved or 'rationed' residue of this desire, and which, as the condition of the existence of the Essence (of) desire, forms phantasmatic desire with it.

2. As for that which is suspended, otherwise suspended by a unilateral and no longer bilateral or topological break like the signifying break (by the 'demand') or like the machinic break (by the 'full body'), it is therefore a matter of the *m*-form of the desire-of-desire (of its PA concept), of that which is concentrated within the *of* of a synthetic and circular intentionality. Can one then conclude that the Essence (of) desire takes as its object the *objet m* or hallucinates it in its one way once it is suspended? Indeed, it is necessary so that the *objet m*, precisely as lost (unilateralised), as inefficacious upon the desire (of) the Other, would be in turn intrinsically transited by the transcendental identity of *Jouissance*, which does not amount to saying that this suspension would be the whole effect and that the desire (of) the Other is fulfilled by the *objet m*. The *objet m* is not an empirical notion or a contingent object; it is the *a priori* of that which is *de jure* suspended within the contingent given of the PA complex: there is therefore *Jouissance*-in-the-last-instance of the *objet m* (in particular of the desire-of-desire, but not only of this object, but of all objects of the PA complex). Once it is dualysed, the notion of the 'desire of the desire of the Other' then takes on another analytically unintelligible meaning: the desire (of) the Other (which is not the desire-of-desire) is the desire (of)

the other, of the *objet a* or *m*, but a desire under its aspect of suspension alone. The circle of desire is finally really broken. We will not say that the *objet m* is a psychically interiorised object, but that its suspension constitutes it as included within the Unconscious or that it is again *Jouissance* which acts within this operation. If you will, it is a question of a 'transcendental hallucination' of the *objet m*, in the sense, however, where this experience designates a hallucination with a transcendental origin or cause and taking the empirical (the *m*-form) as an object; it is not in the sense where one can say that the PA complex and precisely its desire-of-desire are the victims of a transcendental hallucination or appearance of the Real. Finally, one of the components of desire that is added to its essence and overdetermines it all by making it exist is this hallucinating unilateral suspension that is not itself phantasmatic desire (this interpretation would be transferred too closely to the analytic concept of desire), but it is one of its two sides.

3. Its other side, also the work of *Jouissance*, is more positive and requires a preliminary description of the desire-of-desire, its PA concept. As it is perhaps here that the theoretical labour of non-analysis is the most complex and can be pursued, we will be limited to some indications. It is possible to postulate that the analytic experience of desire, at least under its most refined and elaborated form, also emerges from one PA triad: the triad of (organic) need, the demand (through signifying speech), and desire strictly speaking, which nearly signifies the function of the synthetic residue of desire. Altogether rigorously, desire itself should be able to be analysed according to the interiorised dimensions of this triad: need, which provides the object first and aims for it adequately (whether it is satisfied or not); the demand, which aims for it and *de jure* misses it; and finally desire, which adequately aims for this inadequate object (*objet a*). Desire revives and realises need throughout the mediation of demand, which lacks it. The ultimate structure of analysis is woven by philosophical presuppositions under the form of necessary invariants modulated by privational ontology: (1) the intentionality of the object of need; (2) the 'signifying' demand that leads to the break and failure, the substitution for objects; and (3) the desiring synthesis under the form of one desire that participates in the opposites of the dyad: with need insofar as desire is *de jure* incestuous and aims for total possession (of the maternal body), and *jouissance* insofar as desire is satisfied with an object of substitution – desire is satisfied with its insatisfaction. The impossible *jouissance* of the Other is realised as the *jouissance* of the desire of the *objet a*. The set of these premises emerges from the most traditional philosophical axiomatic solely indexed by privational ontology. Desire refuses the real identification of need with its object and registers the impossible real

identification of the total *jouissance* of the Other (incest); it gives birth to the repression of this double satisfaction and realises their synthesis, which is, therefore, the auto-position not of a substance-desire, but of the impossibility of the *jouissance* of the Other or the 'sexual relationship' exercised within the empirical material of need.

On this basis, a new non-analytic elaboration may begin in view of the production of phantasmatic desire. Generally, *Jouissance* (of) the Other contains, on the one hand, one moment equivalent to 'demand', the moment of the unilateral-suspense described above, which no longer belongs to the privational style; and, on the other hand, one relation with the PA complex as the equivalent to 'need', but a relation that precisely no longer belongs to the philosophical dyad but to occasional material; and finally a third moment which it draws from the previous two and which is nevertheless not their synthesis, the non-analytic form of the synthesis of desire: this is the extraction throughout this PA triad of the invariant moments that constitute it (need/demand/desire) but under a form henceforth deprived of the *objet m*, that is, the PA auto-position that is 'lost' (and hallucinated as lost). What is it then that *Jouissance* as the Essence (of) desire or desire (of) the Other can extract and make itself manifest (on the 'stage' of the Unconscious) of the analytic triad? It extracts invariant, non-auto-positional *a priori* functions from it, therefore from the same nature as itself or conformal with the typical mode of being given of the Unconscious. We will call them the dimensions of the Unconscious; if you will, they substitute themselves with the two axes of the differential signifier (succession or metonymy; substitution or metaphor) yet without at all constituting the essence of the Unconscious. They are rather the specific dimensions of existence of its essence. From this point of view, the *Jouissance* organon extracts from need (assumed to be one ingredient constitutive of PA desire) the *a priori* dimension of a position of the object, a calm and adequate position, here as simple or non-auto-position, without an internal and refolded division. From demand, *Jouissance* extracts the *a priori* dimension of a privational exteriority, more than a substantial exteriority or alterity, but a non-auto-positional depriveness which is nothing more than one particular overdeterminant dimension of the Unconscious, rather than its essence as it is in the PA complex that restrains it. Finally, from desire strictly speaking or desire of the *objet a*, *Jouissance* extracts the main or first *a priori* dimension (the dimension of a 'transcendental *a priori*') of a One-as-Other (explicitly as Other), but of a One as depriveness. Let us recall that non-analysis neither negates nor denies analysis (by what right? From where? What substitutes it?), nor is it an analysis of the *non*, but it works with the help and occasion of its material. Non-analysis proposes a theory and identically a pragmatics, a theoretical use of analysis that it eliminates from its sufficiency alone, or under the condition of the loss of the *objet m.*

The Identity of the Non-Analyst: The Sembled and the Semblant, and the Performational Identity of Theory and Practice

1. As analysis could incite us in saying, we do not say that the *objet m* is the unique object of *Jouissance,* thus distinguishing it from the Other. We renounced the Other (= unconscious)/other (= *objet a*) doublet, the splitting of the symbolic and the real in the privational mode. For *Jouissance* (of) the Other, that which is manifested as a ration is its direct and positive, not lost, object. The *objet m* does not itself escape from *Jouissance,* at least its being-lost. The duality is the duality of the identity of unilateral being-lost and the identity of the being-rationed. Both emerge from the phenomenal-being-given of *Jouissance* and emerge within this phenomenality.

Within our problematic, analysis would unitarily identify *Jouissance* with one of its transcendent forms, surplus-enjoyment alone, and its object with the *objet m* alone. In reality, the identity (of) *Jouissance* has two objects also in a unilateral duality, the rationed or the Other and the loss of the *objet m.* This is to avoid a triple reduction of the Unconscious to lack, to the hole of structure; *Jouissance* with surplus-enjoyment alone; but also the non-analyst in the sole place of the *objet m* as analysis does, which institutes the analyst representing the *objet a* and identifies them finally with the 'privational' function of lack or this energy that lack is. How does one define the posture of the non-analyst in relation to the posture of the analyst? The problem of the non-analyst as such, the problem of the theory and use of their identity, by definition excludes a process of identification with 'surplus-enjoyment' alone. They are the Subject itself, that is, they assume not the *Joui* – which does not 'belong' to them properly, and which 'falls outside' of non-analysis – but the organon of the *Joui, Jouissance* in its transcendental identity, but more than them assuming the transcendent identity of surplus-enjoyment. They also assume the position of the *objet m* in the stead of PA sufficiency and resistance, but here they exercise it nevertheless dually without being taken up within the auto-privational circle of the partial and the hole, loss by detachment and *jouissance* by lack.

2. We know that the subjective position of the analyst in their relation to the analysand combines a feigned indifference and receptive availability: it is a matter of the 'semblant' (Lacan). Philosophy knows of similar postures, such as the phenomenological suspension, the Cartesian feint or fiction of doubt,

the forgetting of traces and the Nietzschean 'branding' [*étiquette*] of consciousness, and even Heideggerian 'serenity'. Among the analyst or the philosopher, these postures define an appearance of a subjective posture that is required by the first object of their thought, which, in some way, 'responds' to them. The symptom contains in particular a semblant-suspension complex, the objective semblant (of) a suspension. It is here important to detect conforming to the triadic logic of lack two fundamental traits: (1) a suspension of re-semblance, the analyst not transferring their posture from that of the analysand, not identifying themselves with the analyst, and the semblant truly speaking being the identity of a mimetic identification and resemblance but deprived of identity and resemblance, deprived of mimesis because it is related to lack; (2) a quasi-phenomenological, dis-interested availability, otherwise more 'Heideggerian' than 'Husserlian', for the given and givenness, this given being of the 'privational' order: the speech of the analysand at the point of its rupture or failure, its hesitation or breaking point. The semblant is therefore the phenomenon of the subjective posture of the analyst, more than broken up or hesitant, almost prohibited, when the phenomenon is thus at first glance hidden or dissimulated as lack is or the forgetting makes itself forget.

The subjective posture of the non-analyst exercises the semblant and the phenomenalising suspension otherwise. If identification or resemblance are suspended, then it is less by the effect of a differe(a)nce or even a depriveness, than it is by the effect of *Jouissance* as identity, nevertheless a de-auto-positioning identity, which itself holds its phenomenality (of) identity of the *Joui* rather than the lack of the *Joui* that, let us recall, is not the 'subject' of non-analysis. The position of the subject is held rather by *Jouissance*. Therefore, non-analytic availability is not for the phenomenon *par excellence* of the Given-without-Givenness which is the cause and has no need for the operation of the semblant. It is included within *Jouissance* as the unilateralising suspension, opened by the radicality of the phenomenon itself. The operation (of) *Jouissance* is indeed the operation of a uni-dentification that is also a transcendental suspension exercised upon the PA complex. As a transcendent identity and the phenomenal kernel of resemblance and identification, the semblant is determined by the phenomenon itself or, if you will, to use our axiomatic style of invention, by the Sembled-without-semblance, the immanent Sembled that is the *Joui*. Perhaps we must indeed dualyse the semblant between the Sembled (the *Joui*, the already Sembled-without-semblance-or-semblant) and Semblance (*Jouissance* as determined-in-the-last-instance by the Sembled). The operation could be renewed by the phenomenological suspension, to dualyse in accordance with the priority of the phenomenon over its phenomenological givenness.

3. Does non-analysis tolerate a process of 'supervision' similarly to how one analyst supervises another? With the risk of meta-analytic pretension or auto-positional mimeticism (auto-vision or super-position, it is of little importance) being entirely inapparent regardless of the analytic point of view itself, non-analysis nevertheless manifests it as the avatar of analytic sufficiency. For its account, it is because the problem of the multiplicity and the formation of the non-analyst begins by not being posited. Indeed, the Real escapes from the predicates of the one and the multiple: it is one 'condition' of non-analysis which does not fall under the problems raised by it and *a fortiori* by analysis; the *Joui* thus allows us to posit that the problem of the formation of non-analysts begins by not being posited. It is only posited with *Jouissance* and its intrinsic dual order, yet it is then resolved within and by the immanent exercise of non-analysis because *Jouissance* is *de jure* multiple, it is existence-as-multitude. Of course, the problem of an 'empirical' formation, beginning and exercise of non-analysis ends by being posited within terms borrowed from philosophers and analysts, but it is precisely a matter of the problems bound to the conditions of the PA existence of this exercise, which do not belong to its essence and do not define it. Said otherwise, these problems do not form the law as in the institutional idealism of analysis, and they must be first dualysed in turn or made into the object of a non-analysis.

4. Among the amphibologies of psychoanalysis or the PA complex, the amphibology between knowledge and truth is not the lesser one even if their distinction is an obligatory exercise of Lacanianism. Knowledge and its closure must let themselves be affected by 'truth effects', that is, essentially, being pierced by lack. As for truth, it is confused with the privational ontology that innervates knowledge and is uniquely manifested by 'effects'. Analytic theory formulates a knowledge that delimits the real and *jouissance* in their ineffability, all by being affected by them. The theory is thus the articulation of the privational style of knowledge and truth, and it is undoubtedly one of the most fruitful and most pertinent inventions of Lacanianism that analysis has conceived as a theory, rather than as a system. Non-analysis can do nothing but accentuate this aspect against the inanity that consists in opposing the 'lived experience' to the 'matheme', although on the condition that this universalisation of theory penetrating *Jouissance* would be conceived as an effect of the lived experience, itself radicalised as the Real (of the) *Joui*, which determines-it-in-the-last-instance. Unconscious *Jouissance*, the Unconscious as universal, is intrinsically and identically theory (and) practice, it is fully performational or actual. Instead of lack being still more or less reciprocally

determined with knowledge, the One (of the) *Joui* unilaterally determines not the theory also assumed as 'lived' but the lived experience or desire of theory. *Jouissance* is the identity of practice and theory, desire and dualysis.

What is the truth? It is the fact . . . for *Jouissance* to be determined unilaterally by the Real outside-truth as much as outside-knowledge. Yet what is the mode of the being-given of truth, its phenomenon, if it is not the proper phenomenon of the *Jouissance* (of) the Other, its being-given as is, as a non-auto-positional transcendence and therefore in a sense emptier still, more multiple yet more positive than lack? The truth does not pierce: it dualyses PA knowledge. It maintains with completed non-analytic knowledge a double relationship. On the one hand, rather than the 'subject', it is the cause or organon of this knowledge, consuming the old knowledge, dualysing it and producing with it a new knowledge. On the other hand, it is enveloped or overdetermined by this knowledge, not that it is held in withdrawal behind it, like a transcendent metaphysical essence, and manifesting itself in 'appearance' or in 'effects' – psychoanalysis in effect – but as a phenomenon which, given in its essence as it is (the as it is is the essence (of) the given of the Real, the Given-without-Givenness or the Manifest-without-manifestation, here the *Joui*), is nevertheless not confused with the Real itself and, like transcendence, requires an operation of manifestation as such. This operation is conditioned by knowledge and included within its production. From this point of view, there is no dialectical circulation between theory, practice and the givens, but inferences which hold to induction and deduction. The articulation of truth and knowledge within non-analysis therefore emerges from a unilateral duality rather than a signifying disjunction overdetermined by lack. The point is to do without the amphibology of knowledge and truth, not completely, but to do without its pretension and sufficiency, rather than to de-port or dis-located within 'effects', operations which let its transcendental illusion subsist. This is the absolute condition so that 'theory' finally becomes 'practice' fully or performational and, without being at all confused with or exhausted in the 'effects' of knowledge – this is its inalienable identity – it does not determine it, but dualyses rather than 'piercing' it. Thus, theory stops being limited to its operation, which is to revolve around an impossible real as to revolve around knowledge, blending these two imaginary circles in the hope, failing to reach the real, of intervening in the illness and unbinding [*illimiter*] it by being disguised as a cure. Used under its own conditions of the analytic act, non-analysis also produces a 'non-therapeutic' order where therapy is determined by man rather than the inverse, the only possible 'cure' of the appearance that fascinates analysis.

The Non-Analyst's Phantasy: The Facticity of the *objet m* as a Support of *Jouissance*

1. Can non-analysis problematise the phantasy, making a place for it by dualysing its analytic concept? Is there within it a 'subject' susceptible to identifying themselves with the *objet a qua* lost? Can one, for example, first say that the PA complex behaves like a 'subject' (through auto-position) and then loses this subject-form? Maybe not. Let us recall that non-analysis does not intervene within analysis – but it makes use of it to produce another order of experience. It cannot both suspend the *objet m*, that is, the auto-positional sufficiency of the PA complex which is precisely where it is a subject, and to then assume that this subject subsists and is identified with the *objet m*. If a subject is affected and interested by this loss, it must be situated within the very element of non-analysis, and it is necessarily *Jouissance* which is the subject or 'organon'. Nevertheless, the loss that it imprints upon auto-positional/privational sufficiency of the PA complex, thus transforming it into the *objet m*, does not let itself be co-determined by the *m* itself circularly (as analysis supposes that the *a* co-determines it). It is a loss of a transcendental origin, the identity of an operation (of) loss which is held and remains near itself all by affecting the PA complex. *Jouissance* is enough to 'practically' determine loss and affect its object – this is the first central point of a real critique of Pure *Jouissance*, the other point being that it is also enough to draw from PA material a residue that it allocates and presents within the element of unconscious phenomenality. It also makes the vicious or specular circle appear – of a privational type, no doubt – which is at the basis of the theory of the *objet a*: the object is a part of me that I lose, that I am by losing it, and that I finally have. How can the I thus understood really lose something or have what it never really lost? The subject of loss, 'subject to' loss, should not – rigorously – be the same, to some near nuance even if it were this intra-philosophical nuance that is depriveness, as the subject that co-determines loss, for this subject is also present in all operations of possession, loss, being and having . . . Loss, the object of loss, and the subject of loss are not dually distinguished. A rigorous, unilateral loss comes to the PA complex from somewhere other than it, from *Jouissance*, and *Jouissance* does not make a circle, more or less broken or distanced, with the *objet m*. To summarise this real critique, we will say that analysis, it is true, has conducted a pertinent critique of Cartesianism, but it could only produce a broadened Cartesianism.

In these conditions, we could redefine and relocalise a phantasy called 'generalised' or the phenomenal kernel of the 'restrained' phantasy of analysis. It cannot consequently be the *Jouissance* (of) the *objet m qua* lost, definitively or absolutely distanced. Without a doubt through this absolute, unilateral distancing, *Jouissance* neither negates nor annihilates the *m*-form, but it is not identified with it or is no longer appropriated by it. In a general way, the operation of *Jouissance* is below the disjunction between having and being, a disjunction which reflects, as one may doubt, in each of its terms (the *objet a* is a part of me = I have it/I am it at once; then I lose it = I no longer have it and no longer am it; I am it = the *objet a* has me and is me; and finally I have it = I am no longer it). It is the identity (of) being and (of) having, but also the identity (of) the loss of being and the identity (of) the loss of having. More profoundly still, the being-lost (not that which is lost) is itself already manifested, as we previously said, in the element of *Jouissance*. As an *a priori*, it does not fall outside it or the Unconscious, but finds its transcendental identity within it, and therefore is not 'caused' except in an 'occasional' way by the *m*-form – that which is lost.

In a sense, therefore, nothing seems to respond to the 'signifying' dialectic of being and having, the subject and object, necessary for the production of the phantasy, except to recognise that this identity (of) *Jouissance*, which is the identity of the being-lost, is *only* the condition of its production in the sense of its manifestation. The phantasy would result from the identification of *Jouissance* not with the being-lost that it already 'contains' but with *that which* is lost. One distinction of a similar type reigns within analysis: loss is *jouissance* itself in its excess, in its surplus-enjoyment or its maximal intensification, and we must distinguish it from *that which* is lost, the partial object or the hole of the symbolic. This distinction is then reciprocal or bilateral. By contrast, within non-analysis, if that which is lost and its being-lost are indifferenciated, if their distinction makes no sense from the transcendental point of view or for *Jouissance* for which there is therefore no phantasy from this point of view, a now unilateral distinction can be made by contrast from the point of view of the 'content' (that which is lost), more exactly, the contingent givenness of the PA complex, of the 'there is some analysis and some philosophy rather than nothing' [*il y a de l'analyse et de la philosophie plutôt que rien*]. Under this lens, the contingency or facticity of the *m*-form that is lost or invalidated, not pertinent, for the theory of the Unconscious, is a formal trait that can become the object of one identification. The fact of being lost does not remove anything from its contingency as occasion. If the PA complex within its sufficiency motivates non-analysis, then this sufficiency – once led to its loss – remains the contingency or givenness of this sufficiency itself and it is with it that *Jouissance* had to already let itself be taken or identified, without being able to negate it as 'unreal' or without consistency in the name of its own immanence.

The problem is the following: as Ego (of the) *Joui*, why does one go beyond this essence and 'enter' into non-analysis? This is undoubtedly because of the resistance (*de jure*, not contingent or accidental) of the PA complex to the *Joui* and also to the idea of the *Joui*. Resistance is identical to auto-position, or to the *m*-form. By inferring itself (in a solely transcendental way) from this situation, *Jouissance* has already reduced or 'lost' the *m*-form. However, what *Jouissance* cannot reduce is this ultimate or first contingency of the *m*-form, the most encompassing invariant form of the PA complex and whose factual givenness is at the origin of resistance. Resistance can be reduced, but there was a given that can serve it as a 'support': this is what non-analysis must admit or receive as the cause of resistance. The relative autonomy of the PA complex (there is one such complex) is at stake – in relation with the absolute autonomy of the Real and the absolute autonomy as well (yet already relative to the Real) of *Jouissance*. It is not a matter of the syntactic content of the *m*-form but its facticity. One will conclude that non-analysis is inseparable from its identification with this facticity of the *m*-form, of which it suspends resistance but whose existence it cannot suspend, itself subject to perishing or abstractly affirming itself like a new transcendent philosophical thesis. The human essence cannot be assumed under the form of non-analysis unless the non-analyst, the Subject, is constituted as a phantasy or as the *Jouissance* of the facticity of the *objet m* as of its occasional cause. Phantasy is not constituted from the identification with the *objet m* but the deeper identification with the 'material' cause of the *objet m*. In reality, it precedes as causing the loss of the object, but the loss of the object reveals it or manifests it from within itself. This is not: 'the subject is identified with the object', a formula nearly unthinkable or too thought out already likely as it is full of philosophical presuppositions, but *Jouissance* is pre-transcendentally identified with the *objet m*, an identification which the loss of it manifests or finally makes appear.

2. A non-analytic idealism – which would be nothing but a psychoanalytic normalisation of non-analysis – would attempt to deduce non-analysis, therefore deduce it from the *Joui* alone, which, nevertheless, does not produce anything beyond itself. *Jouissance* or the Unconscious is inferred from a double causality, not only one, and the secondary or 'occasional' causality is exercised across the phantasy or is identical to it. The phantasy is obviously distinct from its analytic concept, which is rather circular to a near signifier, restrained consequently and at the same 'primary' level as the other objects of analysis. If the *objet a* is truly speaking the energetic-type cause of the phantasy and the signifier its efficient cause, the *objet m* provides the phantasy its facticity as an 'occasional' cause (it is no longer of the circular ontological

or metaphysical type) and the dual signifier its cause-of-the-last-instance, identically of unconscious desire and syntax. The phantasy, far from being anonymously 'enjoyed' outside of any subject by transcendent causes or objects, is 'enjoyed' by man himself who is obviously not confused with the PA 'subject', but if *Jouissance* is the subject (of) the Unconscious, its very existence as an organon, it is determined within its own manifestation, otherwise within its phenomenal reality *en-Joui*, by its prime identification with the facticity of the PA complex. *Jouissance*, *qua* transcendental, is unilaterally identified with this facticity as to a 'support'. Therefore, we will not say that *Jouissance*, if it is the *jouissance* (of) the being-lost, is also the *jouissance* of this facticity, but rather that it finds within it a moment of its own constitution necessary for its transcendental nature. However, the correlation of the facticity of the *m* and transcendental immanence of *Jouissance*, far from being of a circular type which imposes the PA dyads and the signifier (empirico-transcendental doublet), is one effect of the very finitude of the immanence of the *Joui* and therefore of *Jouissance*. This intrinsic finitude renders necessary, at least for the manifestation of it, that it maintain an originary bond with facticity rather than it being constituted by the forgetting or rejection of it. The so-called occasional causality is exercised as it is as a phantasy or a subspecies of phantasy, but it is not really mysterious or miraculous, being the correlate of the Determination-in-the-last-instance which is the order of the *Joui* and *Jouissance*. Said otherwise, the Given-without-givenness of the *Joui* leaves a free place for a Given-through-givenness, a 'there is' which is not of a simple indifferent ascertainment but to which *Jouissance* must already be identified from the point of view of its manifestation, if not of its essence.

The Body (of) *Jouissance*: Analysis as the Incomplete Critique of Philosophy

1. If *Jouissance* presupposes a body, if this body postulates that non-analysis cannot be of the PA order but must be called 'universal', what exact relation does it maintain with the Unconscious and *Jouissance* itself? Against the disjunction between the 'signifier' and '*jouissance*', the Other and the body, the *Joui* involves, as we have said, the concrete identity of these two aspects yet, as well, a new definition of their content, a new 'syntax' and a new type of lived experience. If there is a body (of) *Jouissance* and therefore the Unconscious, we will say that it is subjective or 'enjoyed' in-the-last-instance alone and that, otherwise, it is woven by a non-auto-positional objectivity. It is consequently impossible to begin by disjoining it into a speaking body and a

sexual body under the pretext that the distinctions between the object-body and the subject-body or the body 'proper' are insufficient. The body (of) *Jouissance* is universal insofar as this universality, having its cause within the *Joui*, is transcendental and therefore not divisible into whole/part or any such division (duality is an identity, not a division). It is therefore neither global nor specific, neither 'full' nor 'partial', neither subjective nor objective – the organicist model just like the signifying model must be suspended – and it is furthermore not distributed between the 'symbolic' body and the enjoying body, a signifying body of speech and the orificial body of sexuality. If it is subjective, then it is subjective in-the-last-instance alone, yet it is subjective radically. If it is objective, it is of a simple exteriority that self(-)enjoys without partialising, folding and thickening itself like the full body or emptying itself like the hole: it is an intrinsically infinite and non-auto-positional body. If it is sexual, it is of a sexuality that does not fail as a pretension towards incestuous totality nor does it succeed as partial: it is universal sexuality in its transcendental identity. If it is signifying, it is dually, as a body which is manifested as a ration or absolutely emergent ahead of and, therefore, under this condition, beyond its PA forms. The body postulated in an immanent way by non-analysis does not represent one subject for another body, or another body part, yet emerges within its identity each time for the first time at the same time as the transcendental appearance of the PA body is lost and given to the phenomenality of *Jouissance* as lost. The subjective-body-in-the-last-instance is indivisible into three instances like the 'real' body of *jouissance*, the 'symbolic' body, and the 'imaginary' body; it crosses otherwise, as dual, these three transcendent instances which are not topologically 'knotted' but pre-knotted within an identity, so that the 'enjoying' body is identically the 'signifying' body and also the 'imaginary body' but within relations of identity and duality.

2. Psychoanalysis suffers from an insufficient critique of the 'total' as a philosophical category, a critique in the name of the partial and the hole, the partial even if it were One each time or again positivised under the form of constitutive partial objects, for example, of 'desiring machines'. It is a transcendent machine running on lack, revolving around a hole, constituted by transcendent orders more or less cleverly adjusted in the name of the clinic and theory together (but not identical in-the-last-instance). Insofar as the 'big Other' does not exist as Lacan argues, if not as a fiction, is still to grant the fiction of the Other as total and its pretension constituent. The analysis of the mirror stage has not been pushed to term or has been poorly engaged: it still presupposes, like the deconstruction of the self, the validity of the image of a

total body as constitutive, under the heading of the 'imaginary', of the being-human-of-man. And likewise, the image of the global body of the mother, as fictive as the object of an impossible incestuous *jouissance* would be, is one of these phenomena of the imaginary with which analysis cannot not attempt to constitute this essence. The whole (as full or even as lack) and the partial, the ultimate great philosophical oases of analysis, can no longer be constitutive of the process of a non-analysis and belong to the objective PA appearance, a transcendental appearance. More generally, the unitary hierarchies of the 'real', the 'symbolic' and the 'imaginary', the hierarchies which must circulate rather than being fixed to the benefit of one of their terms, are replaced by an order-without-hierarchy, a priority-without-primacy of the Real over *Jouissance* or the Unconscious, and the Unconscious over the PA imaginary.

Unitary Narcissism and the Narcissism of *Jouissance*: System and Theory

1. What is to be done with the 'split' – primary and secondary – narcissism of the PA body? Non-analysis conducts a triple operation. (1) It treats the PA body as a contingent given, without making a new hypothesis about its essence in-itself and thus adding to its sufficiency: there is this double and unique narcissism, but in the sense this time of the given properties that the point is to explain through a hypothesis of an entirely other nature than narcissistic or other this narcissism, therefore to withdraw from it its character of auto-foundation. (2) It precisely detects the true meaning of these forms of narcissism within a more powerful or 'unitary' narcissism of which analysis cannot make a theory for because it is the narcissism of the PA body itself. It is a matter of auto-position as a broadened narcissism or the element of spontaneous PA sufficiency. It is a first step within the explanation of restrained or split narcissism, an explanation which therefore begins by treating this mixture as the identity of a universal *a priori* of experience that must obviously 'refer' to the transcendental identity of *Jouissance*. (3) Nevertheless in these limits alone, it can make a supplementary hypothesis of a still philosophical type or one that is ultra-PA concerning the causes or origin of it. In the same way that the mirror stage is an absolute, auto-foundational structure that in reality explains nothing but that is only the object of commentary, interpretation and functioning because it is content with folding narcissism back upon itself and tautologically doubling it, likewise we are able in turn to seek an auto-foundational structure of the broadened narcissism of auto-position. It can no longer be the effective mirror, but this 'broadened' mirror: language. Non-analysis could formulate and describe a language stage (of which the

'linguistic turn' is but one recent form and a specific case) within the formation of thought 'explaining' the narcissistic constitution of the PA body, which, in this perspective, would represent an 'infantile' stage of thought. The PA body would constitute itself as thinking across its identification with the Other insofar as the Other is already given by language, in the mirror of language as auto-reflexive *par excellence*, and therefore already virtually constituted as total meaning, *logos*, or 'Being'. We will remark that this type of hypothesis, the hypothesis of the mirror stage and the hypothesis of the language stage which generalises the first, explains nothing: they are simple tautologies or *petitio principii* because they already assume given, of which they are responsible to explain its genesis: the ego [*le moi*]. Indeed, how would the child identify their ego, the ego of the image as being their own (under the form of another) if they did not already possess the knowledge? Therefore, it is a simple recognition. And likewise, thought cannot recognise itself in the auto-reflection of language because it already knows that which is in question. The ego does not recognise in the mirror except what it has put there before. Said otherwise, the true meaning of these hypotheses is that the 'total' I is an *a priori* of experience. Let us explain these hypotheses.

The indestructible mixture of philosophy and analysis is reflected within the theory of narcissism, which is at the crossroads of the philosophical triad and its sexual modalisation, so that at one level of a sufficiently radical examination of presuppositions, the sexual theory of narcissism does nothing but vary or interpret a universal narcissism of a philosophical essence that one will call 'unitary' and that is the essence of its 'primary' and 'secondary' forms. There are two proofs of this indissociability:

a. Primary narcissism or auto-eroticism of drives and partial organs, a pre-egoic narcissism, is not observable. It is here a 'hypothesis' in the sense, however, of a structure that we must assume given as such to elaborate upon it, as upon an absolute soil, a non-amendable knowledge, rather than a scientific and 'falsifiable' type of hypothesis that one could annul or integrate within a more general hypothesis. It is a foundation that is auto-legitimated, not a hypothesis capable of induction and deduction. The PA body in general presents itself as already given: there is the already legitimated PA and in particular there is narcissism in the sense where it is, for itself, not only a simple *datum* but rather already a *factum*, an auto-donative fact that already possesses a certain self-knowledge.
b. Primary and secondary narcissisms form an interlocking of split dyads and triads (hence, apparently, four terms). The first dyad, the dyad *par excellence*, is the dyad of partial drives and the object; the second, the dyad of partial

drives and the ego; the third, the dyad of the object and the ego (obtained by the identification with the 'traits' of the lost objects); the fourth, the dyad of the object and the ego ideal [*l'idéal du moi*]; the fifth, the dyad of the I and the ego ideal - all dyads which make up triads by reflecting themselves or 'referring' to one another, firstly closer and closer, and secondly in and through the third instance *par excellence* of the ego ideal. The ego ideal finds its respondent itself at the starting point within the assumed partial auto-eroticism of organs satisfying itself upon the supposed body proper. Among all these instances, splitting into two and specularity (to varying degrees, for example the images of the ego within the Other and in the mirror, between the Other and the mirror), weave a philosophical substance that entirely exceeds the concepts of the ego as the reflection of the object, the identification of the ego with the ego ideal then with the object, and the reversibility of the libido of the object and the ego, which are nonetheless only effects.

Freud's rigour, his philosophical rigour or his rigour of thought, obviously finds itself accomplished in Lacan, who more explicitly renews the philosophical triad and the ontology of depriveness, and it is completed by closing up despite everything into a system which should perhaps have been nothing but a theory. On the one hand, the symbolic instance of the ego ideal records and resumes, by displacing it, the dual conflictedness of the ego and the ideal ego, conforming to the most invariant essence of philosophy. Once more, the imaginary and the symbolic make a circle, mediation or system: it is within the imaginary relation of the ego with the Other that the symbolic order of desire is inscribed and incarnated and this order, in turn, comforts the imaginary relation, preventing it from sinking into its own specular inessentiality. On the other hand, the imaginary forms a system with the real, needing its own sustenance and not only from the symbolic to be able - the imaginary or the mirror stage - to produce that which it produces. The hole of the real or the drive must affect specularity or not be overlapped by the image so that the image and desire circulate; there is some sexuality that 'de-completes' the image and enters into discordance with it, but which sustains it and makes it 'function'.

2. There are several consequences: unitary narcissism and aggressiveness under the form of antinomies and self-misunderstanding [*méconnaissance de soi*] obviously make up a system within the constitution of a subjectivity proper to the PA. Indeed, there exists a subjectivity of the PA body that is not confused with the 'subject of the unconscious', but it is actualised as the sufficiency and conflictedness of auto-position or auto-givenness. By virtue of the

previous meta-PA hypothesis, we must postulate that the PA body grasps its total image within the mirror of lingual auto-reflexivity, and it is experienced within a certain discordance between its effective and 'regional' means or objects of thought and this 'fundamental' image, within which its totality to come is actually presented. The PA body is also 'partial', 'fragmented', made with motley and tinkered theoretical pieces, but it is unified within an image that is presented to it by language. This imaginary ego is captured by language and frozen under the form of a meaning given as general and total, a fetishised image whose only becoming now depends on lingual production and its variations. Indeed, this subjectivity has as its unique content a pretension or a sufficiency – it is the broadened or transcendental imaginary which non-analysis postulates – and remains foreign to the order of science and knowledge. The subjectivity of philosophy (rather than an intra-philosophical subject like the *cogito*) or analysis (rather than an intra-analytic subject like the unconscious) is only an imaginary and narcissistic capture by language and without a relation to the Real nor to effectivity, contrary to what both claim. Hence, the 'broadened' or transcendental paranoia, the self-misunderstanding which is one with philosophy and psychoanalysis and what non-analysis strives to manifest (even if it is not authorised to investigate the effective cause of this auto-position within the specular fascination for language). The PA 'theory' of narcissism – and other PA objects – is therefore not an authentic theory, but a system where the 'empty case' of depriveness and lingual production give the appearance of the theoretical hypothesis and the production of knowledges. The lack is split into two between the real and the symbolic, analysis is an auto-position of lack and the system of an auto-depriveness which mimics theory.

3. If the explanation by the mirror or lingual specularity is a meta-philosophical 'hypothesis' that is not necessary for non-analysis, it is because non-analysis considers the narcissism of the PA body as not being really explicable in this way, except in a sense to reproduce it, and being content with taking it first as it is given with its pretension and then as it is given under the phenomenalising conditions of *Jouissance* or the Universal Unconscious, postulating that it is not explicable by itself but by a hypothesis with a non-narcissistic essence which obviously belongs to the *Joui*. The One-in-One as *Joui* is the surest guarantee against the auto-manifestations of narcissism and the only real or practical critique of PA auto-position. However, if narcissism can be vanquished where it is, elsewhere from its terrain, non-analysis can dualyse its concept and distinguish from its PA form another form by which it belongs to *Jouissance* itself. It evidently abandons its unique and split form (primary/secondary) to receive an undivided transcendental identity. We will

then conceive it as the specific 'auto'-reference of *Jouissance*, which, insofar as it is distinct from the *Joui*, which is nothing but given-without-givenness, must be given in a givenness or manifested within a manifestation. Nevertheless, this distinction and correlation of the given and givenness cannot be a specular mirror structure or auto-reflexive language but, through its real cause in the *Joui*, what we will call a uni-flection, a property by which *Jouissance* is immediately self(-)related without a relation. Besides the *Joui* that purely and simply excludes all narcissism, and besides the narcissism of a specular nature but also origin, insufficiently 'criticised' and delimited by 'depriveness' and lack, there is a universal-unconscious form of narcissism specific to *Jouissance*. Neither being a real (there is none) nor imaginary narcissism, it is a transcendental narcissism in the now known sense of this term, and consequently it does not represent a synthesis of the two other ones. Together, these instances do not reconstitute a triad and even less a dialectic, but unilateral dualities.

Hence, a new organisation of the Real, the Dual Unconscious, and PA Appearance. The intra-PA explanation through the identification with lingual specularity is in any case insufficient and itself depends in-the-last-instance on the invisible (of) the Real, an invisible more radical and more positive than any depriveness or hole within the imaginary. As for it, the 'loss' of the *m*-form to which the Unconscious *Jouissance* proceeds is furthermore not a hole within the PA body and obliges thought to disbar itself . . . from this pseudo-theoretical imaginary. By definition, the essence of *Jouissance* is not exhausted or understood by PA appearance, but it is enveloped and specified by that which it extracts from this support, and this is the intrinsic finitude of its cause, the *Joui*, which requires this 'coating'. The relationship between these two instances is not unitary, not belonging to a direct causality from a substance or hole, but it is dual and theoretical, not schematisable by any such figure, topological or not, even if *Jouissance*, subject to being a transcendent entity, does not exist without this envelop extracted from the PA complex. Inversely, the narcissism (of) *Jouissance*, uni-flection such that it has its cause *en-Joui*, therefore 'de-narcissised' if you will, or de-specularised, is the transcendental (real-in-the-last-instance alone) organon that extracts from the complex what we may still call images, but under two conditions: (1) these images are themselves de-specularised, non-auto-positional, uni-(reflections), impossible to grasp or double in a mirror; this is the 'non-imaginary' phenomenal kernel of imagination; and (2) they are universal or *a priori* images, in no way belonging to a 'psychological' imaginary. As for the non-analyst, they are not narcissistic subjectivity, a special mode of PA auto-specularity; they do not emerge from the identification with an assumed real language: these are definitively transmitted by self-misunderstanding. They are only efficacious when they assume the organon of *Jouissance* and its transcendental or immanent narcissism. Therefore, it is not a matter of a smooth mirror nor as a choke hole, a pierced surface (see Wittgenstein and Lacan) directly affecting images, de-completing them and making them circulate once more around a hole, but as a subjective body in-the-last-instance alone which induces and deduces images. The non-analyst does not make desire circulate: they manifest it and know it as it is. This is to be done with the appearance that essentially makes up PA thought.

Non-Castration: Transcendental Incest and Detriangulation

1. We call non-castration the unity of operations of loss and the *objet m* and the manifestation as such or unconscious manifestation of the identity of each of the sides of any such of the antinomies of the PA complex. Through its function, non-castration does not designate the refusal or assumed absence of castration, nor a castration of the analyst *qua* analyst – a meta-castration – but the immanent transcendental universalisation of castration that is identically valid for the philosopher and analyst independently of philosophico-analytic difference, and valid for man and woman independently of sexual difference. Far from being determined by these differences and in particular sexual difference (to the symbolic benefit of the masculine libido), like castration itself, the universality of non-castration exceeds this determination without however being indifferent to any difference (now reduced to a simple material). Non-castration is lived-*en-Jouissance*, from the outset unconsciously, rather than it being a psychic interiorisation of an effective and/or imaginary event. Provided its type of universality, non-castration is valid for each of the terms in presence and, in particular, determines the analyst towards the assumption of their human identity as non-analyst, likewise determining man or woman towards assuming their own identity.

Through its content, this concept first designates the unilateralising suspension of analytic sufficiency, or the *m*-form, a suspension at the end of which the analyst admits as such no longer the PA antinomies or sexual difference (the question of the analyst's sex or the question of the phallic essence of their libido as analyst), but the unilateral duality of the experiences of *Jouissance* and '*jouissance*'. The spontaneous analytic regime belongs to sufficiency, that is, to the assumed omnipotence of the analyst as to the Real – even if it were precisely thought as 'impossible' and analysis being 'limited' by this 'real'. The desire of analysis exceeds the desire of the Other that it thematises; it is the desire-of-the-real as possibly (or not) determinable. By contrast, for non-analysis, even the desire-of-the-real, by definition, is a transcendental appearance or is not the

Real: there is no desire of the Real, the contrary belief that grounds analysis emerges from an objective illusion susceptible of taking on contrasting forms, in particular the thesis that there is an incestuous desire of the real except that the real is impossible, and so on. In the non-analyst's posture, the analyst assumes an intrinsic finitude or identity that has the effect of the loss of the *m*, that is, the non-castration of the PA body. If it was affected by lack, however chastened or cut off, the desire of the real is not yet adequate to the essence of the Real. The Real is not adequately thought unto its essence unless it is the Real that is determinant of castration as non-castration and unless it de-realises the PA body. The PA triangulation exceeds the Œdipus complex and gives it its genuine transcendental or philosophical horizon. It is not the Œdipus complex that is dissolved (in man) or, to the contrary, initiated (in woman) as it does so with castration; rather, it is the armature of philosophical triangulation, the *m*-form itself, which is led to its loss by *Jouissance*, but not 'lost-for' it. Said otherwise, we will not confuse non-castration as a transcendental universalisation (neither real nor effective, but for the PA effectivity) with a meta-, super- or hetero-castration. Non-Castration is not founded on a meta-, a super- or a hetero-psychoanalysis (nor otherwise a non-analytic 'supervision' of the analyst), which are all attempts to potentialise or magnify it. Rather, non-castration is a de-potentialisation of desire and *jouissance* within their analytic experience, their unilateralisation suspended by *Jouissance* as *Joui*(-)power [*force (du) Joui*].

2. It would be tempting to say that analysis is the infantile theory proper to non-analysis, but this thesis makes no sense. By contrast, if the non-analytic theory is left in turn to be seduced and bewitched by analytic sufficiency, then we will say that it is a matter of an infantile illness of non-analysis. Besides, without this formula having an indirectly pejorative or derogatory meaning, we can characterise the PA complex as broadened infantile theory as is in its mode, and to the nearest depriveness which is not differenciating or pertinent enough; it reproduces an incestuous and specular invariant ground – beyond depriveness precisely – which makes it into the thought of 'big children'. Like the philosopher, the analyst postulates that the desiring essence of man resides within the total scope of an Other, either One-as-Being (philosophical logocentrism), or One-as-Other strictly speaking, in which this Other gives rise to affirmation, if not to a position (deconstruction) or to an affect of lack and depriveness (analysis) at the point where this Other is reputed inexistent or impossible. In the same way that analysis broadens the reality of incest into a mythical figure and structure, likewise we can broaden – nevertheless without rupture – up to the figure of a transcendental incest the One-as-Being or as-Other that philosophy and analysis postulate as being the desired object constitutive of the human essence. A theory of

desire stops being infantile and idealist to become universally human when it infers desire from the Real or from man and determines desire by the Real; likewise when it stops, as we have said, being abusively phallogocentric or masculine when sexual difference is nothing more than a material for *Jouissance* rather than the essence of sexuality, which, as well, must be inferred in priority from the *Joui*. Therefore, non-analysis pursues incest at the heart of philosophy and psychoanalysis.

Therefore, the point is not to perforce constrain the analyst to accept in their work as an analyst technical modifications and the abandonment of analytic sufficiency, to intervene within it by breaking in or capturing, but to do it also or equally within an otherwise human and theoretical order: the order of *Jouissance* wherein the PA complex is the object. The PA symptom cannot enter into this order unless its limits are assumed within the Unconscious and, under these conditions, unless it recognises that its desire of the impossible or missing real is not yet the Real. This delimitation is not carried out within the topological figure of the limit, the edge, the hole, the band, and so on, but through the insertion of the PA complex within a new use. The analyst's resistance is so absolute – it is a foreclosure – that there will never be any reason to 'get out' of it, to displace it and choose the intrinsic finitude of the most human *jouissance*. By contrast, the analyst for their account 'chooses' between the total and incestuous metaphysical desire of the real (even if it were declared imaginary, unsatisfactory and utterly prohibited), which is nevertheless the evil *joui*, the non-humanly *joui*, and desire reduced to the Unconscious and accompanied by a simple becoming-material of the PA complex. It is then no longer necessary – it is more insufficient – to prohibit incest, even the figure of a transcendental incest, to demonstrate the finite essence of desire because it secures from itself a universal castration (in a radical transcendental mode, not in an empirical mode, extension or comprehension).

3. The auto- and hetero-critique of the PA complex can, under certain conditions, pass for a preparatory process towards non-castration. From within and without the PA complex simultaneously and, in particular, from within and without philosophy, threats against the desire of an incestuous omnipotence of thought are profiled, wounds even cuts which, blended according to the *m*-form in the analytic sense of castration and separation, lead to the constitution of a 'superego' of the PA system. We can isolate some important historical and systematic stages in this process of auto-/hetero-castration:

1. The 'Kantian' and modern emergence of the 'subject' as the first form of a non-substantial alterity albeit still included within subjective interiority; this is 'finite human reason' which is itself posited however in its finitude.

2. The strictly speaking analytic affect of depriveness or loss, which gives its main meaning to castration and is still immediately associated with one philosophy or one ontology that it de-substantialises in an even more radical way than 'rational finitude' does.
3. The post-modern, post-Nietzschean emergence of an Other as such, more transcendent, irreducible and extra-territorial than the previous one, without however stopping from manifesting itself, at least by its effects, from within philosophy and now within the PA complex (for example 'deconstruction' and the attempt at a 'deconstructionist psychoanalysis').
4. Finally, a fourth form threatening philosophical authority and susceptible to interest non-analysis, even if it remains still from our point of view interior if not to psychoanalysis, at least interior to philosophy: this is the threat of a subtraction of Being from being [*Étant*] or the Multiple from the One, a materialist and opaque ordeal of the identity of the in-itself, the identity of Being or the Multiple without difference.

On the basis of the PA mixture, it is no longer sexual difference that modulates the castration complex and the Œdipus complex; it is another difference, Ontological Difference, which passes through these four forms of alteration and threat. Being and being, like man and woman (and perhaps at the same time), each have their way of suffering and assuming the threats which are Finitude, Castration, Deconstruction and Subtraction. We cannot specify here as one must, in particular, the way in which Being and being, without speaking of the One, within Ontological Difference are affected by these operations that rather have the general meaning to de-triangulate philosophy itself, to de-Œdipalise it, but which finally, through a new twist of fate, assure the philosophical assumption of the triangulation, that is, a 'superior' form of incest – a transcendental incest. The mixture is not capable by itself – even if it were magnifying its forces by one another – of really resolving, that is, to invalidate, philosophical triangulation. It 'resolves' it like philosophy resolves its antinomies and analysis resolves its complexes: by re-dividing them, broadening them, softening them, infinitising them, and so on. It is as though Œdipus is not abolished [*levé*] within its ultimate foundations.

4. The theoretical problem of non-castration is to know if – by affecting the PA complex in any case – it is solely lived-*en-Jouissance* or if we may say that it is subjectively affected by it and at what level of subjectivity, because we have said that even unilateral loss is not an intervention within analysis but the passage to an emergent order. The assumption not of the *Joui* but *Jouissance* as such is carried out within non-analytic theory and practice, for they

are effective or are related to a material (they are not indifferent and abstract) thanks to the universal phantasy, as we have suggested. In this phantasy, *Jouissance* is identified – in the transcendental and unilateral mode – by the *m*-form and the diversity that it informs, more exactly by their contingency or relative autonomy as by a support, but in no way by their resistance, which it suspends. The suspension of resistance bound to the exercise of the *m*-form does not belong to the material, that is, the blend of the diversity and the *m*-form, without which *Jouissance* would stop being a transcendental force to become a transcendent or metaphysical entity. Therefore, non-castration affects the 'subjectivity' *par excellence* of the PA complex, that is, its most proven and deepest claim, because it affects its resistance, but it does not intervene as philosophy or even analysis or 'another' analysis does in the PA mechanism in view of dismembering and making it function otherwise with the same claims and within the same resistance. Non-analysis affects the PA resistance, that is, the only relation of the PA to the Real and *Jouissance*, and it uses the *m*-form for its own account (*Jouissance*), what resistance prevented it from doing, but leaves the PA complex intact.

5. It is self-evident that with non-analysis, PA resistance passes a qualitative state: the state of universal, ultra-Œdipal triangulation (or an Œdipus generalised in a differential mode) in relation to the state of 'logocentrism', 'metaphysics', 'presence' or substance against which the intra-PA threats are exercised. The unconscious *Jouissance* produces a sort of radicalisation or unblocking of resistance that thus contributes towards assuring – beyond the 'resolution of Œdipus' or even schizo-analytic de-Œdipalisation – the de-triangulation of the PA complex. There is progress in the theoretical elaboration when admitting that castration is not the simple psychic interiorisation of a threat, but an actual fact of the structure under the form of a break or separation bearing not on one term but on the imaginary relation or bond of incest of two terms. However, it only does so to make its ultimate philosophical nature appear (beyond any explicit reference to such and such philosopheme, which here has nearly no importance). The separation (of mother and child) is undoubtedly not simply a substantial, positive division that still bears on unity or synthesis; it is overdetermined by depriveness and is as much entailed by being as having (the phallus). It is neither being nor non-being, neither having nor non-having, but still another process that deprives antinomies of their immediately antinomic aspect. However, it does nothing but result in repressing their essence as antinomy without really invalidating them. Only a thought of the radical determination-in-the-last-instance of being and having can make these limits of an ontology of depriveness appear. If the process

of non-castration affects the resistance bound to the *m*-form, it therefore affects all the antinomies – hard or soft – of the PA complex. Its effect is the equivalency of identities, not the abstract equality, but the equality through suspension of the *m*-hierarchy, such that it henceforth places the terms of the antinomy in relation; it is specific to identities, of-the-last-instance, the dual or unilateral relation and therefore without possible exchange or permutation. Œdipus and even generalised triangulation as a simple difference of philosophy and analysis – or man and woman – are thus suspended within one unified theory, whether it is the unified theory of philosophy and analysis or the unified theory of man and woman.

The Transcendental Phallic Identity: Saving the Phenomenon of Desire and the Pragmatics of Sexual Difference

1. If the most human desire does not know the restrained and transcendent form of castration symbolised by the 'phallus' as assumed constitutive of human sexuality, the universal pragmatics of castration must be prolonged by the pragmatics of the phallus or its analytic use. The point is to define a transcendental phallus, the immanent cause of desire and what, with it, contributes towards forming the content of *Jouissance*.

Philosophical thought is organised around the explicit or implicit yet universal prevalence of the One-that-is, in the sense where even the One that is not, or the One that is the Other, and so on, still assumes that it would be inserted within an ultimate reciprocal reference to Being rather than thought as One-in-One. This thesis in its universality belongs to a non-philosophical or non-analytic origin. It is then divided between the One-that-is in the narrow sense of presence or the convertibility of the One with Being valid for the ontology of the Ancients but also the Moderns; and the One that is not in the sense where the One is the Other or convertible with the Other valid for the ontology of the post-moderns, that is, deconstructions and psychoanalysis. It is their most universal invariant, as it specifies this schema through the Lacanian institution of the phallus, more exactly of a lack-phallus opposed to the substantial phallus of classical ontology; and the exclusively masculine character of the libido at the centre of Freudian theory – a thesis which is therefore also one of philosophy though on another mode. In both cases and not only in the case of analysis, it concerns an imaginary (and/or substantialist) and symbolic representation, indeed of a theoretical concept, one that is in any case belonging to a structural function rather than a real-empirical description. The phallus responds to the One-as-Other by specifying it ontologically by lack and the signifier – this is the One-of-the-lack, so that the mixture of onto-phallogo-centrism emerges from privational ontology but obeys the ultimate amphibological and antinomic invariants of philosophy – in the *m*-form. From this perspective, the 'Western' thought of love is governed by two models, two very simple schema that non-analysis will distinguish itself from: a Greek androgynous model of the separated or divided One, the dyad that aspires to become what it is, that is, the triad; and the transcendent phallic model, the model of the One-of-lack which prohibits substantial and reconciliatory love. However, they belong to one and the same invariant, even if the second would be opposed to the first, the invariant of the love-of-the-One as love-of-love. On this plane, non-analysis' problem is to define an essence of love that would not itself be 'amorous' or auto-erotic, in some way a non-love which would be love's Essence (of) love.

It neither belongs to the definition nor to the tasks of non-analysis to critique, through a contrary hypothesis about the in-itself of sexuality, this Freudo-Lacanian thesis and attempt to make woman 'exist'. On the one hand, this thesis is consonant so perfectly – this is its solidity and coherence – with the exclusive definition of philosophy by the One-as-Being or as-Other, by the One such that it is given in transcendence and with it, that we must rather pose the problem in its full philosophico-analytic amplitude: the problem of the phallogocentric primacy characteristic of philosophy. Yet above all, rather than stating in turn 'woman exists' or 'there is a sexual relation' and to play sexual difference against this thesis, at risk in resulting in a simple inversion to that of an anti-phallism or a differe(a)nce of the phallogocentric which would do nothing but broaden it in reality, generalising and rendering it inexpugnable, non-analysis postulates: (1) that the human essence, man's essence (of) man is not constituted by nor constituent of sexual difference, that sexual difference is only determinant for the conditions of existence and knowledge of this essence; (2) that there is no doubt something of sexual difference that analytic theorisation – if it is rigorous, that is, philosophico-analytic – inserts within it like an indissoluble mixture but which, if it is taken as an 'in-itself' attribute of man, then escapes from non-analysis; and (3) that, by contrast, there is precisely some theory of sexual difference and that it is one of the possible data of non-analysis. To sum this up, the One is in-One rather than in-Lack or the Lacking, and the phallus, if we keep to conserving this 'name', must be removed from the privational ontology of sexuality and tested as a transcendental organon, as a function, if we may say, of *Jouissance* with regard to the PA complex.

2. Regardless, what would correspond to the phallus as One-of-lack, if it is dualysed, is the constitutive transcendental Identity of *Jouissance* that we may say – in view of producing effects of analytically unintelligible statements

– that it is an immanent phallus or a phallus of-the-last-instance. This phallus no longer regulates *Jouissance* as a repression but informs it interiorly as identity or the simplicity of a radical exteriority – a phallus-organon, rather than a phallic organ. This transcendental phallus is not itself intrinsically transcendent, but it is the transcendental identity (of) identity and that which supports it, that is, contributing it to the region of transcendence. By contrast, analysis supports it from the hole that is assumed surreptitiously *de facto* auto-positional or of a depriveness that makes it protrude within transcendence and, detaching it from the Real or the *Joui*, completes by unrealising it, transforming it into the symbol of unreality and inessentiality where the signifier and appearance which is supported by it sinks. Determined by the Real itself, the phallus is indivisible in the imaginary and the symbolic, and stops being affected or divided by these empirical cleavages but is all the more universally valid for these spheres.

The problem of the transcendent phallus as the correlate of lack is indeed that it is de-magnified in an ultimate way, despite everything, in a specular mode. The imaginary phallus of the incestuous and narcissistic relation is doubled by a symbolic phallus, so that it plays two antinomic roles: both what makes the object of castration and what symbolises the Law, the symbolic limit or break linking the imaginary. The essence of desire such that analysis apprehends it is decidedly the circle of a difference that we, perhaps, may not call phallo-phallic, but more profoundly phallo-andro-logical. If non-analysis prohibits itself any contrary or different hypothesis concerning the essence in-itself of human sexuality and aims by way of essence only by what is given in an immanent or phenomenal use, it will also distinguish two or three phalluses, why not, but two by two in a dual relation where the 'second' phallus does not co-determine the essence of the first but only serves as a material for the knowledge of this essence.

3. The phallus is definitively de-genitalised and de-symbolised. It is so firstly on the imaginary plane, its identity being henceforth supported by a simple salience which is non-auto-positional. As invested throughout *Jouissance* or the transcendental universal libido, the phallic identity loses its local or partial libidinal charge. As determinant of the *objet m*, it stops being itself threatened by loss, being immediately determined by the Real which is never lack or loss, but positive finitude. It is so secondly on the syntactic or symbolic plane. As the 'radical' type of identity, it stops being a generalised partial object, an object among others which is equivalent and exchangeable within one chain or 'symbolic equation' to be engaged one-time-each-time-without-dividing into each of the desiring actualisations or effectuations of *Jouissance*'s Essence (of) desire

acting as the performativity of desire. It is a cause that agitates desire under the mediation of a form that unifies the multiple: desire is non-consistent and the phallic identity does not contradict this non-consistency. In this way, it maintains desire from inside and keeps it, as the desire (of) the Other, from always sinking once more into the desire of the Other. As the immanent cause of desire (of the Essence (of) desire), it is valid for all objects of the *m*-form, the empirico-imaginary doublets which serve as material for the organon that determines them. Since its origins, it stops being excluded from this series and from becoming the norm and the symbolic measure, both the internal and external cause, both the lack and excess as the One-of-the-lack does that, in this levelling way, renders all objects equivalent. It agitates all the desiring effectuations, the multitudes (of) *Jouissance*; and it acts 'upon' the PA objects through its transcendence (of) the organon, a transcendence which is the organon and which it exhausts in a blow, that it will not redouble. It then acts not as an exclusive or absent cause but as an immanent cause. The distribution of immanence and transcendence is quite distinct from one case to the other. Moreover, it introduces an equivalency through equality of identities, an equality finally without a repressed hierarchy but not without distinction. If hierarchy and primacy are identical to the *m*-form, the transcendental phallus de-hierarchises the works of the transcendent phallus and imposes the ration-form to the PA objects that renders them analytically indifferent and non-analytically equivalent, imposing democracy not within analysis but to analysis itself in its relation to philosophy, a relation which stops being one of a conflicting hierarchy (the conflict of interpretations, deconstruction, schizoanalysis, and so on). As an immanent phallic organon, *Jouissance* stops being a transcendent norm agitating through depriveness, distributing and redistributing everywhere lack and inequality that castration lets subsist.

4. Generally, *Jouissance* is not auto-or-hetero-limited like the illusory *jouissance* of the Other: *Jouissance* is the organon of a unique undivided operation or an operation without simultaneity, as produced and determined, limited, in a transcendental and immanent way. The first test that desire undergoes is to only be from the outset the phenomenon of desire's Essence (of) desire, or the desire (of) the non-auto-positional Other. The impossible *jouissance* of the mother, with castration and renouncement that she pays off, are objective postulations *qua* properties of the PA body, but are not necessary to save the phenomenon of desire, because this is what is in question and analysis has some harm in assuring it. Desire is not completed with its dissatisfaction – still a form of auto-position as auto-depriveness – but immediately coincides with its essence insofar as it is a moment of the immanent phallic organon, rather

than an internal/external referent or measure. Finally, the desire included within *Jouissance* has its essence as an intrinsic finitude adequate to the essence of man because he receives it from his essence and therefore does not need to be 'real' to be limited in exteriority, receiving a mark, a trait a limit, and thus pouring into a linguistic turning or taking on a topological turn.

5. Nevertheless, if it is immanent or unknown, this finitude is received by a heteronomous cause. This is a philosophical paradox. Through its real cause, *Jouissance* is identically cause through immanence and heteronomous (rather than 'immanent') in relation to the PA complex and in relation to itself insofar as it is presupposed. Philosophy and analysis intend to confound heteronomy and transcendent exteriority, the phallic organon and its withdrawal, its auto-positional redoubling. Non-analysis necessarily distinguishes the mere salience, the immanent phallus-organon and the auto-salience typical of analysis. The immanent phallus is valid universally or transcendentally for sexual difference. In particular, it is no longer the imaginary and symbolic interiorisation of masculine genitality that no doubt erects [*lève*] genitality but universalises the masculine essence of desire. It is not only de-genitalised but torn from its auto-privational context and thus said as 'de-phallicised'. We will say the same thing about sexuality, which is an objective property of the theoretico-factual form under which we understand analysis, but it is not constitutive of the essence of man nor even of desire except in posing, as an axiom, universal or transcendental sexuality identical to *Jouissance* itself and, therefore, 'regulated' immanently by phallic identity; or, again, a non-sexuality and a non-phallus – this is according to the capacity of the 'axiomatic' invention of non-analysis.

Non-analysis then renounces the philosophico-analytic conflict of the sexes, renouncing sexual difference as assumed constituent, renouncing the attempt to absurdly make woman 'exist', but produces the de-hierarchised equivalency, the equality of man and woman without confusion. With regard to *Jouissance*, man and woman are 'equals', but they do not present themselves to it as equals within the PA complex. All that *Jouissance* can do (which we see that the utilised PA material – it is not responsible for it – constrains non-analysis to describe it in terms of the 'phallus') is to unilaterally determine, by imposing the equality proper to unilaterality, the relation or non-relation of man and woman, a relation or non-relation of the sexes; to thus constitute the mixture of sexual difference into the universal *a priori* of experience, giving it a transcendental (radical or simple) identity which it does not have as long as it remains delivered by its spontaneous amphibological and antinomic nature. It is within this identity that each of them integrally receives what they do not share, what woman and man, without ever confounding each other or reducing each other, without entering into consensus for war, are posed in their relative autonomy and find their identity (as) woman or (as) man. A unified theory of woman and man is possible on condition that it would be capable of pronouncing the theoretical and pragmatic invalidation of sexual difference and its use as a simple material in a science of humans.

Transcendent Sublime and the Transcendental Sublime

Non-analytic sublimation is evidently the transformation of its analytic form by *Jouissance*. To the extent where it more precisely defines a de-sexualisation of the original sexuality of drives, we will also call it a non-sexualisation. This term does not designate a final absence of all sexuality, but what the sexuality of the PA body becomes in the gaze of *Jouissance* as unconscious organon.

1. First, we distinguish the intra-analytic concept of sublimation with the philosophical or theoretico-ontological presuppositions that render it possible, that is: (a) the presupposition of partiality or the being-partial of satisfaction (therefore of the impossible totality) that corresponds to the constitutive dyad of the being-PA of the drive in general – this is the dyadic or most general determinant condition of sublimation, its PA 'motor'; (b) the presupposition of the operation of transcendence, that is, the de-sexualisation of the object by the narcissistic ego which withdraws the libidinal investment from it and turns it towards itself; this 'negation' of sexuality simultaneously assures the passage towards an *a priori* universality of the libido in relation to such and such object or particular goal; the ego is thus rigorously the organon of sublimation and makes it pass through a 'meta-physical' or meta-sexual stage; and (c) the presupposition of the unity of continuous synthesis or transcendence of the sexual drive capable of a double substitution of the object and goal, for an object and a goal now assumed non-sexual (but not of a change of a sexual origin and persistence or insatisfaction by virtue of point (a) above): this is the function of the ego ideal as the PA condition of Unity or closure but not the motor of sublimation; but the ego ideal which finalises the sublimation that cannot do anything without the ego-organon.

These three presuppositions form a triad – in particular, the narcissistic ego is identified with the ego ideal, as the organon of the *a priori* is with the transcendental unity – and defines sublimation not as a special type of satisfaction of the drive but as the passage or plasticity from one satisfaction to another. This is why we must understand that the genuine operation of sublimation is not defined by its new, 'non-sexual' and non-'utilitarian' goals or objects, nor by its 'ideal' products (moral, social, artistic values, and so on) and that the genuine work of sublimation is sublimation itself.

2. Besides the intra-analytic, that is, intra-sexual or 'restrained' concept of sublimation as transcendence within sexual immanence, there is indeed the immanence of sublimation itself or a 'broadened' sublimation, its auto-position as immanent to itself and not to sexuality assumed as a separated instance alone, limited to the origin and nature of the drive. This identity of sublimation, but also of its supposed sufficiency, is not perceptible from the PA body that nevertheless spontaneously exercises it, yet without seeing the character of the transcendental appearance and which can only apprehend it from partial outlines. It is not perceptible as such beyond the works to which analytic finalism still reduces it, except from *Jouissance* as the posture of non-analysis. Under this new condition, sublimation changes theoretical status: it is already levied as sufficiency or 'real' pretension whereas it subsists as a support and material for a non-analytic elaboration. The sexuality (of the drive)/de-sexualisation (of its object and goal) couple can also, from this point of view, be 'broadened' into a sexual immanence or a pan-sexuality, whose true meaning is to respond to the formal trait of auto-positionality and in no way excludes, to the contrary, its auto-limitation or its auto-de-sexualisation.

3. Finally, the organon of *Jouissance*, without itself being nothing of a product of sublimation (into its analytic concept), is the instrument of a new type of sublimation that no longer responds to PA criteria. If sublimation is ultimately auto-productive (by the ego) and auto-finalised (by the ego ideal), if it rests upon an ontological experience of sublimity or alterity such as the-other-of-the-other and if it is inscribed within the most universal philosophical matrix, by contrast, sublimation as a non-analytic operation of *Jouissance* presents the following traits:

a. It is no longer sufficient, auto-positional or more exactly auto-transcendent as is the sublimation that renders the supposed sufficient ego ideal possible, but it is second or inferred from the real (of the) *Joui*: regardless of its concept otherwise, analytic or not, it can no longer be the *nec plus ultra* of the destiny of sexuality realising itself under its highest and most excellent form; in a general way, the transcendent immanence which analysis thinks, the transcendent immanence of sexuality, sublimation, and finally of the most creative works, is ordered to the real immanence of the Real. Works are absolutely not autonomous except through a transcendental appearance and must be as well enjoyed-in-the-last-instance – this is their human, non-metaphysical or non-phantastic use – to acquire and manifest their transcendence. Their essence is specified by sexuality, but in no way meta-sexual sexuality as it claims to be in the PA body.

b. *Jouissance* itself is no longer the split and redoubled transcendence of PA sublimation. It also contains the sublime as a dimension of alterity of the Unconscious, but the phenomenal sublime, as it is, or a simple, non-auto-positional sublime, the one-time-each-time transcendence nevertheless in the state of the empirico-transcendental doublet. Regardless, this sublime adequate to the human essence is as sublime as its PA form that bars the humanity of man and confuses the phenomenal identity (of) transcendence with the redoubling of it, the identity of the sublime with an absolutely autonomous auto-transcendent sublimation aspiring interminably unto itself; it confuses flight or withdrawal of transcendence with the essence of it and finally the sublime with a hinterworld. The sublime as it is is not a hinterworld operating within the World.
c. This universal, because transcendental sublime, unlike the *Joui*, which is nothing but given, is nevertheless one with a 'sublimation' this time as the givenness of the sublime. It is a static sublimation, the operation proper to the organon of *Jouissance* and which is nothing but manifestation, finally as such, of the sublime as it is. This sublimation necessarily includes an operation of knowledge upon that which serves it henceforth as material, that is, the transcendent concept of sublimation. We understand that this concept, from its immediately philosophical load, its classical ontological structure and not only by its 'ideal' objects to which it is abusively reduced, could have appeared suspect to some analysts, but a sufficiently summary examination of its requisites demonstrates its necessary belonging to analysis as PA: it is a sublime-sublimation mixture. In non-analysis, it abandons its doublet-form to the benefit of a unilateral duality of the sublime and sublimation as if the former would precede not only *a priori* but unilaterally the latter of which it nevertheless needs to be manifested. Non-analysis places the radical, not 'absolute' in a metaphysical sense, creation, nevertheless the phenomenon of creation, at the heart of the *Jouissance* of the Unconscious and their form of narcissism. The really sublime creation is the identity of discovery and invention, as it is performed within *Jouissance*, but creation is not yet the work, the latter presupposes the rationing of a material that the PA symptom [*symtôme*][10] furnishes. The operation of *Jouissance*, transcendental sublimation, unilaterally suspends desire with the *m*-form issued from this PA symptom [*symtôme*], but it also manifests the sublime itself thanks to the *a priori* and 'simple' images which it extracts from it. The work, as a correlate of creation, produced by the organon, has no imaginary except the material that serves it as a support and specification. In its

[10] Translator's note: The reader may safely assume that this is a typo for the French *symptôme* as Laruelle did not introduce this as a term or concept.

phenomenal or real, non-specular kernel, it is in-the-last-instance a lived experience (of the) invisible *Joui* and, in its specific essence, it is a radically multiple void like the Unconscious is – in some way a void without a hole that is incarnated in *a priori* representations of an imaginary origin that makes it exist as transcendence.

The Amphibology of the Concept of Identification: Identity and Identification

1. The varying types of identification distinguished by analysis are modes of one philosophical invariant. Let us recall that by this very general 'thesis', we do not intend to give a new philosophical interpretation of analysis, but to demonstrate that philosophy and analysis are in an invariant way narrowly entangled and even inseparable, even if they are locally distinct. What we call the PA body is this distinction and this inseparability of two disciplines, and it is the objective material to which non-analysis is *de jure* related as a unified theory of philosophy and psychoanalysis. These types of identification are therefore entirely grounded upon an assumed constitutive distance of identity, whether this ontological distance would be psycho-sociologically modulated or unconscious and among unconscious instances, whether it would be ordered by already constituted terms (the ego-instance is transformed by the identification with the given object) or by terms constituted to the contrary in and through this distance (a causation by the object of the unconscious ego), therefore whether it is classically philosophical (subject → object) or inverted (object → subject), or even whether it is asymmetrical apparently in one direction [*sens*] or another, and so on, these distinctions are only important for the intra-analytic labour, but they are without pertinence for a unified thought or theory of analysis (and philosophy). Indeed, they continue to obey certain typical traits of the most universal structure of philosophy: (1) the primacy of the object over the ego or the subject, and finally the 'objectivation' of the subject of the unconscious (the philosophical 'subject', as we know, is as much an object as a subject); (2) correlatively, the constitutive or determinant function of the distance, that is, transcendence, within the reality or identity of the instances; (3) the auto-positional nature of this distance and therefore of unconscious instances among which identification is produced; consequently it is a false unilaterality and an effective reciprocity of this distance more or less dissimulated but *de jure*, which can go, beyond analysis and into schizoanalysis, up to an affirmed reversibility of identification; (4) the insertion of the previous traits within the philosophical dyad of the partial and the total (the total and partial identification, the latter in

turn reflected within the triad of the symbolic, the imaginary and the phantasmatic, and generating the distinction of the subspecies of the partial: the salient trait, the global image and the local image); and (5) the modalisation of the ensemble of this structure and in particular the assumed real distance by auto-depriveness, which now makes the real stand out beyond identifying distance, not substantially modifying, as we have said, this simply foreclosed philosophical structure, 'repressed' in the background of analysis, nevertheless always efficacious.

2. Of course, we will finally characterise analysis itself, beyond its varying concepts of identification, as an auto-identifying process that passes through the stages as much of the partial as the general and the total or the local and the global. As a 'broadened' identification, it is another way of conceiving the sufficiency of the PA body, for despite its 'holing' through lack and depriveness, it remains a simply repressed or inhibited auto-identification. One of the proofs of it is that identification, inverting its classical or Freudian vector, ends by reclaiming a genuine, yet transcendent causation enclosed within a dyad: either the symbolic causation of the subject by the signifier; or the imaginary causation of the ego by the image; or again the phantasmatic causation of the identity of the subject of the unconscious and the *objet a*.

3. For its own account, non-analysis makes a hypothesis of another experience of identification. (1) It unilaterally, without reciprocity and therefore without hierarchy, subordinates any kind of identifying distance not only to identity but, consequently, to the Real, which is not 'impossible' but unconstituted and inconstitutive and which therefore is responsible for determining this distance itself and removing it from the illusions of its auto-position or its constitutive power. (2) It recognises within the real identity or within the *Joui* a radical 'subjectivity' or more exactly the real phenomenal kernel of any subjectivity and therefore gives it a definitive priority (rather than a primacy), the priority of the 'subject'-organon over the 'object'. (3) It conceives unconscious *Jouissance* (identical to the Transcendental Unconscious) as the organon of identification, and identification as the very operation of *Jouissance.* (4) It subordinates identification to identity, identification remains a distance yet without reciprocity or auto-positionality; consequently, it makes use of instances which are neither positional at all (the *Joui*) nor auto-positional as transcendent entities would be ('transcendent' is not a critique of the unconscious in general, but of the PA conception of the unconscious); it is therefore the identity within the term, rather than the term itself assumed already constituted, which precedes identifying distance.

If the *Joui* is identity-without-identification, *Jouissance* is itself identity and identification, but without reforming within it a mixture or a doublet, but a relation which we have called uni-flection. It is identity as it is, though transcendental or said of identifying distance, but it is the identification of *Jouissance* itself. Enjoyed-in-the-last-instance, *Jouissance* does not operate except by making an appeal to PA material upon which it exercises a labour of identification precisely in the narrow sense, associated with a labour of suspension and loss. The labour by which it is the organon of identification consists in extracting moments corresponding with the PA body modalities or kinds of identification that are this time *a priori*. Being given that non-analysis is an affect, a use and a theory of identity, it is crucial in general for it to suspend the mixture of auto-identification *qua* superior form of all known concepts of identification; to declare it a transcendental appearance and order identification to identity. The psychoanalytic idealism passes through the amphibology of identity and identification; its destruction will pass through the subordination to the Real of identifying causality. From the Real, *Jouissance* is henceforth the unique incumbent below the transcendent tripartition of the symbolic, the imaginary and the phantasmatic. However, if non-analysis succeeds in finally thinking the identity of identification itself, it does so by liberating dualities of the types of identification as we have described them schematically.

Index

EU Authorised Representative:
Easy Access System Europe Mustamäe tee 50, 10621 Tallinn, Estonia
gpsr.requests@easproject.com

Printed and bound by CPI Group (UK) Ltd, Croydon, CR0 4YY
13/01/2026
02034695-0008